DAVID BOWIE MADE ME GAY

100 Years of LGBT Music

DARRYL W. BULLOCK

DUCKWORTH
OVERLOOK

LONDON
30 Calvin Street, London E1 6NW
T: 020 7490 7300
E: info@duckworth-publishers.co.uk
www.ducknet.co.uk
For bulk and special sales please contact sales@duckworth-publishers.co.uk

A catalogue record for this book is available from the British Library

Typeset in Dante by M Rules

Printed and bound in Great Britain
by Clays Ltd, Elcograf S.p.A.

HB ISBN: 978-0-7156-5192-6
PB ISBN: 978-0-7156-5299-2

3 5 7 9 10 8 6 4 2

Contents

This book is dedicated to the families and friends of the people who lost their lives, or who were injured, in the Pulse Nightclub shootings in Orlando, Florida in June 2016. We are family.

A Note on Sources

All quotes from k anderson, Andy Bell, Blackberri, Guy Blackman, John 'Smokey' Condon, Ray Connolly, St. Sukie de la Croix, Sean Dickson (HiFi Sean), Alix Dobkin, Robbie Duke (Patrick Pink), Patrick Haggerty, Drake Jensen, Dane Lewis, Mista Majah P, Holly Near, Andy Partridge, Tom Robinson, Paul Rutherford, Paul Southwell, Rod Thomas (Bright Light Bright Light) and Cris Williamson, unless otherwise credited, are taken from exclusive interviews conducted by the author. The interview with John Grant was conducted by Ian Leak, and is used by permission.

N°22

GAY NEWS

15p

Bowie
Extravaganza
To
Rock
Gay
Ghetto

Fleet Street
Freedom
Shock
Page 3

Jenny
Fabian
Sex
Surprise
Page 10

EUROPE'S BIGGEST SELLING INDEPENDENT NEWSPAPER FOR HOMOSEXUALS

David Bowie on the cover of *Gay News*, 1973

INTRODUCTION

Once upon a time, in a disco far, far away . . .

'When I asked him what kept him going to discover new music, John Peel looked at me, smiled, and said: "The next record I hear might be the best record I have ever heard". Since that moment that has been my life's motto'

Sean Dickson, a.k.a. HiFi Sean[1]

N ow, I know what you're thinking: surely the world doesn't need another book about music, does it? Well, maybe it does.

Over the centuries, countless volumes have been written about the lives of the musicians and composers who have enriched our world with their performances, and we have become accustomed to lapping up the lurid minutiae of our favourite musicians' lives. We have all heard the (completely false, of course) story about Mick, Marianne and the Mars Bar, and we are intimate with the childhood traumas of the individual Beatles. We (quite literally) know what Elvis' last movements were before his fiancée discovered his lifeless body – assuming, of course, that you believe Elvis did in fact die in 1977 and he isn't still wandering in and out of the crowds that gather at Graceland daily as a white-haired man in his 80s. Yet although the lives of many mainstream artists have been laid bare in print, there have been surprisingly few attempts to document the influence of gay, lesbian, bisexual and transgender musicians on the development of the music we listen to today. True, for years now tabloids and newsstand weeklies have been filling their pages with such trivia as Elton's latest falling-out with Madonna, lists of Freddie Mercury's former sexual partners or stories about what really caused George Michael's tumble onto the tarmac, but while celebrity spats and the more sensational aspects of someone's sex life or drug use may grab the headlines, the contributions that many LGBT recording artists have made in propelling popular music forward have been all but ignored.

Obviously, there were LGBT writers and performers before wax cylinders and shellac discs became the norm. Seventeenth-century baroque composers Jean-Baptiste Lully and Arcangelo Corelli were both gay; Tchaikovsky, despite his disastrous marriage to 'a woman with whom I am not the least in love' (as he described her),[2] and all Soviet efforts to portray him as heterosexual, had a string of male lovers – including his own nephew. Both Schubert and Handel have been outed by biographers, and even during the Victorian period, when urban myth would have you believe that the redoubtable monarch refused to believe that such a thing existed, lesbian composer Dame Ethel Smyth was already making a name for herself for her operatic and sacred scores.

The discovery, in the second half of the nineteenth century, of a method to record and preserve sound meant that music quickly became much more accessible to a vastly wider audience. Suddenly, LGBT musicians were no longer limited to the music hall stages or opera houses of the world's major cities; they could reach into the homes of everyone coming to terms with their own sexuality. Sitting in your room scared and confused, hearing a voice on a record telling you that you were not alone, was like having a comforting hug from a friend. And just as everyone who bought the first Velvet Underground album or attended the Sex Pistols' legendary gig at Manchester's Lesser Free Trade Hall is said to have gone on to form their own band, those voices that came crackling through the horn, out of the speaker or over that transistor radio would influence every generation of LGBT musicians that followed.

The LGBT community has spent over 100 years pioneering musical genres and producing some of the most lasting and important records of all time. However, even though every music mogul worth his wage packet (and, sadly, even today it's almost invariably a 'he') is fully aware of how important the Pink Pound is in supporting the careers and record sales of their 'gay-friendly' acts (do you really think that Cher, Madonna or Kylie would have lasted as long as they have in the cut-throat music industry without their fiercely loyal LGBT fan base?), far too many LGBT musicians have seen their stories 'straight-washed' or completely brushed under the carpet. The roles of LGBT people in the theatre, in the cinema, in photography and in classical music have been thoroughly examined by worthy writers, but the contributions of members of our community in the fields of pop, folk, punk, electronica and so on have been all but ignored, unless you happen to have been lucky enough to be one of the handful of artists to make the big time. It hasn't helped that, until very recently, pop music has been seen as second-class, ephemeral and disposable; a victim of snobbery and of its own success.

And that is simply not fair: LGBT people were there as jazz gestated. We were in the maternity ward during the birth of the blues, and in the first few decades of the twentieth century, many LGBT performers enjoyed a level of fame and a freedom that would not be seen again until the 1970s, when a new wave of politically active gay musicians demanded to be heard. We dominated the disco era, and the pop charts of the late 1980s and early 1990s would have been barren without our influence: the hit-making machine that was Stock, Aitken and Waterman (with over 100 UK Top 40 hits to their collective names, including seven Number One singles) freely admit that their signature sound was developed from the Hi-NRG music they had witnessed filling the floors of gay clubs.[3]

Yet while they were happy to camp it up on stage in some of the world's biggest arenas, many LGBT artists struggled to come to terms with their own sexuality – or remained in the closet at the behest of their management team. Andy Fraser, producer and co-author of the massive rock standard 'All Right Now', did not come out until 2005, and by that time he was already fighting AIDS. Freddie Mercury, the man for whom the word 'flamboyant' seemed to have been invented, never fully came out to his adoring public. The day before his death (which came, according to his death certificate, as the result of bronchial pneumonia brought on by AIDS), he still felt unable to admit to the world that he was gay, even when he asked fans to join him and his medical team 'in the fight against this terrible disease'. George Michael only revealed that he was gay after he was forced to by his arrest in a public convenience in California. At least Fraser and Michael had the opportunity to discover how liberating coming out can be. Rob Halford, the frontman of the devil-baiting hard rock act Judas Priest, says that outing himself (during an interview in 1998) was 'the greatest thing I could have done for myself. It didn't affect Priest one iota: the record sales didn't plunge, the show attendance didn't plunge. Unconditional love will accept you for who you are, and I think that was the blessing I had from the fans'.[4] Michael Stipe was the singer and spokesperson of the biggest band in world when he admitted to being 'an equal opportunity lech';[5] a year later, R.E.M. signed what was then the biggest recording contract ever awarded (estimated at some $80 million) and their next album was an international Number One hit. Like Stipe, who prefers the word 'queer' when describing himself, Elton John has proved beyond doubt that a gay artist can have a worldwide fan base and still be open and honest about their sexuality although, as many of the bigger LGBT acts have discovered, he can still only get radio play (and, subsequently, hit records) by singing songs about the opposite sex – especially on the ultra-conservative American airwaves.

The world tends to view the Stonewall Riots in 1969 as the dawn of our age of empowerment, yet gay, lesbian, bisexual and transgender musicians have been causing a scene for a whole lot longer than the last 50 years. LGBT musicians have powered many of the most important stages in the development of music over the last century, and that music has, in turn, provided a soundtrack for our community as it has struggled for acceptance and fought for equality across the globe. As we carry on fighting for our basic freedoms in many countries around the world, music continues to inform, inspire and – above everything else – unite us all. This book is not intended as a fully comprehensive guide to every LGBT musician who has ever entered a recording studio, but it is my hope that, through its pages, you will discover some of the people who spent their lives fighting for us to be heard.

Dusty Springfield press advert, 1966

CHAPTER 1

David Bowie Made Me Gay

'There is old wave, there is new wave and there's
David Bowie'

RCA promotional advertisement, 1978

2016 was a terrible year for the entertainment industry. For a while, it seemed that every time you opened a newspaper, or every time your smartphone signalled an update from Twitter or Facebook, the noise heralded the death of yet another great: in the first five months of the year alone, the music world lost Prince, Maurice White of Earth, Wind & Fire, Glenn Frey of The Eagles, Jefferson Airplane's Paul Kantner (coincidentally on the same day that Signe Anderson, the Airplane's original singer, also passed away), Keith Emerson of ELP (his erstwhile musical partner, Greg Lake, would follow him through the pearly gates in December), Beatles producer Sir George Martin and so many more that people started taking bets on who we would lose next. By the end of the year we had also lost Leonard Cohen, Pete Burns of Dead or Alive and George Michael.

It wasn't just the music world, of course. Authors, entertainers, sports personalities, film and television stars and more were dropping like ninepins, but none of them (with the possible exception of Sir George) had the cultural impact and not one evoked the devastating feeling of loss quite as much as the death of David Bowie. With a recording career spanning 52 years behind him, and a heartbreaking new album ★ (*Blackstar*) issued less than 48 hours before his untimely passing, Bowie's death resonated around the world. For many people, the death of the man born David Jones in the London suburb of Brixton signalled the end of an era. And it was.

His decision to die offstage, to keep his private health battles to himself, coupled with the fact that his career had recently been undergoing a renaissance, only served to amplify the sense of shock. These days we are bombarded with the ins and outs of so-called stars' private lives; for Bowie to swear the few who knew about his terminal cancer diagnosis to secrecy meant that when the announcement of his death was made, it was almost as shocking as the assassination of his friend and occasional collaborator John Lennon had been in December 1980. Like Lennon's, Bowie's death had a far greater impact than that of most musicians – greater even than that of Queen frontman Freddie Mercury, who in 1991 became the first major rock star to die from AIDS.

It somehow seems right that a wider audience would mourn Bowie, for he was more than a musician. David Bowie was an actor, a writer, a painter, a fashion icon and a trendsetter . . . and he was directly responsible for the proliferation of lesbian, gay, bisexual and trans musicians we have today. 'David Bowie was the perfect fantasy and foil for the teenage gay kid at the time,' says Kid Congo Powers, former member of The Gun Club, The Cramps and Nick Cave and the Bad Seeds, and currently fronting Kid Congo Powers and the Pink Monkey Birds. 'He was a rock star, androgynous, hedonistic and an alien from outer space, typifying exactly what a gay teenager experienced. We felt like aliens growing into our bodies and experimenting with alcohol and drugs. I could relate to the Bowie image – hook, line and sinker.'[1]

In January 1972, less than five years after a change in UK law meant that gay men were no longer to be persecuted for simply having sex, Bowie told Michael Watts, a journalist from the *Melody Maker*, 'I'm gay and always have been, even when I was David Jones,' a statement that would resonate with a number of young people and have far-reaching repercussions.

'I was desperately searching for some kind of gay identity when I was a teenager, and books and films and pop music were one of the ways I found that,' Frankie Goes to Hollywood's Holly Johnson told *Gay Times* in April 1994. 'It was like that feeling the very first time you go to a gay club: you realise that there are other people like you. It was all quite a revelation. David Bowie, Marc Bolan, Roxy Music, Lou Reed. I used to tell people "Oh, I'm bisexual, just like my hero David"!'[2] To Paul Rutherford, he 'was too wonderful. He was like a gift from the Gods, with that kind of talent'.[3]

The use of gay imagery on the *Hunky Dory* track 'Queen Bitch' (one of Bowie's attempts to out-Lou his idol Lou Reed) did not go unnoticed, nor did his penchant for performing mock fellatio on stage with guitarist Mick Ronson. Bowie's accessible androgyny appealed to all: you didn't have to be gay to appreciate it. 'The first time I recall having my ears truly tickled by Bowie was when I was on holiday in Weymouth with my parents in a wretched caravan,' reveals XTC frontman Andy Partridge.

On a Saturday morning the radio was on and the BBC played 'Andy Warhol' [also from *Hunky Dory*]. I vaguely knew who Andy Warhol was by then but what I was taken with was Bowie's flamboyant singing, a sort of gulping yodel that caught me aside swipes. A mental note was made about this boy. I was up in London, shopping for clothes in Kensington Market in the summer of 1972, and was having a burger for lunch in a café there, when a record stall a few feet away put on the just-released *Ziggy Stardust* album, very loud. Man, I was in heaven. I'd just bought a sailor jacket, which I was to dye red (it went pink!), and I was having a burger and a milkshake, with 'Moonage Daydream' bending my brain. It was the same record stall that featured in the *Clockwork Orange* film. Seriously. It was all too perfect.[4]

When Bowie draped an arm around Ronson on the BBC's flagship music show *Top of the Pops* a few months later, a nation was outraged. Well, the majority of the nation, anyway: there can be little doubt that the indignation of their parents only helped to endear the otherworldly Bowie to young viewers. For the generation that would spawn the out-gay pop stars of the 1980s, Bowie's outrageous campery and sexual androgyny was a revelation, and for many watching that Thursday evening as David and Mick pushed the bounds of acceptability during their performance of 'Starman', Bowie's current hit single, their own personal journey began. 'Bowie did not make me gay,' says Andy Bell of international hit act Erasure, 'but it was pretty staggering seeing him perform on *Top Of The Pops*. The music was for a slightly older crowd in school who tended to over-intellectualise; as a boy from a council estate I felt a bit out of my depth'.[5]

'I first saw David Bowie as Ziggy Stardust, performing at Lewisham Odeon in 1973 just before my twelfth birthday,' Boy George revealed in a touching tribute to his hero published just two days after his death. 'I have been a loyal fan since that first concert. As a teenager growing up in Suburbia, I was very much the odd one out and Bowie was the light at the end of a very grey tunnel. He validated me and made me realise I was not alone.'[6] Fellow hit-maker Marc Almond felt the same way. 'He was so much more important to me than my teachers,' he told *The Guardian*'s Jude Rogers. 'He got me into books, music, films – that's what great pop stars can do'.[7] For a nation brought up to laugh at the colourless campery of John Inman, Larry Grayson and Melvyn Hayes (early evening television was full of nancy boys in the 1970s), David Bowie exploded from the TV set like a rainbow-coloured angel. The opening couplet of 'Rebel Rebel', where he sang 'got your mother in a whirl; she's not sure if you're a boy or a girl', simply cemented his stature as the figurehead of the disenfranchised.

'It was only really on discovering the music of David Bowie that music suddenly was about me instead of about somebody else,' says singer-songwriter, broadcaster and human rights activist Tom Robinson. 'That experience, of hearing music that I loved and having it emotionally resonate with me, was an enormously important factor for me, and I did say to myself in my early 20s that if I ever had the chance to make music that would also resonate with people like me – rather than people like them – then I would do that. And over the years that's what I've tried to do. I was able to write songs where, ultimately, the relationships were kind of same-sex, implicitly or explicitly.'[8]

Bowie may have backtracked on that later, telling *Playboy* in 1976. 'It's true – I am a bisexual' (and admitting that his first sexual experience, at 14, was with 'some very pretty boy in class in some school or other that I took home and neatly fucked on my bed upstairs'),[9] and seven years later confiding in journalist Kurt Loder that talking to *Melody Maker* was 'the biggest mistake I ever made. Christ, I was so young then. I was experimenting,' but it did not really matter. In her 1993 book *Backstage*

Passes – Life On The Wild Side With David Bowie, the Thin White Duke's first wife Angie insisted that she had caught David in bed with Mick Jagger; other biographers have made similar claims. Bowie's backing singer Ava Cherry stated that Angie did indeed find the two rockers in bed together – but that she was also there: 'They made love to me,' she told the *New York Post*. 'It's called a cookie. I was the tasty filling. It was wonderful, just like it should have been – everybody on their respective side doing whatever they do. We were friends'.[10] Gay, straight or bisexual: whatever word Bowie chose to define his sexuality, this particular cat was out of the bag – or rather the closet. He'd said it, in print, and for thousands of young LGBT people across the world, life was suddenly a little less suffocating.

Whatever side of the sexual fence he fell on, Bowie's death heralded an understandable outpouring of grief, and social media platforms were littered with comments from straight, gay, trans and bisexual writers, artists and performers whose lives had been affected by him. Stars including Bruce Springsteen, Paul McCartney, Madonna, Bono and Lady Gaga paid homage in print and on stage. Many echoed Marilyn Manson's sentiment about how Bowie 'changed my life forever,'[11] including film director Guillermo Del Toro, who said that 'Bowie existed so all of us misfits learned that an oddity was a precious thing. He changed the world forever'.[12] It may sound like a bold claim, but it's true: although others had been gingerly trying to prise open the closet door before him, Bowie was the first rock icon to discuss his sexuality in such open terms in those post-Wolfenden Report years.

Two years after Bowie broke down the door, Freddie Mercury told the *New Musical Express*. 'I am as gay as a daffodil, my dear'.[13] No one seemed to notice and, unlike Bowie's shock disclosure, no one seemed to care. 'I like that Freddie,' said Little Richard. 'But he was not a queen!' Revisionists have insisted that this was Mercury coming out; others have claimed that the band's 1975 mega-hit 'Bohemian Rhapsody' was Mercury's attempt to out himself to his audience. This simply isn't the case: Mercury was playing with the *NME* reporter and stopped short of outing himself proper. He coyly admitting to being 'camp' and he claimed that at boarding school he had acted 'the arch poof'; bandmate Roger Taylor echoed his words, adding, 'Freddie's just his natural self:

just a poof really,' but the meaning was clear: he's outrageous, but he's not 'bent', and the revelation barely got a reaction – even when he 'pranced around the stage in a ballerina outfit that made him look like a moustachioed Tinkerbell'.[14] The year after, Bowie's friend and fellow glam idol Marc Bolan (who, like Bowie and Mercury, used make-up to enhance his androgynous appeal) admitted to being bisexual, but again this went almost unnoticed. The world, and especially the British media, was either not ready or simply not interested. It all seemed a little calculated, fake even. As Marc Almond says: 'It didn't strike me then that Freddie was actually gay'.[15]

Besides, Bowie, Bolan and Mercury all had women in their life. Mercury was already known for his outré stage persona, and although he would continue to camp it up, he would never open up in public about being homosexual. 'I remember back in an interview where I said, "I play on the bisexual thing,"' he recalled in 1976. 'Of course I play on it. It's simply a matter of wherever my mood takes me. If people ask me if I'm gay, I tell them it's up to them to find out.' Apparently, those around did not need much convincing. When Mercury split from his long-term girlfriend Mary Austin, saying he thought he was bisexual, Mary is reported to have told him 'No, Freddie; I think you are gay'.[16] Even his later lover, the German soft-core porn star Barbara Valentin, described him as 'mostly gay'.

Mercury's sexuality was no secret to those who knew him; as he became more comfortable in his private life, he also became far less guarded about how he was perceived by the public and the press and, for the most part, they left him alone. However, once he started making more headlines for his hedonistic lifestyle than for his music, the British tabloid press began circling. The message was clear: do what you like in private, but if you dare to bring your sexuality in to the real world we're going to pounce. When, in 1986, the *News Of the World* ran a story claiming that Mercury had recently undergone an AIDS test, the article outed him as bisexual. Subsequent stories in the same newspaper, and in sister publication *The Sun*, continued to dig around in his sex life, finding his former personal manager Paul Prenter willing to spill so long as the reporters kept opening their cheque books: Prenter himself died of AIDS, outlived by a few months by his former employer. On the

Freddie Mercury performing in New Haven, 1977

day Freddie Mercury died, the *News Of the World* (which went to print before his death was announced) quoted him as saying: 'I've had a lot of lovers. I've tried relationships on either side – male and female. But all of them have gone wrong.'[17] That last sentence was not quite true. Mary Austin, the woman Mercury had referred to as the love of his life, has stayed loyal to this day, refusing all requests for interviews. Eight years before he died Mercury met Jim Hutton; the pair became lovers and Hutton moved into his house, finally bringing some stability in to his life – although as far as the public and press were concerned, Hutton was simply Mercury's gardener.

Bowie may have been open with some of the intimate details of his sex life, but he was not the first superstar of the music industry to attempt to poke a stiletto heel through the closet door. In September 1970, 16 months before Dame David had been summed up in Watts' *Melody Maker* article for being 'a swishy queen, a gorgeously effeminate boy . . . as camp as a row of tents, with his limp hand and trolling vocabulary'[18] – and 10 months after she and Bowie had shared a stage at the London Palladium – Dusty Springfield, one of the biggest stars of the 1960s, came perilously close to revealing that she was bisexual. In an interview with Ray Connolly of *The Evening Standard* she owned up to sharing her home with another woman – American singer/songwriter Norma Tanega – and told him, that 'so many other people say I'm bent, and I've heard it so many times that I've almost learned to accept it. I don't go leaping around to all the gay clubs but I can be very flattered. Girls run after me a lot and it doesn't upset me. But I know that I'm as perfectly capable of being swayed by a girl as by a boy. More and more people feel that way and I don't see why I shouldn't.'[19] Although she was hailed as Britain's 'best ever pop singer' by *Rolling Stone* magazine, as Connolly reveals, 'by 1970, when we spoke, her career in the UK was already in decline. In those days, stars had to keep churning out hit singles at a rate of three or four a year and Dusty was hardly releasing any singles at all. I don't believe that the article affected her career adversely. Much more damaging was her decision to go off to California in 1971, abandoning her fan base in the UK.'[20]

She would not enjoy another major chart hit in her home country until her rediscovery by a new, gay-friendly audience, thanks to her association with the Pet Shop Boys in 1987. Purely coincidentally, Bowie worked with the Pet Shop Boys himself, on 1996's 'Hallo Spaceboy'.

Springfield's admission, couched though it was, was a brave move and one she knew would likely alter people's perception of her. 'D'you realise,' she told Connolly, 'what I've just said could put the final seal to my doom? I don't know, though. I might attract a whole new audience.'

'I never knew why she decided to say what she did to me,' Connolly adds, 'but she actually goaded me into it. So she obviously wanted it out.' Like Bowie, she struggled with the straitjacketing, telling *The Los Angeles Free Press* in 1973, 'I mean, people say that I'm gay, gay, gay, gay, gay, gay, gay, gay. I'm not anything. I'm just . . . People are people . . . I basically want to be straight . . . I go from men to women; I don't give a shit.' A decade later, she took part in a symbolic marriage to her then-lover, actress Teda Bracci, on a mutual friend's California ranch. Battling depression, drink and drugs (the pair first encountered each other at an Alcoholics Anonymous meeting), the couple's relationship was always volatile and often violent. Prone to self-harm and with her career at an all-time low, on one occasion Dusty was admitted to Cedars-Sinai hospital with her face swollen and blackened and her front teeth missing after the two women had fought using saucepans and skillets. The resultant plastic surgery altered Dusty's appearance forever. Understandably, the relationship did not last.

Deported from South Africa in 1964 for refusing to perform before segregated audiences (apartheid reminded the singer, born Mary Isobel Catherine Bernadette O'Brien, of the prejudice shown back in England to homosexuals), no pop singer before her, at least not one who had enjoyed such mainstream success, had dared to even suggest that she (or he) may be a 'queer'. Raised a Catholic, her choice of material in her later years showed that she was becoming much more comfortable with her position as a gay icon: 'Closet Man' (from the 1979 album *Living Without Your Love*), 'Soft Core' (from 1982's *White Heat*), and others answered any questions people still had about where her sympathies lay. Sadly for Springfield and her legion of fans, the singer, who died from breast cancer in 1999, was subject to homophobic abuse for years. As recently as 2014, Roger Lewis, writing in Britain's *Spectator* magazine, chose to use a review of a biography about Springfield as an opportunity to poke fun at a her and many other celebrity lesbians: 'You can always spot a lesbian by her big thrusting chin. Celebrity Eskimo Sandi Toksvig, Ellen DeGeneres, Jodie Foster, Clare Balding, Vita Sackville-West, God love them: there's a touch of Desperate Dan in the jaw-bone area, no doubt the better to go bobbing for apples.'[21]

*

Of course, there were other gay, lesbian and bisexual people in the music industry before David or Dusty. Just a few years before either of these pop idols opened up, the Beatles' manager Brian Epstein had died after an accidental overdose, his pill-popping exacerbated by his closeted homosexuality and having to deal with blackmailers including his former lover, the out-of-work actor Dizz Gillespie. Epstein's death came just two weeks after the grisly discovery of the bloody corpse of gay playwright Joe Orton, bludgeoned to death in a jealous rage by his lover Kenneth Halliwell. The same year that Epstein and Orton died (Orton had been having talks with Epstein about writing the script for the next Beatles movie; his body was discovered by a chauffeur who was to relay Orton to a meeting with the group), the pioneering British record producer Joe Meek took a gun and killed first his landlady and them himself. Epstein, Orton and Meek all knew each other and had all been persecuted because of their sexuality. Like Epstein, Meek, who scored a pre-Beatles Number One single on both sides of the Atlantic with 'Telstar', had been the victim of blackmail. It's no wonder, then, that it was widely accepted that coming out would mean the instant death of one's career – or worse.

But it wasn't always that way.

CHAPTER 2

Pretty Baby

'You can talk about your jelly roll, but none of them compare with Pretty Baby...'

From the unpublished original lyric to 'Pretty Baby' by Tony Jackson, c. 1911

O ur story begins in the red-light district of New Orleans, an area no bigger than 38 blocks that was formally designated as The District but, in a sarcastic doff of the cap to city councilman Sidney Story, was known to one and all as Storyville.

Founded by the French (as *La Nouvelle-Orléans*) in 1718, New Orleans is a city with a colourful, confusing and occasionally violent history. In 1722, it became the capital of French Louisiana, but over the next 180 years, the area was first surrendered to the Spanish Empire before being handed back to France and finally, in 1803, being sold by Napoleon to the United States for a total of 68 million Francs.

New Orleans quickly became the largest port, as well as the biggest and most important city, in the South, exporting most of the country's cotton as well as other products to Europe and New England. Unfortunately all of this new wealth and trade had an unpleasant consequence: by the middle of the century there were over 50 slave markets dotted around the city. Hot and humid, the 'Big Easy' grew rapidly with

Opposite: Tony Jackson

the arrival of American, African, French and Creole people, attracted to the business opportunities (legal and otherwise) to be had. Refugees fleeing from the revolution in Haiti brought slaves with them and massively increased the city's French-speaking population.

As well as being prosperous, New Orleans was also one of the most dangerous cities to live in. Devastating fires in 1788 and 1784 saw the majority of the city's original wooden buildings razed to the ground. Relationships between the different races were often tense (spurred on by the State of Louisiana's attempt to enforce strict racial segregation), and race riots, marches by white supremacists and mob lynchings happened all too frequently. Despite this, with a large, educated coloured population that had long interacted with the whites, racial attitudes were relatively liberal for the Deep South. Regrettably, this liberal attitude did not carry through to all aspects of life: the Territorial Convention of 1805 imposed harsh sodomy laws, with a mandatory life sentence for indulging in 'the abominable and detestable crime against nature'; however, before the end of the century this penalty was reduced to a maximum of ten years in prison.

The progressive Sidney Story noted the success of port cities in European countries that had legalised prostitution, and it was he that penned City Ordinance 13,485 – the guidelines that would legalise vice and would have to be followed by the people plying their trade in The District. These guidelines were adopted on 6 July 1897 and, by limiting prostitution to one area of town where authorities could monitor the practice, within three years Storyville had become the number one revenue centre of New Orleans. For 25¢, you could buy a copy of the *Blue Book*, a directory listing houses of ill repute as well as the names and addresses of the women who worked there. Black and white brothels existed side by side, although perversely black men were barred from using either by law, and dozens of restaurants and saloons opened up to cater for the huge influx of sex tourists. The great and good of other cities were shocked at the goings-on in New Orleans, so much so that in 1913 the National Commission for the Suppression of Vice, backed financially by John D. Rockefeller, sent a crew to Storyville to make a film about a good girl from New York's fall from grace, which was screened around the country as a warning to others not to follow the lead of this modern-day Sodom and Gomorrah.

By 1910 The District housed 200 brothels with 2,000 women, and there was at least one house – run by an effeminate man known as 'Big Nelly' – which provided boys rather than girls for entertainment. The bars, bordellos, honky-tonks and dives of Storyville offered more than sex: the better – and more expensive – establishments would hire a piano player or a small band to accompany dances and provide amusement for their guests. Houses like Lulu White's Mahogany Hall, on the notorious Basin Street, were grand buildings with ornate fireplaces, coloured tilework, sweeping staircases and expensive drapes. Paintings in gold frames adorned the walls of the elegant parlours filled with velvet-covered chairs. Black, white and Creole musicians rubbed shoulders and a newly emergent style of music, which by 1915 had been christened jazz, flourished. Buddy Bolden (considered to be the first bandleader to play jazz), Jelly Roll Morton, Pops Foster and many others got their first break in Storyville, as did a young man by the name of Tony Jackson, one of the most accomplished musicians working in that part of town. As New Orleans banjo player Johnny St. Cyr told music historian Alan Lomax, 'Really the best pianist we had was Tony Jackson'.[1]

Jackson (born Antonio Junius Jackson and alternately referred to as Tony or Toney) had been born into poverty in New Orleans on 5 June, 1876 (according to his sister Ida) – or was it October 1882 (as claimed in the 1910 census), or perhaps it was 25 October 1884, the date that appears on his draft card and which he signed to confirm it. Trumpeter Bunk Johnson, in a letter to noted jazz historian Roy J. Carew, was adamant it was the former: 'I think he is a few years older than me. I was born December 27, 1879.'[2] Yet Bunk Johnson's memory was, at best, unreliable: author Donald M. Marquis has proved quite convincingly that Bunk added a decade onto his own age, and that he was actually born in December 1889, making the date that the infant Jackson drew his first breath much more likely to be 1882.[3]

Whatever his true birth date may have been, Jackson was the sixth child of a freed slave and one of a pair of sickly twins: his brother, Prince Albert, died when Jackson was just 14 months old. An epileptic since birth, legend has it that at around 10 years of age he constructed his own keyboard instrument out of junk found in the backyard and taught himself to play. Jazz historian Bill Edwards (writing at www.ragpiano.com) adds, 'within a short time an arrangement was worked out with a neighbor exchanging dishwashing duties for time on the neighbor's old reed organ,' however his sister Ida claimed, 'Tony never had any lessons. He taught his own self with the help of God.'⁴ One thing is certain: by the age of 13, he had landed his first job playing piano at a honky-tonk: just two years later he was already considered one of the best – and consequently most sought-after – entertainers in Storyville.

Described (by Tim Samuelson in the 2008 book *Out and Proud in Chicago*) as the 'musical bridge between the multicultural sounds of his native New Orleans and the emerging syncopated music of his adopted Chicago,' before he became the toast of Storyville, Jackson and his family had been living in a small apartment at 3920 Magazine Street. That apartment was a couple of miles from Storyville but less than ten minutes' walk from one of his earliest regular gigs: Bunk Johnson recalled that 'Tony Jackson started playing piano by ear in Adam Oliver's tonk on the corner of Amelia and Tchoupitoulas. That was between 1892 and 1893.'⁵ Again, this date is probably out by a few years: Bunk claimed that he and Tony played together in Adam Oliver's band in 1894, but this has never been substantiated. If they did appear together, it was probably around 1904.

Around the same time, a young boy, barely in his teens, could be heard playing piano in a local brothel. Ferdinand Joseph LaMothe, later to find fame as Jelly Roll Morton, was overawed by Jackson – and why wouldn't he be? There was no one to touch him. Morton looked up to Jackson (who was the best part of a decade older than him) and is quoted as saying that he was the only pianist better than he was. For a man as prone to self-aggrandisement as Morton (this is the same man that claimed to have single-handedly 'invented' jazz), that's quite something. Jackson became mentor, tutor and surrogate father to young Ferd (as he was known to his friends), and their friendship was untouched by the racial, sexual and religious taboos of the time. Jackson was black, the child of a slave family, and openly, almost defiantly homosexual; Morton was a Creole-born Catholic and fiercely heterosexual. If he had not already been thrown out of the family home for playing 'the Devil's music', there can be no doubt that his God-fearing relatives would have ensured that he had nothing to do with a ne'er-do-well like Jackson.

It would not take long for Jackson and Jelly Roll Morton to become favourites with the patrons of Storyville, and the pair were employed by the better-class white houses; according to Bunk Johnson, Morton and Jackson were the only black players able to work the white-run brothels. They dressed well and were paid well, too. Jackson, who could pick up almost any tune by ear, was known as 'Professor', an honorary title given to the best of Storyville's piano players. 'Tony Jackson played at Gypsy Schaeffer's,' Morton told Alan Lomax:

Walk into Gypsy Schaeffer's and, right away, the bell would ring upstairs and all the girls would walk into the parlor, dressed in their fine evening gowns and ask the customer if he would care to drink wine. They would call for the "professor" and, while champagne was being served all around, Tony would play a couple numbers. If a naked dance was desired, Tony would dig up one of his fast speed tunes and one of the girls would dance on a little narrow stage, completely nude. Yes, they danced absolutely stripped, but in New Orleans the naked dance was a real art.[6]

Schaeffer's house, on Conti Street, had a raised step (or banquette) in front, and it was standing there that Roy J. Carew first heard Tony Jackson play. Writing in *Jazz Journal* magazine (in March 1952) Carew recalled:

The piano was in the front parlour next to the street, and consequently a sidewalk listener could receive the full benefit of Tony's performance, which always seemed to me to be perfect. I didn't go inside, where I could watch as well as listen ... those establishments were strictly business places. The house provided entertainment, but always at a substantial price, and patrons were expected to spend freely. So I took my fill of listening from the banquette. Some time later, however, I was pleasantly surprised while passing the corner of Franklin and Bienville Streets, to hear Tony performing in the café on that corner, lately identified as Frank Early's Café. This was my opportunity, for it was a café for white patrons, so I strolled in, bought a drink at the bar, and took a seat at the little table close to the platform where Tony was playing the piano.

Legend has it that Tony wrote an early draft of his biggest hit, 'Pretty Baby', at Frank Early's, and he was famed locally for the obscene variations on, and parodies of, popular songs that he would improvise at the piano.

Jackson's standing on the local circuit increased, and in 1904 he was chosen to accompany the Whitman Sisters New Orleans Troubadours on their national tour. A high-class vaudeville show, it is said that 'the singing of Tony Jackson and Baby Alice Whitman usually brought down the house'.[7]

Carew remembered how most people thought Jackson was ugly 'largely because his rather weak chin accentuated the prominence of his lips. At that time, around 1905, he already had the little tuft of prematurely grey hair in his forelock. But Tony's lack of beauty was immediately forgotten in his flawless performance, and his happy, friendly disposition. He was a happy-go-lucky person, and his actions seemed to evidence the fact.'[8] It seems that most people remembered him as 'happy-go-lucky' with 'not a care in the world,' but as Al Rose put it in his definitive book *Storyville, New Orleans, Being an Authentic, Illustrated Account of the Notorious Red-light District*:

> Oh, to be an epileptic, alcoholic, homosexual Negro genius in the Deep South of the United States of America! How could you have a care? Anyone would be happy, naturally, being among the piano virtuosi of his era, permitted to play only in saloons and whorehouses, for pimps and prostitutes and their customers. How could he be anything but "happy-go-lucky"? Tony Jackson discovered early in life that a young man of such beginnings as his, such "advantages," had to try to please everybody simply to survive.[9]

Life certainly was not easy for a black male homosexual at a time when same-sex attraction was considered either criminal or a mental illness.

After hours, Jackson and his friends used to congregate at The Frenchman's saloon, a known haven for cross-dressers where a number of musicians went. Every inch the flamboyant showman, a prostitute named Carrie recalled that 'all them dicty [a slang word meaning well-dressed or pretentious] people used to hang by the Frenchman's to hear that fruit Tony Jackson best of anybody. He play pretty, I give them that.'[10] Composer Clarence Williams backed this up: 'at that time everybody followed the great Tony Jackson. About Tony, you know he was an effeminate man – you know. We all copied him. He was so original and a great instrumentalist. I know I copied Tony.'[11] Clarinettist George Baguet remembered how Tony would 'start playin' a Cakewalk [a dance that had been popular with slaves and which found its way into minstrel shows], then he'd kick over the piano stool and dance a Cakewalk – and never stop playin' the piano – and playin', man! Nobody played like him!' Jackson's exhibitionist style presaged the piano pyrotechnics of Liberace, Jerry Lee Lewis and Keith Emerson by decades.

It is Morton that we have to rely on for much of what we know today about Tony Jackson, and specifically the series of interviews he gave to Alan Lomax in 1938, which were later edited for the book *Mister Jelly Roll*:

All these men were hard to beat, but when Tony Jackson walked in, any one of them would get up from the piano stool. If he didn't, somebody was liable to say, "Get up from that piano. You hurting its feelings. Let Tony play". Tony was real dark and not a bit good-looking but he had a beautiful disposition. He was the outstanding favorite of New Orleans, and I have never known any pianists to come from any section of the world that could leave New Orleans victorious. Tony was considered among all who knew him the greatest single-handed entertainer in the world. His memory seemed like something nobody's ever heard of in the music world. There was no tune that would ever come up from any opera, from any show of any kind or anything that was wrote on any paper that Tony couldn't play from memory. He had such a beautiful voice and a marvellous range. His voice on an opera tune was exactly as an opera singer. His range on a blues would be just exactly like a blues singer.[12]

Carew recalled how 'his repertoire included all types of music, anything a customer might ask for: ragtime songs, waltz songs, march songs, ballads, semi-classics . . . and he executed them all in his matchless style;

he even sang duets, taking each part with equal facility. His voice was of an exceptional quality, clear and vibrant, of good timbre and wide range.'[13]

Jackson was tiring of playing bordellos in Storyville. He was earning good money, the tips were often huge (Morton boasted of earning up to $100 a night in tips alone) and he was easily able to support his family, yet he wanted more. Morton told Lomax that Jackson decided to move to Chicago because 'he liked the freedom there,' and on the original recordings (which still exist in the Library of Congress), Morton and Lomax joke about Jackson's sexuality. When Morton reveals that 'Tony happened to be one of those gentlemen that a lot of people call them a lady or a sissy or something like that, but he was very good and very much admired,' Lomax counters this with 'so was he . . . was he a fairy?' Morton, laughing, replies, 'I guess he was either a ferry or a steamboat, one or the other, I guess it's a ferry because that's what you pay a nickel for'.[14] The inference is clear: Tony Jackson's sexual favours were available to those with money in their pockets and could be bought for a lot less than the hookers he played piano for.

No one can seem to agree on when exactly Jackson moved to Chicago; however, his influence on the city's music scene, and on every jazz pianist that came after him, is undeniable. He helped to lay the foundation for Chicago's reputation as a jazz capital, and other musicians – including Morton – soon followed him there. Jackson found acceptance in Chicago's Bronzeville neighbourhood, where the LGBT community flourished in the pre-war years. As well as enjoying the freedom that his new home afforded him, he found plenty of work amongst Bronzeville's cabarets, theatres and cafes – and would have no doubt have taken advantage of the opportunity to socialise with other gay men. Black men and women were more than simply tolerated in Bronzeville, where prostitution, interracial relations and visible same-sex couples were the norm. 'Chicago was segregated: the South Side was black and the North Side was white. It's still a lot like that, but back then it was even more strict,'[15] says historian St. Sukie de la Croix. 'Right up until the 1960s, the black gay community and the white gay community were completely separate entities. The only blacks that appeared in the bars on the North Side were drag queens and piano players. All the bars were run by the

Mafia. Bronzeville was entirely black: that's where all the black clubs were. It was a great place, and white people were welcome there, but black people could not go to the North Side'.

Jackson lived in an apartment on the ground floor of 4111 South Wabash Avenue, Chicago, where he was joined by two of his sisters, a brother-in-law, a nephew and two nieces (according to his draft card, issued in 1918, the whole family later moved to 4045 South State Street). He tickled the ivories at venues including the Elite Café on Chicago's South State Street (there were two Elite Cafés, both on State Street; Tony played at both) – often as part of a three-piece band with Oliver Perry (violin) and percussionist Charles Gillian backing singer Sallie Lee Johnson – and at Russell & Dago's Grand Buffet: an advertisement for Russell & Dago's features a photograph of 'Toney' above the state-ment, 'Mr. Jackson is one of the best entertainers in the city, and is well liked. He is a good card.' He quickly earned himself a reputation, not only for his playing but also for his manner: writer Columbus Bragg referred to him as 'that spoiled and petted Black Paderewski,' although he grudgingly admitted that Tony was 'unequalled on the piano'.[16] That part of State Street was known as the Stroll, and Jackson was the king of the Stroll: 'Tony Jackson received an ovation, then played the piano dexterously and just took four bows and then had to do it all over again to please the feverish anxiety of that distinct clientele that patronise the Grand Theatre'.[17]

At a bordello known as Dago Frank's, he met the singer Alberta Hunter, herself a lesbian who – although she had a brief marriage in 1919 – lived for many years with her partner Lottie Tyler. It was Hunter that revealed that Tony wrote 'Pretty Baby' for a 'tall, skinny fellow,' and it was her performances that helped popularise the song. 'Everybody would go to hear Tony Jackson after hours,' she revealed. 'Tony was just marvellous – a fine musician, spectacular, but still soft. He could write a song in two minutes and was one of the greatest accompanists I've ever listened to. Tony Jackson was a prince of a fellow, and he would always pack them in. There would be so many people around the piano trying to learn his style that sometimes he could hardly move his hands – and he never played any song the same way twice.'[18] One of his other compositions, 'I've Got Elgin Movements in my Hips with

Twenty Years' Guarantee', was plagiarised by a number of performers (Cleo Gibson's 1929 recording 'I've Got Ford Engine Movements in my Hips, Ten Thousand Miles Guarantee', for example) but, unfortunately, Tony's original – which he would sing in a high register, imitating a woman – was never recorded. A third song composed around this time, 'We've Got Him', was written for the now-forgotten female vaudeville duo Brown and Wallace.

'Tony was instrumental in my going to Chicago the first time,' Morton revealed to Alan Lomax. 'Very much to my regret, because there was more money at home. We were very, very good friends and whenever he spotted me coming in the door, he would sing a song he knew I liked – "Pretty Baby", one of Tony's great tunes that he wrote in 1913 or 14 and was a million-dollar hit in less than a year.' Glover Compton, another contemporary of Tony's who had first encountered him at the Cosmopolitan Club in Louisville, Kentucky in 1904, insisted that he wrote 'Pretty Baby' when he was working at the Elite Number Two in 1911. Compton – who also performed with Alberta Hunter in Chicago in the early 1920s – said that his style 'and the styles of Tony Jackson and Jelly Roll Morton were about the same, but Morton played better without songs (i.e. on instrumental pieces), while Jackson was better with songs'. Compton and Jackson became good friends: Tony called Glover 'Bill', and the two of them composed several songs together. Jackson wrote the song 'You're Such a Pretty Thing' for Compton's wife Nettie Lewis, and the men kept in touch: Compton played at Jackson's funeral. Once, when Tony sent Glover a photograph of himself with an unidentified male friend, he wrote, 'That medal you see on my coat I won down here in a contest on the piano'. Morton told a story about how he bested Jackson in a competition: 'I finally stayed for a battle of music that came up and I won the contest over Tony. That threw me first in line, but, even though I was the winner, I never thought the prize was given to the right party; I thought Tony should have the emblem.' Roy Carew, writing in *The Record Changer* in 1943, recalled how Morton 'told me with considerable pride that he had beaten Tony once in a contest. Jelly Roll said that, as the other contestants were seated on the stage while Tony was playing, he (Jelly) was seated near enough to the piano to keep telling Tony, sotto voce, "You can't sing now ... You can't sing now." I don't know if that affected Tony's playing any, but Jelly Roll won the contest.' Perhaps the medal Tony wore so proudly in that photograph was for second place, and Morton's admission that Jackson should have won the competition was his way of assuaging his guilt.

It's thanks to Morton's Library of Congress recording that we have the only example of Jackson's original lyrics:

> *You can talk about your jelly roll*
> *But none of them compare with pretty baby*
> *With pretty baby of mine*
> *Pretty baby of mine*

Those words might seem pretty tame by today's standards, but '*jelly roll*' was a slang term for both the penis and the vulva: Jackson's words reveal that he was not interested in sex with anyone else, as they could not measure up to what he was getting at home. Although Tony wrote 'Pretty Baby' around 1911, the song as it exists today was copyrighted in 1916, is credited to Jackson, Gus Kahn and Egbert Van Alstyne and features very different lyrics to those Jackson first penned. The song was originally about one of Jackson's male lovers: in his book *Vaudeville Old and New: An Encyclopedia of Variety Performances in America*, Frank Cullen states that the song 'was inspired by a young male prostitute to whom Jackson was attracted'. The chances are that one cynical line that remains in the sugary confection we now know as 'Pretty Baby' – 'Oh, I want a lovin' baby and it might as well be you' – is one of the few phrases to remain from Jackson's original.

Kahn and Van Alstyne first heard Jackson performing his version of the song (then, according to Kahn's son Donald, known as 'Jelly Roll Rag') in a black nightclub in Chicago, and they persuaded their publisher to buy it. After forking over the fee (a paragraph in the *Xenia Daily Gazette* of 15 January 1917, claims that he 'only received $45 for the great song hit' and that he was 'still pounding the piano every night for a few dollars'), Van Alstyne rewrote some of the music, adapting one of his own earlier songs, and Kahn set about cleaning up Jackson's somewhat bawdy lyrics. The new version of the song first appeared in *The Passing Show of 1916* (also known as *A World of Pleasure*); it later

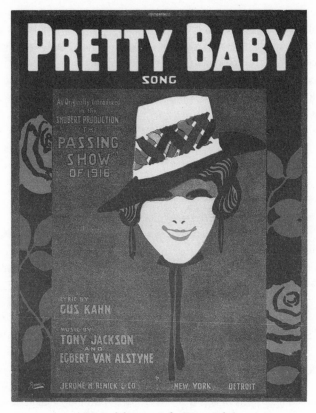

Original sheet music for 'Pretty Baby'

featured in the MGM musical *Broadway Rhythm*. In the years that followed, Van Alstyne and Khan were often accused of plagiarism, but this is simply not true. Tony was no fool, and it was common practice for songs to be rewritten to suit their purpose. 'Pretty Baby' debuted in a musical revue where it would have been wholly unacceptable to use a song that repeatedly used the phrase 'jelly roll'. Jackson certainly didn't feel cheated, as he collaborated with the pair again the following year on the song 'I've Been Fiddle-ing'.

One of the many stories about Jackson is that he would not allow his songs to be published, saying that 'he would burn them before he would give them away for five dollars apiece' [19] but this is not borne out by the facts. Following the success of 'Pretty Baby', a number of Jackson's songs were made available as sheet music, including 'Some Sweet Day' (first recorded in 1917 by Marion Harris: Louis Armstrong recorded a version in 1933. His version 'provides a direct link with music performed in New Orleans before the turn of the century,' according to jazz historian Floyd Levin), 'Ice and Snow', 'Miss Samantha Johnson's Wedding Day', 'I've Got 'em! There Ain't Nothin' to That', 'Waiting at the Old Church Door', 'I'm Cert'ny Gonna See 'bout That' (recorded by Fats Waller) and 'Why Keep Me Waiting So Long?' (which was popularised by Sophie Tucker). 'Why Keep Me Waiting So Long?' is the story of young Mandy Brown, a girl who is desperate to understand why her beau refuses to make love to her when her 'poor heart cries out for loving, good and strong'. Was Tony alluding to his own sexual desires in his lyrics?

Unfortunately, Tony Jackson never recorded, and sadly it appears that no examples of his playing have been preserved for posterity on piano rolls, unlike that of fellow ragtime maestro Scott Joplin. However, several of Jackson's tunes were transcribed for player piano in 1916 by Jackson's contemporary, the Chicago-based pianist Charley Straight, and listening to these 'recordings' is probably the closest any of us will ever get to experiencing Tony's style. While he may not have recorded the song himself, 'Pretty Baby' became a jazz standard and has been recorded by dozens of acts from the Emerson Military Band and Billy Murray (who released the first recorded versions of the song in 1916), through to Al Jolson, Dean Martin, Bing Crosby, Judy Garland, Doris Day and Brenda Lee. Murray, one of the most popular singers of the early recording era, deserves special mention for having recorded the song 'Honey Boy' in 1907, a song about a girl missing her sailor boyfriend which, when sung by a male vocalist, takes on a whole new meaning.

By 1917, Jackson was back in Storyville, playing piano in a house owned by the opera loving and cornet-playing Madame Antonia Gonzalez when the US Navy – concerned at the open availability of prostitution to its young sailors – closed the area down for good. 'Some sailors on leave got mixed up in a fight and two of them were killed. The navy started a war on Storyville,' wrote Louis Armstrong in his autobiography *Satchmo: My*

Life in New Orleans. 'The police began to raid all the houses and cabarets. It sure was a sad scene to watch the law run all those people out of Storyville. They reminded me of a gang of refugees. Some of them had spent the best part of their lives there. I have never seen such weeping and carrying-on.' [20] Tony Jackson packed up his few belongings and returned to Bronzeville: Lulu White and her girls moved to Bienville Street, a hovel compared with her former palace of passion, where she was regularly arrested and charged with 'operating a disorderly house'. 'Chicago was different,' recalled jazz clarinettist Willie Humphries, who grew up around the musicians of Storyville and – like countless others – blew into the Windy City after the red-light district was forced to clean up its act. 'It was wide open. We took root there. [But] The District's where we learned to play the music that could corrupt the angels.' [21]

In August 1919 – the year that the city saw its worst race riots after 17-year-old Eugene Williams was killed by a hostile crowd of whites – Jackson was arrested in connection with a spate of recent murders on the South Side of Chicago. He was released without charge, but life in Chicago was becoming tougher: a stray bullet killed Alberta Hunter's accompanist and she fled for New York. The introduction of prohibition in January 1920 – and the criminal activity, illegal underground drinking establishments and speakeasies that went hand-in-hand with the ban on the sale of alcohol – only made the city even more difficult to get by in, especially for a black man who was openly homosexual.

Although he was not yet 40, Jackson's health was in steep decline. On 17 February 1921, knowing full well that the end was near, some of his friends held a fundraising benefit for him. The All Star Tony Jackson Testimonial took place at the Dreamland Café on South State Street, Chicago, arranged 'as a proper and fitting demonstration of their loyalty and friendship' to raise enough money to send Jackson on 'a long and much needed vacation at Hot Springs'. The benefit, which raised $325, all of it handed over to Jackson,[22] featured 'one of the greatest programs ever arranged, in which the leading cabaret and vaudeville stars, as well as several boxers and wrestlers, participated'.[23] Unlike many other jazz musicians, Tony Jackson was not interested in drugs, however he was a heavy drinker (in *Hear Me Talkin' To Ya* Alberta Hunter is quoted as saying, 'he always had a drink on the piano – always!'), and there's no way of knowing what damage illicit liquor was doing to his already weak body. Jackson died in April 1921; the official line is that his rather bizarre end came as the result of a seizure after suffering 'eight weeks of the hiccups which the efforts of doctors could not relieve'. Several accounts state that he was also suffering from the ravages of syphilis.

Outside the recollections of Carew and Morton, Tony Jackson would have been wiped from history had it not been for the many recordings of his most popular song. In 1978 'Pretty Baby' provided the inspiration for the Louis Malle film of the same name, with the director describing Jackson as 'a very extravagant, very brilliant, and quite extraordinary character'.[24] The film, which outraged audiences by having a 12-year-old Brooke Shields portray Violet, a child prostitute working in a New Orleans brothel, featured Antonio Fargas (star of TV's *Starsky and Hutch*) as Professor, a whorehouse piano player loosely based on Tony. In 2008, the year that playwright Clare Brown debuted *Don't You Leave Me Here*, a dramatisation of the relationship between Tony and Jelly Roll, 'Pretty Baby' was used in the British TV soap *EastEnders*, during a heart-breaking tour de force by the actress June Brown.

'Tony was a versatile performer,' theatre manager Shep Allen told George W. Kay (in an interview for *Jazz Journal* magazine, February 1963). 'As a singer, he sounded something like Nat "King" Cole but he had more power and greater range. He could reach very high notes without getting a falsetto. He could play a great piano and he could play anything.' His influence on jazz, and on the musicians coming out of New Orleans and Chicago, is immeasurable: Professor Longhair, Fats Domino, Huey 'Piano' Smith and many, many more owe him a huge debt. 'People believe Louis Armstrong originated scat,' Morton told Lomax. 'I must take that credit away from him, because I know better. Tony Jackson and myself were using scat for novelty back in 1906 and 1907 when Louis Armstrong was still in the orphans' home.'[25] 'Pretty Baby' may be the only song people remember, but many others have been attributed to him, including 'Michigan Water Blues' and 'The Naked Dance' (both recorded by Morton). Morton may have described him as 'real dark and not a bit good-looking,' but, as Carrie the prostitute and jazz trumpeter Bunk Johnson noted, Tony was 'dicty', and the way he dressed came to define the archetypical image of the ragtime pianist, with his bowler hat, diamond pin, waistcoat and sleeve garters. In his later years, Tony often performed, as if a concert pianist, in a dinner jacket and black tie, and it was said of other jazz pianists that if you couldn't play like Jackson then you could at least look like him.

In 2011, some 90 years after his death, Tony Jackson was inducted into the Chicago Gay and Lesbian Hall of Fame. He was honoured for his musical contributions and for living 'as an openly gay man when that was rare. His influence on Chicago's music scene was immense [and he] helped to lay the foundation for Chicago's reputation as a jazz capital.'[1]

CHAPTER 3

Bull Dyker Blues

'I went out last night with a crowd of my friends. They must've been women, cause I don't like no men'

'Prove it on Me Blues' by Ma Rainey

Written histories have tended to straightwash the stories of the female pioneers of the blues, yet many of these women were either lesbian or bisexual, and sang openly and joyously about having sex with other women. Around the time that Tony Jackson wrote 'Pretty Baby', two women who were instrumental in popularising the blues had their first encounter. Bessie Smith was just 14 (some reports say she was as young as 11) when she first met Gertrude 'Ma' Rainey, but the older and more experienced woman quickly became her mentor, instructor and – more than likely – her lover, as Rainey's guitar player Sam Chatmon revealed.[2] Both women were bisexual and did not care who knew, although both would marry men who would exert a massive influence on their lives and careers.

With its roots in African American work songs and European folk music, from its earliest days the blues included elements of spirituals, work songs and storytelling ballads. Emerging towards the end of the nineteenth century, the songs were originally performed by one singer accompanying themselves on guitar or banjo, or by a singer accompanied by a pianist. With raw, simple lyrics full of emotion, blues songs dwelt on love and loss, with singers recounting tales of loneliness and injustice, of hard-done-by women and their cheating men. Named, if you believe her own story, by Ma Rainey sometime around 1902, blues is the music of the oppressed, of the experiences of black people at a time when they were considered by many to be second-class citizens. With the majority of singers and musicians all but illiterate, these songs were passed orally from musician to musician, adapted and improved along the way, with ribald slang and double entendres often used to get the far more risqué meaning of many of the songs past censors. The blues quickly became the most listened-to music (with the possible exception of gospel) by black audiences. 'The Blues,' poet, novelist and playwright Langston Hughes wrote in his 1927 collection *Fine Clothes to the Jew*, 'unlike the spirituals, have a strict poetic pattern: one long line repeated and a third line to rhyme with the first two. Sometimes the second line in repetition is slightly changed, and sometimes, but very seldom, it is omitted. The mood of the Blues is almost always despondency, but when they are sung, people laugh.'[3]

Hughes is describing the 12-bar, call-and-response music most of us recognise as the blues, yet the genre also encompasses folk-blues, country-blues, urban and electric blues. Although it grew from the cotton fields of the South this music developed in northern cities: in New York (specifically around Harlem), in Detroit where the production lines of the motor manufacturers desperately needed workers, and in Chicago alongside jazz. It was the pop music of its day, and its stars – far from the ragged minstrel described by W. C. Handy in his autobiography *Father of the Blues* – were well-regarded and occasionally highly paid.

At the end of the nineteenth and in the first decades of the twentieth century, Harlem had become one of the chief destinations for black migrants from around the US and a centre for African American culture. The Harlem Renaissance was fuelled by black intellectuals, including writers, artists, musicians, photographers and poets – many of them gay (like Langston Hughes), lesbian or bisexual – who filled the formerly white, middle-class district. As writer and painter Richard Bruce Nugent put it, 'Harlem was very much like a village. People did what they wanted to do with whom they wanted to do it . . . You just did what you wanted to do. Nobody was in the closet. There wasn't any closet.'[4]

The antics of Harlem's lesbians provided fuel for gossip writers, including Archie Seale, whose *Man About Harlem* column often featured salacious – and anonymous – stories of the area's ladies, and Geraldyn Dismond, a reporter on the African American paper the *Inter-State Tattler.*

Some venues in the notorious Jungle Alley district, including the world-famous Cotton Club, only welcomed white audiences even though they featured many of the most popular black entertainers of the day, among them Duke Ellington, Cab Calloway and Louis Armstrong (Bessie Smith played there, while on the comeback trail, in 1935). Photographer and writer Carl Van Vechten was famously turned away from the Cotton Club because the party he arrived with was racially mixed; he vowed to boycott the club until black patrons could hear Ethel Waters singing there. Yet although racism, segregation and bigotry was rife throughout the country – even among the many black Americans who aspired to join the middle classes – for the most part, gay men, lesbians and bisexuals were an accepted part of the Harlem scene. Waters, who began her recording career in 1921 with the jazz number 'The New York Glide', but was signed as a blues singer by The Aeolian Record Company when they launched their race records line in July 1923,[5] had been a fixture in New York since the beginning of the 1920s and was often seen fighting in public with whoever was her girlfriend at the time. For many years she lived openly with her lover, the dancer Ethel Williams, a relationship that led to them being nicknamed The Two Ethels. The hugely popular Drag Balls, which had thrived underground for more than three decades and had provided a haven for people of all races and all sexual persuasions, became more prominent. Often referred to disparagingly as the Faggot Ball (the first appearance of the word 'faggot' in print came in the sentence 'All the fagots (sissys) [sic] will be dressed in drag at the ball tonight,' in Jackson and Hellyer's 1914 book *A Vocabulary of Criminal Slang*), one such event was held annually at the Savoy Ballroom and attracted many high-society voyeurs, black and white, gay and straight, among them Van Vechten, the novelist Max Ewing and the 'poet laureate of Harlem' Langston Hughes. Harlem's Renaissance Ballroom and Casino hosted the Hamilton Lodge's annual masquerade, which began in the 1890s and was infamous for the number of both white and black men dressed as women: 'It seems that many men of the class generally known as "fairies", and many Bohemians from the Greenwich Village section took the occasion to mask as women for this affair. They appeared to make up at least fifty per cent of the 1,500 people who packed the casino, and in their gorgeous evening gowns, wigs and powdered faces

Brevities, March 1932

were hard to distinguish from many of the women,' reported the *New York Age*.[6] By the middle of the 1930s, the Hamilton Lodge ball had moved to the Rockland Palace, a building more suitable for its ever-growing attendance. As *Brevities* (formerly known as *Broadway Brevities*), the scandal sheet that called itself 'America's first national tabloid weekly' crowed: '6,000 crowd huge hall as queer men and women dance ... crowds of spectators gather to witness the horrible orgies of the perverted. Stern men and simpering women who show the marks of passion make up the crowd. Appearances are deceiving. Most of the "women" in attendance at the orgies are men in disguise. A majority of the people wearing tuxedoes are female.'[7] 'Harlem is the one place that is gay and delightful however dull and depressing the downtown regions may be,' Max Ewing wrote in a letter to his parents. 'Nothing affects the vitality and the freshness of Harlem'.[8]

Thanks to her constant touring, Ma Rainey was quickly becoming the first nationally recognised star of the blues era. Born Gertrude Pridgett (in Alabama in 1882; some sources state that she was born in Columbus, Georgia in 1886), Ma joined the travelling tent show the Rabbit's Foot Minstrels (aka the Rabbit's Foot Company) after marrying William 'Pa' Rainey in 1904. She wasn't pretty, but she liked to dress up and she loved jewellery, wearing gold coins on long chains around her neck and ostrich feathers in her hair: 'When she came out everybody was astonished, she was that ugly,' Ruby Walker told Bessie Smith's biographer Chris Albertson in 1971. 'If you wanted to make a performer mad in those days you would say: "you look like Ma Rainey"!' That didn't matter. You didn't go to look at her dreadful horsehair wigs or the mouthful of gold teeth: people flocked to the tent shows that featured Ma because of her voice: 'when they hear and see "Ma" Rainey they just do not associate the voice with the person before them'.[9] Full and strong, she would soon become known – thanks to a Columbia copywriter's gift for hyperbole – as The Mother of The Blues.

Advertised (in 1910) as 'our coon shouter,'[10] by 1914 Ma and Pa were being billed as Rainey and Rainey, Assassinators of the Blues. Rabbit's Foot was the premier black touring revue, and owner Pat Chappelle was recognised as one of the 'wealthiest colored citizens of Jacksonville, Fla., owning much real estate. He was very successful as a showman, and made considerable money touring small towns in the South.'[11] In 1909, Chappelle commissioned the Pullman Company to build 'the finest sleeping car used by any show,'[12] for his troupe to travel in. In the year that Bessie joined the show, Pat Chappelle died from tuberculosis, and his wife sold the Rabbit's Foot Company to F. S. Wolcott Carnivals.

Bessie Smith auditioned for Rainey some time around 1911 (different accounts state 1912 or 1913) and joined the company immediately. Smith had already been gaining quite a reputation as singer in her hometown of Chattanooga, Tennessee, singing on street corners for small change, when her older brother Clarence arranged for the fame-hungry young girl to audition for Ma. The older woman was impressed, but initially took her on as a dancer, not as a singer. A popular story had it that Rainey had Smith tied up in a sack (her niece Ruby Walker insisted that Smith had been kidnapped by gypsies), kidnapped her, forced her join the Rabbit's Foot Minstrels, and taught her to sing the blues. It wasn't true, but the rumours did the show no harm and neither woman bothered too much to correct them. Smith became Ma Rainey's apprentice and stayed with her for around four years before branching out on her own. In 1917, she was booked into the Paradise Club in Atlantic City, and shortly afterwards she established a base in Philadelphia.

Black women's voices were the first that the majority of the record-buying public heard singing the blues. The first recording to include the word 'blues' in its title, an instrumental version of W. C Handy's rag 'The Memphis Blues', had appeared in 1914 (Morton Harvey's vocal version followed in 1915), but it was Mamie Smith's debut recording – 'That Thing Called Love' and 'You Can't Keep a Good Man Down' made in 1920 for Okeh Records in New York – that proved that the blues could be anything more than a local novelty. It could have all been so different: Mamie Smith's pioneering recording session only happened because the singer who had been scheduled to record the songs – the stage star Sophie Tucker – fell ill and Mamie was called in to replace her. Before Mamie Smith came along, every blues singer that had been captured on record was distinctly Caucasian. Her follow-up, 'Crazy Blues', was a million-seller, and the success prompted record companies – principally Columbia and Paramount – to seek out and record other female blues singers for their new 'race records' imprints. Now-forgotten singers were quickly snapped up: Sara Martin, Eva Taylor and Virginia Listen all recorded for Okeh in the early 1920s; Clara Smith (no relation) was picked up by Columbia. Rainey (often billed as Madame Rainey and even on occasion the Million Dollar Highbrow) and Bessie Smith soon followed suit, and both were popular with the record-buying public. Spotted by Frank Walker of Columbia Records while singing in a small club in Selma, Alabama, Bessie Smith made her first recording, 'Downhearted Blues', in New York on 16 February 1923. The original recording of the song, released the previous year by Alberta Hunter (a one-time lover of Ethel Waters and former protégé of Tony Jackson), had sold well, but Bessie's recording (backed with 'Gulf Coast Blues') sold an unheard-of 780,000 copies in less than six months and went on to sell two million.[13]

In 1922, Columbia had issued seven blues records; in 1923 it was three dozen, including fourteen by Bessie Smith,[14] and the company launched a major campaign to promote their race records stars:

Special material, including a complete campaign of advertising mate-rial is now being issued by Columbia Graphophone Co. in connection with its "blues" recordings made by negro artists. For more than two years the sales volumes of this class of records has increased rapidly, and among the Columbia headline artists today are Bessie Smith and Clara Smith. Records by these artists are meeting with popular recep-tion everywhere, especially in the South, where it is not surprising to hear of dealers ordering as many as 2,000 of a selection within a period of a week or two.[15]

Bessie's fame spread so quickly that, by June that year while on a tour of the Southern States, 'a midnight performance was given by the [Atlanta theatre] 81 for white people, and the house was packed to full capacity. It was estimated by the officials of the theatre that one thousand people were unable to gain admittance.'[16] Smith's show was 'the first "Midnight Frolic" for white people ever offered in Atlanta'.[17] Arguably the most popular female blues singer of all time, she cut 160 sides for Columbia and soon became the highest-paid black entertainer of the period, earning $1,500 a week at her peak.

Two other things happened in 1923: Smith married a security guard named Jack Gee and Ma Rainey recorded her first eight sides for Paramount in Chicago (she recorded a total of 92 songs, all for Paramount). At that point touring with the John T. Wortham tent show with her act Madam Rainey's Gold Beauties, so huge was Rainey's following that sales of her discs were not harmed by her regular run-ins with the law, even after her arrest following a raid by police at her home during a lesbian orgy in 1925:

> It seemed that Ma had found herself in an embarrassing tangle with the Chicago police. She and a group of young ladies had been drinking and were making so much noise that a neighbor summoned the police. Unfortunately for Ma and her girls, the law arrived just as the impromptu party got intimate. There was pandemonium as everyone madly scrambled for her clothes and ran out the back door. Ma, clutching someone else's dress, was the last to exit, but a nasty fall down a staircase foiled her escape. Accusing her of running an indecent party, the police threw her in jail, and Bessie bailed her out the following morning.'[18]

That incident inspired Rainey's most obviously and outlandishly lesbian-themed recording, 'Prove It On Me Blues'. Just in case the message was lost on anyone, when it was first issued, 'Prove It On Me Blues' was advertised in the press accompanied by an illustration of Ma dressed in a fedora and three-piece suit, flirting with a couple of feminine young ladies while a cop watches suspiciously from the other side of the street. That year, crowds of both black and white blues fans besieged the Broad and Market Music Shop in Newark, New Jersey when Smith made a public appearance: 'the store was packed . . . outside in the streets similar crowds jostled, straining to hear'.[19]

Although Smith was married to the possessive and physically abusive Gee, she was hardly what you would call discreet. When appearing in Detroit she would take her favourite girls and hang out at buffet flats. Described as 'an apartment to which people come to sit around, eat, drink, talk, sing and dance' and 'the modern counterpart of the salons of classical France' by the *New York Recorder*,[20] buffet flats were, in fact, small, unlicensed clubs in private homes where customers could drink and gamble, eat and sleep ... and enjoy watching (or even joining in) every kind of sex act imaginable. She was also known to have had a relationship with male impersonator Gladys Ferguson.[21]

In January 1927, just a few weeks after Smith and Rainey had collaborated on the latter's song 'Don't Fish In My Sea', one of Smith's lovers, Lillian Simpson, attempted suicide after the pair had a fight. Lillian had been a schoolmate of Ruby Walker's, and her mother had once been Bessie Smith's wardrobe mistress; it was natural that she would join Smith's troupe. However the two women soon entered into a tempestuous affair that Smith tried unsuccessfully to hide from Gee. Once, when she made a very public play for the younger girl, Simpson refused her advances. 'The hell with you, bitch,' Smith is reported to have said. 'I got twelve women on this show and I can have one every night if I want it'.[22]

Blues singers were soon using words such as 'sissy' or 'bulldagger' in their songs: in 'Foolish Man Blues' Bessie sang about 'mannish actin' woman and a skippin' twistin' woman actin' man'; in the song 'Sissy Blues', Ma Rainey complained of her husband's infidelity with a homosexual called Miss Kate who can 'shake that thing like jelly on a plate'. Lucille Bogan (aka Bessie Jackson) warned her listeners that 'B.D. [bull dagger or bull dyke] women sure is rough' in 'B.D. Women Blues', and told them quite categorically that 'Women Don't Need No Men' on her 1928 Paramount release of the same name. Like Bessie and Ma, Lucille Bogan had also begun her recording career in 1923 (for Okeh) and was an uninhibited bisexual famed for singing some of the most notoriously dirty blues songs of the era, including the frankly obscene 'Shave 'Em Dry': 'I got nipples on my titties big as the end of my thumb, I got something 'tween my legs gon' make a dead man cum'. Often included with Ma and Bessie as the 'big three' of the vaudeville-inspired urban blues, Lucille Anderson was born in Amory, Mississippi in 1897 but grew up in Birmingham, Alabama. So many of her self-penned songs are concerned with the seedier side of sex ('Tricks Ain't Walking No More', for example) that it has been suggested that she may have worked as a prostitute before (or possibly during) her marriage to railway worker Nazareth Bogan. She recorded around 100 sides during her career for companies including Okeh and Paramount, but none of her releases emulated the sales of Smith or Rainey.

The best-known LGBT hangout in Harlem was the Clam House, described by *Vanity Fair* columnist Charles G. Shaw as 'a popular house for revellers but not for the innocent young'.[23] A tiny club with just eight tables for its patrons, Beatrice Lillie and Tallulah Bankhead were known to frequent the Clam House, where Gladys Bentley, big and black and dressed in a white top hat and tails, would hold court, belting out the Kokomo Arnold song 'Sissy Man Blues' and risqué versions of popular songs such as 'Alice Blue Gown' or 'Sweet Georgia Brown': 'If ever there was a gal who could take a popular ditty and put her own naughty version to it, La Bentley could do it,' wrote Bill Chase in the *New York Age* in October 1949. Open all night, the venue soon became known as Gladys' Clam House; Bentley provided the inspiration for the singer Sybil and the venue appeared thinly disguised as The Lobster Pot in Blair Niles' 1931 novel *Strange Brother*.

Born in Philadelphia in 1907, Bentley was an out – and outrageous – lesbian who made a name for herself at such venues as the Ubangi Club (formerly known as Connie's Inn, where you could also see a female impersonator from Chicago who went by the stage name Gloria Swanson), the Log Cabin Grill (better known as George Wood's), the Red Rooster and the Rainbow Gardens. One of the many scandalous stories told about Bentley was that she married another woman (a white woman, no less) in a ceremony held in Atlantic City, New Jersey. Initially using the stage name Barbara 'Bobbie' Minton, Bentley was a favourite attraction who would flirt outrageously with the prettiest women in her audience and who could often be heard slamming on the piano and belting out a tune at a local rent party when she was not on stage. Although she recorded several sides during her career, none of them were anywhere near as outré as the material she sang in her nightclub act, nor did they challenge the sexually themed records cut by Bessie Smith, Ma Rainey or Lucille Bogan, yet in spite of this her fame, and her earning power, rose quickly. Before long, Bentley was boasting of living in a rented apartment on Park Avenue with her own servants and chauffeur-driven car, and was appearing regularly on radio.

Of course it was not just the women: in his song 'Say I Do It', Waymon 'Sloppy' Henry sang about using a powder puff and wearing lace; singer Frankie 'Half-Pint' Jaxon, a 'close friend and admirer' of Bessie Smith[24] caused a sensation in Chicago where he often appeared in drag. As the vocalist of Tampa Red's Hokum Jazz Band, Half-Pint had a hit with the song 'My Daddy Rocks Me', a reworking of Trixie Smith's 'My Man Rocks Me', which is often cited as the first song to pair the words 'rock' and 'roll' in a sexual context. Jaxon's party piece was a duet, with him singing both the male and female parts. In 1930, singer George Hannah – accompanied by pianist Meade Lux Lewis – released 'The Boy In the Boat', a song about lesbian sex (the phrase 'boy in the boat' is a euphemism for the clitoris and the clitoral hood). Hannah recorded for Paramount between 1929 and 1931 and also had a hit with the self-penned 'Freakish Man Blues' (listed on the disc's label as 'Freakish Blues'), a song about a man who has no interest in having sex with his woman. Very little is known about Hannah, but 'The Boy In the Boat' had been standard material for LGBT blues singers for a number of years: the aforementioned drag artiste who used the stage name Gloria Swanson (a number of drag acts named themselves after famous Hollywood actresses) is known to have regularly performed the song from around 1920. According to Jazz historian Frank Gillis, the originator of 'The Boy In the Boat' was none other than Tony 'Pretty Baby' Jackson.[25]

Bessie Smith's life, and her career, were spiralling out of control, aided and abetted by her increasing reliance on alcohol. Changing tastes meant that her records were not selling in as large a number as they had been, and her fiery temper and unreliability caused major theatre owners to stop booking her. In an attempt to manage her own affairs, she went back to the tent shows she knew so well, but even these were struggling. Audiences were turning away from vaudeville and minstrel shows towards more sophisticated entertainment, and increasingly to radio and the movies. Courting the new medium, Bessie starred in her own two-reeler, *St. Louis Blues*, in 1929. The film, shot with an all-black cast, was based on the recording she had made in 1925 with Louis Armstrong. Having made her last recordings in 1928, Ma Rainey returned to the tent show circuit before retiring for good in 1935. She went back to the house she had built for her mother in Columbus, Georgia, where she took over the ownership and management of a couple of local theatres, the Lyric and the Airdrome (after many years of neglect, the house is now home to the Ma Rainey Museum). Paramount, the company she recorded for and who billed her as their biggest star, closed in the early 1930s, another victim of the Depression. She drifted into obscurity until the 1950s, when Riverside Records licensed some of her recordings for reissue. Lucille Bogan retired, too, although she remained involved with the blues scene as manager of her son's band Bogan's Birmingham Busters.

In the late summer of 1937, Benny Goodman and John Hammond arranged for Smith to record for Columbia again: she had not set foot in the studio since laying down four sides for Okeh in November 1933. With a big promotion campaign planned, it looked like the Empress of the Blues was going to reclaim her throne. But sadly that would never happen. On 27 September, Bessie died after the Packard she was driving collided with a parked truck near Clarksdale, Mississippi. Horribly injured, with her arm partly severed, her niece, Ruby Walker, insisted she bled to death after a whites-only hospital refused her admittance. In truth she was taken directly to the Afro-American Hospital in Clarksdale, Mississippi, where she died seven hours later. The myth that she was refused entry to the whites-only hospital stems from in an article by John Hammond which appeared in the November 1937 issue of *Down Beat* magazine entitled 'Did Bessie Smith Bleed to Death While Waiting for Medical Aid?' Although her biographer Chris Albertson has proved this was not the case (and Hammond later admitted the piece was based entirely on hearsay), even noted columnist Walter Winchell referred to her death as 'murder' (in his syndicated column *On Broadway*, 22 December 1946), and playwright Edward Albee used this as the basis for his hit play *The Death of Bessie Smith*.

Seven thousand mourners attended her funeral. 'We gave Aunt Bessie a big send-off. Everything was done properly,' her nephew Buster Smith told *The Philadelphia Enquirer*,[26] although her estranged husband refused to foot the bill for a headstone: 'After paying funeral expenses, we had nothing left,' Fred Gee claimed.[27] Presumably the budget had been eaten up by the gold and velvet trimmed coffin her body rested in. The grave of Lucille Bogan, who passed away on 10 August 1948, also went unmarked. Ma Rainey died of heart disease in December 1939, but the scene was already over – destroyed by the Depression, the repeal of prohibition, increased persecution and the new conservatism sweeping the country. Soon McCarthyism would herald a new witch-hunt, with LGBT entertainers – and even those simply suspected of being homosexual – targeted. The hunt for 'perverts', who were presumed to be subversive by nature, resulted in thousands of innocent men and women being harassed and denied employment. In 1948, some of Bessie's friends held a memorial concert in New York to raise funds for a headstone. The concert was a success, but it seems that Jack Gee pocketed the proceeds and promptly disappeared. He resurfaced in 1952, when it was reported that he had sold 42 recently discovered and previously unrecorded songs written by his late wife.

Referred to in the press as 'the masculine-garbed, smut-singing entertainer,'[28] in her later years Gladys Bentley attempted to clean up her act and straighten herself out – in more ways than one. In the space of three years, she claimed to have been married to three different men. In 1952 Bentley penned an article for *Ebony* magazine titled 'I am a Woman Again' in which she wrote that she had 'violated the accepted code of morals that our world observes but yet the world has tramped to the doors of the places where I have performed to applaud'. She called her life 'a living hell as terrible as dope addiction'.[29] Two years later, *Jet* magazine reported, 'The lives of some strange women, however, have happy endings. Gladys Bentley, entertainer, says injections of female sex hormones three times a week hastened her return to womanhood.'[30] Her self-pinned memoir, *If This Be Sin*, remains unpublished: Gladys died during a flu epidemic in Los Angeles in January 1960. Ethel Waters also ended up marrying three times and renouncing her once-flaunted sexuality. Born in 1900, the product of a knifepoint rape when her mother was just 13, she turned from singing to acting, and in 1929 appeared in *On With The Show!* the first all-talking, all-colour feature length movie. Waters died in near-poverty in 1977.

Despite being cited as an influence by artists including Billie Holiday (who began her recording career in the same week that Bessie had her final studio session) and Frank Sinatra, interest in Bessie, Ma and the rest of the original blues singers waned until its resurgence in the 1950s with the birth of the electric blues, and later still in to the following decade, when folk singers and pop acts began to cite them as influences. In 1970, Bessie's grave in Sharon Hill, PA, finally got a headstone thanks to contributions from long-time fan Janis Joplin, Juanita Green (president of the North Philadelphia chapter of the National Association for the Advancement of Colored People [NAACP] who, as a child, had done housework for Smith) and Columbia's John Hammond. Smith had been a huge influence on Joplin, who saw her as something of a role model and had even told friends that she felt she was Bessie Smith reincarnated. Sadly the marker, engraved with the legend 'the greatest blues singer in the world will never stop singing,' got the date of her birth wrong. Joplin, herself bisexual, died from a heroin overdose a few months later, but her influence is still being felt today.

Gladys Bentley

CHAPTER 4

The Pansy Craze

'PANSY PLACES ON BROADWAY: Reports are around
that Broadway during the new season will have nite places
with "pansies" as the prime draw. Paris and Berlin have
similar night resorts, with the queers attracting the lays.
Greenwich Village in New York had a number of the funny
spots when the Village was a phoney night sight seeing
collection of joints, The Village spots died away, as only the
queers eventually remained the customers and they were
broke. The best entertainer In the Village joints along the
pansy lines was Jean Malin'

Variety, 10 September 1930

The 1920s saw an explosion of bohemian enclaves. In cities around
the world – especially in dilapidated but formerly upmarket areas
like New York's Greenwich Village – artists, writers, poets and musicians
were lured by cheap rents and an increasingly wild and lawless lifestyle.
A gay migration was taking place, with LGBT people flocking to New
York and other cities, attracted as much by the nightlife as by the promise
of being able to connect with others in areas of the city 'now filled with
smart little shops, bachelor apartments, residential studios and fashionable speakeasies'.[1]

New York has a history of gay-friendly bars stretching back to at least
the 1870s, when Pfaff's Beer Cellar was staffed with effeminate men,
making it popular with both gay men and straight writers and artists,
including Walt Whitman. Another basement bar, Frank Stevenson's

infamous Slide on Bleecker Street, was New York's most notorious, flamboyant and dangerous watering-hole: in 1890 a (presumably off-duty) policeman, Edward Sweeney, shot a waiter named George Rankin, who 'used to entertain people by singing songs in a falsetto voice,'[2] during a drunken rampage. 'It is an alleged boast of its owner that it is the "wicked-est place in a wicked town".'[3] Described as 'the most notorious of all dens of iniquity in the city ... where vice reigns in such a hideous mien that it is impossible to describe,'[4] it was said that 'neither Paris nor London can boast of a resort so openly run and yet so unspeakable in its viciousness'.

When The Slide was closed after a campaign orchestrated by the *New York Herald*,[5] Stevenson and many of his staff moved to a new – and even tougher – bar, the Metropolitan on Bond Street – a place that was 'crowded with the most depraved people of both sexes,' where 'waiters amuse the patrons with ribald songs' and where 'the orgies continue until dawn'.[6] Bathhouses were popular, too, although often raided by the authorities: in February 1903, New York police conducted the first recorded vice raid on a gay bathhouse, in the basement of the Ariston apartments. Twenty-six men were arrested and twelve of them were brought to trial on sodomy charges; seven of those received sentences ranging from four to twenty years in prison.[7] Still, when you consider hospitals were allowed to sterilise or lobotomise men convicted of sodomy, twenty years in prison doesn't sound too bad.[8]

During the jazz era, it was not unusual to hear male singers performing (and recording) songs more usually associated with female vocalists whilst keeping the pronouns intact: music publishers kept a tight grip on their copyrights and would not allow singers to alter a word. LGBT historian and music collector JD Doyle calls these records 'cross-vocals': examples include the fiercely heterosexual Bing Crosby recording the songs 'Ain't No Sweet Man Worth the Salt of My Tears' (1928) and 'Gay Love' (1929), male vocal trio The Rollickers singing lines such as 'I would let him pet me' and 'he drives me wild' on the record 'He's So Unusual' (issued by Fred Rich and His Orchestra on Columbia in 1929) and many, many more examples. It was around this time that homosexual men started to refer to themselves as 'gay' in preference to the usual 'fairy', 'queer' or (in America especially) 'faggot' – the word had already had connotations of immorality (a 'gay dog' or a 'gay blade', for example, was a man who enjoyed a less than monastic life).

Centred around the clubs of Harlem, Times Square and Greenwich Village, the Pansy Craze grew out of a fondness for female impersonators. Men in dresses became hugely popular in the early years of the twentieth century – even Brigham Morris Young, the son of the polygamist Mormon leader Brigham Young, performed publicly under the pseudonym Madam Pattirini from 1885 into the early 1900s – but none were more famous than the massively influential Julian Eltinge.

Before Eltinge, the men who played vaudeville and the British music halls dressed as women had mostly performed as comedic stereotypes: harridans, crones and pantomime dames; Julian's 'illusions' were much more feminine, and he was feted for his characterisations, which often took hours to prepare. 'On make-up alone I usually spend three-quarters of an hour,' he told *Variety*. 'I envy some of those other artists who are able to prepare for the stage in fifteen minutes'.[9] Even though he had his own women's magazine and line of make-up, he did his utmost to cover up his own sexuality, famously saying 'I am not gay, I just like pearls,' and his manliness was unquestioned: 'He has the entire approval of his own sex and the admiration of the women. No one suggests that he couldn't go out into the back yard and saw a cord of wood if he wanted to';[10] 'Eltinge was rather noisily a he-man off stage. In his younger days he engaged in enough saloon brawls to keep any longshoremen happy, mostly in resentment against slurs on his manliness.'[11]

Born William Julian Dalton in Newtonville, Massachusetts in 1881, dressing as a woman made Harvard graduate Eltinge a wealthy man and famous worldwide: he made his London debut in 1906 and was commanded to give a performance for King Edward VII at Windsor Castle. The king later presented him with a white bulldog.[12] He built his own house, Villa Capistrano, one of the most lavish villas in Hollywood, where the confirmed bachelor lived with his mother and entertained extravagantly. He appeared in several silent comedies, including *The Widow's Might*, *The Countess Charming* and *Madame Behave*, and even had a Broadway theatre named after him. For a 1908 publicity stunt, it was announced that Julian was to marry Eva Tanguay, the Canadian singer who billed herself as 'the girl who made vaudeville famous'. The pair had

a mock ceremony, with Eva dressed in traditional male formal attire and
Julian as the blushing bride, but although a ring was exchanged, they
never wed officially.

Eltinge also appeared on the big screen with Rudolph Valentino (in
Over the Rhine, in 1916, later recut and reissued as *An Adventuress* and later
still – after Valentino had broken big with *The Sheik*, *Blood and Sand* and
The Four Horsemen of the Apocalypse – as *Isle of Love*) and cut several sides
for Victor – 'In My Dream of You' in 1913 (an unreleased test recording,

Julian Eltinge as Salome, 1909

with Eltinge performing unaccompanied) and 'Eat And Grow Thin' (with lyrics written by Eltinge) and the Jerome Kern composition 'Two Heads Are Better Than One' in 1916; both of the latter two songs were featured in the musical comedy *Cousin Lucy*.

But times were changing, and the outrageous performances of female impersonators like Bert Savoy, and the drag balls and gay speakeasies of the Pansy Craze made Eltinge seem old-fashioned. He began to drink heavily, lost his money and his luxurious house and, despite a couple of attempts at a comeback (including appearing in a brace of sound movies – *Maid to Order* in 1932 and a brief cameo as himself in the Bing Crosby film *If I Had My Way* in 1940), his career was over. He died in 1941, 10 days after being diagnosed with kidney disease:[13] *Hollywood Babylon* author Kenneth Anger claimed he committed suicide by taking an overdose of sleeping pills.

Eltinge outlived his principal rival, and the one man who did more than most to popularise the type of drag act that has lasted until this day. Bert Savoy's candle burned bright for a few years at the beginning of the 1920s, and his style was diametrically opposed to the more demure style of Julian Eltinge. Savoy died when he was struck by lightning on Long Island on June 26 1923, killing him and his companion Jack Vincent (aka Jack Grossman) instantly. His last words were reported to be 'Mercy, ain't Miss God cutting up something awful?'

His body remained unclaimed by relatives; he had been brought up in an orphanage. Perhaps unsurprisingly, former wife Anna Clamper, who had sued Bert – real name Everett Mackenzie – after he allegedly 'socked her on the skull' and 'presented her with a pair of black eyes'[14] was uninterested, and it was left to his stage partner Jay Brennan to organise the burial. More than 1,500 people attended the funeral, and police had to be deployed to manage the crowd. Writing in his syndicated column *New York Day By Day,* O. O. McIntyre called Savoy 'the gayest of female impersonators,' and claimed that his death so affected Broadway that 'it was as though the same electric bolt that killed Savoy had stunned the street'.[15] McIntyre recalled that 'he told me once with rather pathetic melancholy that he had no friends. "Nobody likes a female impersonator",' he added. Brennan and Savoy had what McIntyre called 'a strong attachment. Several weeks before the tragedy each planned to take out a

$50,000 insurance policy in favor of the other, but neglected the matter. They had a contract binding them together for life.' Jay Brennan was said to have 'aged many years' following the loss of his partner. Savoy's mother later surfaced in Chicago, and immediately employed a lawyer to look into what she claimed was her son's missing money.

Savoy and Brennan's entire recorded output consists of two sides for Vocalion in early 1923: 'You Must Come Over' and 'You Don't Know the Half of It'. The recordings were issued on a double-sided 78 in September 1923, three months after Savoy died. Savoy was the first of what we now accept as traditional drag: the brassy, gossipy harridan who is quite clearly a man in a dress, and a direct influence on the stage persona of Mae West; Mae's oft-misquoted 'Why don't you come up sometime and see me?' is reputed to have been based on Savoy's catchphrase 'you must come over'. Savoy's stage persona would have an enormous influence of the cross-dressing stars of the Pansy Craze, a short period when gay men and lesbians were feted by royalty, courted by Hollywood (before the Hays Code, which effectively banned Hollywood from portraying homosexual characters or movies having positive LGBT storylines) and celebrated nationally for their work. The Pansy Craze was a by-product of the open defiance of America's recently enacted prohibition laws, and the moral crusaders of the Woman's Christian Temperance Union and their allies would have been furious had they realised that their success in banning alcohol sales across the United States would create a thriving black market for bootleg booze, a bustling underground club scene and a vicious criminal underworld. *Broadway Brevities*, an early monthly gossip magazine, ran a series of news items and columns loosely bound together under the title *Nights in Fairyland*, spreading licentious tittle-tattle about the stars and venues, and asking 'when are the local constabulary going to confer a little attention on the rouged youths who have made this place a laughing stock?'[16]

One of the most famous female impersonators of the day, Karyl Norman (occasionally billed as Karol), was a prolific songwriter. Although he never released a record (a story appeared in the *New York Morning Telegraph* in 1922 which stated that he was 'making records for the various phonograph companies,' but to date no recordings have surfaced), several of his songs were committed to shellac by other artists. Born George Francis Peduzzi in Baltimore in 1897, he billed himself as The Creole Fashion Plate (although he was mocked by those less kind as The Queer Old Fashion Plate) and was known for his lavish gowns, most of which were made for him by his devoted mother, who travelled with him throughout his career, and which (in 1935) were valued at $20,000.[17]

Norman began his showbiz career in 1911 and made his debut appearance as a female impersonator in New York City in May 1919. He was an immediate sensation, noted for being able to switch between a natural baritone and his falsetto voice, and for his quick costume changes; in his show *Types* he performed as five different female stereotypes, including the co-ed, the flapper and the debutante. 'Off stage he is a wholesome American youth, who avers he detests femininity in a man,' *The Stage* reported. 'Karyl considers himself thoroughly masculine.'[18] Like Eltinge, Norman was keen to quell rumours about his sexuality, becoming engaged to male impersonator Ruth Budd in 1922. The engagement did not last long: a newspaper report claimed that it was because Ruth Budd's mother wanted to accompany the pair on their honeymoon,[19] and after a breach of promise court case Norman was forced to pay Budd $10,000.[20] As well as performing in vaudeville, Norman appeared in stage plays and musical comedies and toured the world. The actress Fifi D'Orsay, who played with him in the Greenwich Village Follies in 1924, said that Norman was 'marvellous. He was a great performer and I loved him. Karyl Norman was a wonderful guy, beloved and respected by everybody, although he was a gay boy, and for the gay boys in those days it was harder for them than it is today. He did an act with two pianos and those gorgeous clothes. He had such class and he was so divine.'[21]

Norman was known for his stroppy attitude towards uninterested audiences. In Cleveland he admonished his two-thirds full house, telling them, 'we actors expect applause. You people ought to applaud an act whether you like it or not. I've only done half my act and that's all you get!'[22] By the start of the 1930s, his popularity had begun to wane, but he continued to perform and, in January 1931, he was caught up in a police raid on The Pansy Club at 204 West 48th Street, Manhattan. New York, of course, was still in the grip of prohibition, and New York's police commissioner Edward P. Mulrooney planned to impose a 1 a.m.

curfew on the city's nightspots. On the night the Pansy Club was raided, the police also shut down the Calais Club, another venue that promoted female impersonators.[23] Norman was also arrested in Detroit on a morals charge, but apparently was let off with a caution at the behest of Eleanor Roosevelt.[24] He continued to tour and perform throughout the States during the 1930s, but retired after his mother's death and died in Hollywood, Florida, in 1947.

Some of the Pansy acts sailed close to the wind and, as a result, the occasional run-in with the law was not uncommon. In April 1935, impresario Fay Norman (no relation to Karyl) and the entire cast of her Gay Boy Revue were charged with having committed acts of indecent exposure when they played Baldwinsville, New York. The charges were eventually dropped, but not before Judge Charles Hall had admonished the troupe with his personal wish that 'some charge may be found on which I may sentence the whole outfit to the penitentiary'.[25] The stars of the Pansy Craze were not all cross-dressers, but drag – and the blurring of sexual stereotypes – was massively important in the scene's development. Brooklyn native Jean Malin (born Victor Eugene James Malinovsky in 1908), one of the biggest names on the circuit (he was the highest-paid nightclub entertainer of 1930), began his career in drag under the name Imogene Wilson, earning $10 a week in a tiny club called the Rubaiyat,[26] but he found fame in his early 20s as an openly gay man (although he, like many others, would later marry), who bleached his hair platinum blond but dressed in expensive suits and dinner jackets when he performed. After the Rubaiyat was closed by the police,[27] he soon found work elsewhere, and was directly responsible for giving 'Broadway its first glimpse of pansy nightlife. Malin was a tremendous success and other club owners followed the lead. Before the main stream knew what happened, there was a hand on a hip for every light on Broadway'.[28] Acting as emcee and club host at the Club Abbey, and introducing drag acts and other performers whilst mingling with the audience, Malin gained a reputation for cracking risqué jokes and actively encouraging hecklers to have a go at him. Today we would describe the antagonistic audience engagement and vicious verbal put-downs so much a part of Malin's and Norman's acts as 'camp'; that attitude has directly influenced every drag act since. Theatre reviewer Arthur Pollock wrote 'I don't know what Jean Malin is, but he is clever. If his tart retorts were spontaneous, he is a smart fellow'.[29] On hearing that Jean was to marry Lucille Heiman, Walter Winchell cracked the joke 'Did you hear the news about Jean Malin getting married? . . . "No kiddin' – who's the lucky man?"'[30] When Winchell bumped in to Malin a short time later, he dragged the singer off to one side and asked, 'what is this marriage thing anyhow? Why did you do it?' Malin's reply was simple (although Winchell steadfastly refused to accept it): 'Because I love her'.[31] By July, Winchell was crowing that 'the sissylebrity' was already heading towards the divorce court, having been 'served with melting papers'.[32]

That year, the management of the Argonaut, the club Malin was appearing at, threw a huge party for 500 guests to mark his 23rd birthday. Malin was a star, and associating with him could only give your career a boost. The 'gay, glamorous and naughty' singer Nan Blakstone, was a talented pianist and satirist who had appeared with Malin at the Argonaut, one of the clubs owned and operated by former movie actress 'Texas' Guinan, a 'big, loud lesbian' who was tight with the mob, according to writer Jimmy Breslin.[33] Hailed as 'the world's greatest interpreter of sophisticated song,' Blakstone had a successful career of her own, recording for a number of companies and performing in night spots in Chicago, New York and Los Angeles before retiring through ill health in 1949.

Not everybody was a fan. Columnist O. O. McIntyre wrote about how he hated 'the loathsome antics of a Jean Malin or other pansy performers';[34] a few months earlier he had claimed that 'the Narcissus posings of the blond and oyster white Jean Malin in night clubs was a depravity sickening even those hailing it as innovation'.[35] Critic Jack Lait referred to him, poisonously, as 'the quick-witted, Tuxedoed comedienne'.[36] Columnist Gilbert Swan called Malin 'the woops-my-dear- interlocutor'.[37] Press aside, the police in New York were tired of the trouble the pansy clubs gave them, and the authorities did whatever they could to 'put an end to the vogue for lisping, falsetto-voiced young men . . . word has passed around that the officials would frown on further efforts to display the cavortings of the female impersonator type'.[38] In October 1931, Malin, effectively barred from working in New York by Commissioner Mulrooney, went to Boston where, according to the front page of scandal sheet *Brevities* (the recently launched tabloid version of the *Broadway Brevities* magazine) 'Queers Seek Succor! Fairies cruise in daisy beds of Boston, making the city a lavenderish camp of love,'[39] yet by the following March he was back, headlining at the Club Richman on Broadway.

In the early hours of 10 August 1933, Jean Malin was involved in a fatal automobile accident in Venice, California. Patsy Kelly, who at one time was Tallulah Bankhead's companion, told *Movie Mirror* magazine in 1937 that she had a premonition about Jean's death: 'I went down to the Ship Café that night. I glanced up at the flashing sign over the door that said "Jean Malin's Last Night", and as clearly as I'm hearing you a voice said: "be careful. It *is* his last night." He backed his car into the ocean off the end of the pier just one hour later. We were all submerged in the water. Adrenaline worked with me. It didn't with Jean.' Patsy was hospitalised for several days. Jimmy Forlenza, described in contemporary reports as Malin's 'room mate' and 'close friend', escaped from the car with a broken collarbone and severe bruising. According to Walter Winchell, Malin had been contemplating making some major changes to his act at the time of his death: 'Malin wouldn't stick to his set. He wanted to leave all that stuff behind him, he remarked, and I scolded him for it, arguing that his forte was being funny, after his fashion, and not being the dude he tried to be. "You want me to be a great big sissy!" he bellowed, "I want to progress".[40] Within weeks, his brothers, Al and William, and his widow Lucille (Malin sought a divorce in Mexico in November 1932, but at the time of his death the couple were still legally married), filed suits seeking damages for his death.

A large, powerful man who was not afraid to use his fists if necessary, Malin had written the Broadway revue *Sisters of the Chorus* and was originally to have been a featured player in the Clark Gable – Joan Crawford film *Dancing Lady* (1933), but he died three months before the film was released and all of his scenes were edited out. Malin's one record – 'I'd Rather Be Spanish Than Mannish' and 'That's What's The Matter With Me' – was issued posthumously. In 1936, Lucille Malin was charged with being the mistress of three of the 'most exclusive call houses' in New York, for 'sending a girl from New York to Montreal for immoral purposes'[41] and for 'violating the White Slave Traffic Act'[42]. She pleaded guilty.

*

The Pansy Craze was not restricted to New York: while Karyl Norman, Jean Malin and Gladys Bentley made their names in the prohibition-era clubs of the great metropolis, Frankie 'Half-Pint' Jaxon was making his mark on Chicago. Born in Montgomery, Alabama, in 1896, Frank Devera Jackson – who earned his nickname because as an adult he stood no taller than 5' 2" – was raised in Kansas City, Missouri, and he began his singing career there around 1910 before travelling extensively with medicine shows in Texas, and then touring the eastern seaboard. Called 'a freak novelty act'[43] by vaudeville reporter Sylvester Russell, his vocal range and flamboyant manner established him as a crowd favourite. By 1917, he had begun working regularly in Atlantic City (he held a residency at the Paradiso Café in 1920), and in Chicago, often with such performers as Bessie Smith and Ethel Waters, whose staging he helped design.

In the late 1920s, he sang with the top jazz bands that passed through Chicago, and recorded with pianist Cow Cow Davenport, slide guitarist Tampa Red and Thomas Dorsey. Half-Pint released sides on Brunswick, Decca, Supertone (as Cotton Thomas), Vocalion and other labels, both solo and as a featured vocalist for acts including Tampa Red's Hokum Jazz Band, recording the infamous and frankly obscene 'My Daddy Rocks Me With One Steady Roll', and 'How Long How Long Blues' (where Jaxon can be heard faking an orgasm) with the latter. Another Chicago-based act styling themselves The Hokum Boys recorded a version of the song 'Somebody's Been Using That Thing', featuring lyrics about a man 'who puts paint and powder on his face' and 'women who walked and talked like men'. The line-up of the Hokum Boys changed with almost every disc they issued: this particular recording features Georgia Tom (aka Thomas Dorsey, Ma Rainey's long-time pianist and a member of Tampa Red's band) and Big Bill Broonzy. By June 1926, Jaxon was running the show at Chicago's Dreamland Café, and the following year was headlining at the Apollo Theater, producing and starring in his own show, where he was described as 'a fine singer, genuine talented actor and a natural born dancer'.[44] That year, Jaxon recorded his most famous song, 'Willie the Weeper' (itself based on the much earlier 'Willie the Chimney Sweeper'), the tale of a drug-fuelled nightmare that became the basis for Cab Calloway's 1931 hit 'Minnie the Moocher'.

'Within the past six months some 35 new dim lit tea rooms ...
have opened on or near the North Side,' *Variety* reported in December
1930, when writing about the proliferation of clubs in the white part of
Chicago. 'All have waitresses who are lads in girl's clothing ... racket-
eers, who have made the North Side their playground for some years
have gone strong for these boy joints in a big way'.[45] Frankie Jaxon
could often be heard on radio with his own band The Hot Shots (the
band also held down a residency at the city's Capitol Theatre), although
he was suspended from broadcasting for a time in February 1932, with
the gossip pages suggesting something queer was afoot. The following
year Frankie and his band were one of the highlights of the Streets of
Paris, a temporary village that was built as part of the Chicago World's
Fair. Here, for a 25¢ entry fee, visitors could enjoy an approximation of
Parisian cafe society, and for a further $7.50 they could attend a grand
ball with entertainment from 'the hottest jazz band at the exposition,' led
by Jaxon with 'his clarinet, his baton and his yodelling'.[46] Around 7,000
people paid for the privilege of dancing to Frankie and his group, and
'no better music was heard on the grounds that night'.[47]

Known for performing in nightclubs in full drag, and for a show-
stopping performance where he would duet with himself singing both
the male and female vocal parts on songs like 'I'm Gonna Dance With
The Guy Wot Brung Me', in 1941 Jaxon retired from show business
for good and took a job at the Pentagon. A number of other female
impersonators attempted to take his place – chief amongst them Petite
Swanson (who recorded for the Sunbeam label), Valda Gray and a pair
of fellas going by the name of Joan Crawford and Marlene Dietrick [sic],
all of whom could be found strutting their stuff in State Street's Cabin
Inn. Frankie relocated to Los Angeles sometime around 1944, where he
dropped off the radar. He died on 15 May 1953.

Back in New York, things had not been the same since nightclub owner
Charles 'Chink' Sherman had been shot and stabbed during a mob-
related attack at the Club Abbey, where Jean Malin had been performing,
in January 1931. That incident (which was not the first time that the
police had been called to a shooting at the premises), which had seen
'two gangs translate their enmity into a free-for-all battle with revolvers,

knives and fists'[48] and a police officer, Detective John J. Walsh implicated in the gangland goings-on,[49] brought about a 'police edict barring female impersonators from the local nite clubs'[50], and by the end of 1933 the Pansy Craze was all but over in the Big Apple. Soon, the Harlem scene had changed beyond recognition, the white audience had moved on and many of the old clubs had closed. 'Gladys Bentley, who used to sing and play so tirelessly in the Clam House, has gone plumb hinkty [snobbish; aloof] in her shiny tuxedo suit and is a real night club entertainer'.[51] Her star in the ascendant, in 1935 Gladys was invited to take part in the entertainment for a ball held in aid of the Policemen's Benevolent Association of Westchester County. Billed as 'the Brown Bomber of Sophisticated Song,' she was still plying her butch lesbian act in San Francisco in 1942, when she could be seen appearing nightly at Mona's Club 440 on Broadway, whose slogan was 'where girls will be boys'.

After the police clampdown and threatened curfew, Texas Guinan made plans to move her operation to Paris, but she died of amoebic dysentery in 1933, shortly before the repeal of prohibition. In advance of the 1939 World's Fair, the New York State Liquor Authority (SLA) embarked on a clean-up, applying to court for permission to close down bars that were known to serve 'sex variants'. One such venue, the Gloria Bar and Grill on Third Avenue, had its licence revoked because, it was claimed, it allowed 'homosexuals, degenerates and other undesirable people to congregate on the premises'. Unlike most of the bars closed by the SLA (the El Rey Tavern – also on Third Avenue – was raided around the same time), the management of Gloria's decided to contest the case, even though the bar was run by a gay man, Jackie Mason, and was a known draw for gay men and lesbians in the city. Gloria's argued that that the SLA could not prove that staff knew they were serving homosexuals. Their motion to appeal was denied.[52]

Bruz Fletcher and Ray Bourbon were the biggest names of the second wave, reaching fame as the Pansy Craze was dying down but continuing with their careers into the 1940s and, in Rae's case, beyond. Bruz (pronounced Bruce) came from what his biographer Tyler Alpern calls 'one of the wealthiest and most dysfunctional families in Indiana'.[53] The nephew of novelist Booth Tarkington (author of *The Magnificent Ambersons*), his wild, drama-filled life includes running away from home at the age of eight, an attempted suicide as a young teen and a final (and successful) suicide bid at the age of 34. His mother and grandmother killed themselves in a double suicide, his sister spent some years living as a man before she was committed to an asylum and his father lost the family fortune and became an elevator operator.

Bruz Fletcher (born Stroughton J. Fletcher III) lived openly with his partner Casey Roberts, a set designer and former actor. In 1929, aged just 22, he was signed as a songwriter by Los Angeles agent Harry Weber. He had already been writing material for other acts, including the screen star Esther Ralston, and appearing as a pianist and singer in clubs in New York. His 1933 play *Not a Saint* was a hit but the 1936 comedy *Commuting Distance* was poorly received by critics. Fletcher issued many of his urbane, witty (and occasionally catty) songs on 78; his best-known release was probably 'Lei From Hawaii' ('I've wanted a lei for so long. I can't get one here, they're entirely too dear, but Hawaiians get lei-d for a song'). Columnist Harriet Parsons archly pointed out (in her syndicated column of 19 August 1937) that 'Monte Wooley and Bob Benchley [are] mailing Bruz Fletcher's record, "Bring Me a Lei from Hawaii", to all their pals'. It was an open secret that writer and actor Monty Wooley was gay, but humourist Robert Benchley was a famous womaniser, who had many affairs during his married life. Harriet Parsons was telling her readers that she knew exactly what Fletcher meant by the word 'lei'.

'Outrageous, potty-mouthed drag queen'[54] Ray Bourbon claimed to have been born and educated in England[55] but this was not true: he was born Hal Wadell in Texas in 1892. It's hard to build a true picture of him, as he told so many lies about his life and career, any number of which have been accepted as fact. He claimed to have appeared in several films, as a woman, with Rudolph Valentino: he may well have appeared in *Blood and Sand* (St. Sukie de la Croix mentions Bourbon, as a young matador, dying in Valentino's arms), but if he did, he was not included in the credits. What we can be sure about is that by the beginning of the 1930s he was appearing as part of a double act, Scotch and Bourbon, before performing in the revue *Boys Will Be Girls* in San Francisco, which *Variety* labelled a 'pansy floor show,' and which was raided on several occasions by the local police. Trouble seemed to follow Ray Bourbon wherever he went: he was convicted of 'staging an indecent show' in Los Angeles in 1936, and was found guilty by the jury after they heard him perform material from the show in question in court.[56] He was a friend of Mae West: in July 1944 she hired Ray to perform in her Broadway production *Catherine Was Great*. He also appeared in her show *Diamond Lil,* which toured during 1949 and 1950.

In 1956, at the age of 60, Bourbon announced that – after a 'series of operations in Mexico, which he says turned him into a woman' – she was now to be known as Rae.[57] Only a few years before, Christine Jorgensen (given the name George William Jorgensen Jr. at birth) had been the first American to become widely known for having undergone sex reassignment surgery ('sex-change' operations had, in fact, been carried out for decades: Danish portrait artist Lili Elbe transitioned in 1930, and British papers were reporting on a female to male sex-change in 1942). However, although Rae Bourbon issued an album entitled *Let Me Tell You About My Operation,* it appears that Bourbon never actually underwent surgery. Jorgensen had her operation in Denmark: the year before Bourbon made the announcement he had been forced to postpone 'his previously announced trip to Denmark for the usual reason,' when he was arrested and charged with reckless driving. 'You can't arrest me,' he remonstrated with the cops who pulled him over 'I've got to get home and feed the kids!' The 'kids' turned out to be 12 dogs.[58]

Bourbon issued a number of recordings of songs and monologues, mostly sold under the counter or through specialist magazines, but his sex-change act brought about the end of his career rather than re-invigorating it as he had hoped. He was arrested several times for 'impersonating a woman,' and his act was declared 'obscene and profane'.[59] After being banned from performing his 'lewd' act on a number of stages, Bourbon's twisted tale ended in 1971: three years earlier he had been accused of being an accomplice to murder. He had entrusted the care of his dogs (now numbering as many as 70) to an A. D. Blount, a kennel owner in Texas. When Bourbon failed to pay Blount's bill for their upkeep, Blount disposed of the dogs. Enraged, Bourbon hired two men to beat Blount up. Unfortunately Blount died as a result, and Bourbon and his accomplices were arrested, found guilty and sentenced to a 99-year prison term. He died in hospital in Brownwood, Texas in 1971.

Original sheet music for 'Das lila Lied', 1920

CHAPTER 5

Europe Before the War

'London is gayer and more full of people than at any time
since the war. This is the opinion of people who have
known all the capitals of Europe in their greatest and
palmiest days. Vienna, Berlin, Madrid, Paris, all have been
known in their turn as the "gayest city in Europe"'

'London – Gayest City In Europe,'
Adelaide News, 30 June 1932

I n 1835, James Pratt and John Smith became the last men to be executed
in England for committing 'an unnatural act'. Although no man would
again be murdered by the state for the simple act of loving another man,
the death sentence for same-sex acts (specifically between men; sex
between two women was never outlawed) would stay on the statute
books until 1861. Sixty years after Pratt and Smith died, Oscar Wilde was
convicted of gross indecency and sentenced to two years' hard labour, and
despite the three-decade moratorium on murder, there were those who
demanded a rope for his neck. The press, on the whole, was damning, but
occasionally people would speak out in defence of Wilde: Hugh Stutfield
wrote a piece entitled 'What we Owe to Oscar Wilde' for the June edition
of *Blackwood's Magazine* in which he asked the question 'Whence, then,
sprang the foolish fear of being natural?'[1] The general feeling was that the
playwright, poet and aesthete had been too severely punished by the court.

By the start of the new century, change was in the air. Britain had
come a long way in a very short space of time. The educated classes

had begun to discuss the idea of Edward Carpenter, Havelock Ellis and other social reformers that an intermediate or third sex (dubbed 'Uranian' by Carpenter) existed. Attitudes – and tastes – were changing, and Wilde's imprisonment and subsequent death in exile had done much to direct people's sympathies towards the plight of homosexuals.

The British music hall had provided a home for both female and male impersonators since the Victorian era. Vesta Tilley, the undisputed queen of male impersonators, made a number of recordings for the Edison Company in the first decade of the twentieth century, including 'When the Right Girl Comes Along' and 'I'm The Idol Of the Girls', but she was the epitome of womanhood off stage, married to a British politician and dressed in the latest fashions. No one ever questioned her sexuality. Vaudeville and music hall offered a camouflage of sorts and a safe space for gay, lesbian and bisexual artists to express themselves and, during the 1920s and early 1930s, a number of LGBT performers who were out and open enjoyed a level of fame that they would not see again until the 1980s, making records, movies and national headlines. With suffragettes celebrating their victorious campaign for votes for women in both the US (at least as long as you were white) and Britain, songs with titles such as 'Masculine Women, Feminine Men' (1926, written by Edgar Leslie and James V. Monaco) and 'Let's All Be Fairies' (recorded by the Durium Dance Band) were all the rage. Women were wearing their hair short and their skirts shorter, and Hollywood had introduced Middle America to both the well-groomed man and the mannishly attired woman. Garbo, Dietrich and other exotic megastars of the era were challenging perceptions and the world seemed to be becoming more tolerant towards people deemed to be *different*, especially in the bohemian circles of the world's major cities.

But not everyone was prepared to be as broad-minded: homosexuality was still against the law, and governments were keen to crack down on overt displays of perversion. In one of the most famous cases in British history, at a private ball in London's Holland Park Avenue, more than 50 men were arrested in a police raid after two undercover officers had watched them dancing, kissing and, they claimed, having sex wearing make-up and dressed in women's clothes. The organiser of the private event – Austin Salmon, a 23-year-old barman known to his friends as Lady Austin – told officers: 'there is nothing wrong [in who we are]. You call us nancies and bum boys but before long our cult will be allowed in the country.'[2] Thirty-three of the men (and one woman, Kathleen O'Farrell) appeared in court: because there were so many of them they were forced to appear with 'cards around their necks bearing numbers';[3] 27 of them were jailed for up to 20 months apiece. In Liverpool, a man known as Augustine Joseph Hull was prosecuted for 'masquerading as a woman'[4]. Newspapers and magazines were filled with such scandals, and lurid stories began to appear featuring popular actors and actresses of the day. The prurient interest of syndicated gossip columnists in the private lives of famous people would titillate readers around the globe for decades to come.

Fred Barnes, an unashamedly out-gay man who was a huge star of the British music hall, had been sold on the idea of a life on stage ever since seeing Vesta Tilley when he was a small boy. Born Frederick Jester Barnes, the son of a butcher in 1885, and called 'the best dressed man in vaudeville,'[5] Barnes helped popularise the stage perennials 'On Mother Kelly's Doorstep', 'If you Knew Susie', 'Sally the Sunshine of Our Alley' and Irving Berlin's 'When I Lost You'. His big stage hit, a sketch and song titled 'The Black Sheep of the Family' was a self-penned confessional about his own difficulties: 'it's a queer, queer world we live in; and Dame Nature plays a funny game. Some get all the sunshine, others get all the shame.' He was effete and immaculately groomed, and his audience would often heckle him with calls of 'Hello Freda!' Fred's father, seemingly sick of his son's shenanigans, committed suicide with one of his own butchery knives. Barnes inherited his father's not-insubstantial estate and drank most of it away: in 1917 he spent some time 'recuperating' from a mystery illness in Brighton – presumably he was actually drying out.

In 1919, he announced his engagement to an American heiress, Kathleen Aldous (broken off, apparently, because her parents insisted Fred give up the stage)[6] and, in an elaborate hoax, eight years later he faked a marriage to Australian actress Rose Tyson – celebrating the occasion in hotels and restaurants around London before admitting

PHOTO.
DOBSON, LIVERPOOL. MR. FRED BARNES. 495.S.
BEAGLES POSTCARDS.
THE MUSICAL COMEDY STAR IN HIS FAMOUS SONG.
"THE BLACK SHEEP OF THE FAMILY"

Fred Barnes

that the ceremony had never taken place. Fred was a drinker, and less circumspect than he should have been: he walked about London in white plus fours and pink stockings, his cheeks rouged and with a pet marmoset perched on his shoulder. At night, he would cruise the streets of the capital in his Rolls Royce, picking up male prostitutes.[7] In October 1922, he set sail for Australia for a string of engagements; however, his hard-drinking ways caused him to miss a date and he was thrown off the tour after just two weeks; his booking agent took pity on him and found him some dates in South Africa which he fulfilled before returning to England.

While Barnes was drinking his way around the antipodes, back in London, Noël Coward was enjoying his first successes and soon became one of the world's highest-earning writers. Although he would not come out during his lifetime, it was no secret that Noël was gay: 'I should love to perform "There Are Fairies in the Bottom of My Garden" but I don't dare,' he is reputed to have said to a friend. 'It might come out "There Are Fairies in the Garden of My Bottom".'[8] Society was willing to accept homosexuality as a passing fancy of the upper class or the bourgeoisie: Coward's unquestionably louche lifestyle and affectations were simply accepted as 'artistic'. Yet although he was not out, Coward was an essential element of Britain's version of the Pansy Craze, and his songs 'Green Carnation' (from his hit operetta *Bitter-Sweet*), 'I've Been To A Marvellous Party' and 'Mad About The Boy' can be seen in hindsight as less-than-guarded attempts to out himself. Oscar Wilde had popularised the wearing of a green carnation – a flower that does not exist in nature – and it was later adopted as an underground symbol by gay men: Coward similarly adopted Wilde's mantle as the leading light of London for a time. 'Mad About the Boy', first performed in London in the 1932 revue *Words and Music*, was written to be sung by a woman, although Coward rewrote the lyrics for the New York production which were to be performed by a male singer and contained explicit references to homosexuality. This version, which featured the line 'People I employ have the impertinence to call me Myrna Loy,' was never performed.

If Coward's star was in the ascendant, then the one that illuminated Fred Barnes' career was plummeting straight towards earth. A magnet for scandal, in 1924 Barnes was imprisoned for a month for being drunk whilst in charge of a motor vehicle. After knocking a young man and his (stationary) motorbike over, 'he emerged from the car weeping, accompanied by a sailor, whom he met at a bar'.[9] On top of the jail sentence, he was also fined £15 for driving in a dangerous manner. He was lucky to get away so lightly: Barnes had apparently attempted to bribe the arresting officer, hoping to keep the scandal (the sailor was said to be 'half naked') out of the press.[10] Following the arrest, Barnes was deemed 'a menace to His Majesty's fighting forces,' and he was banned from attending the Royal Tournament, a military tattoo held annually in London. He appealed against the charges, claiming in court that he was not drunk when the incident occurred but was suffering from neurasthenia, a medical condition whose symptoms included tiredness, headaches and irritability associated with emotional disturbance.[11]

Barnes recorded a number of sides for His Master's Voice and Regal in the 1920s, but with his drinking and his personal troubles making him less and less reliable, by the end of the decade his career was all but over. In 1927 he received a bequest of $425,000 from a Mrs Gordon Browne, a New York millionairess he had befriended some 11 years earlier during a Zeppelin raid on London. Barnes donated $100,000 to hospitals in Yonkers,[12] and the remainder should have seen him set up for life, however his extravagant ways – at one point he was paying out for garaging for four cars, a liveried chauffeur to drive them, a butler, a maid and an expensive apartment in one of the best parts of London – saw him burn through the legacy in a few short years, and by 1931 he was treading the boards again with old-time variety stars Vesta Victoria, Harry Champion and Fred Russell. Trouble seemed to follow Barnes wherever he went.

With work becoming harder to come by – mostly because his drinking had made him a liability – he moved to a small flat in Southend-on-Sea, which he shared with John Senior, his former chauffeur and now, apparently, his manager and lover; the rent on the apartment was paid by one of his previous managers, Charles Ashmead Watson. Reduced to singing in bars – accompanied by a pet chicken rather than his famous marmoset – and passing the hat around for tips, Fred Barnes died, aged 53 in 1938, 'in a tiny room at Southend. The corpse was found dressed in an immaculate blue suit, overcoat, patent leather shoes, and muffler, surrounded by photographs of bygone stars';[13] the inquest found that he had died of gas poisoning.

One of London's brightest stars was the openly gay British actor and female impersonator Douglas Byng, a close friend of Noël Coward. Billed as 'bawdy but British,' Byng's songs – of which he recorded many – are full of sexual innuendo and double entendres, and he was noted for his camp performances on the music hall stage and in cabaret. In 1925, he appeared in the musical revue *On With The Dance*, in a sketch written by Coward, and shortly after he opened his own nightclub in central London where, in full drag, he performed the camp cabaret songs for which he is best remembered, including 'I'm The Pest Of Budapest', 'Sex Appeal Sarah', 'I'm One Of The Queens Of England' (recorded, in a futile attempt to avoid controversy, as I'm One Of The Queens Of Wengland'), and 'Cabaret Boys'. In 1929, Byng and his performing partner Lance Lister ran foul of the BBC, when a particularly 'daring' broadcast the pair had prepared for their national radio debut had to be abandoned after they were informed that drastic cuts must be made. 'In reply to our protests it was admitted that no complaints about the taste of the turn had been received,' Byng told reporters, 'But after various officials had been consulted, we were told that the cuts must definitely be made, as certain lines were considered too daring for London listeners'. Byng refused to cooperate. 'I replied definitely that the programme would not be given in its mutilated form, as there was nothing left worth broadcasting, and accordingly the turn was abandoned. We were engaged as vaudeville artists, not for a Sunday school concert.'[14] Byng was the first artist to sing Cole Porter's 'Miss Otis Regrets' on stage, a song that has since become an LGBT staple, performed and recorded by Edith Piaf, Charles Trenet, Rufus Wainwright, Billie Holiday, Clare Teal, Ethel Waters and many more.

In 1931, Byng appeared in cabaret at the Club Lido, in New York, and although he claimed to have retired in 1962, he would continue to perform sporadically until the year before his death, aged 94, in 1987. 'I decided to retire because I don't like to see a lot of old people staggering around the stage breaking wind and forgetting their lines,' he told an interviewer from the British gay men's magazine *Gold* in 1978. 'It's no good trying to be an ingénue when you've got a bosom twice the size of the Oval [the famous cricket ground].' Princess Alice and the Duke of Kent were fans: the Duke once suggested Byng write a parody of his old university fraternity song.

When the war came, Coward wanted to enlist; however, Winston Churchill felt he could do more for the war effort by entertaining the troops: 'Go and sing to them when the guns are firing – that's your job!'[15] Coward was popular with the troops, and in 1942 he starred in the patriotic film drama *In Which We Serve*, which proved to be a huge morale-booster. Byng, in his late 40s when the war broke out, was too old to enlist but, with songs full of sexual innuendo and double entendres such as 'Black Out Bertha', he, too, proved popular with the troops.

At the same time that Byng was wowing them in the theatres, a bisexual black man became the toast of London. Pianist and singer Leslie Hutchinson, known as 'Hutch', was one of the biggest cabaret stars in the world during the 1920s and 1930s and is rumoured to have had affairs with Ivor Novello (Somerset Maugham once claimed that Churchill had slept with Novello just to find out 'what it would be like with a man')[16], Noël Coward and Tallulah Bankhead among many, many others. Born in Grenada in 1900, he first came to fame in New York, but his popularity among wealthy white socialites attracted the wrath of the Ku Klux Klan, and he moved to Paris, where he became Porter's lover, and then to London where he soon became the highest-paid star in the country. Hutch recorded a number of Porter's compositions, and camp comic Kenneth Williams often imitated Hutch's trademark vibrato, yet when he died in 1969, just 42 people attended his funeral.

As the Pansy Craze palled, many American performers relocated to Europe. 'Pansies Blow US' screamed the front page of *Brevities*, claiming that artists, scholars and many of the 'prominent pansies of this country are scramming for Berlin and Paris. In these two cities they have found a freedom not granted them in America. Instead of hiding their lavender shade under a fake maleness, they go completely margy and blossom out in all their repressed femininity.'[17] The Texas-born Vander Clyde Broadway became the toast of Paris: performing as Barbette, the female impersonator and trapeze artist appeared in such venues as the Casino de Paris, the Moulin Rouge and the Folies Bergère. He appeared at the London Palladium but his contract was cancelled after Barbette was discovered engaged in sexual activity with another man. He would never perform in England again, but in Paris he became the muse of the bisexual writer and filmmaker Jean Cocteau and was photographed by Man Ray. Paris had a reputation for its free and easy attitude and tolerance. This laissez-faire stance allowed a number of gay and lesbian bars to thrive during the 1920s in and around Montparnasse, the bohemian enclave of Montmartre, and in the nearby Pigalle. In Paris the jazz was hot and the bisexual, cross-dressing Josephine Baker[18] 'the little colored girl from 63rd Street, New York'[19] was the sensational star of the Folies Bergère. In Paris, Baker's popularity had done much to dispel racism, and homosexuality was, to a degree, accepted. La Baker had made her recording debut in 1927 with 'I Love My Baby', a fun little jazz tune on which she appears to switch the gender of her lover from female to male. The disc was coupled with 'I Found a New Baby' which, although uncredited, contained a snatch of Tony Jackson's 'I've Got Elgin Movements in my Hips with Twenty Years' Guarantee'. In 1930, she caused a near riot when she turned up at Paris' famed Théâtre de l'Empire (on l'avenue de Wagram) with her pet panther, Chiquita, and the animal proceeded to attack several members of the orchestra.[20]

Berlin had been known as a Mecca for LGBT people for decades before *Brevities* reported on the city's 'queer resorts' which were 'unrestricted as to the sex of the patrons, either lesbian, fairy or normal sexed are welcome into these gorgeously decorated nite spots'.[21] *Der Eigene* (*The Special One*), the world's first regular gay magazine, began in the German capital in 1896 and the city was widely recognised as being at the centre of European gay culture, with its own village, the Schöneberg (the area Christopher Isherwood wrote about in *Goodbye to Berlin* and *Mr. Norris Changes Trains*, the books that inspired the stage show and movie *Cabaret*). Magnus Hirschfeld's Institute of Sexual Science, a non-profit foundation which campaigned for gay rights and tolerance towards LGBT people, was a forward-thinking establishment that was well-regarded for its efforts to reform attitudes towards homosexuality. Hirschfield had, in 1919, co-written and acted in the ground-breaking gay film *Anders Als Die Andern* (*Different from the Others*).

Originally an anarchist journal, *Der Eigene* published its first gay-themed short story *Echte Liebe* (*Real Love*) in 1898. Publishing the magazine was a courageous move, as sex between men was punishable by a stiff prison sentence. The offices of *Der Eigene* and the home of its publisher Adolf Brand were frequently the targets of homophobic abuse, and police raided Brand's home on many occasions. However the magazine managed to keep going until 1907, when Brand was sent to prison for 18 months after claiming in print that German Chancellor Prince von Bülow had a long-standing homosexual relationship with Privy Councillor Max Scheefer.

Der Eigene resurfaced immediately after the First World War, and if Prohibition kick-started the Pansy Craze in the United States, then the equally liberated scene enjoyed by LGBT people in Berlin was fuelled by the end of hostilities in Europe. The country was broke: millions were unemployed and inflation soared to unprecedented levels. Yet the chance to build a new society gave the German people the perfect opportunity to re-examine their traditional values, and a greater tolerance towards LGBT people emerged. Although it was still illegal for two men to have sex, the police tended to look the other way, and it has been suggested that there were more gay and lesbian bars in Berlin during the 1920s than there were in New York in 1980. In the city's cabaret bars you could hear singers performing 'Das Lila Lied' ('The Lavender Song') which, with its repeated refrain 'We are just different from the others,' is quite probably the first song to directly reference and celebrate homosexuality. With music by Mischa Spolianski (under the pseudonym of Arno Billing) and lyrics by Kurt Schwabach, several versions of 'Das Lila Lied' were recorded in 1921, the year that Berlin hosted the First International Conference on Sexual Reform, an instrumental by Marek Weber on Parlophon and one by an unnamed vocalist on Homokord among them. Lyricist Schwabach would later write the words for Germany's entry for the 1960 Eurovision Song Contest, 'Bonne Nuit, Ma Chérie'.

LGBT artists enjoyed fame and freedom, yet many others regarded the Weimar Republic's tolerant attitude towards homosexuals as a sign of the country's decadence. Hitler's rise to power in 1933 brought about the closure of gay and lesbian bars, bathhouses, hotels, clubs and cafes; the sexologist Magnus Hirschfeld's Institute for Sexual Research was ransacked by stormtroopers (led by a gay man, Hitler's close friend Ernst Röhm) and its archives – including thousands of books, magazines, films and other irreplaceable items – were burned. Luckily, Hirschfeld himself was out of the country at the time; he remained in exile until his death (in Nice, on his 67th birthday) in 1935. Max Hansen, the cabaret star who in 1932 recorded 'War'n Sie Schon Mal In Mich Verliebt?' (Weren't You Ever In Love With Me?), which depicted Hitler as homosexual and a drunk, was forced to make a quick exit from Germany, first to Vienna and then to Denmark. Rumours had circulated for years about Hitler's own sexual proclivities: 'in the Munich days of 1920-22, before the abortive Putsch, everyone knew of his homosexual activities. It was only after he felt certain he was to become a dominating figure in the public eye that he took pains to indulge his vice in secret,' wrote one British newspaper columnist.[22]

Over a six-month period, Adolf Brand's home and offices were raided five times by the Nazis, and his files, equipment and personal archive were impounded. Röhm and his deputy Edmund Heines (who was also gay) were singled out by the British press as being behind the burning of the Reichstag.[23] In October 1936, Himmler established the Reich Central Office for Combating Abortion and Homosexuality; LGBT people were forced out of the country or back into the closet, and those who did neither were at risk of being rounded up and sent to the concentration camps. Tens, possibly hundreds, of thousands of LGBT people (the vast majority men: Hitler did not seem to see lesbians as a major threat) were sent to the camps and forced to wear the pink triangle: many were subjected to humiliating medical 'experiments' and at least 55,000 died, including Berlin cabaret artists Willy Rosen, Max Ehrlich, Kurt Gerron (the star of Kurt Weill and Bertolt Brecht's *Three Penny Opera*) and Paul O'Montis.

Paul O'Montis (born Paul Wendel in Budapest in 1894) had been one of the biggest stars of the era, recording around 70 songs for the Odeon label, including German-language versions of American hits such as 'Ist Dein Kleines Herz Für Mich Noch Frei, Baby' ('I Can't Give You Anything But Love'). Raised in Hanover, he tried his hand at scriptwriting before first appearing on stage in Berlin in 1924. By 1932 he could regularly be heard on radio across Europe.

Openly gay, after the Nazis seized power O'Montis was banned from performing in Germany and fled the country. He went first to Vienna but after the Germans annexed Austria he escaped to Prague, and was arrested there when the German army invaded Czechoslovakia in 1939. He was deported first to Zagreb and then to Łódź in Poland before being sent to the Sachsenhausen concentration camp on 30 May 1940, just 20 kilometres or so north of the cabaret stages he had once commanded. O'Montis died in Sachsenhausen just six weeks later, aged 46. The official reason given for his death was suicide.

Luckily, many of Berlin's lesbian entertainers escaped persecution. Claire Waldoff (born October 1884 as Clara Wortmann), another well-known cabaret performer, lived happily and openly with her lover, Olga von Roeder, in Berlin during the 1920s: the pair were a common sight at the city's many lesbian bars, including the famous Damenklub Pyramide. Unusually for the era, she shunned the sophisticated manner and double entendres that the city's cabaret stars were noted for, instead adopting a mannish, direct approach which often got her into trouble. A contemporary of Marlene Dietrich (the pair shared a stage on more than one occasion), her best-known recording is probably 'Ach Gott, Was Sind Die Männer Dumm' (Oh God, Why Are Men So Stupid). Dietrich, a bisexual who was known to have enjoyed the thriving gay scene and drag balls of 1920s Berlin (she is reputed to have said that 'only pansies know how to look like a sexy woman'),[24] had appeared in a number of cabaret revues, but she had already started to establish herself on the silver screen and moved to the United States in 1930 after her career-defining appearance as Lola Lola in Josef von Sternberg's *The Blue Angel*. The icon is said to have met theatrical costumier James Stroock on her passage to New York and to have tried, unsuccessfully, to seduce his wife Bianca. When the shocked Mrs. Stroock rebuffed her advances, Dietrich simply told her that: 'In Europe it doesn't matter if you're a man or a woman. We make love with anyone we find attractive.'[25] In her first American movie, *Morocco* (1930), Dietrich, who began her recording career in 1928 but who will be forever associated with her theme song 'Falling in Love Again', caused a scandal for the scene where, dressed in a man's black tails and top hat, she kisses another woman. More than half a century later another icon would shamelessly copy Dietrich's style: Madonna's 'borrowing' of Dietrich's look for photo shoots, video performances and the like may be simply seen as an homage, but coming at a time when she was also flirting with lesbianism – suggesting that she was in a relationship with actress and comedian Sandra Bernhard – it seemed more like an attempt to grab headlines than to pay tribute to an inspiration.

Dietrich got out of Germany before the Nazis came to power, but Claire Waldoff ran foul of them on several occasions: a performance at a fundraiser for the communist party earned her a temporary ban, and after further bans, she and Olga left Berlin in 1939, settling in Bayerisch Gmain, near Salzburg. While she was in London to film Alexander Korda's *Knight Without Armour,* Nazi officials approached Dietrich and offered her lucrative contracts should she agree to return to Germany. They promised her that she would become the foremost film star of the Third Reich. Dietrich refused their offers and instead applied for US citizenship. The women survived the Second World War and, after her movie career was over, Dietrich returned to the stage, forging a successful second career as a cabaret singer. Waldoff, who had lived in quiet semi-retirement, lost her money in the West German monetary reform of 1948 and they had to rely on financial support from the state. Waldoff died in 1957 and von Roeder in 1963, and the pair are buried together in Stuttgart. Dietrich lived until she was 90, and died in Paris in 1992.

Liberace, as he appeared on a postcard given away to viewers of his hit TV show in the 1950s

CHAPTER 6

Strange Fruit

"'I made you a man. When your momma brought you home
she brought a boy. If you hadda been a girl she would
have named you Martha. You are a boy." My daddy wanted
seven boys, and that I was messing it up'

Little Richard[26]

Unlike the period following the 1914-1918 conflict, in the years immediately after the Second World War, LGBT performers were sent
scurrying back into their respective closets. Post-war culture emphasised
strong, virile men as being the providers for their families, with women
encouraged to stay at home, cook hearty meals and raise the kids. Any
kind of gender deviance was deemed criminal. Austerity, coming on the
heels of the pre-war Great Depression, only helped further the 'us and
them' mentality.

Where once difference had been embraced, during the post-war
period people were actively encouraged to be suspicious of anything outside the accepted norm. Deviance was not to be entertained. In Britain,
a series of high-profile court cases and a marked increase in the number
of gay men prosecuted and imprisoned drove the country's gay elite and
'bright young things' underground. In 1950s America, homosexuality
was classified as a psychiatric disorder; homosexuals were categorised
as sexual perverts and it was widely believed that homosexuality was a
dangerous, contagious social disease that posed a threat to the family
and to the security of the country. The FBI began to keep lists of people

in the public eye and government office that they identified as homosexual, believing them to be weak and easily indoctrinated by the enemy. McCarthyism was putting what would seem to be the final nail in the coffin for the LGBT community. The Cold War, allied to the fear of the spread of communism and the near-certainty of an all-out nuclear war in the not-too-distant future, saw a new wave of conservatism masquerading as patriotism drive suspected commies and queers from Hollywood, from the radio and from the recording studio.

Yet in spite of this, an underground gay movement sprang up which gave birth to a new language: Polari, a type of slang which had been used in Britain for decades but that reached its apotheosis from the 1930s to the early 1970s in gay pubs, among theatre crowds and on merchant ships. New LGBT-friendly bars opened in cities around the world, there were new publications – such as the rash of pocket-sized physique magazines which legitimised the ownership of cheesecake portraits of virtually naked men – and a market for discs and magazines sold 'under the counter' and through specialist outlets. LGBT people created their own subterranean world, where risqué cabaret performers pushed boundaries (and ran the risk of arrest) and – just as during the years of prohibition – bars were run by a criminal class who cared not where their money came from as long as it came.

In the 1940s, Edythe D. Eyde was 25 years old and working as a secretary at the RKO film studios in Los Angeles. By her own account, she had a lot of time to herself in the office,[1] and so twice a month Edythe 'typed out five carbons and one original of *Vice Versa*,' the world's first lesbian newssheet. Subtitled 'America's Gayest Magazine,' *Vice Versa* (whose first issue appeared in June 1947) was begun by Ms Eyde initially as a way of expanding her social circle: 'I was by myself, and I wanted to be able to meet others like me. I couldn't go down the street saying, "I'm looking for lesbian friends".' She published nine issues of *Vice Versa* before RKO was sold and she was forced her to change jobs. 'I did eight copies at a time (and) I'd run it through twice, that made 16 copies. And after I was through I would just give it to my friends. I never sold it.'

In the 1950s, Edythe began writing for *The Ladder*, the first nationally available lesbian magazine, published by the Daughters of Bilitis, the first lesbian civil rights organisation in the United States. It was while she was writing for *The Ladder* that she adopted the name Lisa Ben (an anagram of 'lesbian'); all nine issues of *Vice Versa* had been published anonymously. While working with the Daughters of Bilitis (and billed as 'the first gay folk singer') Lisa issued her first 45, her own composition, 'Cruisin' Down the Boulevard' backed with a lesbian version of the standard 'Frankie and Johnny': 'I started writing parodies to popular tunes in 1948,' she told writer Kate Brandt.[2]

'I listened to a lot of different artists,' says queer singer-songwriter Blackberri, 'I'm really eclectic when it comes to music, but my favourite vocalist of all time was Billie Holiday. I love her voice. She sings like Satchmo's horn! Her voice has got that kind of feel to it, it's just amazing'. Throughout her tempestuous career, Billie Holiday was openly bisexual and was rumoured to have dated many notable characters, including the actress and wit Tallulah Bankhead. Frank Sinatra called Billie 'the greatest single musical influence on me,' adding 'I think anyone listening to Billie sing can't help but learn something from her'.[3] Etta James was a huge fan, as was Ray Charles, who performed with her at Carnegie Hall in 1959. Diana Ross portrayed her on the big screen in *Lady Sings the Blues*, a highly fictionalised version of her life.

Billie and Tallulah first met in the 1930s, a period when Bankhead could often be found slumming it in Harlem. After suffering a difficult and abusive childhood (she spent long periods in care and had was the victim of an attempted rape when she was just 11) in 1929, Holiday, who was born in Philadelphia in 1915, moved to Harlem, where she worked as a teenage prostitute. Imprisoned for soliciting when she was still only 14, once out of jail the girl born Eleanora Harris began singing, adopting the stage name Billie Holiday from actress Billie Dove and the musician Clarence Holiday, her biological father. By 1931 she was singing professionally, and in 1933 she made her recording debut as vocalist for the Benny Goodman Orchestra's 'Riffin' The Scotch'. She shone at the Café Society in New York, where she introduced one of her best-known songs, 'Strange Fruit', a stinging depiction of a lynching. In the early years of her career she often crossed paths with Bessie Smith, and Holiday cited the Empress of the Blues as a major influence.

It seems that Holiday and Bankhead were more than just friends, and by 1946 they had become lovers: 'It was Billie's deep feeling and originality which moved me from the first time I heard her,' Bankhead revealed.[4] By this time, Holiday had become a major – albeit troubled – star, recording such classics as 'God Bless The Child' (a million-seller in 1941), 'That Ole Devil Called Love' and the haunting 'Strange Fruit'. Working with the best jazz musicians of the day, including Lester Young, Teddy Wilson, Count Basie and Artie Shaw, Holiday was earning more than a thousand dollars a week (according to a 1947 news report she made $250,000 in the three years up to 1947),[5] but she spent a great deal financially supporting her mother and most of what was left went on heroin. Bankhead often attended Holiday's shows, and on several occasions she attempted to sort out her messy life: after Holiday was busted for opium possession, it was Bankhead who posted bail, and it was she who paid for a psychiatrist when Holiday threatened suicide. After Holiday was sent to the Alderson Federal Prison Camp in West Virginia, Bankhead pleaded with FBI Director J. Edgar Hoover (himself rumoured to be gay, although there has never been any real evidence to back up the often-repeated stories about him being a transvestite) that she be spared jail: 'Miss Holiday is a very great artist. She doesn't need to be confined within prison walls. What she needs is understanding, medical help and the warmth of a loving home'.[6] In early 1959, Holiday was arrested again, this time along with her manager John Levy, for the illegal possession of narcotics. Her attorney, Jake Ehrlich, successfully argued that the hearing be delayed so that Lady Day could fulfil a series of live dates already arranged for cities including Seattle, Vancouver and Portland.[7]

By 1952, when Bankhead issued her autobiography *Tallulah*, things had soured between the two women. The book, published at a time when Bankhead was becoming something of a television celebrity and was desperately trying to clean up her act, hardly mentioned Holiday at all, yet when Holiday was featured in a TV special in October 1953, Bankhead was just one of the many celebrities (including Louis Armstrong, Artie Shaw and Count Basie) queuing up to sing her praises.[8] Three years later, Holiday issued her own autobiography (like Tallulah's, ghost-written); Bankhead was furious with Holiday over 'unkind' mentions of her in *Lady Sings the Blues*, and threatened to sue. Bankhead called Lee Barker at Doubleday, Holiday's publisher, and warned him 'If you publish that stuff about me in the Billie Holiday book, I'll sue you for every goddam [sic] cent that Doubleday can make.'[9]

Billie Holiday's life ended ignominiously in New York in 1959; she was just 44. She died handcuffed to a bed in the Metropolitan Hospital, having been arrested on yet another narcotics charge while she lay dying. Legend has it that she only had 70¢ in the bank, but an hour before she died she gave a nurse a roll of $50 bills wrapped tight in Scotch tape that she had kept secreted in her vagina, which she asked her to give to Bill Dufty, the journalist friend who had ghost-written her autobiography and who had been present at the hospital throughout her stay. For many years, Dufty kept the location of Holiday's stash a secret, initially claiming that a nurse had found it taped to her leg. Bankhead sent a wreath of red roses for the casket, which was buried in an unmarked grave next to her mother's: the coffin was exhumed in 1960 and reburied with a headstone which read 'Billie Holiday, known as Lady Day. Born April 7 1915, Died July 15 1959'. Bankhead, who never publicly described herself as being bisexual (she did, however, describe herself as 'ambisextrous' and 'as pure as the driven slush'), died in New York in 1968.

Sister Rosetta Tharpe has been hailed as the 'woman who invented Rock 'n' Roll'; her extraordinary electric guitar-led, gospel-influenced performances were a massive influence on Elvis and any number of early Rock 'n' Rollers. Little Richard called her his favourite singer: in 1947 she heard Little Richard singing and invited him to join her on stage at the Macon City Auditorium. That show was Little Richard's first public performance. When Rosetta decided to pay him, her generosity inspired him to become a performer. Johnny Cash was a fan; Bob Dylan still is.

Rosetta Tharpe (she adapted her stage name from her first husband's surname, Thorp) was born on 20 March 1915 in Arkansas and began playing guitar and singing when she was just four years old. By the age of six she had joined her mother, Katie Bell Nubin, on stage and was performing in a travelling evangelical troupe before the pair moved to Chicago and became featured performers at the Church of God in Christ, with little Rosetta standing on a table so that the congregation could see her. In Chicago she became immersed in jazz and blues.

Not everyone loved her; 'she fluctuates between a Mammy shout and very sad blues crooning,' wrote one critic, noting, however, that 'she's receiving a hearty welcome'.[10] She recorded her first sides for Decca in 1938: one of the songs laid down at that session, 'Rock Me', was a gospel/blues crossover that became the first ever gospel hit. Churchgoers were shocked at the mix of spirituality and secularism; she sounds like Bessie Smith or Ma Rainey but her message is one of redemption in the Lord, not of sex and drugs and pre-rock 'n' roll. Moving on to perform in Broadway's Cotton Club and Harlem's famous Savoy Ballroom, she was a sensation, but embracing secular music hurt her standing in the church, and although she tried to split from her management and return to pure gospel, Tharpe's handlers saw that there was money to be made: she had signed to a seven-year contract and she was going to continue recording the songs they wanted her to sing. The boogie-inflected 'Strange Things Happening Every Day' is proto rock 'n' roll and pre-dates Jackie Brenston's 'Rocket '88' (often cited as the first true rock 'n' roll record) by seven years. When (in 1947) she showcased her electric guitar playing prowess on a re-recording of her early hit 'That's All', she paved the way for a generation of male guitarists including Chuck Berry and Carl Perkins.

Throughout the 1940s, she performed with fellow Church of God in Christ singer Marie Knight, and while the two women were touring, Marie's two children died in a house fire in New Jersey. They were close; it has been suggested that they were lovers and, in 1948, Tharpe bought a house for the pair of them (and Tharpe's mother) in Richmond, Virginia to live in when they were between engagements. However, they split acrimoniously in 1949, with Tharpe taking out notices in newspapers to announce that Knight was no longer associated with her act.[11] Tharpe played several times in Britain: in 1958 a young drummer by the name of Richard Starkey saw her play at Liverpool jazz cellar The Cavern.[12] When she came back to England in 1964 with B. B. King to appear in a TV special for Granada (recorded in a disused railway station), Britain's nascent blues scene sat up and took notice. Although Gospel's first superstar was not out to the public during her lifetime, it has been posthumously claimed that she was much less guarded in her private life and was either lesbian or bisexual, with promoter Allan Bloom claiming to have walked in on Tharpe having sex with other women during the 'honeymoon tour' which followed her third wedding.[13] Sister Rosetta Tharpe died in October 1973, survived by her third husband, who she had married in front of 25,000 people in Washington's Griffith Stadium in 1951. Her old friend Marie Knight fixed Rosetta's hair and make-up for her final journey.

Sister Rosetta Tharpe was hardly the first artist to decide to stay in the closet – although in reality most had little choice in the matter. Władziu Valentino Liberace (known to his family and friends as Lee) made his first recordings in 1946, and as outlandish as he was, he resolutely refused to answer any questions about his sexuality. Revered as one of the world's greatest entertainers, his enormous success – and ostentatious wealth – relied on his position as America's non-threatening, asexual 'mama's boy', and his low-brow popularisation of high-brow music would never have happened if his audience – including the 35 million that regularly tuned in to watch him on TV – had seen him as anything other than sexless. In the process of exploiting his own poor upbringing, he filled his devoted audience with the belief that anyone could make it big. He was the embodiment of the American Dream. Elvis was a fan: until Elvis displaced him, Liberace was the best-loved star in America, and when they met, Elvis made sure to get Lee's autograph for his mother. Associating himself with Elvis was a smart move: the King of Rock may have alluded to homosexuality on his worldwide hit 'Jailhouse Rock', but no one seriously questioned his heterosexuality. Recorded in April 1957, the song's homoerotic lyrics are not exactly guarded, especially in the third verse when one male prisoner opines to another to 'come on and do the Jailhouse Rock with me': for decades the word 'rock' had been used in songs as code for sex.

In 1956 an article in the British newspaper the *Daily Mirror* (by column-ist William Connor, writing under the pen name Cassandra) described Liberace as 'the summit of sex – the pinnacle of masculine, feminine, and neuter. Everything that he, she, and it can ever want ... a deadly, winking, sniggering, snuggling, chromium-plated, scent-impregnated, luminous, quivering, giggling, fruit-flavoured, mincing, ice-covered heap of mother love'. Liberace, at the time the highest-paid entertainer in the world, sent a tongue-in-cheek telegram to the *Daily Mirror* that read: 'what you said hurt me very much. I cried all the way to the bank,' although he would later sue the newspaper for libel, testifying in a London court that he was not homosexual and that he had never taken part in homosexual acts. During a six-hour address to the court, Liberace stated that 'on my word of God, on my mother's health, which is so dear to me, this article only means one thing, that I am a homosexual and that is why I am in this court. "Fruit-flavoured, masculine, feminine and neuter" – all this points to one horrible fact which has damaged me in my career and my reputation, has made me the subject of ridicule and caused me great embarrassment.'[14]

'"Are you a homosexual?" Liberace was asked by [his representa-tive, Gilbert] Beyfus. "No, sir." Said the pianist, looking straight at the bewigged judge, Sir Cyril Salmon. "Have you ever indulged in homosex-ual practices," the attorney asked. "No, sir, never in my life." "What are your feelings about it?" "My feelings are the same as anyone else's. I am against the practice because it offends convention and offends society," the pianist said.'[15]

Lee testified that, at a performance in Sheffield 'there were cries from the audience of "queer" and such things as "go home, queer",' which upset him 'very much, and it upset the audience too.'[16] He won the suit, perjuring himself in the process, and the £8,000 damages he received led Liberace to repeat his new 'I cried all the way to the bank' catchphrase to reporters.

The *Daily Mirror* was not the only publication prepared to take a pop: the headline in the July 1957 issue of the US magazine *Confidential* trumpeted 'Liberace's Theme Song Should Be "Mad About the Boy"!' Once again, Liberace sued, this time filing a $20 million libel suit and telling George Putnam, a reporter for Los Angeles broadcaster KTTV that 'It's real heartbreak to see your life's work destroyed so viciously by a magazine in an article of this kind. It's a lie. It's trash.' He eventually settled for $40,000.

Lee kept up the pretence to the end: even after his former chauffeur and lover Scott Thorson filed a $113 million lawsuit against him (in the first same-sex palimony case in the US), he denied any kind of homosexual involvement. In December 1986, less than two months before he died, Liberace settled the case for $95,000. The week after his death (on 4 February 1987) the *Daily Mirror* made a half-hearted attempt to recover the money from his estate, running the headline 'Any Chance of a Refund'.[17] 'He was a huge influence on me,' Elton John admitted in 2013. 'He wasn't publicly out – but he didn't give a flying monkey about what he was wearing; he just went for it. That, of course, influenced me. My thing was to leap on the piano, do handstands and wear clothes that would draw attention to me because that's the focus for two and half hours. Liberace gave me that idea.'[18]

Cassandra's accusation would not have come as a surprise to the average newspaper reader, as Britain saw a major crackdown on homosexual activity in the post-war years. Home Secretary Sir David Maxwell Fyfe promised there would be 'a new drive against male vice' that would 'rid England of this plague'. In 1947, distinguished army officer Lord Colwyn of the Gordon Highlanders was court-martialled after pleading guilty to 'five charges of gross impropriety . . . in which Italian men were involved during Lord Colwyn's overseas service'.[19] Arrests for importuning were common and high-profile cases made sensational headlines. By the end of 1954, there were 1,069 men in prison in England and Wales for homosexual acts, and undercover police officers would pose as gay men soliciting in places including public lavatories (known as cottages) and cruising grounds in municipal parks in an effort to add to that number.

In 1953, rumours started to circulate that a prominent '27 year-old bachelor peer' had been up to no good. Soon after, Lord Montagu of Beaulieu fled the country, first to France and then to America, from where he knew he could not be extradited. Choosing to return and face his accusers, in December that year the bisexual Montagu was acquitted of committing a serious sexual offence against a 14-year-old boy. Montagu was adamant it was a set-up: he had accused the boy of theft but the police, aware of his position in society and sexual predilections, were after him. Three weeks later, the police came for him again. The media had been tipped off and were on the doorstep waiting when they arrived. Montagu, along with landowner Michael Pitt-Rivers and *Daily Mail* correspondent Peter Wildeblood, was charged with 'conspiracy to incite certain male persons to commit serious offences with male persons' (two young airmen, Edward McNally and John Reynolds). This was the first time that such a charge had been used since the trial of Oscar Wilde almost 60 years earlier. Montagu was the only one of the three men to protest his innocence. 'Because I was,' he told the *Evening Standard* in 2007. 'It was guilt by association'.[20]

The result of this sensational trial would see a peer of the realm jailed for a year (his co-defendants were incarcerated for 18 months apiece): more importantly, it presaged a change in attitudes towards homosexuality in Britain. Partly as a result of the case, in September 1957 the Committee on Homosexual Offences and Prostitution issued a report recommending changes in the law. Better known as the Wolfenden Report (after the chairman of the committee, Lord John Frederick Wolfenden), the report recommended that 'homosexual behaviour between consenting adults in private should no longer be a criminal offence'. It would take a further decade, but the Wolfenden Report eventually led to the passage of the Sexual Offences Act 1967, which decriminalised homosexual acts in private between two men over the age of 21 (the act applied to England and Wales only). Subsequent acts would reduce the age of consent to 18 then, in 2001, to 16 when, for the first time in British history, regardless of gender, the age of consent was the same for both heterosexual and homosexual acts.

When Cole Porter wrote the song 'Farming' for his 1941 Broadway production *Let's Face It*, he became the first person to use the word 'gay' to mean homosexual in a popular song: 'George's bull is beautiful but he's gay'. The word had been used liberally before (by Bing Crosby in his 1929 hit 'Gay Love', for example), but this was the first time it had been used in a pejorative sense; Bing's love had been fun, happy and heady – although at no point does the song mention the gender of the object of Mr. Crosby's affection. 'Farming' used the 'G' word as a way of emasculating the bull in question.

The Broadway musical is as central to LGBT culture as our culture is central to the existence of the Broadway musical: heterosexual audiences may laugh at the endless references to nancy boys, the swishy dance numbers and the effete leading men, but without out (and

LGBT-friendly) writers, composers, costume designers, choreographers, directors and – naturally – actors, the Broadway musical as we know it would simply not exist. This is abundantly clear today, when the biggest shows include *The Lion King* (music by Elton John), *Hairspray* (by out-gay film director John Waters), *Falsettos* (a musical about the AIDS crisis) and *Wicked* (seriously, how could a show with its roots in *The Wizard of Oz* not have been crafted to appeal to both lesbians and gay men? There's a reason that gay men are often referred to as 'friends of Dorothy', you know), but it has always been the case. Porter was married but gay (and would write the outrageous 'Tom, Dick or Harry' for the 1948 production of *Kiss Me, Kate* which includes the repeated line 'A Dick! A Dick! A Dick! A Dick!'), as was Leonard Bernstein, composer of the huge international hit *West Side Story*, and his lyricist Stephen Sondheim, probably the greatest composer of the Broadway musical still living today. Then you have Noël Coward, Lionel Bart, lyricist Lorenz Hart (co-writer, with Richard Rodgers, of *The Boys from Syracuse* and *Pal Joey*; repressing his homosexuality drove the rough trade-loving Hart into the alcoholism that ultimately killed him), John Kander and his lyricist Fred Ebb (*Cabaret, Funny Lady, Kiss of the Spider Woman*), and Ivor Novello. Yet although musicals were dominated by LGBT artists – so much so that Broadway earned the nickname 'The Gay White Way' – it wasn't until the 1959 show *The Nervous Set* and its central song 'The Ballad of the Sad Young Men' that America got to see gay men portrayed on stage as anything but bright, fey and fun young things. A few years later, *Hair: The American Tribal Love-Rock Musical* proved a useful training ground for a number of LGBT artists (Jobriath, Joan Armatrading, Peter Straker and Valentino among them) and included a scene where two men kiss, but Broadway would have to wait until Earl Wilson Jr's 1976 musical *Let My People Come*, which debuted in 1974, and explicitly tackled LGBT issues in the song 'I'm Gay'.

Although he wasn't out at the time, Johnny Mathis recorded several songs with an underlying gay theme, including 'The Best Of Everything', 'All The Sad Young Men', and 'A Time For Us'. When he first signed to Columbia in 1956, being black and gay and out was simply not an option: Johnnie Ray already filled two of those spots for the company; Mathis chose not to hide his sexuality but to not discuss it at all. His non-threatening image and yearning ballads meant that he could appeal to both men and women, to both straight and LGBT audiences. Johnny Mathis was Liberace-safe. After he revealed that he was gay, in an interview with *Us* magazine in 1982, he received death threats. 'A few people in the Southern states didn't like it,' he told Britain's *Sunday Express*. 'I was in no real danger but when you're young it's difficult to get over. It doesn't bother me at all now, and it's not even a big deal any more which is wonderful, but I learned to isolate myself from negative things.'[21]

Born on 10 January 1927 as the second child of farmers Elmer and Hazel Ray, Johnnie Ray's career was anything but conventional. In 1951, shortly before Ray was signed to Okeh records, he was arrested in Detroit for accosting and soliciting an undercover vice squad officer in the restroom of the Stone Theatre, a burlesque house. He pleaded guilty and, offered the choice between 30 days in the slammer or a $25 fine, he wisely paid up and was released. The incident failed to make the news locally, but would continue to haunt him.

Called the 'father of rock and roll' by Tony Bennett, legend has it that before he was three years old, Ray was already playing the piano; however, an accident at 13, when he fell and suffered a concussion, severely affected his heath: crippling headaches and depression followed until his hearing was tested the following year. Damage from that accident had resulted in Johnnie losing around half of his hearing, and he wore a hearing aid for the rest of his life (Morrissey chose to parody this, appearing on British TV show *Top of the Pops* wearing an old-fashioned hearing aid of the type Ray used). Destined for the stage, his career included a short stint as a straight man in a comedy act when he was just 19 years old before he got his big break at the Flame Show Bar, a 'black and tan' night club in Detroit with a mixed-race clientele. Ray fit right in, and he soon came to the attention of a talent scout named Danny Keasler. 'I want you to hear a singer who's terrific,' he is reputed to have told his bosses at Columbia. 'He's a boy who sounds like a girl!'[22]

He recorded his first single, the self-penned 'Whisky and Gin', on 28 May 1951. Within months he had scored his first million-seller, 'Cry', and captured the hearts of screaming bobbysoxers. And almost immediately the stories about his sexuality began to spread.

Known affectionately as the Nabob of Sob or the Prince of Wails, Ray had more than twenty hits during the 1950s. At the highest point of his career he made well over a million dollars a year, sold out shows around the world, and appeared in movies including *There's No Business Like Show Business* with Ethel Merman, Donald O'Connor and Marilyn Monroe. He was often mobbed by his adoring fans: during his Australian tour of 1954 it was reported that he earned around £30 a minute from his shows and that 'he also had three tuxedos and several ties and shirts ripped to pieces by emotional fans'.[23] On a previous visit to Brisbane, 'Ray had a new 15 guinea drape coat ripped up the back, his shirt torn and the tassels ripped off his shoes'.[24] In May 1955, he was knocked unconscious by a mob of screaming fans as he arrived at his Edinburgh hotel.

In the spring of 1952, Ray married Marilyn Morrison. She was aware of Ray's homosexuality but told a friend of his that she would 'straighten it out'. The couple separated before the end of the year and divorced in January 1954. Sixteen months later, he announced his engagement to Silvia Drew, one of his backing singers. In 1959 Ray was arrested by the Detroit vice squad on a charge of soliciting an undercover police officer at the Brass Rail theatre bar, one of the city's gay bars (there were three Brass Rails in Detroit at the time: he appears to have been arrested at the one on Adams St. across from Grand Circus Park). Released after another night in the cells on a $500 bond, this time Ray hired an attorney and fought the charges. 'I can only say that the whole thing is a complete misunderstanding,' he told reporters. 'I have witnesses to testify to the validity of anything I say at my trial'.[25]

'I was sitting at the bar signing autographs when this man came up and asked me to autograph his handkerchief, which I did. Then we talked and had some drinks. All of us were going over to the Statler [hotel] for a nightcap and I asked him if he wanted to join us guys. The fellow said he did, and walked out with us.'

Ray had been the victim of police entrapment, an all-to-frequent device used to arrest gay men – and the jury felt he had been coerced, taking less than an hour to find him not guilty. Still, the damage had been done: Ray's career hit a downward slide, and although he kept working, he did not have another chart hit after 1959. Years of heavy drinking eventually took their toll, and he died of liver failure in February 1990.

The Brass Rail, where Johnnie Ray fell victim to police entrapment

If Ray was the 'father of rock and roll', then either Little Richard or Esquerita can lay claim to being the mother. Esquerita (born Eskew Reeder Jr or Steven Quincy Reeder in 1935 in Greenville, South Carolina) was an early rock 'n' roller who inspired the camp approach of Little Richard, although they seem to have influenced each other equally; Little Richard may have 'borrowed' some of his style from the more flamboyant Esquerita, but the latter man did not begin his recording career until long after Little Richard first made it big. A self-taught pianist, Eskew Jr spent his early years playing piano in church before, in his late teens, dropping out of high school and moving to New York to join the gospel group the Heavenly Echoes around the time that they released their 1955 single 'Didn't It Rain'/'Your God is My God Too'.

Inspired by the 'dirty blues' of Ma Rainey and Lucille Bogan, Eskew left the Heavenly Echoes and began playing his own, raucous music for just about anyone who would put him on a stage. Discovered playing in a bar by Paul Peek, Gene Vincent's rhythm guitarist, he was signed to Capitol Records (Vincent's label) and recorded his first session for the company in May 1958. His debut album, *Esquerita!* featured Elvis' backing vocalists the Jordanaires.

Over the next decade, he would record for a variety of labels and with a number of up-and-coming players, including Big Joe Turner and Allen Toussaint. In 1963, he recorded an unreleased session for Berry Gordy's Motown label and the following year played with Jimi Hendrix on *Little Richard's Greatest Hits,* an album that consisted of re-recordings of Little Richard's biggest songs for his new label, VeeJay. Sadly, and not through lack of trying, Esquerita never really made the grade as a solo artist. Changing his name to The Magnificent Malochi, he signed with Brunswick Records in 1968, releasing the one-off 45 'As Time Goes By'/'Mama, Your Daddy's Come Home' which featured famed New Orleans keyboardist Dr. John on organ. Reissues of his classic 1950s material followed, but if they made any money, none of it filtered down to the artist himself.

During the 1970s and early 1980s, he did what he needed to do to get by, often playing in dives in New York for little money; at one point he wound up in prison. Esquerita died of AIDS in October 1986 in Harlem, and was buried in a pauper's grave. In 2012, Norton Records issued a new Esquerita album, *Sinner Man: The Lost Session.*

'Little' Richard Penniman freely admitted that Esquerita influenced his wild style of piano playing, and he also told interviewers that the first time he clapped eyes on Eskew's exotic look he was blown away. Little Richard told Charles White, author of the excellent biography *The Life And Times Of Little Richard: The Quasar of Rock,* that he had met Reeder at the Greyhound bus station in his home town of Macon around 1951:

> One night I was sitting there and Esquerita came in. He was with
> a lady preacher by the name of Sister Rosa, whose line was selling

blessed bread. She said it was blessed, but it was nothing but regular old bread that you buy at the store. Esquerita played piano for her and they had a little guy singing with them by the name of Shorty. So Esquerita and me went up to my house and he got on the piano and he played "One Mint Julep" way high up in the treble. It sounded so pretty. The bass was fantastic. He had the biggest hands of anybody I'd ever seen ... I said, "Hey, how do you do that?" And he says, "I'll teach you". And that's when I really started playing.[26]

Little Richard, a man who has clearly struggled to define his sexuality but has at times been happy to admit to being gay, began recording that same year and was a huge influence on another genderfluid icon, David Bowie. When asked who or what made him first want to sing, Bowie said:

Little Richard. If it hadn't have been for him, I probably wouldn't have gone into music. When I was nine and first saw Little Richard in a film that played around town—I think it was probably *Girl Can't Help It*—seeing those four saxophonists onstage, it was like, "I want to be in that band!" And for a couple of years that was my ambition, to be in a band playing saxophone behind Little Richard. That's why I got a saxophone.

Bowie told *Vanity Fair* in 1998 that his most treasured possession was 'a photograph held together by cellophane tape of Little Richard that I bought in 1958,' and he admitted, 'when I heard Little Richard, I mean, it just set my world on fire'. Bowie later said that, after his father bought him a copy of Little Richard's 'Tutti Frutti' that 'I had heard God'. 'Tutti Frutti' was originally about anal sex between two men, but the original lyrics – 'Tutti Frutti, good booty/If it don't fit, don't force it/You can grease it, make it easy' – were cleaned up for mass consumption by songwriter Dorothy LaBostrie.

As the man who (in his early years) performed in drag as Princess Lavonne once said, 'Elvis may be the King of Rock and Roll, but I am the Queen.' He told filmmaker John Waters (for a 1987 *Playboy* interview), 'I love gay people. I believe I was the founder of gay. I'm the one who started to be so bold tellin' the world! I was wearing make-up and eye-lashes when no men were wearing that. I was very beautiful; I had hair hanging everywhere. If you let anybody know you was gay, you was in trouble; so when I came out I didn't care what nobody thought. A lot of people were scared to be with me.'

Along with Buddy Holly (with whom Little Richard once claimed to have enjoyed a threesome), Carl Perkins and Elvis, Little Richard was one of the biggest influences on the Beatles. The flamboyant legend's dress sense and wild, powerful voice are credited by Rolling Stone Keith Richards for making 'the world change from monochrome to Technicolor'.[27] But his difficulty in reconciling his deeply felt religious beliefs (at the height of his fame, Little Richard gave everything up to go in to the church) with his homosexuality has caused him to vacillate between being out and diving back in to the closet. 'I used to be a flaming homosexual from Macon, Georgia, until God changed me,' he declared from the pulpit of a New York church.[28]

Jazz, with its casual attitude to drink, drugs and sex, provided a number of gay and bisexual musicians with cover, yet on the whole the post-war jazz scene was fiercely homophobic, in startling contrast to its early years. One of the few out-gay musicians of the time was pianist and composer Billy Strayhorn, who teamed with Duke Ellington and wrote hits such as 'Lush Life' and 'Take the "A" Train'. Ellington didn't care about colour or sexuality, he was only interested in musicianship, and Strayhorn was incredibly loyal to the man whose support enabled him to live his life openly, even if it meant Ellington receiving the credit for much of Strayhorn's work. As one of his friends said: 'The most amazing thing of all about Billy Strayhorn to me was that he had the strength to make an extraordinary decision – that is, the decision not to hide the fact that he was homosexual. And he did this in the 1940s, when nobody but nobody did that.'[29] For almost a decade, Strayhorn lived openly with his partner, pianist Aaron Bridgers. The couple were introduced by Ellington's son, Mercer,[30] and only split after Bridgers decided to move permanently to Paris. They would remain friends for the rest of Strayhorn's life. The last piece Bridgers wrote and recorded, 1999's 'Phil', was dedicated to Strayhorn.

There can be little doubt that, if Ellington had not protected Strayhorn, he would not have been able to enjoy as active and open a sex life as he did. Being out of the limelight helped: there's no way that someone with a profile as high as Miles Davis could have come out as bisexual during his lifetime (he was outed posthumously by comedian Richard Pryor).[31] Likewise, much has been made in recent years of singer and pianist Nina Simone's bisexuality, although for most of her career she was married to a psychologically and physically abusive ex-policeman, Andrew Stroud.[32] Vibraphone player Gary Burton turned professional before he had finished his teens (his first recordings were issued in 1960, when he was still only 17) but it took two marriages and a whole lot of soul searching before he was finally comfortable enough to come out publicly, which he did in 1994 after having been in a gay relationship for a number of years. 'I have been asked what it's like being white in a field of music that's considered African-American,' he told Francis Davis of *The New York Times*. 'I think it would be equally valid to ask me what it's like being gay and playing a form of music that's seen as macho. It's interesting that the subject never seems to come up'.[33] Burton married his long-time partner, Jonathan Chong, in 2013. Band leader and pianist Billy Tipton, whose performing career began in the 1930s, spent his entire adult life hiding a secret from his audience – and from the women he shared his home with. Billy had been born a woman, Dorothy Lucille Tipton. Tipton went to great lengths to pass as male, binding his breasts and telling female partners that his genitals had been damaged in an accident. The Billy Tipton Trio recorded two albums of jazz standards in 1957, but it wasn't until he passed away (in January 1989 at the age of 74) that his common law wife and adopted sons discovered that he had been leading a double life. 'No one knew,' said Kitty Oakes, the woman Tipton claimed to have married in 1960. Although the couple had separated some 10 years earlier, Oakes refused to talk about their life together, saying that Tipton died with the secret and that should be respected. 'The real story about Billy Tipton doesn't have anything to do with gender,' she added. 'He was a fantastic, almost marvellous, and generous person.'[34]

Would it surprise anyone to know that George Cory and Douglass Cross, the men who wrote the music and lyrics to '(I Left My Heart In)

San Francisco' were a gay couple? Written in 1953 for the singer Claramae Turner, the song became a worldwide smash and multi-million-selling hit when it was recorded by Tony Bennett in 1962. The men met during the Second World War and spent the rest of their lives together. Friends of Billie Holiday (according to Bennett, who is a huge Holiday fan), the couple also knew Bennett's pianist Ralph Sharon, who brought the song, originally called 'When I Return To San Francisco', to the singer. The pair composed the song in a moment of homesickness, having moved to New York to try to make it in Tin Pan Alley. In 1969, 'I Left My Heart In San Francisco' was named the city's official song. Douglas Cross died in 1975, and Cory – broken-hearted after losing his partner of 30 years – committed suicide three years later . . . a short time after he had returned to live in San Francisco.

For many decades, LGBT people have identified with the autobiographical songs and tragic life of French chanteuse Édith Piaf, one of the many women seduced by Marlene Dietrich according to her daughter Maria's biography – and Maria Riva Dietrich was no fan, referring to Piaf as a 'guttersnipe' in a 2003 interview with CNN's Larry King. However Piaf, whose singing career began in the smokey jazz and cabaret clubs of the Pigalle and Champs-Élysées is better known for her tempestuous relationships with men, some (including the actor-singer Yves Montand) bisexual themselves, than for having a string of girlfriends. Although 'the little sparrow' moved freely through Paris' LGBT underworld and Piaf was no stranger in the Pigalle's lesbian bars, if she was indeed bisexual then she kept quiet about it. Dietrich, incidentally, was Piaf's matron of honour when she married Jacques Pills in 1952.

When Lesley Gore hit the big time in 1963, the same year that Piaf died, she was still just 17 – the perfect age for the protagonist in her first million-seller 'It's My Party'. Less than a year later she scored big with 'You Don't Own Me', a fantastic proto-feminist disc that was denied the Number One spot in the US by the Beatles and 'I Want to Hold Your Hand'. The singer, who was born Lesley Sue Goldstein in Brooklyn on 2 May, 1946, realised that she was a lesbian when she was in her 20s, and although there was no public announcement, it wasn't exactly a secret either. 'I just never found it was necessary because I really never kept my life private,' Lesley admitted. 'Those who knew me, those who worked with me were well aware'.[35] As well as maintaining a recording and composing career – she co-wrote several songs for the soundtrack of the hit 1980 film *Fame* – she also acted (she appeared in two episodes of the *Batman* series in 1967, and in several episodes of the TV soap *All My Children*) and from 2004 hosted the PBS television series *In the Life*, which focused on LGBT issues. Lesley, who died in 2015, spent the last 33 years of her life in a committed relationship with jewellery designer Lois Sasson.

Presenting...
CAMP
RECORDS

RACY...RIBALD...MADLY GAY...WAY OUT!

Alone or with your friends, these records make every moment a party moment!

Be one of the first in your crowd to have and hear these mad-cap – strictly adult and sophisticated recordings.

We're so happy to present to you, our customers, the worldly-wise humor of these enticing albums and singles.

EVERYONE–BUT EVERYONE will revel in the delights of this modern Rabelaisian humor!

Each and every record is a full scale production recorded in vivid, vibrant high fidelity. Every record features well-known Hollywood personalities performing specially-written excitingly daring new material!

Owning one of these records will make you want them all. Don't wait – Get in on the action today!

Use the handy order form to find out for yourself about these scintillating records. In fact, the record covers themselves are worth the price of admission!

Camp Records order form, c. 1965

CHAPTER 7

Camp Records

'He's well adjusted, I suppose; he doesn't care if the whole world knows. He goes cruising every night, wearing pants that are too damn tight...'

'Homer the Happy Little Homo' by Byrd E. Bath[1]

At the beginning of the 1960s, the American men's magazine *Adam* lent its name to a series of stag party albums; records designed to be played at bawdy, boozy all-male gatherings. Issued by the Fax Record Company, dozens of these discs, by mostly anonymous performers, appeared, containing ribald songs interspersed with slices of blue humour. One of these albums, *Sex Is My Business*, was, according to the sleeve notes, 'the result of actual interviews with prostitutes, homosexuals, pimps and "Johns" in which we hear them tell the fascinating and almost unbelievable story of their lives; their experiences, how they work, what they do and why, the money they receive and the money they pay; their fears, anxieties, hopes and strange loves ... all in their own words in a frank, graphic and revealing description of a way of life few of us know or understand.'[2] Another, *Nights of Love on Lesbos*, claimed to be a 'frankly intimate description of a sensuous young girl's lesbian desires':[3] in reality it was a recital of parts of French poet Pierre Louÿs' *Songs of Bilitis*, but in an attempt at achieving some mark of respectability its sleeve notes were penned by Frederick van Pelt Bryan, the US District Court judge who was instrumental in allowing the publication of *Lady Chatterley's Lover*. Sold under the counter in specialist shops or, more usually, through adverts in men's magazines, these albums spawned several imitators, with other companies eager to tap into the titillation. It's here, in the land of slightly risqué mail order, that the Camp label was born.

Although in the strictest sense the modern-day use of the word camp derives from the French *se camper* (to pose in an exaggerated fashion), in gay circles since at least the early years of the twentieth century the word has meant one thing only: effeminate. In places where people spoke Polari, this flighty, limp-wristed aesthetic got its name from the acronym KAMP, an effeminate man who was *Known As a Male Prostitute*. The actor and comedian Kenneth Williams wrote that 'To some it means that which is fundamentally frivolous, to others the baroque as opposed to the puritanical and to others – a load of poofs'[4] and he should have known: the closeted Williams and his out companion in comedy Hugh Paddick (who spent the last 30 years of his life with his partner, Francis) made a bona little living, thank you very much, as the über-camp Julian and Sandy, stalwarts of the hit Brit radio show *Round the Horne*. It's very clear from listening to the material where the little-known Camp Records label got its name.

Originating from a company called Different Products Unlimited in Hollywood, California, Camp Records (run by the elusive E. Richman) specialised in producing gay-themed novelty records which they advertised, under the banner 'racy … ribald … madly gay … way out!' in the back pages of publications such as *Drum: Sex in Perspective* (a revolutionary magazine from the Janus Society with a national circulation of around 15,000), *One* and *Vagabond*, a mid-'60s catalogue aimed exclusively at gay men. Mail order businesses that specialised in gay and lesbian books, such as Washington DC's Guild Book Service (run by gay publishing pioneer H. Lynn Womack), San Francisco's Dorian Book Service and Philadelphia's Lark Publications also carried stock of the discs. The releases were, naturally, 'shipped postage paid, in sealed plain package'.

Described by their own press releases as 'wilder, madder (and) gayer than a Beatle's hairdo,' Camp Records issued ten 45s. None are dated, but according to correspondence on the company's headed notepaper, the first two releases (the single 'Leather Jacket Lovers' and album *The Queen Is In The Closet*) seem to have been issued around July 1964 and the third, the 45 release 'Ballad of the Camping Woodcutter'/'Scotch Mist', was released at the end of November. The only ads that have surfaced for the label were published in 1964 and 1965. No new releases appeared after late 1965. The material typically consisted of parodies of well-known songs with their lyrics rewritten to reflect a camp sensibility: 'I'm So Wet (the Shower Song)' is a rewrite of the French folk song 'Alouette'; 'London Derriere' is a rewrite of 'Danny Boy' (aka Londonderry Air . . .), and 'Scotch Mist' is 'The Bonnie Banks o' Loch Lomond' (better known perhaps as 'You Take The High Road') with new lyrics. Some of the discs featured new songs in various styles including rock 'n' roll ('I'd Rather Fight Than Swish' and 'Leather Jacket Lovers'), Sinatra-style crooner-pop and Latin jazz.

The lyrics comically portrayed the homosexual subculture in America at the time, using broad stereotypes, gay slang and double entendres. Where artists are credited, their names are badly executed puns: Byrd E. Bath and the Gay Blades, Sandy Beech, The Gentle-Men. The name Rodney Dangerfield crops up on several releases and he's even credited as performing the tap dancing solo on 'Homer The Happy Little Homo' ('a daring, madcap romp right from the pansy patch,' went the advertising blurb for that particular oddity), but the name is a pseudonym, one that had been in popular use for at least three decades prior to its appearance in the Camp catalogue; Jack Benny had used it for a character on his popular 1940s radio show. The Rodney Dangerfield that recorded for Camp Records is not the late Jewish comedian who found mainstream fame in frat house flicks in the 1980s. It's no surprise that the performers and producers of these discs were happy to go about their work uncredited. In fact, it was important that the entire operation was kept as anonymous as possible in order to avoid trouble: the company was operating in a time when the production and distribution of recordings like this could lead to arrest for possession and distribution of obscene material. Different Products were only contactable via a PO Box number: Richman kept an office on Hazeltine Avenue, Van Nuys, but no address or telephone number appeared on the company's letterhead.

Depending on how you view these things, these records are charming period pieces, badly dated *Carry On*-style comic cuts or complete anachronisms of a thankfully bygone age. Lispy, wispy and fey, and about as sophisticated as a hammer blow to the head, the humour, such as it is, is broader than the side of a barn. More mainstream record companies would echo that same broad humour throughout the 1960s. Record producer (and former Republican governor) Mike Curb issued *These Are The Hits, You Silly Savage* by Teddy & Darrel (in fact the documentary maker Theodore 'Teddy' Charach and his friend Darrell Dee, who both appeared with Curb on the soundtrack to the 1967 movie *Mondo Hollywood*), featuring camped-up covers of recent hits, and a string of camp 45s appeared on both sides of the pond, The Butch Brothers' 'Kay, Why?' (on Thrust Records), singer Steve Elgins' 'Don't Leave Your Lover Lying Around' (a silly song about bed-hopping issued in 1974 on Dawn Records), Yin & Yan's 'Butch Soap' (on the giant EMI), and 'The Ballad of Ben Gay' by Ben Gay and the Silly Savages (seemingly unconnected to the Teddy & Darrel record) among them. Many camp actors and comedians issued records: in the UK alone, Kenneth Williams, Frankie Howerd, John Inman and Larry Grayson all put out novelty songs that pandered to their camp but closeted persona and that were meant to appeal to either children or grandparents, two demographics unlikely to blush at the tired single-entendres in a song like Inman's 'Are You Being Served Sir?' ('I'm sorry that this fitting room is dark and rather chilly, just try these on and mind that zip in case you catch your . . .'). What made records like 'Butch Soap' or 'Kay, Why' different is that they were advertised – like the Camp Records output – exclusively to the LGBT community through the pages of papers such as *Gay News*. In 1975 Oscar, a Manchester-based five-piece band working out of 10cc's Strawberry Studios in Stockport, issued a cover of Noël Coward's 'Mad About the Boy' on Buk records through the major Decca Records company. The song seemed an odd choice for five straight lads from Manchester and it was not included on their debut album, even though that album's cover featured a band member on the front in white tie and tails, sporting one of Wilde's green carnations. Oscar, who claimed that they wanted their style of presentation to 'create an aura of Victorian elegance, splendour and chivalry,'[5] soon left Buk to join Elton John at DJM, but their camp/rock aesthetic failed to ignite the record-buying public. Shortly after, the band reverted to its earlier name, The Royal Variety Show, and returned to the northern pub and club circuit, their dreams of major stardom sadly unfulfilled.

Camp Records released two full-length LPs: *The Queen Is In The Closet*, which consisted of ten songs culled from the singles, and *Mad About The Boy*, a collection of ten popular torch songs which would usually be sung by a woman but recorded instead by a male vocalist without changing the lyric's genders, similar to the cross-vocals of the 1920s and 1930s. This produced what the album's sleeve notes called 'a wonderful pot-pourri of love songs done in a most unique way' and, unlike the rest of the releases on the label, this album eschewed the campness for a much more direct approach.

Two years before *Mad About The Boy* was issued, a similar album, *Love Is A Drag*, had appeared on the Lace Records label, featuring 12 songs including 'The Boy Next Door', 'Can't Help Lovin' That Man' and, of course, 'Mad About The Boy'. Neither album dared to credit the vocalist, musicians, producers, arrangers or engineers. To this day we still do not know who sang any of the Camp Records output, although the sleeve notes – and flyers issued by the company – allude to some pretty big names being involved in what, for them, would have had to have been a covert project. However the cool, sophisticated torch song singer on *Love Is A Drag* (subtitled *For Adult Listeners Only: Sultry Stylings By A Most Unusual Vocalist*) was finally revealed (by LGBT archivist JD Doyle) as Gene Howard (born Howard Eugene Johnson in Nashville, Tennessee), a straight, married professional singer who had worked with a number of big jazz names including Gene Krupa and Stan Kenton.[6] The idea for the album came from Jack Ames, founder of Edison International Records, who created the Lace Records imprint specifically for this one-off release. The album, long out of print, was reissued by Modern Harmonic in November 2016.

'The primary reason for doing this album,' wrote the anonymous author of the sleeve notes to *Mad About The Boy* 'was to prove that good songs could and should be sung by everyone. Gender should not be the determining factor as to who should sing what.' Similarly, the uncredited sleeve notes on *Love Is A Drag* boasted that 'at long last a male vocalist with great talent has decided to take the big step – that is, to perform these classics using their original lyrics, In doing so, he has broken the barrier which has confronted so many other great singers who, for lack of courage, have not attempted.' The covers of both albums echo classic torch song collections: *Love Is A Drag*, with its moody, out-of-focus late-night jazz feel could house any similar album on a major label. *Mad About The Boy* features illustrations from another Different Products item, a desk calendar called Roy's Boys: E. Richman and his co-conspirators seem to have felt that using these images would made the album appeal to an audience already familiar with Julie London's 1956 album *Calendar Girl*. Very few copies of these records were pressed: even fewer have survived the past half-century.

Gay porn star Edward Earle Marsh, better known as Zebedy Colt, began his career as a child actor in Hollywood before moving into stage work. After a number of small roles in musicals and reviews – and an appearance (as Edward Earle) on the 1967 LP *Noël Coward Revisted* – he recorded his 1969 album *I'll Sing for You*, (later reissued as *Zebedy Sings For You*) with the London Philharmonic Orchestra. Like the earlier *Love Is A Drag* and *Mad About the Boy*, the album consisted of songs originally sung by women ('The Man I Love', 'I'm In Love With A Wonderful Guy', Billy Strayhorn's 'Lush Life' and so on) along with a few original, gay-themed songs written by Earle himself: 'at last some guy had the balls to stand up and sing "The Man I Love" and mean it,' the promotional blurb ran. By 1975 he was starring in straight porn (under the Zebedy Colt pseudonym) while still appearing on stage and off-Broadway as Edward Earle. He died in 2004, aged 75.

Born in 1909, Sir Robert Helpmann was an Australian dancer who became an international ballet star and choreographer as well as a noted actor and director. Openly gay (he lived with his partner, Old Vic producer Michael Benthall for 36 years) and with a ostentatious sense of theatricality, Robert had been on stage since the age of eight. 'When he was a little chap,' his mother, Mattie Helpman, once revealed, 'he used to take away my stockings and use them for tights. He would tie feathers round his head, too, and go roaming round the streets until I'm sure people thought I had a lunatic in the family.'[7]

Named 'Australian of the Year' in 1965 and knighted in 1968, during the 1930s and 1940s Helpmann was one of British ballet's premier male dancers. Noted as 'a dancer who could act and an actor who could dance,' his personality and talent played a vital part in helping to establish ballet in Britain. After studying briefly with Anna Pavlova in Melbourne (arranged by his rather dour father), Helpmann went to London in 1933 to study and perform with the Sadler's Wells Ballet, now known as the Royal Ballet. He was the leading male star with that company from 1934 until his resignation in 1950, frequently appearing with his long-time dancing partner Dame Margot Fonteyn. In the 1937-38 season, he beat Laurence Olivier for the part of Oberon in *A Midsummer Night's Dream* at the Old Vic, playing opposite Vivien Leigh. He later repeated that role opposite Moira Shearer at the Metropolitan Opera House and on a US tour in 1954.

During his years with Sadler's Wells, Helpmann took occasional leaves of absence to act, most notably in the classic Michael Powell and Emeric Pressburger film *The Red Shoes*, a stylish, highly influential movie about backstage life and backstabbing in the ballet. Years later, when an interviewer asked him whether the high-pitched portrayal of the events and lives of the dancers were exaggerated, he replied, 'Oh, no, dear boy, it was quite understated'. Other film credits included multiple roles in the *Tales of Hoffmann*, the Bishop of Ely in Olivier's *Henry V* and the terrifying Child Catcher in the classic *Chitty Chitty Bang Bang*. In 1995, Marilyn Manson paid tribute, of sorts, via the EP *Smells Like Children*, with Manson dressed as the Child Catcher on the sleeve.

During his career he starred in Puccini's *La Boheme* and Rimsky-Korsakov's *Coq d'Or* for the Royal Opera House, Covent Garden and T. S. Eliot's *Murder in the Cathedral* for the Old Vic and directed the musical *Camelot* on stage. In 1955, he co-starred with Katharine Hepburn, touring in three Shakespearean plays in Australia, and from 1965 to 1975 he was co-director of the Australian Ballet. The public did not seem to mind about Robert and Michael's relationship: in 1958 an article in the *Australian Women's Weekly* reported on the pair's domestic status in such a matter-of-fact way that barely a head was turned. However even the Aussies balked at the sight of 'homosexuals, lesbians and babies being born on stage' when Helpmann became director of the 1970 Adelaide Festival of Arts[8] and commissioned a performance of Thomas Keneally's apocalyptic melodrama *Upstairs*.

But here's one thing you'll struggle to find a mention of in his official biography: in 1963 Helpmann recorded four surf-themed tracks for HMV in Australia. Seriously. Someone at HMV thought the camp, 54-year-old Helpmann could pass as a teen idol and ride on the coat tails of the Beach Boys, Jan and Dean and the like in to the charts. Two cuts from the session were issued as a 45 the following year (the year he was appointed CBE) – 'Surfer Doll' and 'I Still Could Care' – with the second pair – 'Surf Dance' and 'Let-A-Go Your Heart' – issued the following year. Helpmann appeared on an Australian teen entertainment show miming to 'Surfer Doll', shoeless and with his hair dyed blond dancing an approximation of the twist while riding an invisible surf board: the man was certainly game for a laugh. The first 45 was also issued in the US, on Blue Pacific Records, and all four tracks were collected on the Raven EP *Sir Robert Helpmann Goes Surfing* in 1982. 'I definitely will not record any more,' Helpmann said in 1966. 'I am sick of that bit now. I did it all for fun, but it is only fun when it surprises people.'[9]

Helpmann died in Sydney on 28 September 1986, just two months after his last stage appearance, after a long battle with emphysema caused, it seems, by a lifetime of heavy smoking. He was 77 years old. Prime Minister Bob Hawke said, 'He was a true achiever in his field and a fine ambassador for Australia who helped to demonstrate to the world the diversity of our talents and our capabilities as a nation'.[10] A grieving nation organised a state funeral for the 'distinguished Australian dancer, actor, producer, director and choreographer,'[11] and hundreds of people, including state and federal politicians, filled St Andrews Cathedral, Sydney on 2 October to send him off in style.

'I was decadent when it wasn't permissible,' Australian singer and songwriter Peter Allen (born Peter Woolnough in 1944) once claimed. 'I have a feeling that it's more decadent to be normal now'.[12] Peter came to international prominence when, during a tour with his act The Allen Brothers in 1964, he met Judy Garland and her then-husband Mark Herron. Three years later, Peter married Judy's daughter, Liza Minnelli. On the night of their wedding Liza found Allen in bed with another man. Herron and Allen had a sexual relationship throughout their respective marriages: Garland divorced Herron in 1967, although Minnelli stayed married to Allen until 1974. In 1996 Liza told Judy Wieder, editor of *The Advocate*, that she 'married Peter and he didn't tell me he was gay. Everyone knew but me. And I found out . . . well, let me put it this way:

I'll never surprise anybody coming home as long as I live. I call first!'[13] According to contemporary press reports, within hours of their divorce Allen was in the audience of New York's Grand Finale cabaret bar cheering on Daphne Davis, a Liza Minnelli impersonator.[14] The star act at the Grand Finale was Gotham, an openly gay comedy troupe and vocal trio who issued several disco records (including 'I'm Your AC/DC Man') and who played sell-out shows at Carnegie Hall and the Kennedy Centre in Washington DC.

In the 1970s, Allen – whose father, a grocer, committed suicide when Allen was just 13 years old – became a cabaret star, as big in Australia as Liberace was in the States: 'I was out on stage before anyone else,' he would later claim.[15] In 1973, he met the former model Gregory Connell, and the two became lovers. Although he did not make it as a recording artist, he co-wrote a number of big songs, 'I Honestly Love You', an international hit for Olivia Newton-John, 'Don't Cry Out Loud' (a UK hit for Elkie Brooks) and others, and appeared in the ill-fated musical version of the Beatles' *Sgt. Pepper's Lonely Hearts Club Band*. His 1976 album, *Taught by Experts,* went to Number One in the Australian charts as did its accompanying single, 'I Go To Rio'. Yet although his performances were well-received at home, he had a harder time trying to make it in the States. 'I tried to work a little on the gay circuit around the country and I bombed terribly,' he explained. 'No one came. No one liked me. The only bad reviews I got were from the gay press. They get nasty and insinuate in ways I never get from the straight press.'[16] Still, he persevered and by 1979 was packing them in on The Gay White Way. In 1980 he wrote 'I Still Call Australia Home', regarded by some as the country's real national anthem and followed that up with a co-author credit for the Oscar-winning song 'Arthur's Theme (Best That You Can Do)'. Allen gave his last performance in January 1992 in Sydney and died in San Diego, California, on 18 June 1992 from an AIDS-related throat cancer, eight years after Connell, his partner for more than a decade, had also succumbed to AIDS. Allen's life was the subject of the 1998 musical *The Boy from Oz* which, in 2003, became the first Australian musical ever to be performed on Broadway. 'There was something courageous in the way Allen gave Australia the permission to be camp,' says Brisbane-based writer Peter Taggart. 'He dragged us out of a dim, buttoned-up

Chart # 41   **Week Ending April 29, 1967**

JACKIE SHANE

Although currently touring in California, Jackie calls Toronto his home. His recording of "Any Other Way", still rates as one of the top selling R&B singles of all time in the Toronto area. Jackie Shane's live performances will long be remembered by thousands of Torontonians who saw him during his ten week engagement at the Saphire Tavern. If R&B fans in Toronto have any say, you can bet your bottom dollar, that Jackie Shane will be back in Canada shortly, satisfying souls and handing out soul blessings. Sales of his latest MODERN recording prove that!

Jackie Shane

Englishness and took us on a permanent summer holiday, with maracas, leopard print and Bob Fosse by way of Rio.'[17]

But the most outrageously camp – and openly gay – performer of the period was probably the Toronto-based Jackie Shane. Born in Nashville in the early 1940s, Jackie was a talented singer who sang like James Brown or Otis Redding but whose look would put both Little Richard and Esquerita to shame. Around 1960 he joined saxophone player Frank

Motley's touring band before moving north of the border. A regular performer at Toronto's Saphire Tavern, part of the city's infamous Yonge Street strip, Shane made no bones about his sexuality and he would always look meticulous on stage, in full make-up, sequins and very 'girly' hair. He covered the William Bell song 'Any Other Way', and when he sang the line 'tell her that I'm happy, tell her that I'm gay/Tell her that I wouldn't have it any other way', the inference was clear. Although 'Any Other Way' was a massive local hit, reaching Number Two on Toronto's radio charts in early 1963, Shane recorded just six 45s and one album (taped live at the Saphire and released in October 1967)[18] before he left the city for good. Unusually, the sleeve notes to *Jackie Shane Live* made knowing reference to his homosexuality: 'the only problem is when Jackie suggests "let's go out and get some chicken after the show", you can't be sure what he has in mind'; 'people who deserve your friendship will accept you for yourself'.

One television appearance still exists: grainy 1965 footage of Shane with Frank Motley and his band performing 'Walking the Dog' on a late-night Nashville chat show. He looks amazing, his hair piled high in a pompadour that emulates Little Richard, with full eye make-up, earrings, a sequinned top and a feminine collarless jacket. He looked like no one else making records at the time, yet for some unknown reason he did not record again after 1969. Leaving his showbiz life behind him, he moved back to Nashville. Rumours circulated that he had committed suicide or had been murdered but neither was true: he shared a home with his aunt and lived openly, albeit reclusively, as a woman.[19] When last heard of, he was still there.

CHAPTER 8

Do You Come Here Often?

'I was on holiday with Brian Epstein in Spain, where the rumours went around that he and I were having a love affair. Well, it was almost a love affair, but not quite. It was never consummated'

John Lennon[1]

Open 24 hours a day, Holloway Express, at 304 Holloway Road, North London, is the ideal place to pick up a pint of milk and a loaf of bread on your way home or a quick bite to eat on your way to a football match at the nearby Emirates Stadium. It's an unimposing shop on the ground floor of an unimposing building. Before Holloway Express opened its doors, the premises had housed a bike shop, a branch of Lloyds Bank and, back at the beginning of the 1960s, it was where Albert and Violet Shenton plied their trade, selling handbags, suitcases and other travel goods. All very pedestrian and unexciting.

Yet for almost seven years, on the three floors immediately above A. H. Shenton Leather Goods, 304 Holloway Road is where magic was made.

In Britain, during the dark days of the 1950s and 1960s, those bleak years after the Second World War but before the Wolfenden Report,

Opposite: Joe Meek graffiti near his old Holloway Road address

being homosexual was akin to having the plague. Gay people were spat upon in the street, beaten up and even imprisoned for their sexuality. Outside a foreign film in an arthouse cinema, you would never see LGBT people portrayed in a positive way in the media – although certain gay stereotypes (especially that of the effeminate man or violent butch dyke) routinely provided source material for comedians, and these grotesques often appeared in movies or on television.

It hadn't been that long since medical researchers working in some European clinics had been implanting the testicles from corpses into the bodies of gay men – almost always without their knowledge – in an effort to boost testosterone levels. In the prison hospitals of post-war Britain, men convicted of homosexual acts were routinely forced to undergo aversion therapy: electric shocks were administered, hallucinogenic drugs given and men – whose crime had usually been no more than simply seeking sex with their own kind – were subjected to the kind of brainwashing techniques usually reserved for Hammer horror movies.

Without the freedom that had been afforded LGBT performers before the war, it became necessary to invent a new way of living, and an underground social network sprang up where men and women conducted their lives away from the prying eyes of the public and the police. LGBT people soon had their own places to go (which were often seedy and always prey to the criminal classes), their own language to use and their own entertainment to enjoy – from the politically subversive to the outrageously arch.

Gay men dominated the pop music scene in the UK during the 1960s: although no British artist would dare to come out to the media, the music industry was, in effect, run by a cabal of high-profile gay men. These included the impresario Larry Parnes, whose stable of singers featured many of the most successful British rock singers of the period (Tommy Steele, Billy Fury, Joe Brown and Marty Wilde among them), composer Lionel Bart (who, before penning the musical *Oliver!* wrote chart hits for Cliff Richard, Tommy Steele and Adam Faith) and Sir Joseph Lockwood, the all-powerful chairman of EMI. Then there were the managers such as Brian Epstein (the Beatles, Cilla Black), Andrew Loog Oldham (the Rolling Stones), Kit Lambert (the Who), Kenneth Pitt (who managed David Bowie early in his career) and Robert Stigwood (Cream, the Bee

Gees). By a not-so-strange coincidence, all of these men were at one time or another involved (in a business sense at the very least) with the magician of Holloway Road, the legendary producer Joe Meek.

Meek was the brilliant but troubled *enfant terrible* of British record production, the maverick would-be mogul who was responsible for some of the most intriguing and innovative sounds of the 1950s and early 1960s. Born in Newent, Gloucestershire, Robert George "Joe" Meek was the creative genius behind such hits as 'Telstar' and 'Johnny Remember Me'. He was also psychotic, possibly an undiagnosed schizophrenic or suffering from what we now recognise as bipolar disorder (or manic depression). It's been documented that young Joe's mother – who already had two sons – wanted a daughter and dressed him as a girl for the first four years of his life.

Meek wrote, arranged, engineered and produced an amazing body of work: although it did not receive a full release during his lifetime (just 99 copies of one EP and 20 test pressings of the full album were ever produced) *I Hear a New World*, his visionary 1960 outer space opera, is now recognised both as the first true concept album of the rock era, and as a ground-breaking piece of electronica which has been 'a profound influence' on artists including Steven Stapleton and St. Etienne.[2] His patronage helped make stars of people like Deep Purple guitarist Ritchie Blackmore and Led Zeppelin's Jimmy Page, and he pioneered independent distribution, setting up his own label when he could not find support for his 'way out' sounds from the major companies of the day – although that attitude quickly changed once he started to have chart success. Between 1960 and 1963 Meek scored an impressive 32 Top 50 hits in the UK. His influence was enormous, but his single-mindedness and need for control over every aspect of his recordings often led him astray. He may have had an ear for a hit, but he managed to turn down Rod Stewart and David Bowie (he worked with Bowie's band, the Konrads, after David left the group), and legend has it that he tried to persuade Brian Epstein not to sign the Beatles. What was the point of signing a group that consisted of four strong-willed young men when you could create your own and control every aspect of their career?

His studio, above the Shenton's shop, was stuffed with primitive electronic equipment. Utilising every bit of available space, it was not unusual to find vocalists recording their part in the lavatory whilst the future heavyweights of heavy metal plucked their guitars in the stairwell. Working in this archaic, anarchic milieu, he was rewarded when, in 1962, he managed to give his in-house band The Tornados (fronted by bass player Heinz Burt, with whom Meek was infatuated) a Number One single on both sides of the Atlantic with the instrumental 'Telstar'. Often cited as the first US Number One by a UK act (it wasn't: that honour went to clarinettist Acker Bilk, whose 'Stranger on the Shore' made the top of the Billboard charts six months earlier), 'Telstar' – a rousing anthem created for the eponymous communications satellite – was an enormous international hit, selling in excess of five million copies. His acts may have disparagingly referred to the studio as 'the Bathroom' but Joe refused to move: 'this old dump has been lucky for me,' he once said.

From that point on, things should have been easy for the man dubbed 'Britain's Phil Spector', but in November 1963, at the height of his fame, he was arrested outside a gents toilet in Madras Place (just a few minutes' walk from his studio) for 'persistently importuning for an immoral purpose'[3] and fined £15 (equivalent to around £300 today), an incident that collaborator Geoff Goddard isolated in the 1991 BBC documentary *The Strange Story of Joe Meek* as the turning point in his often tempestuous life: 'This appeared in the newspaper and he was terribly upset about that. From then on everything went wrong.' From that day forward, he would never be seen outside of his studio without his trademark sunglasses. Wracked with guilt and shame over his sexuality, it's hardly surprising that he – like so many other gay men of the same period – would suffer mental health issues.

Goddard was, for a time, Meek's favourite collaborator: although he issued four singles under his own name, he was best known as a songwriter, penning 'Johnny Remember Me' and Heinz' hit single 'Just Like Eddie', playing keyboards on 'Telstar' and, after permanently falling out with Meek, writing for Cliff Richard. His deep interest in spiritualism, an interest that Meek shared, influenced much of his work. The pair claimed to have warned Buddy Holly of the date on which he would die and, after the plane crash, they would have regular conversations with him from beyond the grave. Certainly a large percentage of

Meek/Goddard material shows a heavy Holly influence, including the Mike Berry hit 'Tribute to Buddy Holly' and the hiccoughing vocal on Goddard's own single 'Girl Bride'. Goddard and Meek's successful partnership was brought to an end when Geoff attempted to sue Joe over the Honeycombs' hit 'Have I The Right', which Meek produced and which provided him with his last Number One single. Goddard believed 'Have I The Right' was cribbed wholesale from his own song 'Give Me The Chance'. They would never speak again. From 1964 to 1967, Joe only hit the charts eight more times, and only three of those singles went Top 30. The highly ambiguous lyrics of 'Have I The Right' were written by the gay songwriting team of Ken Howard and Alan Blaikley: according to Blaikley the song was inspired by the last paragraph of Radclyffe Hall's classic lesbian novel *The Well of Loneliness*.[4]

Goddard's lawsuit was only one of many: Meek was already being pursued through the courts by French composer Jean Ledrut, who accused him of plagiarism by claiming that the tune of 'Telstar' had been copied from his own 'La Marche d'Austerlitz', a piece Ledrut had written for the 1960 film *Austerlitz*. There is a striking similarity, but as the film was not issued in Britain until after 'Telstar' had been a hit it seems unlikely Meek – although never one to shy away from a spot of sonic theft – did actually crib Ledrut's composition.

In a life dotted with the bizarre (one of Meek's hobbies was to take his recording equipment into graveyards in the hope of capturing the voices of the dead. On one occasion he was convinced that he recorded a talking cat), Joe's next step along the road towards career suicide was probably the strangest of them all.

For a while The Tornados played as the backing band for British rocker Billy Fury, but Meek was obsessed with establishing his protégé Heinz as a solo star; he scored big with his second release 'Just Like Eddie' (he didn't actually sing on the first disc credited to him, 'Country Boy'), but soon went down the drain. Although Heinz (who died in 2000) and his wife Della always denied that there was anything sexual to their relationship, Heinz lived at Holloway Road with Meek for the best part of three years. Joe created a 'monster', Tornados' drummer Clem Cattini told the *Daily Express* in June 2009: 'Heinz was talentless and that's being kind. It dawned on us rapidly that we were a vehicle for his career.'[5] In 1965, Cattini left, going on to became the most successful session drummer in British chart history, with 40 Number One singles to his credit. When Meek made an abortive attempt to resuscitate his own flagging career by relaunching The Tornados, none of the original members of the band were involved.

An entirely new line-up (referred to by Joe as Tornados 65 or The New Tornados) recorded what proved to be the final single released under the Tornados moniker. 'Is That a Ship I Hear' was a dismal instrumental that Joe hoped would prove a hit with the pirate radio stations – especially as its release (according to Meek's assistant Patrick Pink) was influenced by Joe's friendship with Radio London DJ Tony Windsor. 'Tony and Joe had a bit of a thing,'[6] he explains, 'And I think it was done to please him'. Joe had previously drip-fed Tony exclusive material from his artists, including The Tornados, for use on his show. 'Is That a Ship I Hear' did not exactly make waves on the water or over the air, however the B-side of the 45 may have put a smile on the face of Windsor (real name Tony Withers), the man who presented a strand on Big L called *Coffee Break*, sponsored by the appositely named Camp Coffee.

After a couple of minutes of cheesy cinema intermission organ, 'Do You Come Here Often' drops an outrageous bombshell. Suddenly we are in a gay bar in London, eavesdropping on a private conversation between two very outré and gossipy old queens. The entire conversation lasts for around 45 seconds, and it's fair to say that if only a handful of people heard the track then fewer still would have understood that 'see you down the "Dilly"' was a knowing nod to the gay men who cruised the area around Piccadilly looking for sex. While it was the radio comedy *Round the Horne* that surreptitiously brought Polari into the homes of middle England via the camper-than-camp characters of Julian and Sandy, it was Joe Meek who first put two bitchy, effete types on a mainstream pop record. Although giving a writer credit to the group, and composed around a motif that keyboard player Dave Watts had come up with, that section was written by Dave Watts, guitarist Robb Huxley and Meek. The two members of The Tornados had no idea at the time, but the lines that Joe wrote – coupled with his insistence that they drop any references to the opposite sex – made 'Do You

'Do You Come Here Often', 1966

Come Here Often' the most 'out' gay record released by a gay man in
the UK in the '60s.

As critic Jon Savage wrote: '"Do You Come Here Often" was an
extraordinary achievement: the first record on a UK major label –
Columbia, part of the massive EMI empire – to deliver a slice of queer
life so true that you can hear its cut-and-thrust in any gay bar today'.[7]
Many years later, Dave Watts admitted he

> had no idea what "see you down the 'Dilly'" meant when I recorded
> the voice. I was more concerned about getting Joe to let me play a
> slightly jazzy piece on the organ. I don't think he noticed what I was
> playing as he was giggling so much when we did the overdub with the

talking. Robb Huxley [and I] didn't have a clue that it was something to do with [being] gay. Robby and myself were blissfully unaware of the fact at the time. We were talked into doing it by Joe, but it was a laugh doing it all the same.

Huxley, committing his memories to his website, recalled that 'Dave and I never thought that we were portraying a couple of gay guys but at the same time if it came across that way it was OK, it was fun and we thought we were being cute.' [8]

According to Huxley, 'Joe was getting very hot on the idea of us becoming a comedy act. We toyed with the thoughts of making an LP all based on comical songs, and which Joe decided would be called *They're Not Just Pretty Faces*. There would be spoken parts as well as music on the record. The closest that we ever got to that was "Do You Come Here Often".'[9] 'I found it strange that even though Joe was gay he did not like the people around him being camp, and yet he came out with that great production,' Patrick Pink (who later changed his name by Deed Poll to Robbie Duke, one of Meek's many pseudonyms) adds. Oblique references had been made in pop records before but, issued in August 1966 before the decriminalisation of homosexuality, the release of 'Do You Come Here Often' was a brave, even foolhardy move. Yet within a few months none of that mattered anyway.

Burned by his association with the music industry, Geoff Goddard retired: his final job was working in the kitchen at Reading University. While there, he discovered that his old composition 'Johnny Remember Me' had been covered by Bronski Beat with Marc Almond, that the record had been a sizeable hit and that there was a large royalty cheque and a platinum disc waiting for him. Sadly, Meek did not fare so well. Although he was still on friendly terms with people who could help him (like Epstein, who took Meek to see Bob Dylan at the Royal Albert Hall in 1966 and Lockwood, who offered him a job as replacement producer for George Martin, who left EMI in 1965 to set up his own company), his world was coming apart.

In January 1967, police in Tattingstone, Suffolk, discovered two suit-cases containing the mutilated body parts of a young man by the name of Bernard Oliver. Unsubstantiated rumours quickly reached Meek that he, along with every other known homosexual in London, would be questioned in connection with the murder. This, coupled with the ongoing court cases and his impressive drug intake, was enough for him to lose what little self-control he had left. Unable to get the medical help he so clearly needed and (according to pathologist Professor Francis Camps) suffering from 'delusions of persecution' thanks to his prodigious use of amphetamines, on 3 February 1967 (the eighth anniversary of his idol Buddy Holly's death) using the shotgun left in his flat by his muse Heinz, he took the life of his long-suffering landlady Violet Shenton before turning around and expending the second barrel on himself. Tony Windsor left Radio London the same month.

'I wasn't surprised about the way Joe died because I could never see him dying a natural death,' Cattini revealed.[10] In the days running up to his suicide, Joe had written to friends and colleagues to tell them he was 'not at all well': on the day of his death he barely acknowledged Patrick Pink (who was the last person to record for Meek), communicating with him via a series of scribbled notes, not speaking, as Meek was paranoid about his studio being bugged by people trying to steal his ideas. Things had been very different during the recording of 'Do You Come Here Often' a few months earlier, as Patrick recalls: 'I was in the office and listened to the recordings after they were completed. It was a happy day.' A few weeks later, the lawsuit brought by Jean Ledrut was settled in Joe's favour – unfortunately far too late to be of any help to him 'It has been written that Joe took a tape recorder into a men's toilet in a club somewhere and secretly recorded a conversation which he then used for "Do You Come here Often",' adds Robb Huxley. 'This was absolutely untrue and was just another case of fictitious stories made up by people in order to present Joe as some kind of a perverted individual. He was just a homosexual and probably fought within himself to try to resolve his dilemma. Any time that he could creep out of his closet and create something like 'Do You Come Here Often', and have a fun time doing it, probably brought him a great deal of satisfaction and release. As far as we were concerned we were looking for girls in a club. Joe was looking for something else.'[11]

Today a plaque recognising Joe Meek's achievements as a 'pioneer of sound recording technology' sits between the windows on the first floor of 304 Holloway Road. Until recently, in a deliciously ironic twist, the plaque sat next to a satellite dish. Meek's ghost is reputed to be heard banging about on the floor above the shop every 3 February.

There were LGBT artists, of course, during the swinging Sixties, and Long John Baldry, Dave Davies, Pete Townshend and Dusty Springfield would all come out eventually. Questions about John Lennon's sexuality have been bandied about ever since, at Paul McCartney's 21st birthday bash, he quite literally bashed Cavern Club DJ Bob Wooler about the head (hospitalising the poor man) for gossiping about it. However fashionable it may have become for biographers and filmmakers to suggest (in several cases, to insist) that Lennon had a brief dalliance with manager Brian Epstein, there is not one scintilla of evidence to back these stories up; however it has been suggested that the Lennon-McCartney composition 'You've Got To Hide Your Love Away' was written for Epstein ('Baby You're A Rich Man' definitely was: as the song fades out the acid-tongued Lennon can be heard to sing 'Baby, you're a rich fag Jew').[12] It's interesting to note how every single song the Beatles recorded, from their Decca audition on New Year's Day 1962 through to and including their fifth album *Help!* (outside a three or four cover versions) is about boy meets girl; bands like the Kinks and the Who were singing songs about inner conflict, of being outsiders – and both bands featured bisexual men. True, neither Dave Davies (in his 1996 autobiography *Kink!*) nor Pete Townshend (in a 1989 interview with radio host Timothy White) would come out for years, yet the clues are there in some of their earliest compositions. Townshend was one of the first pop hit writers to broach the subject of queerness in 'I'm a Boy' in 1966, and the Who were the first band to take a song about cross-dressing to Number Two in the UK charts. Coincidentally, 'Lola', the Kinks' international pop hit that dealt with cross-dressing and transvestism two years before Lou Reed's 'Walk On the Wild Side', also reached Number Two in the UK singles chart. By a twist of fate, both 'Lola' and 'Walk On the Wild Side' were at least partly inspired by Candy Darling, the American transgender actress (name assigned at birth James Lawrence Slattery in November 1944) who was a member of Andy Warhol's Factory and starred in his films *Flesh* (1968) and *Women in Revolt* (1971).[13] Inspired by the success of 'Lola', Martin Murray, former leader of Joe Meek's hit band the Honeycombs, issued a

45 in 1971 called 'Sex-Change Sadie'; keen to trade on former glories, he christened his new outfit Honeycombak (the Honeycombs' drummer, Honey Lantree, had been Murray's girlfriend). Even the Hollies got in on the act with their tale of a cross-dressing Rock 'n' Roll singer, 'Hey Willy'.

Shel Talmy, who produced both the Who and the Kinks as well as Dave Davies' brace of solo singles, also produced The Creation, a band whose (posthumous) B-side 'Uncle Bert' (1969) features a line about Bert coming home with his trousers hanging down after being caught cruising on Hampstead Heath. Fittingly, in 1965 he also produced two of the earliest 45s by David Bowie, 'I Pity the Fool' (as the Manish Boys) and 'You've Got a Habit of Leaving' (released under the name Davy Jones). Talmy had once been approached, early on in their career, by British folk rock band The Strawbs. Led by Bowie's friend Dave Cousins, the act lampooned Bowie as a glitter-encrusted sexual predator on 'Backside' (credited to Ciggy Barlust & The Whales From Venus): 'The boy stood on the burning stage, his back against the mast; he did not dare to turn around 'til David Bowie passed'. The bitter attack came after Bowie had poached both The Strawbs' producer, Tony Visconti, and their keyboard player, Rick Wakeman. Perhaps unsurprisingly, Bowie would not talk to Cousins for years afterwards.

Long John Baldry is probably more famous for the artists he discovered than for his own career, but without him the lives of Elton John, Rod Stewart, Jeff Beck, Ginger Baker, Brian Auger, Julie Driscoll and the Rolling Stones would have been very different. Nicknamed 'Long John' because he stood 6' 7" tall, Baldry was an integral part of the British Blues boom of the 1960s: a gay man at the centre of a scene whose origins had been dominated by LGBT artists. Pianist Reg Dwight, a member of Baldry's group Bluesology, took his stage name from his mentor and sax player Elton Dean.

He enjoyed his biggest success in 1967, when the single 'Let The Heartaches Begin' reached Number One in the UK: the following year his single 'Mexico' was used by the BBC during their coverage of the Olympic Games. Baldry is said to have been the inspiration behind Elton John's hit 'Someone Saved My Life Tonight' when he stepped in to prevent his piano player from marrying a woman he wasn't in love with. 'I was going to marry her because she said she was pregnant,' Elton told biographer Paul Myers. 'John had said to me "Why are you getting married to this woman? You're more in love with Bernie [Taupin, Elton's songwriting partner] than you are with this woman" . . . That song is about John Baldry saying, "You've got to call the wedding off". He really did change the course of my life.'[14] Like many of the other gay acts of the era, Baldry fell victim to blackmail. 'John was blackmailed on a couple of occasions,' his sister Margaret told Paul Myers. 'I used to meet a lot of these young guys who were way beyond their years, and they were clearly out to get his money'.

In 1979, he released the album *Baldry's Out!* The album featured the song 'A Thrill's A Thrill', an obvious pastiche of 'Walk On the Wild Side' both musically and lyrically and Baldry's coming-out song. He had been out to family and friends for years (he was noted for his occasional camp mannerisms and never tried to hide his sexuality from those who knew him, even during the pre-Wolfenden years), but this was the clearest indication yet to record-buyers that he was gay. On the title track of *Baldry's Out!* Baldry sings that 'they took me away to the funny farm': a second coming-out of sorts, as he had suffered from episodes of cripplingly dark depression for most of his life which would result in the occasional violent outburst and he spent part of 1975 in a psychiatric unit. Around the same time that the album (and Baldry) came out, he moved permanently to Canada and met New York-born Felix 'Oz' Rexach: the two became lovers and would remain together until Baldry's death in 2005, after a four-month battle with a chest infection. He was 64.

Born in a dressing room trunk in New Orleans (if you believe record company hyperbole) and at one point Jimi Hendrix's flatmate, Jack Hammer (Earl Solomon Burroughs) began his recording career in 1956. Although he scored a few novelty hits in Europe at the beginning of the 1960s, his fame came not as a performer but as a songwriter, writing 'Fujiyama Mama' when he was just 14 and, later, 'Great Balls Of Fire' (with Otis Blackwell). Biographers have claimed he wrote the Coasters' 1958 hit 'Yakety Yak': he didn't, although he did write a song called 'Yakitty Yak', a B-side for the Markeys that same year.

A painter, poet, tap dancer and multi-linguist, his free jazz/soul album *Brave New World* (issued by Polydor in the UK in 1966) tackled such subjects as the Ku Klux Klan, religion and teenage crime and featured the

Northern Soul stomper 'Down in the Subway', later a hit for Soft Cell. Described by Jack himself as 'contemporary folk tunes, depicting life as it really is, pulling no punches,' the album also included the song 'When a Girl Loves a Girl' – a ballad about lesbianism from the perspective of a confused but broad-minded man: 'ignoring all the shame it brings . . . she lives and dreams; her love is not just what it seems. Her heart is dizzy, in a twirl, when a girl loves a girl'. Hammer was straight – he went on to father seven children – but his plea for tolerance and understanding in this *Brave New World,* released in the same year that a new organisation called the National Organization for Women (NOW, a precursor to the Women's Liberation Movement) was formed was a prophetic assessment of things to come.

Someone who would have benefited from a little tolerance and understanding was Arthur Conley, whose urgent 'Sweet Soul Music' lit up jukeboxes and shot up singles charts around the world in early 1967. A protégé of Otis Redding's, any chance the sensitive and deeply closeted Conley had of building on the massive success of 'Sweet Soul Music' was dashed when Redding was killed, aged just 26, in a plane crash later that same year. After several attempts to reignite his career failed, Conley moved to London and then to Amsterdam, where he changed his name to Lee Roberts and met the textile designer Jos, who became his life partner. He continued to perform throughout the 1980s, and spent the rest of his life happily living as an out-gay man in a country with some of the most progressive thinking on LGBT rights in the world.

Walter Carlos press advertisement, 1972

CHAPTER 9

Electronic Sounds

'Walter Carlos' "Switched-On Bach" has won critical raves and become the No. 1 best seller on the classical charts. It's "the record of the year," says Bach interpreter Glenn Gould, who then immediately adds, "No, let's go all the way – the decade"'

'Moog Music Breaks Sound Barrier', Peter Benchley,
Newsweek Feature Service, 28 February 1969

In late 1968 and early 1969, while the Beatles' monolithic, mesmerising *White Album* nestled at the top spot, a rather unusual recording – played entirely on the new Moog synthesiser – appeared on *Billboard* magazine's Top 10 albums chart. At the same time, the disc topped the magazine's classical album chart . . . and stayed there for over two years. The album won a gold award (for selling in excess of 500,000 copies) in August 1969, won three Grammys and in 1986 became the first classical album in the history of the Recording Industry Association of America (RIAA) awards to go platinum. Canadian pianist Glenn Gould, whose 1955 recording of Bach's *Goldberg Variations* established him as one of the most brilliant classical performers of all time, called the record 'one of the most startling achievements of the recording industry in this generation and certainly one of the great feats in the history of keyboard performance.'[1]

That record was *Switched-On Bach* by Walter Carlos, and it was still on the classical chart when the follow-up, *Switched-On Bach II*, was released five years later.

*

The Moog synthesiser made its mainstream debut on the Monkees' November 1967 album *Pisces, Aquarius, Capricorn and Jones Limited*, played by Monkee Micky Dolenz and Paul Beaver (the Moog had also been employed on Pierre Henry's best-known work, *Messe Pour le Temps Présent*, issued that same year, but that really did not hit mainstream consciousness until Christopher Tyng liberally adapted the track 'Psyche Rock' for the theme to the animated TV show *Futurama*). Beaver had previously used the Moog to treat Jim Morrison's vocals on the Doors album *Strange Days*, and he also played the instrument on the soundtrack to the Jack Nicholson/Roger Corman movie *The Trip*. That year, Beaver and musical partner Bernie Krause issued *The Nonesuch Guide to Electronic Music*. Beaver and Krause's album is a sonic soundscape, a soundtrack to an unrealised sci-fi film. *The Nonesuch Guide to Electronic Music* is experimental; all buzzes and whistles and a close cousin to Louis & Bebe Barron's all-electronic *Forbidden Planet* soundtrack, or to the sounds Delia Derbyshire had been conjuring up throughout the decade in the BBC's Radiophonic Workshop. Hit pop album it ain't.

Electronic music wasn't exactly 'new': the Theremin – used to great effect on the Beach Boys' 'Good Vibrations' – had been around since the 1930s. That decade, the advancement of magnetic tape as a recording medium had made it possible to manipulate sound and to make multi-track recordings, and John Cage and (later) Karlheinz Stockhausen would begin their musical experiments. Soon came the Chamberlin and its cousin the Mellotron, two keyboard instruments that used tape loops to recreate the sounds of other instruments and, in 1957, the RCA Mark II, the first programmable electronic synthesiser, was installed at Columbia University. The Mark II was a breakthrough but, at the size of a Transit van, not exactly practical. Beaver and Krause's work with the much smaller (although still enormous) Moog was interesting, important and Art with a capital A, but none of it (outside the few swoops and bleeps which graced the odd pop album) remotely accessible to a conventional audience. With *Switched-On Bach* the world got to see (and hear) exactly what a synthesiser could do. *Switched-On Bach* quite literally turned the world on. Walter's pioneering keyboard works would inspire musicians across the globe to plug in: Kraftwerk may have claimed Stockhausen, with his otherworldly *musique concrète* compositions, as their maestro, but it wasn't until Robert Moog and Walter Carlos began to work together that the world first got to hear the endless possibilities that electronic music promised.

George Harrison bought a Moog and was taught how to use it by Bernie Krause. Harrison's second solo outing, *Electronic Sound* is played entirely on a Moog series III: Krause composed and played one side of the album ('No Time Or Space'), but his name (which is included on the inner sleeve) was removed from the album cover. He later sued Harrison for using the recording, which, he stated, was edited down from his demonstration of the keyboard's capabilities and was never intended for release. The instrument would also appear on the Beatles' swansong recording *Abbey Road*, and on any number of late 1960s and early 1970s rock albums. No Moog, no *Dark Side of the Moon*.

Studying at Columbia University under electronic music pioneers Otto Luening and Vladimir Ussachevsky (in the department that housed the colossal RCA Mark II), it was Carlos who urged Moog – who had started his electronic equipment business selling Theremins – to incorporate a conventional keyboard into his new instrument. Bob Moog (the surname rhymes with 'vogue', in case you were wondering) had never thought of his synthesiser as anything more than an aid for the musician: 'There was never a notion that a synthesiser would be used by itself for anything,' he once said.[2] It was Carlos who saw the potential, inspired by an early love of pipe, fairground and Wurlitzer organs. Moog saw his invention as another piece of equipment in the traditional electronic music studio. Initially inspired by the work of Pierre Henry and other *musique concrète* composers, Carlos heard the future: a future where electronic music would have a lasting influence on the world of popular music, and where Walter would become Wendy.

Called 'perhaps the most important performer in the synthesizer's evolution from a 60's audio novelty to a common piece of the modern instrumental arsenal,'[3] you cannot overstate the importance of Wendy Carlos' work in the field of electronic music. As well as working with Robert Moog on her synthesiser the pair were instrumental (if you'll excuse the pun) in developing the vocoder (and, consequently, kind of responsible for the all-pervasive menace that is autotune) as a musical instrument, with Carlos utilising it on her iconic soundtrack to Stanley Kubrick's *A Clockwork Orange*. The groundbreaking classical crossover albums she created with long-time collaborator Rachel Elkind are wholly responsible for establishing an entirely new genre in music, and Wendy's 1972 instrumental album *Sonic Seasonings* set the stage for what, in the 1980s, would become known as Ambient and/or New Age music. *Switched-On Bach* was responsible for dozens, if not hundreds, of *Moog* this and *Switched On* that albums, with other (often lesser) performers using synthesisers to cover everything from Beethoven to the Beatles. The electronica acts of today owe an enormous debt to this pioneering keyboard work. Carlos' influence permeates glam rock, disco, house, Hi-NRG and every electronic keyboard-based music form, and electronic music is seen as offering a sanctuary for LGBT artists, as Rod Thomas, aka Bright Light Bright Light, explains: 'There's kind of a safety in doing electronic pop music, because historically people like Erasure, Jimmy Somerville, Elton and the Pet Shop Boys and others who have worked in that world have made that a nice, safe space. Open-minded people are drawn to that kind of sound and ethos.'[4] Sadly even today, in a field dominated by LGBT musicians, prejudice is still common. In 2015 Lithuanian producer Ten Walls (Marijus Adomaitis) who had recently scored a Top 10 hit in Britain with 'Walking With Elephants', wrote a homophobic rant on his Facebook page that compared homosexuals to paedophiles and referred to the LGBT community as 'people of a different breed' that need to be 'fixed'.[5]

The recipient of a Lifetime Achievement Award by the Society for Electro-Acoustic Music in the United States (SEAMUS) for her 'contribution to the art and craft of electro-acoustic music,' Wendy was born on 14 November 1939 (name at birth Walter Carlos). Carlos studied piano and began to compose music at an early age. After high school, she attended Brown University, finishing with degrees in both music and physics, before moving to New York, where she studied music composition.

In 1964, Carlos began a four-year association with Benjamin Folkman, a musician and musicologist who shared her interest in electronic music. Together they made various experimental recordings using the equipment at the Columbia University electronic music studio, including some arrangements of pieces by Johann Sebastian

Bach. Carlos' first compositions appeared the following year, on the album *Electronic Music*.

As a child Carlos suffered from gender dysphoria, a medical condition where a person experiences discomfort or distress because of the disparity between their biological sex and their gender identity. Put simply, someone with gender dysphoria may have the anatomy of a man but identifies as a woman – or vice versa. Carlos was 'an unhappy, suicidal man' who, from a young age, 'felt female'.[6] It was while working on *Switched-On Bach* that she sought counselling, turning to the pioneering Dr Harry Benjamin, author of *The Transsexual Phenomenon*. Benjamin's treatment included oestrogen supplements and, in 1972, Walter underwent sex reassignment surgery. By coincidence, another musician given the same Christian name at birth also transitioned that year. Angela Morley (who had been christened Walter 'Wally' Stott) made a name for herself in post-war Britain as a gifted musician, arranger and conductor. In 1953, the Dutch electronics company Philips launched their own record label in England, and Stott – who had worked with several popular orchestras of the day – was appointed musical director; the following year she was both arranger and conductor for a group of sessions with Noël Coward which produced two singles and the album *I'll See You Again*. She also worked with Marlene Dietrich when she came to London in 1955 to record for Philips. Whilst with Philips she kept up a second career, writing music for BBC television and radio (including for comedy pioneers The Goons and Tony Hancock, and for the TV series *Doctor Who*), as well as for several films. Later in the 1960s she went on to produce Dusty Springfield and former Walker Brothers singer Scott Walker, whose Jacques Brel-inspired albums were a major influence on David Bowie and Marc Almond.

In 1972, the news broke that Stott had undergone sex reassignment surgery. Re-emerging as Angela Morley, she went straight back to work, orchestrating and arranging the music for the film version of the Lerner and Lowe musical *The Little Prince* and arranging and conducting the music for the hit musical version of Cinderella, *The Slipper and the Rose*. Angela wrote the music to the hit animated feature *Watership Down* before moving to the United States, where, as well as winning several Emmys for her work on US TV shows including *Dallas, Dynasty, Cagney*

& Lacey and *Wonder Woman*, she also worked with composer John Williams on soundtracks for blockbuster movies including *E.T. the Extra-Terrestrial* and *The Empire Strikes Back*.

Both women were lucky in that they had the support of the two women closest to them. In Morley's case, her second wife Christine Parker, who she had married in 1970 – the year that she went to Casablanca to transition – stayed her side as she transitioned, and continued to be her staunchest ally and closest friend.[7] Angela died, after a fall, in 2009 and was survived by Christine: 'Angela and I stayed together because we had a great relationship,' Parker told Jack Curtis Dubowsky. 'We saw no good reason to divorce'. In 1966, Carlos met Rachel Elkind, who was working at Columbia Records as an assistant to the company's president Goddard Lieberson: 'It wasn't until I met Rachel that someone had the courage to tell me I should be doing more than fooling around'. Elkind convinced Carlos that a full album of Bach's music arranged for and played on the Moog would provide the record-buying public with the ideal introduction to electronic music. Rachel would become an integral part of Wendy's life, setting up (initially with Benjamin Folkman) a creative partnership they dubbed Trans-Electronic Music Productions, Incorporated (TEMPI). Carlos and Elkind moved in to a house together, converting one floor into a studio that Carlos could have 24-hour access to.

Carlos, however, felt that the world was not ready to meet Wendy: although she was now living privately as a woman, albums continued to appear under her deadname and, on the rare occasion she had to face an audience – or when she met with film director Stanley Kubrick – Wendy would use make-up to affect a five o'clock shadow, add stick-on sideburns and appear to the public as male. Carlos and Elkind worked together on the soundtrack for Kubrick's 1971 film *A Clockwork Orange*, processing Elkind's singing voice through a vocoder, created by Bell Laboratories in the 1930s but modified by Carlos and Bob Moog for musical purposes in 1970. The vocoder that the pair developed was employed by German electronic music pioneers Kraftwerk on their groundbreaking *Autobahn* album before turning up on recordings by Pink Floyd, Giorgio Moroder, the Alan Parsons Project, the Electric Light Orchestra and countless other hit-makers. When Moroder linked his Moog to an analogue sequencer to create the bubbling synthesiser lines that dominate Donna Summer's 'I Feel Love', a whole new genre was born. Bowie, living and working in Berlin at the time, recalled that collaborator Brain Eno (whose work with Roxy Music had been influenced by Wendy's pioneering experiments) 'came running in and said "I have heard the sound of the future". He puts on "I Feel Love" by Donna Summer and said "this is it, look no further, this single is going to change the sound of club music for the next 15 years", which was more or less right.'[8]

Carlos and Elkind's final collaboration was for another Kubrick soundtrack, *The Shining*. While working on the soundtrack, Carlos decided, in an interview with *Playboy* magazine in 1979, to finally discuss her transition. It was time for her to stand on her own: Rachel was now married and she and her husband would move to France shortly afterwards.

The press, naturally enough, were all over the story, however to her astonishment the media were surprisingly understanding: 'Carlos' latest creation is himself – or rather herself';[9] 'Walter Carlos, best known for creating *Switched on Bach* has pulled a switch on himself and is now Wendy Carlos'.[10] 'The public turned out to be amazingly tolerant or, if you wish, indifferent,' she later told *People* magazine of her decision to go public. 'There had never been any need of this charade to have taken place. It had proven a monstrous waste of years of my life.'[11]

Wendy Carlos' recordings popularised the use of electronic keyboards, and her development work with Bob Moog helped make the equipment accessible to a whole generation of musicians. Before the 1970s were over, the Fairlight CMI, which paired a polyphonic synthesiser with a digital sampler, would herald the next revolution in electronic music. By the mid-1980s, the machine could be heard on hit records by Peter Gabriel, Kate Bush, David Bowie, Frankie Goes to Hollywood and countless others, but it was prohibitively expensive for most musicians; they had to go to a studio which had one or employ a producer (like Trevor Horn) who had invested in one. All that changed with the Prophet-5, the first totally programmable synthesiser on the market that – importantly – was both portable and affordable. Soft Cell, the Pet Shop Boys, Erasure, Patrick Cowley and many more invested. In a hat-tip to tradition, the Prophet-5 came with a wooden casing – just like a Moog.

*

Still living and working in New York, Carlos has continued producing original music (she scored the Disney sci-fi film *Tron* in 1982), has overseen a reissue programme of her vast archive and has worked on a number of classical arrangements using the latest digital advances. Still in the thrall of technology, more recently she has been developing a new type of synthesizer, the WurliTzer II, marrying pipe organ technology to a digital instrument. Although Wendy has given a number of interviews over the years, she guards her privacy and shies away from any discussions regarding her sexuality and transition, as is her right. 'They don't even wait until I'm dead to slander me, when it no longer would be considered slander,' she wrote in an open letter on her website (www.wendycarlos.com). 'That makes it inevitable that when I do die my sexuality will constitute their one phrase clichéd description of me, the bastards. Watch if I'm not right on this, when I won't be here to do it myself . . .' She has very little patience with writers and media outlets who misrepresent her, either:

They have tried to turn me into a cliché, to treat me as an object for potential scorn, ridicule, or even physical violence by bigots (no joke in these dangerous times of beatings and deaths at the hands of the intolerant). It's no fun to discover someone else's fetishistic hang-ups, to inadvertently confront an unsuspected slice of unwholesomeness in another. Even less amusing is to find yourself the target of painful bigotry and prejudice.

At the end of the 1990s she was unwillingly thrust back in to the spotlight when she sued Scottish musician Nicholas Currie, aka Momus, over the lyrics of his song *Walter Carlos*. The case was settled out of court in Wendy's favour.

The Campaign for Homosexual Equality march, London Pride 1974

CHAPTER 10

After Stonewall

'I'm sure gay rock will be the next thing. Now that gay is open they need their own music and their own bands to follow, just like everyone else. Why not?'

David Arden of Jet Records[1]

28 June 1969 – the date of the first night of direct action in the Stonewall Riots – is often referred to as the most important date in the modern LGBT movement. While it's certainly true that the riots, a reaction to years of police oppression, were a catalyst for the start of the Gay Liberation movement, in truth the people were already massing, learning valuable lessons in how to protest effectively from the Civil Rights Movement, Women's Lib, the anti-war protests of the mid-1960s and the civil unrest seen on the streets of Paris in May 1968.

Police raids on LGBT bars were commonplace in America in the 1950s and 1960s, and several other violent protests had already taken place: in Los Angeles in the spring of 1959 at the all-night coffee shop Cooper's Donuts[2] and in August 1966 at Gene Compton's Cafeteria in San Francisco's Tenderloin district. But when the New York City Police Department decided to raid the Mafia-run Stonewall Inn on Christopher Street, the members of Greenwich Village's LGBT community that used the bar as its base decided they had had enough, and the violent demonstrations that erupted are now enshrined in history as the most important event in the fight for LGBT rights in the United States, if not the world.

Three important things happened after Stonewall. Firstly, there was a palpable change in attitude from LGBT activists. Polite requests for better treatment of LGBT people, such as the annual picket outside Philadelphia's Independence Hall (organised by the Mattachine Society, an early gay rights organisation established in Los Angeles in 1950), were quickly replaced with more militant action from a politically aware community who had experienced the success (in media terms, anyway) of the mass demonstrations against nuclear weapons, the Vietnam War, police brutality and racism. Secondly, LGBT people became more visible: in Canada the first 'legal' gay wedding took place, between singer Michel Girouard and his accompanist Rejean Tremblay (same-sex marriage was not recognised, but Quebec's Civil Code allowed for a legal partnership similar to marriage, regardless of sex), and *le couple* issued an album in celebration. LGBT characters were seen in the cinema and, in 1972 the hit Australian soap opera *Number 96* – which regularly attracted around a fifth of all Aussie TV viewers – became one of the earliest prime-time TV shows to introduce a gay character, the lawyer Don Finlayson 'in his natural surroundings and behaving just like an ordinary person'.[3] Ellen DeGeneres may have grabbed the headlines when she came out on her self-titled sitcom, and there's no doubt that she lowered the drawbridge and allowed *Will and Grace*, *Queer Eye for the Straight Guy* and so on to traverse the ramparts of Castle Primetime, but *Number 96* beat her by a quarter of a century. Finally, just a week after the riots began, the Gay Liberation Front was formed by a politically active splinter group of the Mattachine Society in New York; on the first anniversary of the Stonewall Riots the world saw the first ever Gay Pride marches, held simultaneously in Chicago, Los Angeles and San Francisco. In October 1970, Aubrey Walter and Bob Mellor founded a British branch of the Gay Liberation Front; London saw its first Gay Pride march in 1972, the same year that *Gay News*, Britain's first widely available LGBT newspaper, was founded. Other countries soon followed suit.

Alongside all of this political upheaval, LGBT music started to infiltrate the mainstream. In 1969, American singer Jewel Akens, who had a Top Three hit in 1965 with 'The Birds And The Bees', recorded 'He's Good

For Me' for the small West One label. Reissued in 1973 to cash in on the publicity David Bowie, Lou Reed and the rest of the new crop of LGBT acts were receiving, the disc was marketed in the pages of *The Advocate* as 'the first gay rock single 45'.[4] Jewel was married and insisted that he was not gay himself, but he took a co-composer credit on the 45 and followed up the release with the sexually ambiguous 'What Would You Do'. Swedish singer Johnny Delgada's 'Vi är inte som andra vi' ('We Are Not Like The Others') was an early (1970) attempt to write a ballad specifically for gay men. Also issued in Germany as 'Wir Zwei, Wir Sind Nicht Wie Die Andern' – both countries put the record out in a picture sleeve featuring two naked young men cuddling up to each other – it was an odd career move for the singer and composer better known in his home country as Johnny Bode who had begun his recording career in 1929. Sterilised while undergoing treatment in a psychiatric hospital, at one point Bode enlisted with the German army and apparently was sent to the Grini concentration camp – although he was known to be a pathological liar, so any of the above could be untrue.

London-born singer-songwriter Labi Siffre, who scored his first chart hit in 1971 with 'It Must be Love' (also a Top Five hit for Madness a decade or so later), met his partner Peter John Carver Lloyd in July 1964. The pair would remain together until Carver Lloyd's death in 2013, having been a couple for 49 years. Labi Siffre was an anomaly: an openly gay, mixed-race singer whose work tackled homophobia and racism head-on and who had several UK chart hits, including four Top 30 singles. In 1998, ten years after he had his last chart single, his 1975 song 'I Got The' was sampled by Eminem for his international hit 'My Name Is'; Siffre originally refused to allow his work to be sampled until certain lyrical changes were made. Siffre also wrote the anti-apartheid anthem '(Something Inside) So Strong', which in 1987 provided him with a Top Five hit of his own and won an Ivor Novello award, presented annually for songwriting and composing and named in honour of the Cardiff-born gay composer. In recent years, Siffre has turned to other forms of writing, issuing three collections of his poetry and producing the play *Deathwrite*.

Suddenly, LGBT-themed songs, and LGBT performers, were every-where. A reviewer in *Gay News* called Lou Reed's 'Make Up', from his

Bowie-produced album *Transformer* (which features the line 'We're coming out, out of our closets'), 'the best Gay Lib song I have heard,' going on to say that '*Transformer* is an essential record. The record sleeve, especially the reverse side, is remarkable too'.[5] The back of the sleeve featured Reed's roadie Ernie Thormahlen sporting a very visible erection: photographer Karl Stoecker would later reveal that this was, in fact, a plastic banana that Ernie had thrust down the front of his tight jeans.[6] Reed's international smash 'Walk On the Wild Side' provided a window onto the gender-bending antics of various members of Andy Warhol's Factory, and in doing so opened up an exotic new world of possibilities, one where you could change your look, change your name and even change your sex if you wanted to. Formerly singer, guitarist and songwriter with the Velvet Underground (a huge influence on Bowie, who recorded a cover of Reed's 'I'm Waiting For my Man' in 1967 with his band, former Joe Meek protégés the Riot Squad), as a teenager, Reed suffered a breakdown and was forced to undergo electroshock therapy; an experience he described in detail in the book *Please Kill Me*: 'They put the thing down your throat so you don't swallow your tongue, and they put electrodes on your head. That's what was recommended in Rockland County to discourage homosexual feelings. The effect is that you lose your memory and become a vegetable.'[7] He would also document the experience in his song 'Kill Your Sons'.

Although it was widely assumed that Reed, like Bowie, was bisexual, in an incendiary 1973 interview he told writer Lester Bangs, 'The notion that everybody's bisexual is a very popular line right now, but I think its validity is limited. I could say something like if in any way my album helps people decide who or what they are, then I will feel I have accomplished something in my life. But I don't feel that way at all ...' adding that in future he 'may come out with a hardhat album. Come out with an anti-gay song, saying, "Get back in your closets, you fuckin' queers!" That'll really do it!'[8] Tom Robinson remembers, 'For those of us involved with Gay Liberation, this was disappointing at best and at worst, downright betrayal. Had a queer hero deceived us, or deceived himself? Or had Lou been a heterosexual impostor all along, only in it for the money?'[9] After his death (on 27 October 2013), his sister Merrill Reed Weiner wrote:

It has been suggested that ECT was approved by my parents because Lou had confessed to homosexual urges. How simplistic. He was depressed, weird, anxious, and avoidant. My parents were many things, but homophobic they were not. In fact, they were blazing liberals. They were caught in a bewildering web of guilt, fear, and poor psychiatric care. Did they make a mistake in not challenging the doctor's recommendation for ECT? Absolutely. I have no doubt they regretted it until the day they died.[10]

Glam rock gave men an excuse to wear make-up, don outrageous satin clothes and stick sequins on their faces. The glittery icons on *Top of the Pops* may have looked like dockers underneath the glitz, but this manufactured androgyny created a safe space to camp it up without necessarily getting beaten up. In its own way, glam rock (or glitter rock as it was referred to in the States) subversively blurred the fine line between straight and queer. The New York Dolls were not averse to using the new trend for gay rock to further their career; in fact they embraced it, donning street-gutter drag and glitter-rock make-up for the cover of their debut LP. Briefly managed by Malcolm McLaren, the Dolls' look and sound owed a lot to both Lou Reed and shock-rocker Alice Cooper. Cooper, mostly because of the name and the make-up, was routinely being 'outed' by the press. Even before he (then leading the band of the same name) had even had a hit, when he/they were still signed to Frank Zappa's Straight Records label, Cooper was talking about how 'biologically, everyone is male and female . . . what's the big deal? Why is everyone so uptight about sex?'[11] In August 1974, in an incredible interview in *Spec* magazine, the former Vince Furnier revealed the truth:

'I'm straight . . . but if I could have chosen my own sexuality, I think I might have chosen to be bisexual . . . I think in the future everyone will be bisexual. And everything would be so much simpler then – you'd just make love with anyone you liked, and it wouldn't matter what sex they were, and maybe it also wouldn't matter what color they were, or what age, or anything, except that you liked them . . . I actually prefer the concept of pansexuality, rather than bisexuality. The prefix "pan" means that you're open to all kinds of sexual experiences, with all kinds of people. It means an end to restrictions, it means you could relate sexually to any human being, it means an end to unreal limits. I like that idea.[12]

The unbridled sexuality of the New York Dolls, Alice Cooper, Lou Reed and the like was more about androgyny (or, as Cooper put it, pansexuality) than about being gay or bisexual. In an interview with Ted Castle, David Johansen – the Dolls' singer – said, 'sexuality is a very personal thing ... whatever you perceive as sexuality, that's what it is. And it's not for one person to say that they're heterosexual or homosexual or bisexual, because none of those things are real. People are just sexual.'[13] In 1974, during an unguarded moment backstage in Hamburg, teen heartthrob David Cassidy came out to the German monthly *Du Und Ich*. 'I've nothing at all to hide,' he told reporter Valentino Rhonheimer. 'I have many friends, men friends who I sleep with – and I enjoy it. I don't let anyone dictate to me who I shall sleep with, just as I don't tell anyone who they should sleep with. I only know that I wouldn't want to sing to audiences who didn't like me just because I had slept with a man.'[14] Gossip about his sexuality has followed Cassidy for all of his life, but in this instance he may have been simply kidding around: although he has gone on record on many occasions to say that he supports LGBT rights, in his 2007 autobiography he backtracked on his candid admission, saying, 'I had some thoughts about homosexuality – I'm sure we all have some thoughts about it as we're growing up, finding ourselves. So I was, at times, unsure. It was only when I was actually confronted with the situation that I realised ... I'm really just not into it.' The book is surprisingly frank about his sexual exploits and his close friendships with a number of LGBT celebrities and, as he wrote, what did it matter 'if I slept with men, women, snakes or sheep' anyway? One thing the book did reveal was that his father, the actor Jack Cassidy, was also bisexual, and that dad had enjoyed a long affair with Cole Porter.[15]

The inference was obvious: sexuality was fluid. Or at least it was so long as that fluidity helped sell records and gain column inches in the press. When the actor and singer Peter Straker appeared as a woman who is really a man (though it's never made clear in the movie whether Jo is the son or the daughter of a West Indian High Commissioner, or if in fact they are trans) the issue of androgyny left the recording studio and the concert stage and became comedic fodder for the big screen. Straker had his first stab at pop stardom as part of the original London cast of *Hair: The American Tribal Love-Rock Musical*, which opened at the Shaftesbury Theatre on 27 September 1968 and ran for almost 2,000 performances.

The US and UK productions of *Hair* provided a training ground for a number of actors and musicians, and would also bring Richard O'Brien and Tim Curry together for the first time, five years before they would collaborate on *The Rocky Horror Show*. Born in Jamaica, Straker released a one-off single for Polydor (a version of the Jacques Brel song 'Carousel') and appeared in the aforementioned movie *Girl Stroke Boy* (as the girl/boy of the title) before signing to RCA, who issued his first album, *Private Parts*, in 1972. All of the songs on the album were written by gay songwriting duo Ken Howard and Alan Blaikley, who had written the British Number One single 'Have I The Right' for the Honeycombs; the pair based the songs on aspects of Peter's own life, including the death of his father. 'The album is very personal,' he told Peter Holms and Denis Lemon of *Gay Times*. 'I discussed everything with Ken and Alan. We tried to be explicit – as explicit as Jacques Brel.'[16]

The startling cover, featuring a naked Straker with a map of Hampstead Heath projected onto his body, made it fairly evident what audience RCA were looking for, and as the concept album dealt with issues including bisexuality, early sexual experiences and death, the company marketed *Private Parts* almost exclusively to a gay audience, with a number of ads for the album and subsequent singles in the gay press. Despite a well-received performance with full orchestra at the Queen Elizabeth Hall, *Private Parts* didn't sell, and it would be five years before Straker got to record again.

A long-time friend and collaborator of Freddie Mercury, Straker's next album, *This One's On Me*, would be co-produced (and financed) by the Queen frontman and issued by the band's label, EMI. Again the album, and its single 'Ragtime Piano Joe' bombed (although the single did make the Dutch Top 30), as did the follow-up, *Changeling*; moving to Elton John's Rocket Records (Elton and Queen were both managed by John Reid at the time, and Reid and John were lovers for several years), Peter issued his fourth album *Real Natural Man*. Straker appeared in the video for Mercury's 'The Great Pretender' single, sang backing vocals on his

Barcelona album and is still performing today. A few years after *Girl Stroke Boy* bombed at the box office, comedian Red Foxx starred in the movie *Norman ... Is That You?* (based on the play of the same name), which switches this around a little but intrinsically plays with the same idea. Thelma Houston, whose next single would be the huge international hit 'Don't Leave Me This Way', recorded the song 'One Out Of Every Six' for the soundtrack. Howard and Blaikley's next project was writing for a duo named Starbuck: their singles 'Do You Like Boys', 'Wouldn't You Like It' and 'Heartthrob' were aimed squarely at gay record-buyers but, like the Straker recordings, failed to sell.

Private Parts came out at a point where RCA, buoyed by the success of David Bowie and Lou Reed, would sign pretty much anything that could potentially be marketed to an LGBT audience. The company had a Filipino-born singer Junior (aka Antonio Morales), whose 'Excuse Me For The Strange Things I Do' (an English-language version of the Spanish hit 'Perdóname') was offered free to 'all gay discos, clubs and bars' to promote.[17] Junior had been a member of Spain's biggest pop band, Los Brincos, and his single, co-written by out-gay manager and songwriter Simon Napier-Bell (who, during his long career in the music industry has managed Marc Bolan, the Yardbirds, Boney M, Sinitta, Wham! and many others) had provided him with a huge hit in Brazil and in other South American territories, but British fame eluded him.

Brought up in the West Country, Steve Swindells moved to London in 1973, when he was 21. Then a member of Bristol-based rock band Squidd, the out-gay Swindells persuaded the band to play at one of the earliest fundraising benefits for the Gay Liberation Front at Fulham Town Hall. Approached by Mark Edwards ('a posh, gay hippy from Dorset with a pretentious beard'),[18] who had produced Curved Air's *Air Conditioning* album and who had worked with Howard and Blaikley (on the 1968 singles 'The Tide is Turning' and 'Uh!' by The Barrier), he was quickly signed as a solo artist to RCA, releasing the album *Messages* the following year. Pictured on the cover as a leather boy, a judge, a piano player and in full drag, and with songs about Earl's Court (London's gay ghetto), the album was unlikely to find mainstream acceptance.

A second album was recorded but remained unreleased until 2009. Splitting from Edwards, who he branded 'a junkie, an alcoholic and a psychopath', Swindells joined the UK chart-toppers Pilot before becoming the keyboard player for the Hawklords, a band formed by former Hawkwind members Robert Calvert, Dave Brock and Simon King. Since then he has written for Who vocalist Roger Daltrey (he contributed the song 'Bitter and Twisted' to the soundtrack of *McVicar*), formed the short-lived band DanMingo with Culture Club drummer Jon Moss and tried his hand at DJ-ing and club promotion, as well as becoming a regular contributor to gay magazine *Attitude*.

In their desperation to sign anyone who would appeal to this emerging new market, RCA offered out-gay actor Peter Wyngarde a contract, and the resulting eponymous album is one of the single most peculiar things you are ever likely to hear. Central to the album is a song called 'Rape', which manages to incorporate huge gobs of racism and sexism and so offended Alan McGee (the owner of Creation Records and manager of Oasis) that he refused to reissue the album. *Peter Wyngarde* is also notable for 'Hippie And The Skinhead', the tale of young Billy, a 'queer, pilly, sexy hippy' who 'one night went to troll the "Dilly"' (the use of Polari echoing its appearance in the Tornados' 'Do You Come Here Often') and picked up a skinhead called Ken. It was only when the two of them engaged in their rough sex games that Ken discovered that Billy was actually a woman. Billy, apparently was a cross-dressing bisexual, or quite possibly transgender; Ken it would seem, was a latent homosexual. Wyngarde's career – up until that point he had been one of the biggest stars on British TV thanks to his starring roles in *Department S* and *Jason King* – was all but over after he was arrested for importuning in a bus station in Gloucester. Although he would later appear (behind a gold mask) as General Klytus in the movie *Flash Gordon*, the former lover of actor Alan Bates would never fully recover from the ignominy.

The company also bankrolled brothers Clive and Peter Sarstedt and Junior's manager Simon Napier-Bell, who together produced the album *Fresh Out Of Borstal* by the band Fresh. Coming just a year after Peter Sarstedt had enjoyed the huge hit 'Where Do You Go To, My Lovely', *Fresh Out Of Borstal* is a bizarre semi-documentary of life in an all-male remand home and one of the songs, 'And The Boys Lazed On the Verandah' (covered by pop singer Lou Christie in 1971) made very explicit references to gay sex. Fresh made a second album, *Fresh Today*, but their odd skinhead/glam sound failed to ignite much interest. Clive, who was originally managed by Joe Meek, changed his name to Robin Sarstedt and had a solo hit in 1976 with 'My Resistance Is Low'.

With a career that spans five decades and worldwide sales in excess of 300 million units, Elton John – the man Bowie called 'the Liberace, the token queen of rock'[19] – is the most successful out-gay musician of all time. His re-recording of 'Candle In the Wind', released as a tribute to Diana, Princess of Wales, is the world's best-selling single; he has had seven consecutive Number One US albums and 58 *Billboard* Top 40 singles, including nine Number One hits. In Britain, as of December 2016, he had clocked up seven Number One albums and 69 Top 40 singles, including seven Number Ones. In 1998 he was knighted by Queen Elizabeth II, making the man born Reg Dwight Sir Elton John.

In 1976, at the height of his fame and on the eve of the release of his latest album *Blue Moves*, John gave a candid interview to Cliff Jahr of *Rolling Stone* magazine (sadly, Jahr died of AIDS in August 1991). He talked openly about going to New York gay disco 12 West, about his adventures with John Waters' leading lady Divine at another gay club, Crisco Disco, and that he believed, 'There's nothing wrong with going to bed with somebody of your own sex. I think everybody's bisexual to a certain degree. I don't think it's just me. It's not a bad thing to be. I think you're bisexual. I think everybody is.'[20] John was lonely; he was tired of the constant cycle of touring and recording and he wanted someone to settle down with. 'But . . . as soon as someone tries to get to know me I turn off. I'm afraid of getting hurt. I was hurt so much as a kid. I'm afraid of plunging into something that's going to fuck me up. Christ, I wish I had somebody to share all this with.'

The backlash wasn't immediate. 'Sorry Seems to Be the Hardest Word', his next single was still a sizeable hit, and *Blue Moves* made the US Top Three. However, it came at a time when he was ready to make changes, splitting with long-term writing partner Bernie Taupin, dismissing members of his band and coming off the road for a period. Was it the change in direction, or were tastes simply changing? For whatever reason, his career in America hit a major trough after the interview, and *Blue Moves* would be his last Top 10 album in the States until 1992's *The One*.

John would dominate the pop charts in the 1970s, but it was his close friend Rod Stewart who, in 1976, became the first major star have an international hit with an unambiguously gay-themed song. 'The Killing of Georgie' tells the tale of a young man who is kicked out of his family home for being gay. He moves to New York and finds love, only to die at the hands of a gang, the victim of a mugging gone wrong. Stewart's song was based on a true story: 'George was a friend of mine,' he told Keith Howes of *Gay News*.[21] 'I'd forgotten all about him until I moved to America. America just encourages you to write more radical things because it's all killing and death and robbery and violence. I'm surrounded by gay people so there were no objections.' It was the most overly romantic song on an album scarred by misogyny (on one song, 'Ball Trap', Stewart tells his girl that he would 'rather see you dead with a rope 'round your neck'); in the same interview, Stewart admitted to going to bed with a pre-op transsexual in Melbourne and to being sexually attracted to the model and singer Amanda Lear, widely believed at the time to be transsexual.

Chris Robison, a former member of Steam and Elephant's Memory (a band who had played on John and Yoko's *Sometime In New York City* and Yoko's *Approximately Infinite Universe* and had issued their own self-titled album on the Beatles' Apple label), issued his first album *Many Hand Band* in 1972 and, although he was not signed to a major (Robison issued the album on his own Gipsy Frog label; it has since been reissued by Chapter Music), he was the first musician to issue a gay-themed rock album. 'The lead track was "I'm Looking For A Boy Tonight,"' says Tom Robinson. 'It was just a quite crude, country-picking song, not particularly interesting musically, but it was blatant, out there and without precedent as far as I know. Then there was Steven Grossman, who made one album called *Caravan Tonight*. It was standard kind of wimpy acoustic singer-songwritery love songs, except that they were about his boyfriends. That was pretty courageous for the time.'

Brooklyn-born Steven Grossman's *Caravan Tonight* (1974) was the first album dealing with openly gay themes and subject-matter to be released on a major label, Mercury, and came out within months of *Jobriath*, the eponymous album from the Bowie clone born Bruce

Wayne Campbell in Philadelphia in 1946. Often credited as the first openly gay man to be signed to a major company (Elektra), there can be no denying that his *Jobriath* has a gay aesthetic, but when Jobriath introduced himself to the world with the head-turning announcement, 'I am the true fairy of rock,' no one took him seriously. This was Bowie-lite, music swathed in the pomp of glam rock but with a staged, unnatural feel and sexually ambiguous lyrics. Grossman's words made it very obvious who he was attracted to. Jobriath sang about three-legged aliens, movie stars and the history of Rock 'n' Roll; only one song, 'Blow Away', used the 'G' word. Critics accused him of being 'the ultimate in hype, [an] unscrupulous plagiarist who just happens to have had a great deal of promotion'.[22]

Performing in gay clubs such as The Firehouse, in coffee shops and at open mic nights in folk clubs including Gertie's Folk City in New York, in 1973 Grossman answered an advert in *The Village Voice* for 'a singer-songwriter who writes about the "gay experience"'.[23] His tender, heartfelt songs were heavily influenced by the big singer-songwriters of the day: if you ignore the fact that he's clearly singing about men having emotional issues with other men, you could just as easily be listening to songs written by Joni Mitchell or Cat Stevens. This 'meek and gentle man' had 'both the innocence of a child and the pain of one who has been through it all and has somehow emerged reasonably unscathed'.[24]

Coming out at a time when Bowie, Cooper, Reed and the Dolls were wilfully blurring the lines between masculine and feminine, and promoting casual sex with just about anybody you fancied the look of, *Caravan Tonight*'s songs about looking for love and wanting acceptance sounded dated, but the album pulled in excellent reviews. 'I don't know Bowie's material because I politically disagree with his whole trip,' Grossman told an interviewer in 1974 'It's all right to encourage role reversal by dressing the way he does, and by wearing make-up, if that's what he's doing: if he's using it as a gimmick, though, I think it is a gimmick that perpetuates a certain stereotype of gay people, that disallows the possibility that you can be gay and be whatever you want to be.'[25] Jobriath, on the other hand, milked it for all it was worth – or at least his manager did.

Bruce Campbell's mother left the family home when she became pregnant with another man's child. They later reconciled, and when

Bruce went AWOL from the army he became Jobriath Salisbury, adopting his mother's maiden name as his new surname. The musician and keen amateur painter reinvented himself as an actor, appearing in the Los Angeles production of *Hair*, before joining the band Pidgeon who signed to Decca and released their only album in 1969. The album was nothing special, but Jobriath was proving to be an accomplished piano player and a decent songwriter. Jerry Brandt, manager of Chubby Checker and Carly Simon, heard Jobriath's demo (Clive Davis, then head of Columbia, famously dismissed the singer as 'mad, unstructured and destructive') and decided to track him down. Finding him living and working as a houseboy-cum-male prostitute in Los Angeles, he signed him to an exclusive contract. One of the first things Brandt did was secure a spot for his new protégé on the PBS television series *Vibrations*.[26]

Recording at the fabled Electric Lady Studios in Greenwich Village (with a backing choir that included Vicki Sue Robinson – who had a huge disco hit with 'Turn the Beat Around' – and actor Richard Gere), Jobriath (now using the surname Boone) and Brandt took any and all of the press they could get in an effort to break into the public consciousness. It didn't matter to them that the media thought he was a joke, so long as people bought the records and came to the shows. Sadly, they didn't. 'Elektra Records signed another new weirdo for $300,000 down,' wrote King Features' syndicated columnist Jack O'Brian. 'Jobriath, who swung right off boasting he's a "true fairy" and insists "the energy force today comes from homosexuals and Puerto Ricans"'.[27] Brandt, a man with a habit of referring to himself in the third person, was an unashamed huckster intent on promoting Jobriath as bigger than Bowie. In an interview conducted with the pair of them, Jobriath said, 'Asking me if I'm homosexual is like asking James Brown if he's black. There's a lot of people who are running around, putting make-up on and stuff just because it's chic; I just want to say that I'm no pretender.' A huge promotional push in the UK prior to Christmas 1973 – including ads on the side of London buses, adverts in the mainstream media and posters in record stores – did nothing to break him in Britain. A promised four-night stint at the Paris Opera House, featuring Jobriath 'performing his own music backed by a rock band, 12 dancers and $200,000 worth of sets he designed himself'

and ending with him recreating the death scene from *King Kong*[28] failed
to materialise. The records were not selling, the tickets were not selling
and there was no money to make it happen. An appearance on the late-
night TV show *Midnight Special*, hosted by a clearly confused Gladys

Jobriath *c.* 1974

Knight, did nothing to help bolster his already-flagging career. 'I recall that The Old Grey Whistle Test played a clip from the Midnight Special show that he did, performing "Rock of Ages",' says fan Andy Partridge of English rock band XTC. 'He's in a segmented clear space helmet; he presses a button on the top and it opens down like a flower, or a Terry's chocolate orange! I really liked the song and I thought the band looked great, a bit like The Impossibles, a US cartoon pop group from the 1960s that I liked. It was all very choreographed but no more than the Beatles or Bowie and a host of others.'

Critics were, naturally, divided: 'This is a very good album – an excellent first effort';[29] 'the record contains very little out of the realm of the ho-hum'.[30] 'Every track on the first Jobriath album is a classic,' says Partridge.

They're show tunes from Saturn! I remember being aware of a ruffle of negativity and scorn, in the music papers when his first album came out. Stuff about a sort of an American Bowie clone, but his first album became one of my favourite albums and I played it constantly. I could see why he got hackles rising in the macho denim 1970s. Songs like "Blow Away" with the lines "It's very gay . . . to blow away" must have tipped a few over. Anyway, I really loved the first album and had to pick up the second one after my conversion, so I had them both. The inky music press in the UK seemed to have a down on him, probably more for encroaching on home hero Bowie's territory than anything else – a protective jealousy maybe? Perhaps he wasn't "rock" enough for them, a bit too "show tunes"? That was fine by me, as I love show tunes, and nothing about his cosmic camp bothered me. Hey, it's show business; if my mum can love Liberace, why can't I love Jobriath?

'It's gay time and I think the world is ready for a true fairy,' Brandt told the press. 'My fairy is a writer, a composer, and arranger, a singer, a dancer . . .' the money that Elektra advanced Brandt was gone in three weeks.[31] Both Morrissey and Marc Almond have named him as an influence, but his first album sold next to nothing; the follow-up *Creatures of the Street*, ostensibly compiled from leftovers from the sessions for *Jobriath*, sold even less. Sessions for a third album had to be aborted:

Jobriath's increasing drug intake made it impossible to get much sense out of him.

Steven Grossman, on the other hand, was the critics' darling. Stephen Holden of *Rolling Stone* hailed *Caravan Tonight* as 'one of the most auspicious singer-songwriter debuts of the '70s,' and praised his 'poignant but not self-pitying' songs.[32] *The New York Times* music critic John Rockwell noted, 'Homosexuality in Grossman's case has nothing to do with glitter or trendiness: these are real efforts to compose love songs and set down personal impressions from a homosexual perspective'.[33] Reviewer Bill Adler called it 'a record of huge historical import' and said that it would 'most likely serve as a lavender flag of hope to other gay artists,'[34] but, like *Jobriath*, despite having the clout of a major company behind it, the album sold poorly. Mike Gormley, head of publicity at Mercury at the time, told Adam Block of *The Advocate* that the album sold '5,000 to 6,000. 50,000 would have been acceptable, 100,000 would have made us very happy; but 6,000 just wasn't in the ballpark.'[35] Mercury didn't know how to market him: there was no major gay press at the time outside *The Advocate,* which published a lone advert for the album, and no radio stations would play Grossman's songs, even though a promotional single featuring the title track coupled with 'Christopher's Blues' was issued specifically for airplay. Despite his having cost them $30,000 to sign in the first place, Mercury quietly dropped the talented Grossman.

Actress and model Twiggy recorded a cover version of 'Caravan Tonight' for her first solo album, *Twiggy,* released internationally by (ironically) Mercury in 1976, but Grossman quickly disappeared into obscurity. After attempting to shop around some new songs to an indifferent industry, he moved to San Francisco and became an accountant, putting his songwriting days behind him. In 1979 he was the victim of a gay bashing and lost an eye. Having split from his long-term partner, Grossman – whose early life had been scarred by familial abuse – entered a downward spiral of depression, drugs and unprotected casual sex.

As Steven Grossman was hitting rock bottom, Jobriath was attempting to reinvent himself. Bottled off the stage at the Nassau Coliseum, Jobriath had been dropped by Elektra while he was still under contract to Brandt, who in turn derided him as 'a fucking alcoholic asshole'.[36] He auditioned for the role of the transgendered character Leon Shermer in the film *Dog Day Afternoon*, but shortly after he failed to win that he and Brandt finally called it a day; Brandt opened a nightclub, the Erotic Circus, which Jobriath was convinced he had funded using his money.

Jobriath Boone became the louche pianist Cole Berlin, writing a musical *Sunday Brunch*, residing at the famous Chelsea Hotel and playing at various venues in New York; he would also appear under the name Bryce Campbell and wrote the score to a musical adaptation of Moliere's *The Misanthrope*. He gave a rather disturbing interview to *Omega One* magazine in 1979 in which he exhibited all the symptoms of someone suffering from multiple personality disorder, and dismissed his time as Jobriath as 'retarded. His music is confused, eclectic and debauched. It seems like a long time ago.'[37]

Around the same time, another young man was starting to make a name for himself on New York's LGBT circuit: Tom Wilson Weinberg began singing his original, queer-themed songs in coffee houses and at Gay Pride events in the late 1970s, issuing his debut album *Gay Name Game* (as Tom Wilson) in 1979 and a second, *All-American Boy* in 1982. *Gay Name Game*, an album of sensitive, predominantly acoustic songs with out-and-proud lyrics (à la Steven Grossman), featured a song called 'Lesbian Seagull', later recorded by Engelbert Humperdinck for the soundtrack of the 1996 movie *Beavis and Butt-head Do America*.

In July 1983, the New York Police Department sent three officers to break in to the pyramid room on top of the Chelsea Hotel. According to press reports 'the stench was so foul that they all vomited. The man inside – a man with several names – had been dead and forgotten for over a week.'[38] Jobriath had died from an AIDS-related illness, one of the earliest of a long line of gay musicians lost to the disease. Jim Campbell, Jobriath's father, destroyed most of his son's personal effects, including his diaries and most of the material related to his musical career. He was buried as Bruce Wayne Campbell, Private, US Army. Nine years later, Morrissey, unaware of his hero's death, attempted to track Jobriath down in the hope that he could persuade him to join him on tour.

By 1986, Grossman had cleaned up his act and was performing sporadically again: he had a new partner and things were really looking up; however, the new man in his life was soon diagnosed HIV-positive and, sadly, Steven tested positive too. Steven Grossman died in 1991, aged just 39. Two months earlier, his friend, the singer-songwriter Judith Casselberry, had persuaded him to record some of his recent songs. Twenty years after his death, a second album made up of recordings from those sessions, *Something In The Moonlight*, was issued by Significant Other Records. In 2002, gay singer Mark Weigle released a cover of Grossman's song 'Out', featuring him duetting with Grossman on the track.

When Grossman passed through San Francisco, he would often share a stage with Blackberri, a gay black singer-songwriter who first appeared on the local scene around the time that *Caravan Tonight* came out. Born Charles Timothy Ashmore in Buffalo, New York, he grew up in Baltimore, Maryland and was discharged from the navy in 1966 for being gay: 'I was placed under investigation because one of my shipmates turned me in. They put a tail on me, and when they thought they had enough evidence, they arrested me, went through my personal belongings and found incriminating letters and other things.'[39]

Moving to Arizona, Blackberri began singing with a local three-piece blues outfit. 'I started doing out-music in Arizona. I was in a rock band in Tucson called Gunther Quint and I started writing songs for the band. The first song I wrote was called 'Frenchie', about some boy I'd had a one-night stand with and then he kicked me out. All the guys in the band were straight, but I was out and they supported me and some times they defended me. When people would say: "well, why are you playing with that gay man?" they'd tell them: "he's a good musician, that's why"!' He adopted the name Blackberri when living as part of a feminist collective; the whole household decided to take names that were not gender-specific. (He has since legally changed his name to Blackberri.) After the band broke up:

I went solo and I started playing coffee houses, and I was writing queer songs then. I was writing songs about boys I had fallen in love with. I moved to San Francisco in 1974. I was with this band called Breeze: we had people like the flute player Mindy Canter, bassist Kirk Leonard and Alan Miller on first guitar. Alan was my housemate but then he went back east and we got another blues guitar player called Reiner who just played his ass off. We became boyfriends: I was his first. We weren't making as much music as we thought we would, so I started playing on the streets during the daytime – that's how I got money because I wasn't working. I was busking. People were giving me money and saying: "why are you playing on the streets? You're so good you should be playing in clubs." So that's when I started doing auditions, and every time I did an audition I got the gig, and that got me in to the coffee house circuit and I started to get a following.

In 1975, he and Grossman shared a stage at San Francisco's KQED radio station's first gay music concert *Two Song Makers,* and over the years he has played with Carlos Santana, Bo Diddley, Holly Near and many others:

A lot of people have told me that if I hadn't done the gay thing then I would have been really famous; but that was never my thing. I always wanted to be me, and if anything happened then it had to be on my terms, not somebody else's. I didn't write to please other people, I pretty much wrote to please myself. If people liked it then good – and that's what happened: a lot of people liked it. Not all of my songs are about being out, but when I played those songs people were pleasantly surprised and I never got any really negative comments.

One of his songs, 'It's Okay', had already been covered by San Francisco gay men's musical collective Buena Vista, but the first time that an audience outside a coffee shop or Pride event got to hear Blackberri's voice was on the 1979 Folkways album *Walls to Roses: Songs of Changing Men,* the first anthology of 'men's music'. 'Somebody contacted me. I guess my name was thrown about when they were looking for people for the album. They also wanted colour, as everybody else on these was white! I was it: I was the colour!'

The 1981 release *Blackberri and Friends: Finally* was paid for by 'a donation from a man who told me later on he didn't really want the money back. Then we borrowed some money to distribute it.' That album included his controversial song 'Eat the Rich' – a sentiment picked up

years later by heavy rock acts Krokus, Motorhead and Aerosmith.[40]
Issued on his own Bea B. Queen label (someone had once said he was
more B. B. Queen than B. B. King), he says that he is 'incredibly proud
of *Finally:* it's still getting airplay. When I've gotten reviews they have
always been about my musicianship and never about me being queer.
There was mention of that, but the musicianship was what was most
appreciated. I always thought that my music was the lubricant for the
lyrics: my lyrics are kind of out there and hard, but if the music is good
then people can accept what I'm saying.'

Blackberri quickly became a staple of Pride days and LGBT music
festivals, becoming firm friends with other musicians such as Patrick
Haggerty of Lavender Country along the way. He was the only male
artist invited to perform at Boston's I Am Your Sister Conference in 1990,
attended by over 1,000 women from all over the world, but the arrival of
AIDS put paid to any plans for a follow-up to *Finally*, as his focus shifted
from music to community support. Blackberri has been involved with
a number of causes over the years in both in the LGBT and African
American communities, working with anti-eviction charities, in HIV
education and more recently with the Black Lives Matter movement. 'I
had lost so many friends. I used to go on the road every year in the spring
and then in the fall and when I was going across the country I'd see these
holes in my audience and in the community. We lost a lot of people; I
lost people who booked me, I lost people in my audience, I lost people
who I stayed with when I travelled, so my whole life kind of changed.'
His song 'When Will The Ignorance End' was chosen as the theme for
the first National Third World Lesbian and Gay Conference, and in 2002
he was honoured at the San Francisco Candlelight Vigil with a Lifetime
Achievement AIDS Hero Award. His music can be heard in several films
and documentaries, including the award-winning Channel 4 film *Looking
For Langston*, about the gay black US poet Langston Hughes.

In the 1990s, Blackberri discovered Lucumì, a religion also known as
Santeria, a Spanish word that means the worship of saints.

> What brought me to the religion was a friend of mine in New York had
> an altar in his house and I asked him who this was for and he told me:
> "that's Yemayá, the patron saint of gay men". I'd found a religion that

embraced gay men . . . I became a priest in Lucumì [he was initiated in Cuba in 2000]. The *Orishas* [spirits or saints] . . . believe whatever you do is your private thing, it doesn't concern anybody else and as long as you're right with them then it's cool . . . my spirituality and my sexuality complement each other; it's not a conflict at all.

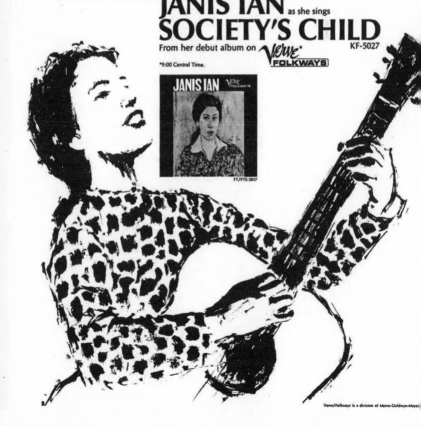

Next Tuesday Night.
April 25.
10:00 p.m.*

On the CBS-TV special, "Inside Pop: The Rock Revolution," Leonard Bernstein will introduce a 16-year-old girl whom he has called the most signficant new talent in popular music.

The highly respected composer-conductor will discuss the work of this controversial *young* composer-singer . . . particularly a song she recently recorded that was banned in some quarters as "too racially provocative."

The ban has been lifted, and on Tuesday night both the singer and the song will explode before a nationwide audience.

Get ready for the resurgence of

JANIS IAN as she sings
SOCIETY'S CHILD

From her debut album on 𝒱𝑒𝓇𝓋𝑒° 𝗙𝗢𝗟𝗞𝗪𝗔𝗬𝗦   KF-5027

*9:00 Central Time.

JANIS IAN

FT/FTS-3017

Verve/Folkways is a division of Metro-Goldwyn-Mayer

Janis Ian press advert, 1967

CHAPTER 11

Living With Lesbians

'We all of us need to be free, yet not add to the burden;
and if you need my voice, it is there, and I will help you find
yours'

Cris Williamson[1]

How can you have the one of the biggest-selling independent albums in the United States and still be virtually unknown? In these days of multimedia, social media and 24/7 entertainment news platforms it seems incredible that any act can be overlooked by the mainstream, yet that's exactly what was happening to pioneering lesbian singer-songwriter Cris Williamson and countless other women in the music industry in the 1960s and 1970s. Today we're used to female artists controlling their own careers – just look at the phenomenal success of Madonna, Rhianna, Lady Gaga and Beyoncé – but in a record industry presided over by men, women were unlikely to get anywhere unless they submitted to what their male overlords wanted (or were convinced that the public wanted). Unless you were in an all-girl vocal group or were a flaxen-haired folk singer, you simply were not going to get signed. Yes, there were exceptions, but by and large if you did not play the game you did not get the all-important exposure. No mainstream record company was going to take a punt on someone like Williamson.

Julie Felix had done it, but she had to move to London to find support. Britain was more open to the idea of women having a musical career on their own terms and it was easier to establish a fan base via TV, radio and the press there than it was in America. In America, you were unlikely to build up anything other than a local following unless you could attract big money via a management deal or by signing to a major label. Joan Baez had the look the bigger companies wanted, but she had a mind of her own and that marked her out as a troublemaker. She did land a contract, but with the independent Vanguard label, not one of the majors; when her boyfriend Bob Dylan signed to a label two years later, it was to the mighty Columbia, then in the middle of a massive expansion programme that would see it establish its own pressing plants and distribution arms in other countries and eventually become part of the biggest music conglomerate in the world. No matter, her albums charted and her mix of traditional folk and political awareness served as a blueprint for many in the Women's Music movement; when Baez admitted that she had a physical relationship with a woman when she was 19, her position as the patron saint of Women's Music was assured. 'If you swing both ways you really swing. I just figure, you know, double your pleasure,' she revealed. The affair 'was lovely and lasted a year,' she added, although she continued 'I've been men-oriented since'.[2]

Janis Ian, who was just 15 years old when she scored her first chart hit, had done it too. 'Society's Child', which she wrote and recorded when she was still only 14, reached Number 14 on the *Billboard* chart. Although she did not come out until 25 years later, Bill Cosby perceived that she was a lesbian and spread the word, resulting in her being ostracised from mainstream television.[3] Undaunted, she kept recording and, in 1975, hit the big time again with her Top Three single 'At Seventeen' and the album *Between the Lines*. In 1989, six years after her divorce from filmmaker Tino Sargo, she met Patricia Snyder, an assistant archivist at Nashville's Vanderbilt University. Ian, who publicly came out in 1993 with the release of her album *Breaking Silence*, married Snyder in Toronto on 17 August 2003.[4]

'We always had freedom, but, in many cases, we did not really know it,' says Cris Williamson. 'Women often felt they needed "permission" to be free. Women – myself included – began to examine and re-examine many of the ways in which we had lived our lives, many of the beliefs we'd come to espouse. Some of these beliefs and ways of living were handed to us by our mothers and fathers; that's the way it's always done, one generation engendering another.' Born in South Dakota, Williamson was influenced by 'every musician I heard, every book I read, every play and movie I'd seen, every person I met, every stone unturned. I truly am made of everything I've encountered. Life itself inspires me every blessed day, from the smallest thing to the biggest feeling. It never goes away and never ceases to amaze me.'

Williamson 's album, *The Changer And The Changed*, remains one of the best-selling independent releases of all time, with sales in excess of a million copies, and the label that issued it – Olivia Records – spearheaded a country-wide movement that would help to change the way women were treated in the music industry. Olivia was set up by a group of 10 women from Washington DC in 1974 as a lesbian/feminist collective 'in which musicians will control their music and other workers will control their working conditions. Because we intend to avoid the male-dominated record industry we are setting up a national distribution system that will get our records out to large numbers of women all over the country.'[5] Olivia's journey began with a fundraising 45 featuring Meg Christian's cover of the Goffin-King song 'Lady' backed with Cris' 'If It Weren't For The Music'; the disc made the collective around $12,000, enough to fund the recording of Meg Christian's debut album *I Know You Know* and to invest in some of their own studio equipment. Yoko Ono, who had been recording music with a distinctly feminist bent for a number of years, approached the collective to suggest that they collaborate on a project, however the women at Olivia declined. 'The image that we were projecting was that we had our own music and vision,' co-founder Judy Dlugacz told Jennifer Baumgardner for her book *F 'em!: Goo Goo, Gaga, and Some Thoughts on Balls*. 'I think we weren't smart enough at the time to realise that Yoko could have been a good thing'.[6] Cris had form when it came to independent releases: her first three albums (issued one a year between 1964 and 1966) had been put out – along with a 45 – on Avanti Records of Sheridan, Wyoming, a label created specifically for her. 'I thought it a good idea for us to invent a women's record company,' says Williamson, 'And so we did, along with a distribution system, all of which served the women well. We stopped struggling, trying to fit ourselves in a structure that didn't want us in the first place and created a structure that did, and wanted so much what we had.' Still going strong, to date Williamson has released around 30 albums, several as part of a duo with folk singer, songwriter and producer Tret Fure.

Women had always had to battle to have their voices heard. In the UK (thanks mostly to the huge loss of life during the First World War) women over 30 were grudgingly given the vote in 1918. The nineteenth Amendment to the US Constitution, ratified in 1920, gave some women there the right to vote, but God help you if you had the misfortune to be poor, black, female and live in Alabama: you would not be able to exercise your right until 1965. In France and Italy, you had to wait until 1945 and in Portugal 1976. In Saudi Arabia women were not offered the opportunity to vote until December 2015; even today in Brunei no one can vote at all.

The Civil Rights Movement provided the perfect training ground for a newly emergent feminist movement, then popularly known as Women's Lib. Traditionally, women had always been confronted with more prejudice and more walls to break down than men, and this was no different in the male-centric, misogynistic record industry, where female artists had always struggled to have their voices heard on their terms. The Women's Liberation Movement was intent on changing the world for the better, and women wanted to dance to the beat of their own life-affirming, woman-centric songs. 'Looking back upon it all, I believe all movements lead to more movements, more freedom, because not just one struggle can encompass all of the ways in which people feel enslaved,' Williamson explains. 'You just have to shine where you are, in the time you have, and do all you can to make it better for everyone'. Here was a chance to redefine how women – whose contributions to culture were so often marginalised – were seen in the music industry, and it was a chance, too, for women from different countries and different cultures to band together and support one another. Female musicians and technicians would no longer have to beg at the table for crumbs: they were going to create their own supportive and nurturing industry. No longer would the face on the front of the album jacket be an industry-standard pretty girl who could sing a bit but who had been signed because her look would give teenage boys something to knock one out to. They would not use sex to sell their products. In the new

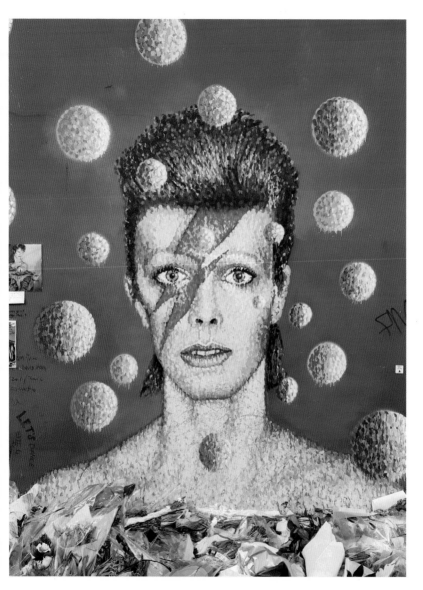

David Bowie mural in Brixton, created by James Cochran in 2013

This daring advert for 'Prove It On Me Blues' (circa 1928) shows Ma flirting with two young women while a cop looks on

Advertisement for Bessie Smith, Columbia, circa 1929

BREVITIES

America's First National Tabloid Weekly

Vol. VIII, No. 9   New York, December 12, 1932   Price 15 cents

BIG BALLS POPULAR

Mammoth Dances Provide Entertainment
Whoopee Seekers Desert Intimate Hot Spots

HOTCHACHA
See Page 2

Wild Honky Tonks Given Cold Go-By
As Hoofers Seek Massive Ballrooms

THE BLOWOFF CAME

By JACK BANNER

NEIGHBOR: *"How's your little boy—the one who swallowed the firecrackers?"*
MR. FROTHINGAWL: *"We're hearing some good reports."*

Big balls have caught on in New York! All over the city—and nation—groups of men are organizing, planning and conducting big balls, hiring the cream of the nation's music masters and radio and screen stars in an effort to put the affairs over with a bang.

Hardly a night goes by in Gotham that some ballroom is not emblazoned with brilliant lights and crowded with thousands of young and old pleasure-seekers, swaying to the rythmic beat of the music.

Even sleepy Philadelphia is bestirring itself. All of the large music halls and ballrooms of the country's first metropolis are booked solid for these events. The same is true of the other large cities throughout the land—Boston, St. Louis, Chicago, San Francisco.

Large business syndicates are behind these big balls. These brainy, affluent men, realizing that in times of depression the public eagerly flocks to any event promising a modicum of pleasure and surcease from the ever-present specter of worry, have invested their time and money and are reaping a golden harvest from their investment.

Mobsters Have Monopoly

In New York the "Drag," or pansy ball, is the biggest and most lucrative attraction. Peculiarly enough, the legitimate business men do not take any part in these affairs. Not that they wouldn't like to, for this type of ball is the biggest moneymaker of them all, thousands of dollars being made at every event. The racket kings of the Lighted Lane have a strangle hold on this particular branch of the business, however, and no one dares to try and break into the charmed circle, for fear of the consequences.

It's a pathetic sight to see the thousands of

(Continued on page 12)

Brevities reports on New York's 'pansy' balls, 1932

Liberace took *Confidential* to court over their cover story and won $40,000 in damages in 1957

COME ONE!
COME ALL!

ONLY

$1⁴⁹

FULL
ORCH. &
CHORUS

A
D
U
L
T
S

O
N
L
Y
!

I'D RATHER FIGHT THAN SWISH!

CAMP records   45-2B1

AMIDST THE SOUNDS OF MOTORCYCLES, CHAINS, AND THE WAILS OF YEAH YEAH YEAH;
COMES A SONG PERTINENT TO TODAY'S WORLD.

THIS HI FIDELITY, PURE VINYL RECORD HAS BEEN PRODUCED FOR PLAY ON ANY
RECORD PLAYER. 45 RPM.

IT'S WILDER, MADDER, AND GAYER THAN THE BEATLE'S HAIR-DO'S !!!

Mail your checks or money orders to:

Enclosed is check or money order for $_____

Name:_____

Address:_____

City:_____

DIFFERENT PRODUCTS UNLIMITED

State:_____

P.O. Box 3213, Hollywood 28, California

* CALIFORNIA RESIDENTS ADD 4% TAX

A rare advertising flyer for Camp Records, circa 1965

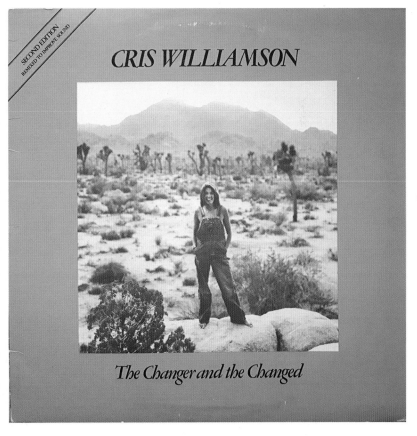

Cris Williamson's album *The Changer and the Changed* (Olivia, 1975) was one of the biggest selling independent albums of all time

Marc Almond on the cover of *Gay Times*, 1987

world of Women's Music, talent and original thought would come first; if you had something to say, at last you could say it. This was music of healing, of solidarity and of independence.

Educator and women's rights activist Madeline Davis could have had no idea that her song 'Stonewall Nation' (released as a 45 in 1971) would become recognised as the very first LGBT anthem. A founding member of the Mattachine Society of the Niagara Frontier (the first gay rights organisation in Western New York), Davis began her musical career singing in choirs before performing solo in coffee houses around Buffalo and in New York City, Seattle, San Francisco and Toronto. She began writing LGBT-themed music in the mid-1960s, while leading jazz-rock band The New Chicago Lunch and, later, her own Madeline Davis Group. In 1972, the year after 'Stonewall Nation', Davis taught the first course on lesbianism in the United States; that year she became the first openly lesbian delegate at the Democratic National Convention, held at the Miami Beach Convention Centre in Florida, where she delivered a powerful and moving speech challenging politicians to fight for equal rights for LGBT people. Although active in the Women's Music scene, it was more than a decade before Davis produced her first album of lesbian-themed music, the 1983 cassette-only release *Daughter of All Women*, a seven-track collection of original songs, included a re-recording of 'Stonewall Nation'. Ten years after that, she co-authored the book *Boots of Leather, Slippers of Gold*, the first written history of Buffalo's lesbian community, and in 2009 she was honoured as the Grand Marshall of that year's Buffalo Pride.

All-female bands like the G.T.O.s, Fanny and the horn-led Isis (who played a residency at the Continental Baths, the infamous New York venue where Bette Midler and Barry Manilow got their first breaks), took a crack at smashing through that glass ceiling, but although each was signed to a 'proper' company, none of them managed it. Fanny came closest, although their breakthrough chart single 'Butter Boy' (about member Jean Millington's brief affair with Bowie) peaked just as the band split. 'They were one of the finest fucking rock bands of their time,' David Bowie told *Rolling Stone* magazine in 1999. 'They were extraordinary: they wrote everything, they played like motherfuckers, they were just colossal and wonderful, and nobody's ever mentioned them.

They're as important as anybody else who's ever been, ever; it just wasn't their time.'[7] Jean and David remained friends: she sang backing vocals on Bowie's 'Fame' single and went on to marry his guitarist, Earl Slick. Jean's sister (and co-founder of Fanny) June went on to work with Cris Williamson and appears on *The Changer And The Changed*.

'I think the world would have been different if bigger companies had been involved,' says pioneering lesbian folk singer Alix Dobkin. 'The mainstream didn't know about us and didn't care about us and didn't pay any attention to us, so there was really no choice other than to do it ourselves. I really wanted a major label, but I couldn't get one for one reason or another – usually my own doing. I wanted to have too much control over the product ... I wasn't about to entrust the precious lesbian, feminist exciting image I had discovered for myself into the hands of these guys.'[8]

During the early years of the Women's Music movement, concerts were small and often held in village halls, gay centres or church basements. They were advertised by word of mouth, by cheaply produced hand-outs or for free on the few radio stations that had LGBT-friendly shows. Concerts were organised by volunteers, and performers often played for free. Organisers provided crèche services, ensured that venues had wheelchair access and even provided sign language interpreters, in an effort to make sure that these shows were as open and inclusive to as many women as possible. Margie Adam (born in 1947 in Lompoc, California) one of the pioneers of the Women's Music movement, insisted on all-women crews during her performances and for her tours, creating a safe space for women performers and their audience as well as work for female technical crews.

'There was a difference between the early lesbian artists and the gay male artists because the lesbian artists had the women's movement to buoy them up,' says Patrick Haggerty of Lavender Country. 'It meant that their music was more widely available. There was an outlet for women's music, but there was not an outlet for gay men's music, in fact it was very difficult for us to make it in any kind of significant way, even in the gay community.'

Cris Williamson explains:

Women needed our music where others did not, so they had to have it. Ginny Berson [concert promoter, educator and co-founder of Olivia Records] was instrumental in the early Olivia days, organising by asking – at a concert, for example – if anyone would want to help us get the music out by going to radio stations and record stores, or have listening parties for women to introduce them to this music. Women

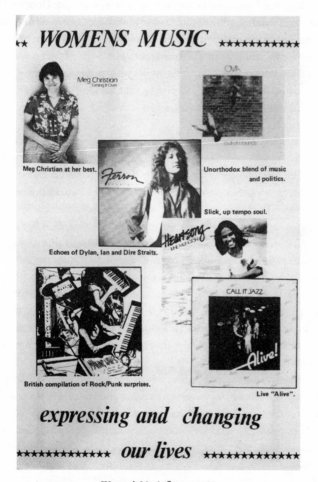

Women's Music flyer, c. 1982

would volunteer to do it with no previous skills most likely, but a deep desire to help women.

Women in the States were the first to curate women-only cultural events, set up women-only run record companies and to encourage other women to learn how to fill the technical and managerial roles in the recording industry, but even within the confines of this female Utopia there were problems. Radical feminist musicians disagreed with some venues that allowed men to attend their concerts, and some Women's Music festivals prohibited men, trans people or even male children over a certain age from attending. 'It was important, especially in those early days, to find women of like-mind who were making their way, making music and art of all kinds,' Williamson adds:

> I think it was echo-location of sorts: sending out signals, and hoping for return, just to know where you were in the scheme of things, or that you were, and that your music mattered an awful lot to other women, and men, too, if they were open to listening, open to witnessing strong women in the house. Being heard, appreciated, loved, helps any artist to grow and further, because she can believe in herself, in her own mystery, her own Self. This was true for me. I was received and passed on as a treasured thing. And still this is true, and still I am inspired.

But as the movement flourished, costs rose: more people wanted to attend so larger venues had to be hired; press advertising was essential to sell tickets to fill the larger venues and the pressing and distribution of records only added to the ever-spiralling costs. Former volunteers wanted (and deserved) to be paid for their time, and artists who were now selling records would no longer play for free (and why should they?) Women's Music was a victim of its own success, and as it became bigger and more influential, the old co-operative or collective ideal was subsumed by a more straightforward business model. Suddenly there were bosses, albeit female ones, to answer to in a field that had once been anti-boss, anti-capitalist.

With these rising costs making it harder and harder for new acts to break through, Women's Music festivals became the way to discover new artists. They were also huge social events, where hundreds of women, many of them lesbian or bisexual, could meet, socialise and support each other. Women's Music festivals began in earnest in June 1974 when Margie Adam, Meg Christian and Cris Williamson co-headlined the first National Women's Music Festival, which took place in Champaign-Urbana, Illinois, but the Michigan Womyn's Music Festival, started by young musician Lisa Vogel and her friends in 1976, quickly became the world's premier space for women's music, and provided a platform for artists from the internationally acclaimed Laura Nyro, Sweet Honey in the Rock, Tracy Chapman, Jill Sobule, Sia, the Indigo Girls and many others to lesser-known acts Bitch and Tribe 8.

'Festivals were a place women could gather together in the summer, somewhere, be together, camp if they wished, eat together, and listen to their artists make the music they'd come to know and love,' says Williamson. 'Only a few festivals maintained their success. There were once producers in each and every major city and some towns in between, and we all went there, did shows, shared profit and loss together, but the music got there and was presented to mostly women audiences.'

The New York-born, Philadelphia-raised daughter of Jewish Communist Party members, Alix Dobkin was a stalwart of the Michigan Womyn's Music Festival from its inception through to the 1990s. She grew up in a musical home listening to everything and anything. 'Broadway show tunes were a great influence,' she reveals, 'and folk music of course, folk music from all over the world,' which included the music of Soviet Russia found in *The Workers Songbook*. By the time she was in her early 20s, she was working as a professional folk singer playing the Greenwich Village scene alongside artists such as Buffy Sainte-Marie and Bob Dylan:

> The Village scene was wonderful; it was a great, supportive, wel-
> coming community – especially in the very beginning when we
> all shared stuff. It was just epic. We met regularly and we hung out
> and we sang and we shared new songs – it was very exciting. I came
> from Philadelphia, which had a very active folk scene, and that was
> also a very caring, supportive community. I had lesbian friends in

Philadelphia, and I knew of people like Frances Faye [the lesbian singer, born Frances Cohen, who began her recording career in 1936], but I didn't have much to do with the gay scene in the Village. The Village really had several, very different artistic scenes; there was jazz, there was the whole gay scene and the folk scene.

For a while, Dobkin was married to Sam Hood, owner of the famous Gaslight Café in Greenwich Village – the place where Dylan would get his big break – but by the early 1970s she was in a relationship with photographer, radio presenter and co-founder of the radical women's quarterly magazine *Dyke*, Liza Cowan. After a succession of knock-backs from major companies, she decided to strike out on her own. 'I wanted to record, like everybody else, and I wasn't having any success,' she admits. 'I didn't have any success at Columbia and I didn't have any success at Elektra, and so I had to do it myself. Judy Collins set up appointments for me because she liked my music. She set up an appointment for me with someone at Elektra – a Vice President or something.' The meeting didn't go to plan. 'I said, "Well, okay, but I have to have women musicians," and he said "fine, no problem," and then I told him that I had to have a woman producer and that was "fine, we'll find one".' However, when she told the label executive that she needed to have control over her own image, things suddenly became less genial. '"Who do you think you are?" he shouted. So that's why I didn't get the contract with Elektra. Thank God!'

In 1973, with flautist Kay Gardner, Dobkin produced *Lavender Jane Loves Women*; two years later she followed that up with *Living With Lesbians*. At around the same time as *Lavender Jane Loves Women* was released, a group of women musicians allied to New York's Lesbian Feminist Liberation group got together to produce *A Few Loving Women*, a collection of original songs sold to raise money for the cause. There had been feminist recordings before: in 1972 the New Haven Women's Liberation Rock Band joined forces with the Chicago Women's Liberation Rock Band and issued the split album *Mountain Moving Day*, but *Lavender Jane Loves Women* and *A Few Loving Women* were the world's first explicitly by-lesbians-for-lesbians albums.

Dobkin and Gardner met at the Manhattan Women's Centre: adopting the name Lavender Jane for their group they advertised in the lesbian press for other women to play music with (and for), and made their live debut at the Women's Centre in August 1973. Once they were joined by bassist Patches Attom, their album was recorded just two months later. Dobkin quickly became part of the burgeoning Women's Music scene on America's East Coast, releasing five further albums. 'I guess there was a gap: none of the music out there really satisfied me in terms of my feminism and lesbianism. So yes, there was a gap that I needed to fill, so I wrote the songs and adapted them to satisfy that.' Musician and producer Gardner (born in Freeport, New York in 1941) later became involved in establishing the Acoustic Stage venue at the Michigan Womyn's Music Festival. An accomplished choral arranger and composer, and early advocate of sound healing, in 1978 she co-founded the New England Women's Symphony. Kay Gardner died of a heart attack at her home in Bangor, Maine in 2002.[9]

Alix Dobkin has performed widely around the world and for many years was an advocate of women-only space, performing only for women and appearing regularly at women's music and lesbian festivals. 'There is a lot of humour; it's the Jewish side of me – you laugh or you cry. Plus it's so funny. A lot of this stuff *is* funny. I learned from Woody Guthrie about that; he has great humour and Dylan has great humour, and, of course, the Broadway musical – the humour and the very subtle literary rhymes. There are all kinds of wonderful ways to get the message across. Music is wonderful but it has always been a vehicle for my politics.'

Cris Williamson says:

I remember thinking I had no political ideas. I had ecological ideas, ideas about the protection of the Earth, the air, the water – but were those ideas political? Some of my fans early on certainly questioned me about them, saying, for instance: "What does water have to do with Feminism?" Now we know, more than ever, that water and its protection is certainly a political and a social issue. I felt free in those days, and in these times as well, to speak my mind, my heart, my soul, and to offer up these thoughts in the shape of music that was palatable, and easily retained. I, like many around me, was making myself up as I went along. The Women's Movement helped us immeasurably

by encouraging us to be as we were, to stop trying to fit ourselves in
an old mould, and create new models of strength and courage that
we could then pass on to society. These new models of behaviour, of
Feminist political thinking have penetrated society, like water drip-
ping upon a stone. There is pride in this: in being whoever you are, as
you are, and being happy in this world on your own merits.

For many women, especially for lesbian musicians, the growing
Women's Music circuit offered more than just the chance to play their
songs; it was a space to breathe. Says Dobkin:

They were family, and it was my tribe. It was like finding your home,
somewhere where, finally, you were the centre. You were important, and we only found that together. For lesbians this was the only
place that we were really important, so it was very exciting. We were
charged up by it. It was the most exciting period in my life. It was
absolutely thrilling to me, as someone who values originality and
uniqueness above everything else to be confronted with this gold-
mine, this field of possibilities. I knew that whatever I wrote about my
life was going to be original; nobody had ever written about it before.
Now that's quite something for an artist, to realise that whatever you
did would be the first. That's pretty amazing. That's what knocked me
out and inspired me, and it was the same when lesbianism met feminism: both had existed for millennia, but never had they combined
before we came along, and that was so powerful.

Maxine Feldman had written what we now think of as the earliest
openly lesbian single, 'Angry at This' (styled 'Angry Atthis'; Atthis was one
of Sappho's many lovers), and debuted the song live whilst performing at
the lesbian bar The Corkroom shortly before the Stonewall Riots in 1969
(she recorded the song in 1972).[10] Feldman, who described herself as a
'big loud Jewish butch lesbian' long before she began recording, had been
performing since the early 1960s, occasionally finding her coffeehouse
bookings refused as she was 'bringing around the wrong crowd'.[11] For a
time she worked at Alice's Restaurant (made famous by the Arlo Guthrie
album and film of the same name) in Massachusetts before she moved to

Los Angeles. 'I went to California and wrote my first lesbian song, "Angry Atthis" in May 1969,' she revealed. 'I wrote it in about three minutes, in a bar in LA. Before Stonewall we had Mafia-run bars where you were a fourth-or fifth-class person. It was the only place for dykes to meet; we didn't have festivals, or women's bookstores.'[12]

In 1976, two years after she shared a stage in Manhattan with Yoko Ono and Isis,[13] Feldman wrote the song 'Amazon', which was quickly adopted as a lesbian anthem and was used to open the Michigan Womyn's Music Festival every year; in 1986 Feldman gave the rights to the song to the festival. Considered too political by the larger Women's Music labels, in 1979 she signed with the tiny Galaxia Women Enterprises and released her sole album, *Closet Sale*. She had opened her own successful Oasis Coffeehouse and performance space in Boston which she used to showcase new talent, but unfortunately her own health problems caused her to stop performing. 'In later years, Feldman explored her own gender identity, but confided in friends that she was too old for surgery. Preferring to use the non-gender specific name Max, Feldman passed away in Albuquerque on 17 August 2007, survived by partner Helen Thornton.' Ironically, in 2015, after it had run for 40 years, the international feminist music event the Michigan Womyn's Music Festival chose to close for good rather than be forced to admit trans performers and audience members: the festival had been facing criticism over its stance for a number of years, since trans attendee Nancy Burkholder was ejected from the site in 1991. In recent years, high-profile acts including the Indigo Girls had withdrawn their support for the festival and its 'womyn born womyn' policy. How would organisers have coped with Max Feldman, their benefactor, if they had still been performing?

In Britain, Women's Music followed a different path: artists were more interested in performing and protesting than recording, and there were no women-run record companies anyway. If British acts did record anything, then more often than not the result was a cheaply put-together cassette with a photocopied insert sold at gigs to help fund the rental of the hall and the PA system. There were some exceptions, but even those that managed to get a record out had to fund the entire operation themselves and handle their own distribution (basically selling copies at concerts, through bookshops or by mail order) and advertising – which meant producing your own flyers or paying for a small ad in *Gay News* or lesbian monthly *Sappho*, just about the only publications which would take an advert anyway. Virginia Tree, a Birmingham-based lesbian musician had previously recorded with the psychedelic rock group Ghost (under her original name Shirley Kent), but in 1975 issued her own (and only) album, *Fresh Out*. Put out on her own Minstrel Records label, Ginny and her partner soon found the promotion and distribution of the record to be a headache; shortly after the album, a well-received collection of romantic love songs, was reviewed in *Sappho* she decided to sell her company and all of the remaining copies of the disc. The record was reissued, with two extra tracks, in 1987 as *Forever A Willow*, credited to Shirley Kent and again in 2000 under its original title.

Six-piece feminist rock band the Stepney Sisters played almost 50 benefits, conferences and festivals during their 18 months together. The band started out as friends from York University who had been sharing a squat in Stepney, London. Intent on forming an all-woman rock band, the members were predominantly straight, although two of them became involved in lesbian relationships during their time in the group and the band were often mocked for being 'middle-class lesbians'. The group was championed by feminist magazine *Spare Rib* and concerts were easy to come by, however their final gig was marred when headline act Desmond Dekker failed to turn up and the women were faced with a barrage of abuse from the predominantly male audience. 'It was ridiculous really because it wasn't like most bands who have to struggle and bend over backwards to get work,' member Marion Lees told *Spare Rib*. 'We didn't have the material or the experience, but before we knew what we were doing we had a lot of gigs'.[15]

Born in 1950 on the island of St Kitts, Joan Armatrading immigrated to England with her family in 1958. In 1970, while in the touring company of *Hair*, she met Guyana-born lyricist Pam Nestor and the two women began collaborating. Together they wrote around 100 songs, several of which would feature on Armatrading's debut album, *Whatever's for Us* (Cube, 1972). Yet that would be their only release. Originally intended as the work of a duo, Cube decided instead to promote Joan as a solo singer and, quite literally, airbrush Pam out of the picture. The album didn't sell, and fights with their management and label over this new direction caused the two women to end their partnership soon afterwards. Joan signed to A&M records, releasing her next album, *Back to the Night*, in 1975, but it was her third album, 1976's *Joan Armatrading* which catapulted the singer into the UK Top 20 and produced her first hit single, 'Love and Affection'.

Despite a media campaign by her record company aimed at breaking her in the States – 'we decided to do whatever we could to bring the name and talent of Joan Armatrading home,' CEO Jerry Moss told *Billboard*, 'so we went on a formidable campaign to achieve this'[16] – massive sales did not follow: only one album (*Me, Myself, I*) went Top 30 and only one single ('Drop the Pilot') graced the *Billboard* Top 100. The problem, it seemed, was that she was difficult to categorise, although lazy comparisons were often made to other black women who played guitar. Praised by critics for 'writing the kind of material that jumps out at you and twists your emotions,'[17] the radio play she (and the label) needed did not follow. Armatrading spent the next few years building a loyal fan base in the UK and a cult following in the US, and the occasional hit single – 'All the Way From America' and 'Me Myself I' in 1980; 'When I Get it Right' in 1981 and 'Drop the Pilot' in 1983 – helped cement her reputation. Although she liked to keep her private life just that, in 2011 she married her long-time partner Maggie Butler.

Although the UK saw a smattering of folk-inspired singer/songwriters like Armatrading achieve success, Women's Music didn't really come alive until punk and new wave saw all-female bands like the Slits, the Bodysnatchers, the Raincoats and Girlschool achieve a level of notoriety. Successful all-female groups challenged the macho norm, and highly visible woman-led bands such as X-Ray Spex, The Pretenders, the Selecter and Siouxsie and the Banshees brought sexual equality into Britain's homes – although few if any of these particular women were either lesbian or bisexual. The chief difference between Women's Music in the US and the UK is that in Britain it did not exist in its own bubble. There was no Women's Music circuit: women were simply part of what was happening and played the same venues as male bands. That many of the women becoming involved in music in the UK were untrained meant that their music was more raw, more urgent. In America, the early stars of the Women's Music movement had come up from the folk scene: in Britain – thanks to punk – girls who picked up electric guitars were automatically musicians, and they brought ideas of social justice, of socialism and feminism with them. The music they made may not have always been pretty, but it was undeniably compelling.

'We believe all women are natural musicians,' Jana Runnalls and Rosemary Schofield of the London-based lesbian feminist band Ova told *Gay Community News*, 'and that one of the purposes of being a performer now is to encourage women to make the connection between their personal/political lives and music'.[18] Jana (formerly Jane) and Canadian-born Rosemary met in London in 1975, fell in love and started a romantic and creative partnership playing contemporary folk songs and songs Runnalls wrote herself. Beaten up and forced out of their North London squat in a homophobic attack, they found a place to live with members of the Gay Liberation Front in Brixton. With encouragement from their new-found, politically active friends, the pair started to use their music as a vehicle to express women- and lesbian- positive ideas.

Ova became a fixture of Britain's nascent Women's Music scene, and the band continued until the pair split up in 1989. During their time together they released four albums, established their own recording studio (like Olivia, the duo helped to train women engineers and producers along the way) and toured extensively around the UK, in Europe and in the US. The duo often found that their own radical brand of feminism was at odds with what other people assumed audiences wanted. On tour in the States, for example, they were told 'by one very well-intentioned and supportive label not to record angry songs because anger doesn't sell over here'.[19]

There was also a strong following for Women's Music in Germany, where the scene was supported by its own magazine, *Troubadora*, and record label Troubadisc. Although established women's acts such as Alix Dobkin, Cris Williamson and Ova dominated, German women had their own acts in The Flying Lesbians, Witch is Witch, Imogen Schrank, Bitch Band #1, and Nichts Geht Mehr. As the Flying Lesbians themselves declared, on the sleeve notes of their debut album *Battered Wife*: 'we are lesbian and feminist and make rock music for women, but we are not professionals. We women are beginning to make our own music and to say in our own lyrics what we are; this is an important part of women's culture.'

Holly Near's career in music and political activism began at just eight years old, when she appeared in a talent contest organised by the Veterans of Foreign Wars. Appearing in school plays and recitals kept her involved with music, and in high school she sang with folk group the Freedom Singers. After school she moved to Los Angeles, studying musical theatre and political science at UCLA. Whilst there, she attended a concert by singer and political activist Nina Simone, and it was Simone's ability to fire up her audience that inspired Holly to think seriously about a career in music. 'My parents loved music and ordered records from various catalogues. These precious packages arrived like gifts from the heavens. I listened to singers creating in many different styles – Lena Horne, Mary Martin, Mahalia Jackson, Patsy Cline – also folk artists like The Weavers.'[20]

Spotted by a talent agent when appearing in a university showcase, Near found herself with an agent before she had finished her studies and in 1968, aged just 19, she embarked on her professional career. As an actress she appeared in a number of US TV shows and, of course, in a stage production of *Hair*, before she became involved with the anti-Vietnam War movement and, through her political activism, in the world of feminist and Women's Music. 'I had already been expressing political beliefs in my work with the anti-war movement,' she makes clear, 'So that part wasn't new. But the expansion of my understanding of what it means to be female added a new dimension and since there was a substantial amount of sexism in the anti-war movement, it became necessary to create some distance in order to think clearly about feminism and how my understanding of feminism was changing my music.'

Like Alix Dobkin, she found that major record companies wanted her to change her style: to be less political and more 'pop'. Undaunted, in 1972 she founded Redwood Records, intent on issuing politically aware recordings from around the world and probably the first independent, artist-owned record company set up by a woman: pretty good going for a 23-year-old. Working from her parents' dining table, Near's experience would inspire Olivia, Ladyslipper (a feminist collective based in North

Carolina that has produced the *Catalog and Resource Guide of Music by Women* since 1976), Sisters Unlimited (based in Atlanta, Georgia and created to press, market and distribute albums of songs by the feminist writer Carole Etzler, creator and producer of a series of radio dramas entitled *Women of Faith*) and every Women's Music label that came after. 'Most of the record company executives and/or managers with whom I met knew there was something worthy of attention, but it didn't sit completely right with them,' Near explains:

> Some said the lyrics were too outspoken, some said there was not enough element of submission in my voice . . . and I'm sure I was also stubborn. I didn't want to take anyone's advice for fear they were messing with my "art" – although the fact is that sometimes it is good to take advice from people who have a different perspective. So somewhere in all of that, I decided to record my own album. In the process I discovered I needed a label, a tax ID, a way to mail out orders for the record – all those practical things. And before I knew it, I had the beginnings of a record company.

In 1975, the year that she played the second National Women's Music Festival in Illinois, Near joined Meg Christian, Cris Williamson, Margie Adam, comedian Lily Tomlin and others at a fundraiser in LA; a year later, Christian, Williamson, Adam and Near embarked on *Women On Wheels*, a seven-city tour of California and the first major tour undertaken by feminist and lesbian artists in the US. That year she came out as lesbian and for several years was involved in a relationship with Christian. She says,

> I didn't know at the beginning that I was moving towards what became known as "Women's Music", I didn't know at first that many people saw me as pioneering that work along with other feminist artists. But once we were able to articulate it, once we gave it a name – the name was first coined by Meg Christian, actually – then that gave us all a calling card. Sections of the women's movement and the lesbian feminist movement began to flock to the songs, to the concerts. It was one way that women got out of the house, out of the bars, out of their

smaller worlds was to come to concerts and meet other like-minded women who were all singing together. It was a very exciting time. In the same way young people gathered to challenge the constricting lifestyles of the 1950s by listening to Janis Joplin or Tina Turner or Bob Dylan, women were finding us and the collective energy gave women the courage to discover themselves more fully. In order to keep up to the emotional demand that was pouring out of this discovery, I had to work hard to keep ahead of the tsunami. I understood early on that feminism for me was not just about white women with guitars. My work in the left had educated me in the arenas of class, race, and international policy so I brought all of that to the table. Everything I knew up to that moment was poured into the songs.

With her media presence and large following, Near became the most visible lesbian singer in the US and, with her deep understanding of the way the system works, she engaged a Hollywood-based PR company to promote her and her work, the company that handled actors Jane Fonda and Alan Alda. One of the first things they did was secure her a guest spot on *Sesame Street*. 'When I go on these TV shows I won't walk right out and say, "Hi; I'm a lesbian feminist",' she told *Gay Community News*. 'I walk out and smile and talk about growing up on a farm, sing a country love song and say "see you next year". Hopefully they'll think that the music is pretty and the next time they go in to a record store they'll buy it. Then they'll get an earful!'[21] 'Holly is the most political of all of the women in the movement, of all the old crew anyway,' says Alix Dobkin. 'She brought her listeners with her when she discovered the Women's Music movement. She was inclined to be a bit more showbiz because that was her experience, she has always done great work and has made a huge contribution. Holly was the most political, and I was the most lesbian!'

'I would not have become the artist I am today had I not crossed paths with feminist and lesbian feminist artists,' Near reveals. 'I am so grateful I turned towards them. We were trying to understand how we would think if we became more "woman identified" and how would that inform our music. I could not have done this kind of critical thinking alone or in isolation.'

Regular headliners of many a Women's Music festival, the Grammy Award-winning Indigo Girls (Amy Ray and Emily Saliers) began performing together while still in high school in Decatur, Georgia. Both out lesbians, although they have never been involved with each other romantically, they released their first self-produced album, *Strange Fire*, in 1987 before signing with Epic Records the following year. After releasing nine LPs with major record labels, including two US Top 10 albums, in 2009 they resumed self-producing albums, issuing them through their own IG Recordings label via Vanguard Records.

With a career that stretches back more than 40 years, Ferron is a long-established part of the Canadian and North American folk scenes. Born Deborah Foisy on 1 June 1952, Ferron made her professional debut in 1975, playing at a benefit for a Vancouver-based feminist publishing house, the Women's Press Gang. Issuing her first album two years later (on her own Lucy Records label), it would take almost two decades of well-received folk club gigs and privately-released records before a major company – in the guise of Warner Bros. – finally noticed the woman that Suzanne Vega, the Indigo Girls and countless others were citing as a major influence and 'an important artist within folk and feminist circles'.[22] Coming off the back of the success of new folk singers like Vega and Tracy Chapman, Warner thought they had a hit on their hands when they signed her. 'This could be the album that breaks Ferron into the mainstream,' said Warner's Brent Gordon, talking about her major label debut, 1996's *Still Riot*.[23] Yet despite being praised by her bosses at Warner Bros. for her creativity and musicianship,[24] it would be her only record for the label. Initially contracted to produce three albums over seven years, Ferron's deal was terminated early and by 1997 she was once again putting out work on her own Cherrywood Station label. 'Warner Bros. didn't know what to do with my voice,' she told interviewer Douglas Heselgrave,[25] Although she had been out all of her adult life, she could not understand why the media constantly referred to her as a 'lesbian singer-songwriter' rather than simply 'singer-songwriter':

> I was thought of only as a lesbian singer. I can remember that the *New York Times* listed *Driver* as one of the top albums of 1994. I was on a plane

flying home when I first read it. I was so happy, but I couldn't tell the guy in the seat next to me about it because under the photo of me was the caption "lesbian singer-songwriter". Perhaps, they felt that I would have taken it as a sign of disrespect if they had not said "lesbian", but they didn't understand that this was not what I was selling. I was selling a way of thinking – a way of getting through a knot in your life.[26]

The company had worked hard to break Ferron via radio, but although she picked up plenty of airplay in California, it did not translate into sales, and the break with Warner Bros. would have massive repercussions. As well as holding the rights to *Still Riot,* the company had also taken over ownership of her previous two albums (which they reissued in remixed form). 'Warner Bros. came along with a deal that broke me at the knees. I ended up losing the rights to my work. I don't think they did anything really awful on purpose. They just do what corporations do: they eat small things. They eat minnows, and for a minute, I was a minnow.'[27]

It took her several years to recover from the experience. Although she continued to perform and record, Ferron also began to teach (at the non-profit Institute for Musical Arts) and to write poetry. In 2008 she released *Boulder,* an album of songs produced by long-time fan turned musical collaborator Bitch, with guest appearances by Ani DiFranco, the Indigo Girls and others. Queer writer, producer and performer Bitch (originally of the duo Bitch and Animal), who became friends with Ferron when they met on the Women's Music circuit, also produced Ferron's 2013 album *Lighten-ing* and the accompanying hour-long documentary film *Thunder.* Bitch (born Karen Mould in 1973), who more recently has been working under the name Beach, had toured with DiFranco, the Grammy Award-winning folk singer, songwriter and multi-instrumentalist (born in Buffalo, New York in 1970). DiFranco released her albums through her own independent label, Righteous Babe, built a devoted following through constant touring and saw the return when nine of her albums made the *Billboard* Top 50. Although for most of her career she self-identified as bisexual, since giving birth to her daughter in 2007 (and subsequently marrying her partner, music producer Mike Napolitano) she prefers not to talk about her sexuality in such fixed terms. 'I think I was in my early twenties when I was having relationships with women.

I'm in my early forties now. I've done a lot more talking about it, funnily enough, than doing it,' she told interviewer Kathleen Bradbury in 2012.[28] She's certainly not the first artist to discover that sexuality can indeed be fluid.

'One of the things that I've always prided myself on is in making public mistakes and being accessible,' says Alix Dobkin. 'It's more honest; it resonates. When songwriters ask me to tell them about how to write songs I say that "if you want me to be interested in your song then send me something only you could have written". I don't want to hear any convention, I don't want to be able to sing along with it the first couple of times I hear it, I'm not interested in that. It has to be original, and if you're really honest then it will be original, because everybody *is* original. If somebody writes from their own true spirit, from their true soul then it's going to be original. That's what I'm interested in, not something that everybody else has done.'

'Of course there is no way to predict how (signing to a major label) would have turned out,' Holly Near adds. 'It could have been wonderful, it could have been a disaster. But this is how my life turned out and it has been full of surprises, challenges, gifts, failures, successes – and music.'

Lavender Country

An Album of Gay Music

By mail: $4.50 postpaid. Wash. state residents add 5.3% sales tax.
Gay Community Services, Dept. G   P.O. Box 22228
East Union Station, Seattle, Wash. 98122

Press advert for *Lavender Country*

CHAPTER 12

Lavender Country

'It don't matter here who you love or what you wear, 'cause we don't care who's got what chromosomes...'

'Lavender Country' by Patrick Haggerty

With talk of a major US music event, the Americana Festival, adding a gay strand to its programme, a high-profile radio and television presenter coming out and LGBT artists finally getting the recognition they deserve, 2017 looks likely to be the year that country music finally wakes up to the needs of its LGBT audience and performers. Sometimes it can take a while to be fully appreciated. Just ask Patrick Haggerty, whose album, *Lavender Country*, was added to the Country Music Hall of Fame collection in 2000, more than a quarter of a century after it was first issued, but who is only now receiving the respect and attention due to him as a pioneer of the country music scene.

Country (Country-Western, Country & Western; for simplicity we'll stick to simply 'country') music has long ploughed its own musical furrow, one where steers, tears and beers – but seldom queers – provide the fuel for singers and songwriters. Originating in the 1920s, although country music is seen as a peculiarly American art form, its roots can be traced through English folk music, Negro spirituals, vaudeville, the blues, Appalachian music (adapted from the music brought over by British immigrants, including traditional Irish and Scottish fiddle music), Hawaiian guitar and even Alpine yodelling. Developing in the Southern states, initially under the names old-time and hillbilly (especially when the predominant instrument was the fiddle), the earliest recordings were made not in country's spiritual home Nashville, but more than 200 miles south in Atlanta (by Fiddlin' John Carson for the Okeh label) in 1923. Ralph Peer, who made those historic first recordings using rudimentary mobile equipment (basically an enormous horn that Carson performed live in front of), would go from Okeh to the Victor Talking Machine Company where, in 1927, he would cut the first discs (out of a makeshift studio in Bristol, Tennessee) from pioneering country artists the Carter Family and Jimmie Rodgers. If the blues was predominantly black, then country was aimed squarely at white, working-class America.

Peer's recordings helped to popularise country, and the fame of the artists involved quickly spread nationwide, thanks primarily to the influence of radio and the nationally available Grand Ole Opry programme, which began in 1925. It would not be long before Hollywood would get in on the act, promoting the image of the singing cowboy in his Stetson hat, elaborately embroidered Western shirt and blue jeans that is still the recognised uniform of the country musician today.

For five decades, country music remained the bastion of hard-drinking, hard-working, womanising 'real men' and their hard-done-by women; if a country song referenced anyone other than a fists first, questions later macho hunk or a broken-hearted woman standing by her brutish husband, it would usually be in derogatory terms, like in Vernon Dalhart's 1939 release 'Lavender Cowboy' (written by Harold Hersey in 1923), which was banned the following year from being played on the radio because of its suggestive lyrics, or Billy Briggs' infamous 1951 recording 'The Sissy Song': 'When I get sissy enough . . . I'll go out behind the old red barn and let a grey mule kick my brains out'.

Then, in 1973, along came *Lavender Country*.

Now in his early 70s and still playing, Patrick Haggerty seems an unlikely musical trendsetter, yet *Lavender Country* truly was a groundbreaking release: the very first out-gay country album. k.d. lang may have hogged headlines when she came out as lesbian in 1992, at the same time as she released her fifth (and still most successful) album *Ingénue*, but *Lavender Country* had started to plough that particular furrow a full

20 years earlier, and today's LGBT artists – including Canadian singer Drake Jensen, Ty Herndon, Billy Gilman, Steve Grand, Shane McAnally and Chely Wright – are proving that a genre that was once seen as the last bastion of 'straight' western music is slowly but surely opening up to everyone.

According to the press release that accompanied its 2014 reissue, *Lavender Country*

> stands as nothing less than an artefact of courage, a sonic political protest document of enormous power, clarity, and grace. At once a scathing indictment of the injustices perpetrated on the homosexual community, a proud proclamation of gay identity, and a love letter of bracing intimacy and eroticism, the album radically appropriates the signifiers of the conservative country genre, queering its heteronormative vocabulary into a deeply personal language.

Brought up on a dairy farm within a loving and supportive family, Haggerty wrote songs for *Lavender Country* that are filled with both humour and deep emotion. With titles such as 'Cryin' These Cocksucking Tears' and 'Back In the Closet Again', the record is very much a reflection of his own experiences, from his upbringing in rural Washington, through his dismissal from the Peace Corps because of his sexuality, his incarceration (at the hands of the family physician) in a mental hospital (an experience he shares with Lou Reed and Tom Robinson) and his struggle to be heard as a young gay man when he came out, empowered by the Stonewall Riots. 'Most of us were angry,' he says of those days. 'I think anger spurred us all on. I'd been kicked out of the Peace Corps and ended up in a mental institution. I spent eight years jobless; no one would hire me because my mouth was so big. All of us knew that we were potentially sacrificing our lives.'[1] Haggerty attests that he had 'more than one personal friend murdered' for being gay.

Now living just outside Seattle with his husband J.B. (the couple had been together for years before J.B. even heard of *Lavender Country*) Haggerty and his friends – keyboard player Michael Carr, Eve Morris (violin, acoustic guitar and vocals) and guitar player Robert Hammerstrom – formed a four-piece band, which he dubbed Lavender

Country. With financial support from Seattle's Gay Community Social Services – who provided counselling, a community centre, health information and more to the local LGBT community – Lavender Country released their sole eponymous album in 1973. Featuring eleven songs, nine written by Haggerty and one apiece from Morris and Hammerstrom, only 1,000 copies of the album were pressed, sold through the pages of gay-friendly publications in the Seattle area. The original sleeve notes confirm the band's desire to 'confront the oppression gay people experience daily and affirm the joys of liberation,' yet when local DJ Shan Ottey (who later directed the documentary *Mom's Apple Pie: The Heart of the Lesbian Mothers' Custody Movement*) played 'Cryin' These Cocksucking Tears' on air her station, KRAB, received an obscenity fine from the Federal Communications Commission and she lost her licence to broadcast.

The group continued to perform together for the next five years, but although they played prestigious dates such as San Francisco Gay Pride, none of the musicians were making a living. Eventually the band fell apart, and Haggerty took a job in the social work field with Seattle City Council's Human Rights department. In the late 1980s, he was one of the founders the Seattle chapter of AIDS-advocacy organisation ACT UP, and he ran for office in state senate and city council elections, both times as a candidate for the left-wing political party New Alliance, which had supported a multi-racial, pro-feminist and pro-gay platform since its formation in New York in 1979.

The album would have been no more than a footnote if it had not been for an article written by Chris Dickinson which was published in the *Journal of Country Music* in 2000. Titled 'Country Undetectable: Gay Artists in Country Music', that piece announced to the world that a new organisation, the Lesbian and Gay Country Music Association (LGCMA), had been formed with the express intention of challenging the boundaries of country music, and belatedly introduced *Lavender Country* to the world. Looking back now, it seems ridiculous that LGBT artists were all but invisible in country music; however, only a few years earlier, country artist Mike Deasy, a guitarist who had played on sessions for the Monkees, the Beach Boys, Simon and Garfunkel, Tiny Tim, Ella Fitzgerald and countless others, recorded the hateful 'God Hates Queer', which featured the lines 'you're going straight to hell and there you'll fry' and 'I don't need no AIDS from no gay plague'; homophobia was still being offered a home in Nashville, and few people were surprised when, just a few months after she began to champion country's LGBT artists, Chris Dickinson lost her job.

Still, her article reawakened interest: *Lavender Country* was reissued (this time on compact disc) and, in June 2000 at Seattle's Gay Pride Day, Haggerty launched a follow-up EP, *Lavender Country Revisited*, featuring re-recordings of three tracks from the album plus two new songs.

'*Lavender Country* might have been forgotten if it weren't for the work of Chrissie Dickinson,' said Doug Stevens, founder and president of the LGCMA and leader of the OutBand. 'Her article shocked the Nashville scene with its celebration of openly gay country musicians. Chrissie wrote about gay country singers with admiration and respect. She celebrated our contribution to the tradition of country music.'[2] Born and raised in Mississippi, in a house with no indoor plumbing but with a colour television,[3] Stevens, a classically-trained counter-tenor, grew up surrounded by country music (his parents and grandparents were all musicians) and pursued a successful career in classical music. In 1990 he received the devastating news that he was HIV-positive: his then-partner abandoned him and he spiralled into what he described as

an eight-month depression. I remembered seeing an interview with Tammy Wynette on TV when I was a kid. She had said that when she was depressed, she wrote a song about what she was feeling and it made her feel a lot better. So, I decided that I would write a song about a man whose lover left him because he was HIV-positive. I thought that it would take a long time to write. I had never tried to write a song before. But I put pen to paper and within 15 minutes I had a nice song. It made me feel much better, so I wrote another one, then another one, and another one. The songs that came out of me were country songs. I saw that gay people didn't have country music about our lives, even though we bought a lot of music. So, I decided to form a country band to perform the music that I was writing about my life and experiences as a gay country man, living in the big city.[4]

Stevens formed the OutBand in 1992 to perform his original, gender-specific songs for primarily gay audiences. 'Just as country music is the most popular music in the US it is also the most popular music among gays and lesbians,' he said.[5] The OutBand played all over the USA, Mexico and Northern Europe; at one point Stevens was fronting two different versions of the band, one in San Francisco and the other based in New York City, and for a couple of years Patrick Haggerty was a member. The two men also toured and recorded together in the band Pearl River. 'The Chris Dickinson article put me in touch with Doug,' Haggerty reveals, 'and I worked with him for a few years. That was good for me because he was a fabulous teacher and he was in touch with some fabulous musicians who believed in me. They took me under their wing – I was really raw and really green and they showed me a lot of good shit!' Stevens retired from recording in 2007, transitioned, and is now – as Teresa McLaughlin – happily married and working as a freelance writer.

The renewed interest in *Lavender Country* lasted a couple of years. 'Around 2004 it went dead again,' Haggerty says. 'I was retired, my husband was retired and I was having a nice life, but I was still singing'. Patrick was playing over 100 gigs a year 'singing old songs to old people in nursing homes and Alzheimer's units' with his musician friend Bobby Taylor. 'I love the old songs, I know hundreds, and that's what those people want to hear – it's joyful'. Then:

> I'd been doing that for like a decade or more, then someone put "Cocksucking Tears" on YouTube. I didn't know anything about it. Someone else heard it and said: "what is this?", went to eBay, found and old, used *Lavender Country* album for sale and purchased it. He was a music aficionado, not gay, and he realised what *Lavender Country* was: he realised its historical significance. He took it to a couple of guys in North Carolina, straight men who had a label ... and I still have no idea that anybody is talking about *Lavender Country*. I don't know anything about what's been happening. But they're all talking to each other. The first time I knew anything was when the label called up offering me a contract. I didn't believe them, I thought they were encyclopaedia salesmen; I thought it was a bunch of bullshit! The furthest thing from my mind would be having some voice on the

phone offering me a record contract. I did not believe a word that was coming out of his mouth!'

The independent Paradise of Bachelors label, which specialises in 'documenting, curating, and releasing under-recognised musics of the American vernacular,' reissued *Lavender Country* in 2014. More than four decades after they first walked into a recording studio together, Haggerty and the rest of the band were about to get the recognition they, and their pioneering record, deserved.

'These people were not gay,' Haggerty adds:

They were straight white men who worked in the music industry. There's not a whole raft of bigots running in to that career; musicians make really poor bigots! Musicians, promoters, people who write about music a lot of them are straight white men and they're the ones who have the power – and the straight white men who occupy positions in the music industry in 2016 are completely different to who they were in 1973 and all of them are down with gay rights and equal rights. The time is right, and it's right because all of these straight white men in the music industry are on board, and they have power and they're going: "I want to stand up. I want to be part of this. I want the world to know what side of the fence I'm on." It's a really nice thing, and these straight white men are making it possible for everybody's ear to open up. *Lavender Country* jumped out of the gay ghetto because these straight men in North Carolina with their brave new label allowed it in to the mainstream. What they're doing is giving a whole bunch of straight people permission to go and listen. We've been doing a lot of shows to general, not gay-specific, audiences, and when people have permission they go nuts!

The careers of Patrick Haggerty and Doug Stevens might seem a little niche, but today more and more country artists – and bigger and bigger names – are finding the courage to come out. If you had anticipated a rush in the wake of k.d. lang's very public self-outing, you would have been sorely disappointed; however, it seems that now – in the second decade of the twenty-first century – the audience is more than ready to accept an out country celebrity or two, and the people who run the business are finally getting there, too.

With a career that already spans more than 30 years, Canadian super-star k.d. lang's androgynous look and punk attitude practically defined alt-country, the musical subgenre that includes artists that incorporate influences ranging from bluegrass, hillbilly and folk to rockabilly and punk rock. After independently releasing her debut album, *A Truly Western Experience*, in 1984 she was signed to a worldwide deal by Sire/Warner Bros. and issued two more albums, *Angel With A Lariat* and *Shadowland* in less than a year. Recorded in Nashville, *Shadowland* was produced by Owen Bradley, who had worked with lang's idol, Patsy Cline. The album, which featured lang singing with country superstars Brenda Lee, Loretta Lynn and Kitty Wells, made the Billboard Country albums Top Ten.

Within a year she was back in the charts with the Grammy Award-winning *Absolute Torch and Twang*, but it was 1992's platinum-selling *Ingénue* (and the hit single 'Constant Craving') that not only established her status as one of the biggest country stars of the day but also helped her cross over into the pop mainstream and gave her the confidence to come out. Described as 'the best singer of her generation' by Tony Bennett[6] (the pair collaborated on the 2002 release *A Wonderful World*), lang's longevity is proof (as if it were needed) that someone's sexuality need not be an issue.

k.d. lang may have been country's first LGBT superstar, but Shane McAnally – who has written or co-written more than half a dozen Number One hits and countless other songs for artists including Kenny Chesney, LeAnne Rimes, Reba McEntire, Kelly Clarkson, Sheryl Crow, Keith Urban and more – is the biggest, and most influential, out-gay man in country music today. The Grammy Award-winner first rocked up in Nashville in 2000, quickly gaining a manager and a minor hit single, but the follow-up album flopped. Disillusioned, he took off to LA, par-tied hard, took a job tending bar and slowly rediscovered himself. After scoring the soundtrack to the gay-themed romantic movie *Shelter,* he felt ready to re-establish himself in his spiritual home, returning to Nashville in 2007 as an out-gay man. Known principally as a hit songwriter – as he says himself: 'When I stopped hiding who I am, I started writing hits'[7] – his lyrics are unusually revealing (as in Jake Owen's mega-hit

'Alone With You') and his music shows influences of everything from Weimar-era cabaret to radio-friendly pop and stadium rock. 'I think gay men by nature are more sensitive,' he told *The New York Times* in 2013. 'I think I'm able to tell a story in a way that relates to both men and women. Guys don't usually sing about the shame or the sadness of sex. But men do have those emotions, those experiences.'[8]

Ty Herndon is a bona fide star, with Number One hits, massive-selling albums and almost 20 singles on the *Billboard Hot Country Songs* chart to his name. His debut album, *What Mattered Most*, was one of the biggest hits of 1995. For half a dozen years, his star shone bright, but his personal life was a mess. In quick succession he had to deal with a divorce from his second wife, bankruptcy, weight issues, a mugging at gunpoint (that, incongruously, occurred while he was promoting his then-current single, 'Heather's Wall', about a man dying of a gunshot wound received in a hold-up), a lawsuit from a California dentist claiming that Herndon had not paid for emergency dental work and another lawsuit from a former manager for breach of contract. In 2004 he admitted himself in to a drug and alcohol rehabilitation facility. This was the second time he had undergone such treatment; the first spell followed an indecent exposure charge (later dropped after a plea bargain) for allegedly exposing himself to a police officer in 1995.

Finally coming out in 2014, having been inspired by his friend and fellow country artist Chely Wright (who came out herself in 2010) and Alex, his partner of six years, Herndon's career – which seemed to be all but finished – is once again on the upturn. Both Wright and Herndon admit that their attitude towards their sexuality was affected by their Christian upbringing and beliefs. 'I was a young, gay, Christian, farm girl from Kansas with dreams of becoming a country music star,' Wright wrote. 'Can you wrap your head around that? I really couldn't.'[9] Wright's inner turmoil brought her to the brink of suicide in 2006: 'I was alone, I was tired, I was hopeless and I was done. Early one cold winter morning in Nashville, I nearly took my life with a gun. Let me be clear, my decision to take my life was not because I am gay. The reason I was ready to end it all was because I didn't know how to be me in this life that I'd carved out. I just didn't know how to make those pieces fit.'[10]

*

Stories of those who have hit the big time and maintained their major
label backing are few and far between, and k.d. lang would not have
enjoyed such a long and successful career if she had not made a successful transition from country to the pop vocal field. The vast majority of
out-LGBT artists who have tried to establish a career in country music
have had to do so without big-label budgets.

After years of struggling to have his voice heard, 2017 could be the
year that Drake Jensen breaks big internationally. His first three, independently released, albums gained him many column inches, huge
amounts of respect and a dedicated fan base, but with the backing of
one of Australia's biggest talent agents and European dates on the hori-
zon, it looks like the time is right for the Canadian country singer: in
December 2016 his single 'Wherever Love Takes Us' broke the Country
Tracks Top 40 chart. His first album, *On My Way to Finding You,* received
positive reviews and sold well, but like Shane McAnally, that was not his
first attempt to start a career in country music. Ten years earlier he had,
under his given name Robbie Meyers, issued a single – a cover of the Ann
Murray hit 'A Little Good News' – which, although it gained some local
radio play, didn't exactly set the world alight.

'That single cost me a couple of thousand dollars,' he says honestly.
'But I was working a minimum wage job and barely surviving at that
time. Somebody opened a door that had been locked to me for my whole
life, and gave me one little glimpse of something that I'd always wanted.
You've got like a day to do it, to see what it's like, and you tick it off
your bucket list and you never think that you're going to do it again.'[11]
It would be a full decade before he dipped his toes in the water again,
but during that period he met and married Michael Morin, who became
his manager and encouraged him to give his music career another try.

Shortly after the release of *On My Way to Finding You,* Jensen announced
that he was gay. In a press release to help promote the album he revealed
that he had suffered severe childhood abuse and bullying, and he dedicated the video of his current single, the title track of the album, to the
memory of Ottawa teenager Jamie Hubley. Fifteen-year-old Hubley committed suicide after having been severely bullied at school; Jamie's father
Allan, an Ottawa city councillor, said that the bullying began when teens
tried to stuff batteries down his throat on the school bus because he was a

figure skater. 'Jamie was the kind of boy that loved everybody,' his father told the Canadian Broadcasting Corporation's Ashley Burke. 'He couldn't understand why everyone would be so cruel to him about something as simple as skating. He just wanted someone to love him. That's all. And what's wrong with that?'[12] Not long after, Drake released a new single, 'Scars' (which would appear on his second album, *OUTLaw*), donating the proceeds to the charity Bullying.org.

'Even when the other kids were beating me up and kicking me in the face I was planning my world domination,' Jensen reveals. 'I was going to be a star. I had that in my head, and it's interesting that all of those people who kicked me in the face are now listening to me on the local country radio station. I've gotten my revenge.' *OUTLaw* received unanimously good reviews, with *Cashbox Canada* calling the album 'eleven perfectly executed songs of love in all its redemptive beauty and a couple of reminders that love hurts, no matter where you find it.'

Jensen's route has not been easy, and he and Michael – who maintains a full-time job as well as spending many hours a day managing his husband's career – candidly admit that they have spent hundreds of thousands of dollars out of their own pockets to get his career off the ground:

> The music business is so expensive for someone who is not signed to a label, but if you do sign to a label then you sign your life away and I just don't want to do it. I don't want to be a slave to that. But every penny I earn goes in to music. What I would like to eventually get is a distribution deal, where we make the product and then they market it, but a lot of people are afraid of an LBGT artist in this genre so no one is willing to take that gamble. Michael and I have talked about not doing this anymore, or just doing local shows but the reach is less, but we both feel like we have a purpose in life with this. It's a bigger thing that me being an artist and making music.

Other acts, including the San Francisco-based singer/songwriter Mark Weigle, have tried to pursue a career in music by going down the independent route, either through choice or because that is the only option open to them. Weigle got good reviews, spent time in Nashville writing songs for his third album *All That Matters* and saw interest from mainstream companies, including MCA and Sony, but that was in 2000, and record company executives simply did not understand how to market a gay artist – or refused to believe that there was a market for them. Despite playing hundreds of gigs and issuing seven albums, in 2007 Weigle called it a day, telling fans via his website that he 'stopped my music career due to lack of support. I dedicated my muse and my career to the gay world, which seems predominately interested in straight celebrities, pretty 20-year-olds, porn stars and drag queens.'

So why choose a career in a genre that is notoriously difficult to make a living in (even if you're not gay), when it may have been easier to try and make it as a pop singer? 'I'd played in pop bands but I returned to country music because as you get older the voice doesn't do what you want it to,' Jensen admits. 'It's very difficult to constantly sing rock or pop music. Country just felt right for my voice . . . that and I always want to piss people off – I like being a thorn in someone's side . . . but I've just been invited into the big country music station here in Ottawa to do a live session, which is amazing. The new single, *Wherever Love Takes Us*, is doing really well, we're getting more radio stations adding us to their playlists, and if we can get enough radio play then we can chart, and if we chart that's pretty momentous because an LGBT artist has never done that in country music before.'

Jensen cuts an imposing figure; a navy reservist with a gym-toned body and an image that feeds in to many gay men's fantasies, he's also incredibly shy and private when out of the public eye:

I've been hyper-criticised about not singing gay songs; you have gay artists in country who will never come out, and that's because when people do come out there's often a big shit storm, with people burning CDs and all sorts. I've always been careful not to shove it in people's faces: I've always said that, you know what, I'm going to sing a love song and you can interpret it any way you want. But I've made it quite apparent that I share my life with a man and there is a threat from that for sure, but that's also part of me being this anomaly – this renegade, maverick kind of guy – but that's who I really am and I've been that my whole life no matter what I've done. I am what you see, and I make no apologies.

For a while I thought that I needed to tame it down, but then I realised that everybody is selling sex, and I'm a business person! I look at my photos and think: "I would buy that!" There's no doubt that 50 to 60 percent of my audience are gay men, and they're buying records based on the hard-on that they get when they see the pictures. They're not searching for gay artists with great music . . . they're horny! Madonna learned that a long time ago, and I've learned that too: sex sells and I've crafted an image.

Going down the independent route isn't easy, and it limits your audience. Just 1,000 copies of *Lavender Country* were pressed initially and it took the album four decades to find its audience. Jensen freely admits, '*Lavender Country* is much more blatant than anything I have done: if that had been my first record it would have shut my career down. But I loved it and I think the concept is wonderful. We hadn't heard of it in Canada when I first came out, it was very obscure. When I found out about it I thought: "wow! This is amazing!" But it's so different to anything I would have done. That's not a soft sell by any stretch of the imagination, but boy, I really respect it.' There are many similarities between the acts: Jensen, like Patrick Haggerty and Mark Weigle before him, is fiercely independent, and he's resolute that he and Michael will make a place for themselves in a genre that has a history of ignoring LGBT artists. 'We've touched many people in our lives; we might not have seen a return in monetary terms, but we certainly have in the satisfaction of knowing that we've made a difference.' Weigle had already experienced similar hardships: 'I've paid to record and produce all the CDs on my Visa, and have run every aspect of a record label by myself. I never wanted to be a businessman, and I'm still paying off debt,' he said in 2007. 'Stopping it all has been an extremely painful decision.' Weigle and his partner Gerry now run a brace of bookshops in California.

Coming out right at the beginning of his career was a bold move, but it's one that Jensen has never regretted:

I didn't think I was going to come out; I was going to keep my private life private. I was going to make music and try and keep it about the music, and then I started to realise that it's really not just about the

Drake Jensen

music. Reba McEntire always talked about her husband, Dolly always talked about her husband – well I had a husband: what am I going to do? Am I going to hide him? Am I going back in the closet and deny who I am, and become something that I'm really not. I've already done that; I've already tried to conform to what my father and everybody else felt I should be. I identified with Boy George: that was me. His father wanted him to be a boxer. My father wanted me to be a man and get married – and I am a fucking man, I'm just a man who likes men.

I came to a point where I thought: "I can't do this". I really want to tell people about how much Michael has helped me, how he has been behind it all, how a lot of his money went to it and I couldn't deny that. Who would I be? What kind of a man would that make me? I think when I put that press release out that was the scariest time of my career. I was coming out for the second time and I knew that was going to take me off the main road and I was going to have to take the long way, but here's the thing about the long way: sometimes it's not as fast, sometimes you'll get stopped and sometimes you'll hit a bump in the road – which I have – but sometimes the most beautiful scenery is along that road., and in the past five years Michael and I have seen many, many beautiful scenes. Would I have changed, would I have not taken that road? The answer is no, because it has helped form the man I am today and the artist I have become. Because it's not just about the music, it's about reaching people and drawing them in.

'There seems to be a rule about it,' Patrick Haggerty adds:

First it was OK to be gay, then it was OK to be gay and be out, then it was OK to be gay and be out and be a professional, then it was OK to be gay and be out and be on TV, then it was OK to be gay and be out and win office – and all of these developments were barriers that needed to be broken down. Well, the barrier that we've been facing all along is that it's OK to be gay but it's not OK to sing about it. That's the barrier, and that's been true my whole adult life. It's OK to be gay but it's not OK to sing about being gay. It has been very, very persistent and very difficult to overcome, and of course the last barrier is Nashville – and even they are crumbling.'

'There have been many times that I've wanted to walk away, because it gets very tiring and I feel like I'm banging my head against a brick wall,' Jensen admits,

but then I think about what questions I'm going to ask myself right before I die. I always worry have I done what I needed to do, and in the end, when you're no longer breathing somebody else takes the big house and the big car and everything else. One of the questions that I ask myself is "what is the legacy?" What about being the guy that allows a 20 year-old to believe that he can do it? One of the people that taught me how to stand up and move forward, no matter what happens, was Boy George . . .

People come up to me all the time to tell me that they love what I'm doing, and that's the gas in the tank. That's how I get it back. One young transgendered girl ran up to me at the last show I did and said "I just want you to know that I follow everything you do. I'm so happy to meet you. You're one of my heroes". And what do you say? I say: "thank you so much, now tell me about you" ... you need to be able to be there for them, that's your job and I think the greatest artists understand that.

In January 2017, Country Music Television's Cody Alan, host of CMT's *Hot 20 Countdown* and winner of the Academy of Country Music's National Broadcast Personality for 2010 and 2013, publicly came out as gay, telling his 132,000 Instagram followers, 'I realised that this could have a great, positive impact on many people who may be country music fans and may feel like they don't fit in. But they see a guy like me on TV who is country and gay, and they recognise that there's a place for you here, and that country music is a warm, welcoming space.'

Patrick Haggerty's re-emergence on the scene inspired filmmaker Dan Taberski to produce the multiple award-winning documentary *These C*cksucking Tears*: 'I'm working with a lot of straight country musicians,' Haggerty adds:

They're way more sophisticated, and way more progressive than the trite, tired and boring lyrics they're being forced to sing, but most of them are doing what they have to do to be heard in Nashville. When they hear something like *Lavender Country* it's like they have been locked up in a stinking basement for 20 years and someone finally gave them a breath of fresh air ... I can really feel the walls tumbling in Nashville. I think that having a gay component to the Americana Festival [an annual, week-long festival and conference for American music fans and industry professionals] is the beginning of the end and the fact that the Americana Festival is being forced to add a gay component has the potential to crack things wide open for everybody. The industry has very tight politics: closet cases high up in the industry are fucking freaked out ... Straight people want to support gay rights, but when they go to gay executives for advice they shut them down ... I'm not speaking unkindly about the gay community; the gay community has made enormous strides and we've done wonderful things and having *Lavender Country* be acknowledged is another wonderful thing that we did.

VILLAGE PEOPLE

Early Village People press photo, 1978

CHAPTER 13

Can't Stop the Music

'The Village People get good reviews because they are a
disco group (gasp) with gay (erk) overtones which straight
rock critics can appreciate for its sense of humor'

'Village People: First Flash Wears Off',
Doylestown Intelligencer, 25 May 1979

In Philadelphia in 1975 Jacques Morali and Henri Belolo, two Morocco-
born but Paris-based business partners, were looking to secure their
first major hit. Private gay dance parties in Philadelphia and DJ and club
promoter David Mancuso's legendary LSD-laced New York loft parties
were giving rise to a new sound, influenced by European pop, soul and
glam rock, and the duo had been drawn to the City of Brotherly Love
in search of 'the next big thing'. The music they heard was music to
dance to, music for all classes and all colours, at odds with the guitar-
heavy sounds that dominated the US airwaves but not a million miles
away from the string-laden pop sounds Morali had been associated with
back in Paris. With records mixed together to provide a continuous
soundtrack, disco dominated gay clubs years before it went mainstream.
The first disco hits that crossed over into the pop charts – the records of
Barry White, George McCrae, Gloria Gaynor and Donna Summer – had
already proved themselves to be huge successes in LGBT clubs and had
helped fill the basement dance floor of New York's notorious Continental
Baths, where a young gay DJ called Francis Nicholls, known professionally as Frankie Knuckles, was making a name for himself.

One of the regular performers at the Continental Baths was the Bronx-born, Puerto Rican singer Joseph Montanez Jr, alias Sir Monti Rock III. Monti had one of the first crossover disco hits when, as the glitter-plastered, feather boa-wearing frontman of songwriter Bob Crewe's studio band Disco Tex and His Sex-O-Lettes, he made the charts with 'Get Dancin'' (released in November 1974) and its follow-up 'I Wanna Dance Wit' Choo', although he had in fact issued his first 45 ('For Days and Days') in 1965. Thrown out of home at 13 for being gay, he worked as a male prostitute before making a name for himself as the hairdresser to the stars. Operating out of a salon in department store Saks Fifth Avenue, Rock became something of a minor local celebrity, appearing on *The Merv Griffin Show* and *Tonight with Johnny Carson* dozens of times. His sexuality was no secret: in 1966, while on *Merv Griffin* with Jayne Mansfield, comedian Henny Youngman referred to Rock as 'Lawrence of Fire Island' (in a reference to New York's well-known gay resort) and made several crude jokes at his expense. 'I was gay, but people didn't mention "gay" in those days,' he says. He was sacked from Saks for appearing nude in a gay magazine's photo spread. Not that it mattered: in 1969 he was cast in the Hollywood movie *2000 Years Later* with Terry-Thomas and Edward Everett Horton. Surely stardom beckoned?

Back in Philadelphia, Morali and Belolo assembled a studio group and recorded an album, *Brazil*, one side of which contained all but instrumental disco versions of classic 1940s songs including 'Brazil' and 'The Peanut Vendor'. Needing vocalists for the project the duo pulled in three women, Cassandra Ann Wooten and Gwendolyn Oliver of the girl group Honey & the Bees, and Cheryl Mason Jacks – and The Ritchie Family was born. The group, which took its name from arranger and assistant producer Richie Rome, took 'Brazil' to Number One in the US dance charts. The following year The Ritchie Family scored again: 'The Best Disco in Town', a medley of recent disco hits, was an international smash, going Top Ten in the UK, Australia, the Netherlands and Norway, and providing them with a second US dance chart-topper.

Unfortunately, things were not going so well for Monti Rock. Following his two hit singles, he put together an outrageous stage show, but his time in the spotlight was up almost as soon as it had begun. His second album, *Manhattan Millionaire,* stiffed and with no records to be made he tried his hand at acting once again, appearing as the DJ in *Saturday Night Fever* and in a 'blink and you'll miss it' cameo in the dreadful *Sgt. Pepper's Lonely Hearts Club Band*. In the 40 years that have passed since then, Monti has attempted several comebacks, issued a one-off single in Germany (1982's 'In Havana') and has become an ordained minister, offering marriage ceremonies in Las Vegas. Name-checked by both Elvis Costello and the Pet Shop Boys, he's still trying to make it big today. 'I'm not a singer. I'm not an actor. What I am is somebody who believes so much in myself that I can make you believe.'[1]

While our Parisian pals were holidaying in New York, the gay Morali (who, after an abortive attempt at a solo career with the 1967 EP *Elle Aime, Elle N'Aime Pas* had moved into writing and production) spotted a man on Christopher Street in Greenwich Village wearing a full Native American costume. The pair followed him into the Anvil, West 14th Street's noto-riously sleazy pick-up joint, where they soon spotted him. They could hardly miss him, for the man they would soon discover was called Felipe Rose had climbed up onto the bar and was shaking his stuff with wild abandon. Inside the Anvil that night the two men saw just about every macho man stereotype they could think of; the bar was full of construc-tion workers, cops in uniform, leather-clad (and heavily moustachioed) bikers, GIs in full fatigues and jolly Jack Tars who had probably never set foot on a ship. Inspired by their visit, Belolo and Morali placed an advert in the *Village Voice*: 'Macho types wanted: must dance and have a mustache'. Around sixty guys showed up at the 'audition'; not one of them made it into the studio for the first *Village People* EP – four songs each depicting an aspect of gay life in the US. The vocals would be handled by Victor Willis, a straight actor Morali discovered in the Broadway production of *The Wiz*: 'I had a dream that you sang lead vocals on my album and it went very, very big,' Morali told him.[2] Felipe, as 'Indian from the Anvil' won himself a small credit for playing 'bells'; he was also the only member of the group to appear on the sleeve. A cheap video was shot for 'San Francisco': of the seven men featured dancing and singing along to the tune only Rose and Willis made Morali and Belolo's final list. At the same time, just a 10-minute walk from the Anvil, at a club called Century 21, a young gay DJ by the name of Walter Gibbons was making a name for himself as a genius on the turntable, stretching out beats and splicing them into other songs to create his own exclusive mixes. Soon he would become the first star DJ commissioned by a record company to create a remix from the original multi-track recording and, with Loleatta Holloway's *Hit And Run*, produced the first proper disco-mix 12" single.

Casablanca, who had already tasted huge disco success with Giorgio Moroder and Donna Summer, signed the new act to a multi-album deal: all Morali and Belolo had to do was find the rest of the singers for the project. Through a further casting session they found Glenn Hughes (the leather man), Alex Briley (the GI) and construction worker David Hodo. Morali found Randy Jones, his cowboy, dancing with Grace Jones. The classic six-man line-up was in place, and Morali and Belolo wasted no time in getting them in to the studio to record the vocals for the first full-length Village People album, *Macho Man*. Everyone involved in the project, bar Morali and Belolo, was surprised when, in September 1978, the title song became a hit, making the *Billboard* Top 30.

In their first two years together, the Village People hit Number One in the UK (and Number Two in the US) with 'Y.M.C.A.', made the UK and US Top Three with 'In The Navy', had a Top 20 hit with 'Go West' (later covered by the Pet Shop Boys), and were awarded six gold and four platinum records, selling over 20 million singles and 18 million albums worldwide. They filled major concert venues, caused near-riots when they appeared in public and were featured heavily on television, in the press and on radio. You simply could not escape them. According to celebrity photographer Mick Rock, Queen singer Freddie Mercury 'was never the same again' after seeing an early Village People performance at the Anvil: 'Freddie was "utterly mesmerised" by the sight of Glenn Hughes. The Anvil experience was presumed to be the inspiration for both the "leather" and "gay clone" looks which Freddie would adopt'.[3] Their massive success with straight audiences and their knowing nod to the gay scene that begat them made them seem subversive: young girls and grandmothers could dance to their non-threatening disco-pop 45s, and gay men could enjoy the scarcely veiled double entendres which filled the group's celebrations of LGBT life. The Village People were fun. 'It's not important who we are and what we are,' Randy Jones claimed. 'Only that people have a good time listening to us'.[4] Then Victor Willis, who co-wrote all of their hits, decided to leave.

Although most members of the group had been guarded about their sexuality ('I never took this job with the idea of becoming a professional pervert or a public sleaze' David Hodo told reporters),[5] the man who struggled the most with the group's gay image was the married Willis, and he was not happy when Morali came out in the press in 1978. 'The group has never performed gay. Nobody has ever come out in drag. The group performs a masculine show. Gay people like us, straight people like us. But we're not a gay group,' he told whoever would listen,[6] although few took his protestations seriously: after all, this was the man who had co-written 'Hot Cop' and 'Macho Man', and had fronted the band's *Cruisin'* album. His departure came just as the group were preparing to star in their first (and, so far, only) movie, the ultra-camp *Can't Stop the Music*, and although Ray Simpson would replace Willis, the Village People would never have another substantial hit. The film's title track failed to chart in their home country and the movie itself, co-starring Caitlyn (then publicly known as Bruce) Jenner, was a box-office bomb. It shouldn't have been: the Village People were hot, the cast was filled out with accomplished talent, it was directed by the award-winning comedy actor Nancy Walker and produced by Alan Carr, who just two years before had backed *Grease*. Unfortunately the Village People themselves stank: 'it's dumb, but great fun . . . musically they are terrific. So what if they can't act?' was one of the kinder reviews.[7]

Willis would return briefly, after the group released their disastrous (and virtually unlistenable) new wave album *Renaissance*, but to no avail. Soon the Village People's original police officer would run afoul of the real cops: in February 1997 he was arrested at Reno's Flamingo Hilton hotel on robbery, drugs and false imprisonment charges and, unable to raise the $56,000 bail, was jailed.[8] Charges for false imprisonment were later dropped but he was arrested again in July 2005 when Californian police found him in possession of 'a .45-calibre handgun as well as rock cocaine and drug paraphernalia'.[9] After several years out of the spotlight, and a number of line-up changes (only Felipe Rose and Alex Briley remain), the band did achieve a renaissance of sorts and – by finally embracing their status as gay icons – have become a staple of LGBT Pride events around the world.

*

If you wanted to meet a member of the Village People then the best place to go – if you were glamorous or famous enough to get past the uppity door staff – was Studio 54. Co-founded in 1977 by gay entrepreneur Steve Rubell, Studio 54 was *the* place to be seen for every hip New Yorker. It was housed in a former TV studio on Manhattan's West 54th Street; on any given night you could see Grace Jones (one fan went so far as to handcuff himself to her ankle during a performance),[10] Donna Summer, Gloria Gaynor, Sylvester and Two Tons O' Fun, The Village People, Klaus Nomi or any one of dozens of other LGBT favourites on stage while you rubbed shoulders with Andy Warhol, Liza Minnelli, Mick and Bianca (or Mick and Jerry), Elton John, Freddie Mercury, David Bowie, Salvador Dali, Donald Trump and just about everyone who was anyone who happened to be passing through the city. Infamous for its excesses (Bianca Jagger rode a white horse into the club on her birthday), the sex and the obscene amount of drugs being snorted in every dark corner, the fun and frolics were short-lived. In 1980, after a disgruntled employee reported the club's shady financial goings-on to the IRS, Rubell and business partner Ian Schrager were jailed for tax evasion and the club was sold.

After a period in Los Angeles, where he 'lived as a woman for a few years'[11], in 1970 Sylvester James moved to San Francisco and became a member of the city's outrageous cabaret collective the Cockettes, occasionally performing a drag tribute to Billie Holiday. Preferring to run his own show, he took on a pair of female backing singers, Martha Wash and Izora Rhodes, who at that time were known as Two Tons O' Fun but who would later find everlasting fame as the Weather Girls and enjoy a huge international hit of their own with 'It's Raining Men'. Openly gay throughout his career (he had left the church to pursue a career in secular music as the congregation disapproved of his sexuality), he said that it was his grandmother – who herself had been a blues singer in the 1930s – who encouraged him to embrace his sexuality. 'She'd met quite a few gay men, and so she saw the signs in me early in my life,' he told journalist Alan Wall. 'When I was in my teens she told me to live the way I wanted to, not to pretend. So I took her advice and did exactly that.'[12] So identified was he with the city that 11 March 1979 was declared 'Sylvester Day' and the singer was awarded the keys to the city by Mayor Dianne Feinstein.[13]

Forever known for his 1979 hit 'You Make Me Feel (Mighty Real)', Sylvester's gay anthem only became a hit after his friend Patrick Cowley, inspired by the electronic disco created by Giorgio Moroder for Donna Summer's epic 'I Feel Love', offered to remix what had been, until then, a mid-tempo gospel tune. Cowley's bouncing synthesiser style became synonymous with Sylvester, and the duo's signature sound has been cited as an influence by the Pet Shop Boys and New Order: in issue 30 of their fan club magazine *Literally,* Neil Tennant and Chris Lowe discussed how their song 'Psychological' (from the album *Fundamental*) was inspired by Cowley's productions.

Like Victor Willis, trouble seemed to follow Sylvester. In 1980 he was arrested and charged with armed robbery and grand larceny after taking part in a swindle involving $55,000 worth of rare coins.[14] He claimed he was the victim of a frame-up, and that the crime had been perpetuated by a lookalike, but he still spent time in jail: 'Sylvester spent his first night in the slammer with an accused murderer and the next few nights with six transvestites accused of prostitution before he was finally set free'.[15] Two years later he sued his (by then former) manager for having had his hand in the till. Sylvester had been signed to Fantasy Records by Harvey Fuqua, a former member of the hit group the Moonglows, who had previously been a talent scout for Motown: soon Two Tons O' Fun were also signed to a separate deal. Yet despite healthy sales and a number of huge hits on the US dance charts, neither act was seeing much financial return and both began to suspect that not everything was right with the deal that Fantasy had given them. Sylvester left Fantasy and in November 1982 filed a lawsuit against them, alleging that the company had failed to pay him all of the money that he was due from the sale of his records. Although it was discovered that Fuqua and Fantasy had withheld more than $218,000 from his star, he was unable to pay more than $20,000 back. Sylvester signed a new deal with Megatone Records, a company that had been co-founded by his old friend Patrick Cowley. Megatone aimed its releases squarely at the gay market, its roster featuring a number of out-gay artists including San Francisco-based singer Paul Parker.

As the demand for disco abated, Sylvester, who had been as noticed for his outrageous, feminine attire (which earned him the nickname 'the Queen of Disco') as he was noted for 'bringing disco to its roots, bringing with it aspects of Rock 'n' Roll, gospel and blues,'[16] dropped the dresses and toned the campery down: 'People used to leave my concerts commenting on the costumes, the make-up, the lights – *anything* but the music,' he told *Gay News*. 'I was more into being a performer; now the music is first and foremost';[17] but as many other acts had found, his straight audience deserted him.

Shortly after Sylvester terminated his involvement with the Cockettes, Harris Glenn Milstead, better known as John Waters' leading lady Divine, also passed through their ranks. Born in Baltimore into a conservative, upper-middle-class family, Harris became the break-out star of Waters' Dreamland set-up, appearing in cult cinematic hits including *Pink Flamingos*, *Female Trouble* and *Hairspray*, and – around 1974 – in several avant-garde performances alongside the Cockettes. In 1980, as Divine, Milstead recorded his first single, 'Born To Be Cheap'. It wasn't a hit, but it managed to get some attention. Soon Divine could be found, squeezed into a far-too-tight animal print dress, strutting her stuff around gay clubs in Britain and America, and this exposure helped the second single, 'Native Love' become a minor dance hit. Divine became a surprise star of Britain's nascent Hi-NRG scene, thanks to her work with dance producer Bobby Orlando, who would also work with the Pet Shop Boys at the start of their career.

Although Milstead saw Divine as a role he played as a character actor, it was Divine the public – and the media – wanted. In 1987, fed up with not being taken seriously, Milstead decided to refuse to do any further media appearances in drag: 'I stopped doing the interviews after I appeared on a show in the States. Tom Schneider was the inter-viewer's name. He said, "Are you a transvestite?", I said no, not at all . . . he then said, "why are you sitting here in a dress?" I of course replied that "well, you insisted that this was the only way I could come on the show"!'[18] A hit act in the UK with seven charting singles, Divine failed to spark as a singer in her home country. In London, Divine appeared at the Hippodrome, riding on the back of a baby elephant. The night she appeared on the British TV show *Top of the Pops* (19 July 1984, lip-synching to 'You Think You're a Man') the country experienced a small earthquake. No doubt veteran morals campaigner Mary Whitehouse would have linked the two seemingly unrelated events. Described by *People* magazine as the 'Drag Queen of the Century', Milstead died from a heart attack in March 1988. He was in Los Angeles to appear, as Uncle Otto, in an episode of the hit US sitcom *Married . . . With Children,* one of the few male roles he had been offered during his career.

John 'Smokey' Condon's life reads like the script to a John Waters movie, full of sex, drugs, prostitutes and wild music. Maybe that's not so surprising when you discover that he – like Waters and Divine – was raised in Baltimore and hung out with the actors from Water's fabled Dreamland stable. Thrown out of his abusive family home for being gay, before he was 16, John was living 'above a nightclub called the Bluesette. I rented a room for $40 a week. I used to hang out with a lot of musicians, jam with them and what have you, and I started hanging out at the bars at a place called Fells Point in the harbour with all kinds of people from Baltimore, all the John Waters people, and partied with them mostly every night of the week.'[19] He continued to attend school, intent on graduating. 'I went to High School whenever I could; it was important for me to graduate. I got suspended four times in my senior year for wearing outrageous clothes and things like that. They just didn't know what to do with me. They said, "you need English to graduate" so I took an English course and I washed dishes in a coffee shop to pay my rent and I graduated.'

For a time, Condon dated Waters' leading man David Lochary, the outlandish star of *Pink Flamingos* and *Female Trouble* (who sadly died in mysterious circumstances in 1977), but Baltimore was becoming a bit too small for him. He explains:

> I hooked up with a guy named Larry, and we started living with a drag queen named Christine. I was like 16 or 17, and I didn't know she was a drag queen! She would go out at night and prostitute so we would sleep all day and stay up all night and party, but she finally had enough of Larry and asked us to leave, so we hitch-hiked up to New York. We got a ride in the back of a vegetable truck. Life is very strange sometimes. We got a ride to the outskirts of New York and we walked for blocks and blocks and got to this nightclub, and this limo pulled up and a friend of mine got out. He took one look at me

and said, "Oh, we've got to go dancing!" I had been sleeping with the manager of *Hair* in Baltimore, and the friend from the limo had been the star of the show, so we lived with him and we partied in New York.'

John Condon arrived in New York a few weeks before the Stonewall Riots. 'The night after Stonewall they had a march,' he explains. 'I made it to the first bar and thought, "That's it; I'm not going any further"!' He quickly decided that New York wasn't for him. 'I went back to Baltimore and I was just hanging out. The Doors were playing at the Civic Centre; I was just hanging outside, and Vince Treanor, their road manager came up to me and said "Do you want to go to Europe with us?"'

After the tour, he moved to LA and met E. J. Emmons. 'E. J. had been a sound engineer for The Doors. I was just part of the entourage, I just hung out with them. I got to meet a lot of musicians, but it was all a bit bigger than life. Vince was in this really crappy apartment and I went out and I got a job as a bartender-slash-go-go boy. I would get in around three in the morning and E. J. used to come over and take pictures of me while I was sleeping! We were partners for eight years.'

And he still had not reached his twentieth birthday.

Now living in Palm Springs, California and working as an account executive for a lighting company, Condon's past life as an outrageously out-gay musician had been consigned to the briefest of footnotes until he was rediscovered by the independent Australian label Chapter Music. Founded by Ben O'Connor and Guy Blackman (himself a musician with several albums to his name), Chapter included Smokey on the 2012 compilation *Strong Love: Songs of Gay Liberation 1972–1981* (which also included tracks by Blackberri and Lavender Country) before, in 2015, they compiled all of his available recordings on the album *How Far Will You Go*. Blackman explains:

Everything Chapter Music does is a labour of love. The *Strong Love* compilation sold reasonably well but not in huge numbers, and didn't quite get the critical response we were hoping for. Maybe we were year or two too early? When the Lavender Country album was reissued a couple of years later people seemed just that little bit more ready to recognise pioneering queer voices. We always wanted to do a full Smokey reissue, as John was one of the wildest and most fascinating artists on *Strong Love*: we even named the album after his song. The five singles, plus all of the unreleased tracks that Smokey's partner/producer E. J. sent through, were incredible and we knew that there was an amazing story behind the music. *How Far Will You Go?* is one of the Chapter releases I'm proudest of having helped to make happen.'[20]

'I had always wanted to sing,' Condon explains, 'Ever since I was three years old. But I never considered myself a gay artist. I sang and did things that came naturally to me, whether that was in the way I dressed and or in my lyrics. The labels came when I hit Hollywood.' When no record company would touch them, Condon and his manager/band mate/lover Emmons started their own label – the provocatively-named S&M Records, whose logo featured a muscled forearm decorated with studded leather and bearing an 'S&M' tattoo. Song titles included 'Piss Slave', 'Leather', and 'How Far Will You Go . . .?' 'I came to Los Angeles in 1971 and I think we recorded "Leather" later that year.' Condon remembers:

E. J. asked me what I wanted to do and I said, "Well, I want to sing" and he asked me "Can you sing?" I said, "I don't know!" so we went in to the studio he had been working in. E. J.'s deal was to get a gig at a recording studio only if he got free studio time; he always wanted to be a producer and I always wanted to make music. He said, "what do you want to sing" and I said, "I don't know", so he said, "well, sing about something you know about" so that's why I wrote "Leather" and why I wrote "Miss Ray". He had been working with a guy named Gordon Alexander, who had a contract with Columbia, so I went in and I recorded "Leather" with Gordon's band. "Leather" was going to be the B-side because we thought that "Miss Ray", a song I wrote about this drag queen that I had lived with in Baltimore, was the A-side. We went in and we did them basically in one take.

It was a time when everybody was handing out cassettes, and saying "listen to my demo". The record people would just throw these cassettes into a big basket and they wouldn't listen to them.

E. J. knew about this pressing plant down the street, a really funky
place where they pressed Mexican records – it was like an auto shop
actually – and so he said, "Let's press up a hundred records and give
them out". I think it cost us about $45. We just started giving them
out and it started to take off, and before I knew it a guy named Nickey
Beat (Nickey Alexander) who was a drummer who went on to play in
several other bands after my group came up to me and told me that we
had a gig booked: "Oh, we're going to play at Rodney's club on Friday"!
I didn't even have a group at that point and he had set up everything!

Condon and Emmons quickly pulled together a live band, which they
dubbed Smokey after John's childhood nickname (not to be confused
with the British pop band Smokie, who styled themselves Smokey until
a certain Mr Robinson threatened to sue). 'Nickey drove a limo for a
hire company,' Condon remembers, 'So I rolled up to Rodney's in this
limo! We had maybe six songs practised, and we played and that's how
it started. And it just kept going after that. It was very strange.'

The band landed a regular spot at the English Disco on the
Sunset Strip, run by the legendary music industry publicist Rodney
Bingenheimer, and although the line-up changed constantly, musicians
who came and went into Smokey's orbit included Randy Rhoads, Adrian
Belew (King Crimson), James Williamson and a teenage Joan Jett, who at
one point ran Smokey's fan club. Joan wanted to play with Smokey, but
Condon felt she was too young. Later she would join all-girl rock band
The Runaways before fronting her own successful band, Joan Jett and the
Blackhearts. Joan is an enigma in rock 'n' roll: despite many attempts to
out her over the years, she has steadfastly refused to discuss her sex life.

'The thing that made it happen was Rodney,' Condon admits. 'Rodney
had a radio show and he played my songs, and he was at every show I
played whether it was at his club or any other club. Rodney was always
there; he was a big contributor.' Like all of their recordings Smokey's
first 45 was laid down in spare studio time. Featuring Williamson on
guitar, the semi-autobiographical song tells the tale of a young man who
moves from Baltimore to the big city in search of a new life. Pressed in
small quantities as and when funds allowed, by 1976 the 45 had started
to gain some notoriety, with reviews in fanzines and healthy sales via the

Tower Records store on Sunset Strip. 'I think they ordered 500 copies, so we had to get them pressed. We went in every week to see how they were selling. I did an in-store signing at Tower and there was a busload of Japanese girls who went nuts over me!'

Life was fun but it wasn't easy; Condon and Emmons were barely scraping by. 'Elton had my records on his jukebox. We did a TV show called *Tomorrow with Tom Snyder* (filmed at Bingenheimer's club in 1974): I was wearing a dress and I had on green eye shadow and Beatle boots and at that time my hair was down to my waist, I was in the DJ booth doing the cancan and they were interviewing Rodney and talking about how David Bowie is really big and he said, "Yeah, Bowie is big but my number one artist is Smokey" and the camera panned to me doing the cancan!' Ironically, it was Bowie who suggested to Bingenheimer that he open a nightclub: the pair had met when Bingenheimer was an intern at Mercury, Bowie's first American label, and remained friends. 'We had a ball. I sang all 18 voices on "Dance The Night Away", we were the first people to use a harmoniser [a piece of studio equipment usually used to process vocals]which has just come in from Europe . . . can you imagine standing in front of nine black dudes singing "Piss Slave"? It was hysterical! These were Jehovah's Witnesses! And we did that in one take! They were really fun times.'

For a time, Condon and Emmons were managed by Dan Bourgoise, who also managed the career of Del Shannon. Condon was enjoying life, rubbing shoulders with stars and partying with David Geffen at Linda Ronstadt's beach house, but things were not right. The reaction he was getting from live appearances, coupled with healthy record sales and a bulging contact book, should have guaranteed him a contract with a major company, but it didn't happen:

There were several thousand people there at my last gig, at a club called Osko's [the club that was used in the movie *Thank God It's Friday*]. I had to have three bodyguards; people were just clamouring to touch me and feel me – it blew my fucking mind, yet I was going home to a garage with nothing in it but a motorcycle and a bed,' he explains. 'I couldn't understand it . . . New Wave was just starting to hit, and big-hair bands like Mötley Crüe, so I don't know if that was the reason it didn't happen for us – by then I had cut my hair and what I was doing was more punk.'

'I got called a fag by record executives: "we like his music but he's gay" and all that kind of shit. I played for Seymour Stein before he signed the Talking Heads and Madonna, but nobody would take a chance. I couldn't understand it. I put my heart and soul into this music and we went from these hole in the wall studios to the best in the world, the Record Plant. In the studio next to me was Fleetwood Mac or Quincy Jones or Bad Company, and it was just weird, because they would all come in and listen to my music and ask, "What label are you on?" And I'd tell them, "I'm not on a label". We kept releasing more and more singles in the hope that somebody would pick it up. I watched people plagiarise me and copy my ideas – it was hard . . . I thought, "Fuck this industry. I've given this everything I had. If you want to copy something and if you want to steal something from me, here, steal this!" We recorded 'Piss Slave' and with that I walked away from it – I'd had enough. It had been ten years, I'd been living in a garage in Hollywood, all I had was my motorcycle and the clothes on my back. I didn't even have running water. I was tired, really tired and I had to pick myself up and move on.'

In Britain, Paul Southwell, leader of gay trio Handbag, was having similar issues: 'I think at that time there was a gay mafia in the music business, and they weren't ready for it. A lot of the record companies wouldn't touch us; it was very disappointing. The music industry was still run by gay men in the 1970s; there were a lot of influential gay people in the music industry and they wouldn't touch a gay act. That was the problem; they didn't want to be dragged out of the closet'.[21]

As innovative as it had been in the 1960s, by the mid-1970s, Motown had become a much more conservative conglomerate, with head Berry Gordy more concerned in pursuing his dreams of making it big in Hollywood than with pushing boundaries with his record releases. Yet surprisingly others within the Motown set-up were still interested in making changes. In 1975, the company issued a pair of genre-defining discs that announced to listeners that even though Hitsville USA may have moved from Detroit to Los Angeles, they still had their finger on the pulse. The Miracles grabbed most of the intention, when the track 'Ain't Nobody Straight In L.A.' (from the platinum-selling album *City of Angels*) issued in September 1975 caused controversy not just for addressing the subject but for insisting that 'homosexuality is a part of society,' but first off the block was a young gay man calling himself Valentino and his song, 'I Was Born This Way'. Billy Griffin, lead singer with the (now Smokey Robinson-free) Miracles, was happy that their record was proving such a hit in the discos. 'When I came to Los Angeles to live,' he told *Gay Times* 'I was exposed to homosexuality. I didn't give it another thought. I've male friends who are very close to me but I've never thought about having a homosexual relationship with them. At least not at present.' He admitted too that he was flattered by the attention the group were receiving from their gay audience: 'Oh yes, It's nice to talk to them. They come up and ask me to go to bed with them all the time. I've become a bit of a gay hero. It's cool. It makes me feel good.'[22]

Press advert for 'I Was Born This Way'

Covered two years later on Motown's main label by Carl Bean (and 35 years before Lady Gaga had a worldwide hit with the similarly titled and themed 'Born This Way'), 'I Was Born This Way' (backed with 'Liberation') was Valentino's first record and the only 45 issued (in both the US and the UK) on Gaiee records, set up by the song's co-author, a heterosexual woman by the name of Bunny Jones – a former beauty salon owner who had a number of gay employees: 'I named the label Gaiee because I wanted to give gay people a label they can call home,' she told *The Advocate*'s Christopher Stone. 'If they're really talented I want to break my neck for them'.[23] After the disc proved to be a hit on the dance floor, and after Bunny had sold a reported 15,000 copies from the back of her car, Motown bought the rights to her label and, more importantly her song.

Advertised as 'the first gay disco single,'[24] with its chorus 'I'm happy, I'm carefree and I'm gay; I was born this way,' the song was a hit in discos but failed to chart on either side of the Atlantic, and a proposed album failed to materialise. Reviewing the disc in February 1975, *Billboard* magazine's Tom Moulton noted that 'feelings on the disc are mixed, as some think it is offensive; others feel it is a great cut. Without a doubt it's a strong disco record.'[25] Born in Alabama in 1952, the man christened Charles Valentino Harris began his career as a dancer and actor, appearing on stage in *Hair* and on television in the crime drama *Madigan*. 'It's not a protest song,' he told *Gay News*' Jeff Grace. 'It's just music with a message. I'm not forcing anyone to turn gay and in the same way no one is trying to turn me straight.'[26] As Charles Valentino, he is still acting today, appearing in the 2015 movie *About Scout*.

Gay rights activist and singer Carl Bean, formerly with gospel outfit the Alex Bradford Gospel Troupe, was singled out by Bunny and Berry as the man most likely to make the song a hit, and that's exactly what he did in early 1978, and again when it was reissued in 1985 (and remixed the following year by Bruce Forrest and Shep Pettibone). An outspoken advocate of safe sex in the gay community, Carl is now an ordained minister: in 1982 he founded the Unity Fellowship of Christ Church in Los Angeles, an inclusive church that actively encourages LGBT members of the African American community. Motown also issued Thelma Houston's 'One Out Of Every Six', taken from the soundtrack of the gay-themed film *Norman . . . Is That You?*, and the company would continue to have a number of high-profile disco hits, including Diana Ross' parting shot to the label she had been with for two decades 'I'm Coming Out'. Composed by Chic's Nile Rodgers and Bernard Edwards and directly influenced by the LGBT scene, the song would become an anthem in LGBT clubs around the globe.

In Britain, discos popped up in every town and city. In a country where the economy was in freefall, where we were getting used to power cuts and three-day working weeks, disco offered people a place where they could – for a few hours at least – forget their troubles and just dance. 'I remember the first time I ever went to my first grownup club,' Jimmy Somerville told journalist Gregg Shapiro:

> I wasn't yet legally allowed to go to a club. I think they liked the look of me at the door. They took one look at me and thought, "What the fuck?" and they let me in. The club was split into two sections. The top part was general kind of chart music and down in the basement it was all disco. I got downstairs and the first thing I danced to was Donna Summer's "A Love Trilogy". As soon as I got on that dance floor I thought to myself, "There is no turning back! Who needs Toto? I've got disco"![27]

What began as an underground musical movement among blacks, Latins and the LGBT community had become a corporate, antiseptic behemoth, packaged for the masses, fronted by the rictus grins of the Bee Gees and their ilk: even Frank Sinatra and Barry Manilow, who had played piano for Bette Midler at the Continental Baths (but who remained tight-lipped about his sexuality for decades) released disco records. Disco went from a joyful expression of freedom among otherwise-repressed communities to closeted gay white men making anodyne black music for straight audiences. No wonder then that there would be a massive backlash that saw piles of disco records set on fire and – at Disco Demolition Night (12 July 1979) – 50,000 people fill Comiskey Park in Chicago to see radio DJ Steve Dahl use dynamite to explode crates full of them. But the final nail in the coffin was just around the corner, and if the hedonism of Studio 54 and the other hyperdiscos could be compared to the revelry that filled the cabarets of early 1930s Berlin, then the AIDS crisis would prove to be as devastating as the fall of the Weiman Republic, bludgeoning the life out of the party.

On 8 May 1982 at the St Vincent's Hospital in Manhattan, George Harris, better known as Hibiscus and one of the founding members of queer performance troupe the Cockettes, died from what was reported as 'a growing threat to the health of gay men: Kaposi's sarcoma and pneumocystis carinii pneumonia. Kaposi's sarcoma is not well understood by medical scientists, but one of the most frightening aspects of the disease is the swiftness with which it kills its victims.'[28] Gay men, sex workers and intravenous drug users had been dying of this mysterious disease in increasing numbers ever since, in 1969, 16-year-old Robert Rayford became the earliest North American victim (Rayford's death wasn't confirmed as being AIDS-related until 1987).[29]

Hibiscus was the first in a long line of musicians to die from the as-yet-unnamed disease. One of his closest friends, Jim Fouratt, an early member of the Gay Liberation Front, a participant in the Stonewall Riots and the former co-owner of New York's mammoth Danceteria nightclub, visited Hibiscus in hospital shortly before he died. 'No one wants to acknowledge that there is an epidemic in the gay community,' he told the *Gay Community News*. 'It seems that it's only when someone famous dies that people care'. Wearing glitter in his beard 35 years before it became 'a thing', Hibiscus left the Cockettes to set up gay cabaret act the Angels of Light before, in 1981, touring the US and Europe with glitter rock act Hibiscus and the Screaming Violets, which featured his sisters Jayne Anne, Eloise and Mary Lou and their brother Fred' Hibiscus was once famously photographed inserting a flower into the barrel of a rifle held by a soldier at an anti-war protest in Washington DC. Three days after Hibiscus died, *The New York Times* ran one of the first articles on the 'new homosexual disorder'.[30] They reported that 'the cause of the disorder is unknown' and that it had 'now afflicted at least 335 people, of whom it has killed 136'. Health practitioners briefly referred to the disease as GRID (gay-related immune deficiency) before, in July 1982 they gave it a new name: acquired immunodeficiency syndrome, or AIDS.

Studio 54 reopened in September 1981, with original business partners Steve Rubell and Ian Schrager initially contracted as consultants, but the heady days were over. Rubell, closeted for most of his life, died from AIDS-related complications in 1989. Although he would continue to enjoy hits on the dance charts, Sylvester would never have another mainstream hit after 1979. He died from complications arising from the HIV virus in 1988, leaving all future royalties from his work to San Francisco-based HIV/AIDS charities. His influence can still be seen today: Jimmy Somerville had a Top Five hit in Britain in 1990 with his cover of 'Mighty Real', and the fierce drag persona adopted by RuPaul (who later recorded with Elton John) echoes Sylvester's own outrageous performances. Patrick Cowley died in San Francisco on 12 November 1982, another early victim of AIDS; he was just 32 years old. After his success with the Village People, Jacques Morali continued to write and produce, co-authoring Eartha Kitt's hit 'Where is My Man' among others, before he too died from AIDS in 1991. When Donna Summer, disco's reigning queen, was widely quoted as saying that 'AIDS has been sent by God to punish homosexuals' she was forced to send a letter to leading gay rights group ACT UP to try to explain the 'terrible misunderstanding'.[31] Three years later, on 29 September 1992, Summer's former collaborator Paul Jabara, the actor and songwriter who had supported her on tour, duetted with her and wrote her hits 'Last Dance' and 'Enough is Enough' (and who also wrote 'It's Raining Men' for the Weather Girls) died at the age of 44 from AIDS-related complications after a long illness. The pioneering DJ Walter Gibbons, who spent much of his short life in turmoil trying to reconcile his fervent religious beliefs with his sexuality, died from AIDS-related complications in September 1994, aged just 40.

Dance music would continue, and the blueprint laid down by people like Cowley and Gibbons would lead to Hi-NRG, a harder dance music dominated by LGBT musicians and producers that, in turn, would be a direct influence on the Stock, Aitken & Waterman (SAW) Hit Factory sound. Dominating the UK singles charts for the second half of the 1980s, SAW's first entry was 'You Think You're a Man', a Top 20 hit for Divine in August 1984. Producer Ian Levine was a huge influence on the sounds being played in discos in the 1980s and 1990s: the self-confessed Northern Soul nut pioneered American-style mixing in British clubs and was the first resident DJ at London's gay super-club Heaven, the first British gay nightclub to seriously rival those of New York, which opened for business in December 1979. 'It became the biggest gay club in Europe virtually overnight,' Levine told *dmcworld* magazine in 2008. 'The first record I played was Dan Hartman's "Relight My Fire".'

After Heaven, Levine helped found Hi-NRG label Record Shack in 1983. Record Shack's first release, Miquel Brown's 'So Many Men, So Little Time', sold two million copies and topped the *Billboard* chart, and while Levine was at Record Shack the label sold 12 million records and had had major hits in almost every country in the world. He went on to work with Bronski Beat, Erasure and the Pet Shop Boys. Hartman, who scored a huge hit with 'Instant Replay' was gay but never came out. Sadly, the disco superstar died of an AIDS-related brain tumour in 1994. 'Dan was an elemental force of nature,' says his friend Tom Robinson. 'He was happy to come in and write with me and have songs that reflected the emotional truth of the time. It's such a tragedy that he died when he did and in the way that he did, but Dan Hartman was a real hero, gone but not forgotten.' Ian Levine suffered a crippling stroke in 2014 but is still working today and has been instrumental in helping the BBC restore or recreate many of its missing *Doctor Who* episodes.

Disco and Hi-NRG would spawn house, Chicago house (helped along by Frankie Knuckles, who relocated to Chicago club The Warehouse), acid house (Heaven's Mark Moore, one of the first UK DJs to play Chicago house in London, had Britain's first acid-flavoured Number One with 'Theme From S-Express'), techno, EDM (Electronic Dance Music), Italo house and Eurodisco – flashy, trashy and ridiculously catchy keyboard-led pop influenced heavily by Bobby O, Giorgio Moroder and the Eurovision Song Contest. The influence of Eurodisco was soon felt in America, where Moroder provided Blondie with their biggest US chart hit ('Call Me'), and Laura Brannigan would also hit Number One with a cover of the Italian pop hit 'Gloria'.

Perhaps the most celebratory of all gay dance acts – at least until the Scissor Sisters came along – was Sweden's Army of Lovers. Formed in 1987, the three members of Army of Lovers had all previously worked together in the group Barbie. Songwriter, philosopher and author Alexander Bard, singer and actor Jean-Pierre Barda and model and singer Camilla Henemark (aka La Camilla) clocked up more than 20 hits across Europe including the Number One hit 'Crucified'. The band's über-camp look, over-the-top videos and infectious beats kept the flag flying for gay disco during the early 1990s, and although they disbanded in 1996 after five albums together, they have reunited on several occasions over the last two decades. In 2013 they attempted to have their song 'Rockin' the Ride' chosen as Sweden's entry for the world's annual celebration of global campery, the Eurovision Song Contest.

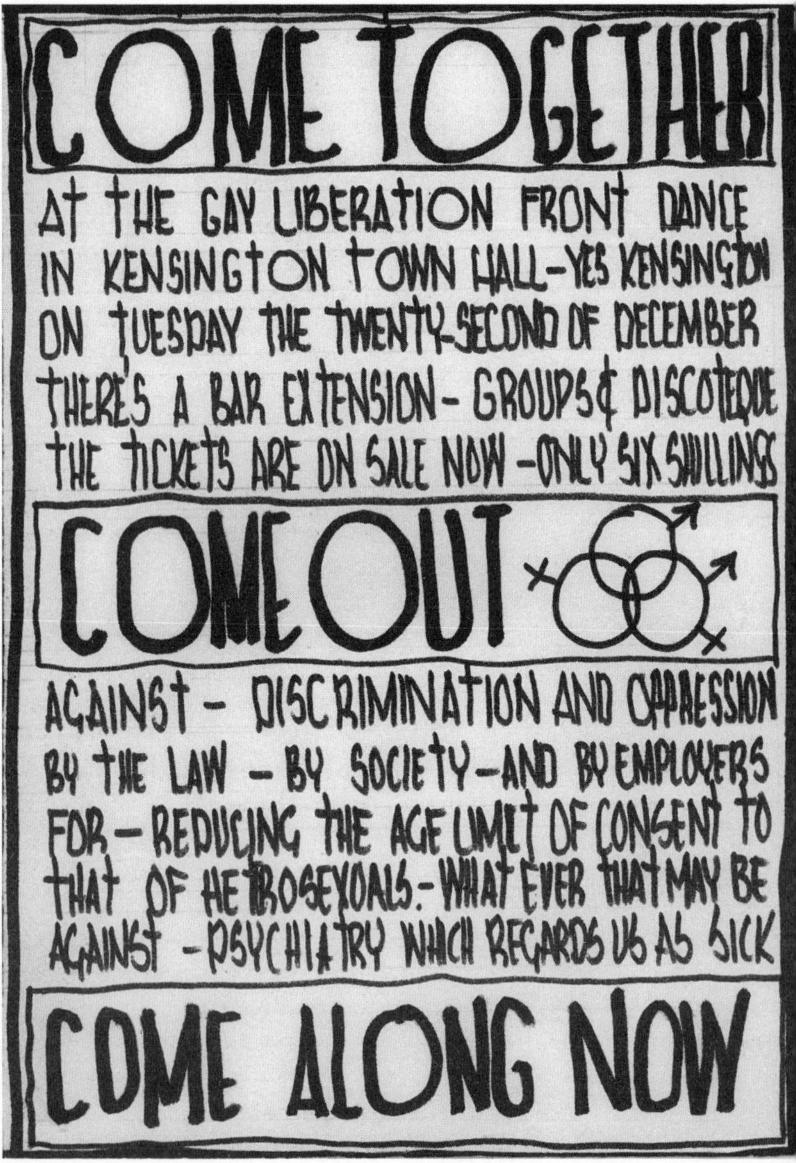

Poster advertising GLF fundraiser, 1970

CHAPTER 14

The 1970s: Political and Pink

'I have never and will never apologise for my sex life. Gay sex is natural, gay sex is good! Not everybody does it, but...'

George Michael[1]

The late 1970s was a time of political awakening on both sides of the pond. In Florida, former beauty pageant queen, singer and orange juice spokeswoman Anita Bryant was heading the political coalition Save Our Children, a right-wing Christian-led campaign to overturn local legislation that banned discrimination based on sexual orientation. Florida had long been vehemently opposed to LGBT rights: like the rest of America, during the 1950s and 1960s the city's officials had been closing down bars and enacting laws to make homosexuality and cross-dressing illegal, and until 1975 the government were legally empowered to refuse employment to anyone thought to be homosexual. Established in 1956, the Florida Legislative Investigation Committee (known as the Johns Committee) hunted down LGBT people in state employment and universities across the state and in 1964 published *Homosexuality and Citizenship in Florida*, more commonly known as the 'Purple Pamphlet', a highly inflammatory document that portrayed homosexuals as predators and a threat to children: 'many facets of homosexual practice as it exists in Florida today pose a threat to the health and moral well-being of a sizeable portion of our population, particularly our youth'.[2]

The title track to Conan Dunham's first album, *Tell Ol' Anita*, was a reaction to Bryant's campaign as well as a document of his own life. 'In 1977, I lost one of the greatest friends a guy could ever wish for,' he said. 'I stood by his bedside in a Sacramento hospital and watched day by day for over a month as he slowly slipped away. The doctors had no idea what caused his death. It wasn't until 1985 that AIDS was discovered to be the culprit.'

Of course, Dunham wasn't the first gay man to be affected by the politics of the time, although he would have been one of the many to indulge in a wry smile when Bryant lost a lucrative TV series on the back of the bad publicity she was acquiring.[3] Political activism has been central to the LGBT experience, from securing the right to vote through to decriminalising homosexual acts; from acknowledging the sacrifices others have made through to railing against the police and state for the way our community has been marginalised. And just as 'straight' songwriters from Woody Guthrie and Bob Dylan to Bruce Springsteen, Steve Earle and beyond have written about the injustices faced by the poor working man, so have LGBT singers and songwriters harnessed their political beliefs to shine a light on the plight faced by their own community. Spurred on by Save Our Children, in June 1977 more than 130,000 people marched to demand equal rights for LGBT people in the United States. 'Marchers waved protest signs attacking former singer Anita Bryant who led a campaign in Florida which saw the repeal earlier this month of a local law protecting the homosexual community. Homosexual leaders said the next step in their fight against discrimination would be to seek court injunctions ensuring equal job rights'. Peaceful demonstrations were also held in London, where around 1,000 turned out to march, and in Amsterdam 2,000 people marched through the city carrying banners that read 'Against the American witch-hunt on homosexuals'. In San Francisco, according to police estimates, more than 100,000 took to the streets; the gay community received heavy support from predominantly heterosexual organisations, including union members and black groups: 'The anger of that city's large homosexual community was heightened last week by the slaying of a homosexual city gardener by a gang of youths who shouted "faggot" as they stabbed him repeatedly'. A Pride parade along New York's Fifth Avenue attracted at least 25,000, and there were smaller demonstrations in cities including Los Angeles, Seattle and Denver.[4]

Then, in February 1978, something quite extraordinary happened: a song about the experiences of LGBT people made the British Top 20.

The song in question was 'Glad to be Gay', the highly charged coming out anthem issued by the Tom Robinson Band on their 1978 EP *Rising Free*. After years of oppression, LGBT people were angry, and they were no longer prepared to be quiet about it, as the demonstrations of the previous summer had proved. Robinson was an early supporter of Rock Against Racism, a campaign set up as a response to an increase in racial conflict and the growth of white nationalist groups such as the National Front in Britain. For the first time pop, rock, punk and reggae musicians were staging concerts with an anti-racist theme and providing a platform for LGBT artists who shared their political stance. Rock Against Racism was also seen as a direct reaction to the right-wing diatribe spewed by such bloated, dated stars as Eric Clapton. At a concert in Birmingham in August 1976 – two years after he had covered Bob Marley's 'I Shot The Sheriff' – Clapton famously ranted from the stage: 'stop Britain from becoming a black colony. Get the foreigners out. Get the wogs out. Get the coons out. Keep Britain white.'[5]

From a man who had spent a lifetime appropriating black culture, his support of Enoch Powell, who had warned of the dangers of immigration in 1968 with his infamous 'Rivers Of Blood' speech, was something of a slap in the face. Elvis Costello, also accused of racism after making drunken, ignorant remarks about James Brown and Ray Charles in 1979, apologised for his actions and worked with Rock Against Racism. Costello received death threats and the incident severely damaged his career in the United States. While recording his *Station to Station* album, David Bowie began to flirt with Nazi iconography and he was photographed – at London's Victoria Station – seemingly giving a 'heil Hitler' salute. When he told *Playboy* that, because of the way he used an audience 'Adolf Hitler was one of the first rock stars,' and that he condoned fascism, he was lambasted by the Musician's Union. He used an interview with *Melody Maker* in October 1977 to insist that he was not a fascist, that he was repelled by racism and that he had been 'out of my mind, totally, completely crazed' at the time.

Over the years, Clapton has been forced to downplay his outburst, and he has claimed that, like Costello, he, too, was drunk at the time,

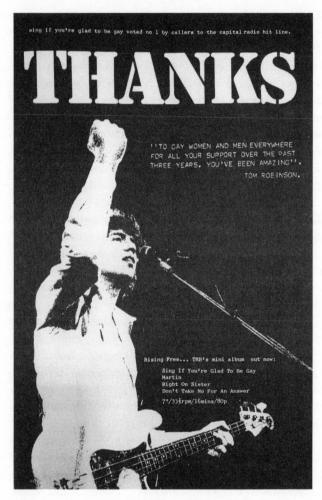

Press advert, 1978

but he has stopped short of an outright apology. When he played, as a guest of Dire Straits, at a concert to mark Nelson Mandela's birthday, organiser Jerry Dammers (of The Specials) offered him the chance to make a formal apology. 'You must be fucking joking,' Clapton told the anti-Apartheid activist.[6]

Robinson's gay hymn was preceded by an earlier, reggae-influenced song also called 'Glad to be Gay', issued to be sold at the 1975 Campaign for Homosexual Equality (CHE) conference in Sheffield, England. Only 300 copies of that disc were pressed: those copies not sold at the conference were later offered for sale through the pages of *Gay News*. 'The idea that we would press up this little thing and sell it at the 1975 conference,' Robinson explains. 'It was just like a bit of optimistic Pollyanna really; it was describing the world as we'd like it to be rather than how it was'. Shortly after Robinson and his group, the three-piece, folk-influenced Café Society, were signed to Konk Records by owner and Kinks frontman Ray Davies:

In those days it was very hard to actually get a foothold in the music industry. I had perfectly clear ideas about what I wanted to do musically, even though my ideas were misguided in some cases while I was trying to find my feet. I was trying all kinds of stuff in lots of different genres and styles and hadn't yet found my own voice. We did record a demo of "Glad To Be Gay" with Café Society – I wrote it when I was still in the band – but we never performed it live. The other guys in the band didn't have a problem with me being gay, but they did have a problem with being perceived as gay themselves because they were both happily married and had kids on the way. So they didn't want to be labelled with my thing when it wasn't their thing, but we did sing the Gay Switchboard jingle in three-part harmony at the shows we did, so there wasn't any kind of "closet-y" thing at all.

'Glad To Be Gay' was inspired by a series of police raids on gay pubs in London, specifically a raid on the Coleherne Arms in Old Brompton Road, Earl's Court that Robinson was caught up in. In June 1976 members of the Chelsea police force were blamed for using violence against LGBT revellers after one man, Roy Lea, was accused of the spurious offence of 'obstructing the footpath'.[7] Police raids on gay pubs and clubs were commonplace and many of them were turning increasingly violent. 'By the summer of 1976, the police in London were completely out of hand,' Robinson reveals. 'They were using the SUS laws – you could arrest anybody on suspicion of anything; if you had a suspicion that somebody might be about to commit a crime you could arrest them – and so black people in Notting Hill Gate and Brixton were being arrested for being black and in charge of a motor vehicle, stuff like that.' The year before, *Gay News* had reported on a series of raids on gay pubs and clubs in London. In one, three coach-loads of police made a midnight raid on the recently opened Rod's Club in Kings Road, Chelsea; the following night, a similar number of police – many of them in plain clothes – raided the Earl's Court pub Bolton's and searched drinkers and staff, ostensibly looking for drugs. Other popular LGBT drinking haunts, including Napoleons and Louise's (both in the West End) had been raided, and agents provocateur were being employed to entrap gay men in the popular cottaging areas of Hampstead Heath and Clapham Common. These raids caused outrage, and prompted people to question whether the Metropolitan Police were involved in a witch-hunt against gay men.[8]

'They were able to swan in and make easy arrests because they figured that gay men in that climate and at that time were very unlikely to contest an arrest in court,' Tom recalls of those days. Paul Southwell, of the gay rock trio Handbag, remembers those days well. 'I was there when it was raided,' he recalls. 'We used to stand outside while that was going on. It was a bloody nuisance, standing outside while the police went in and did whatever they were supposed to be doing – which was fuck all really!'

It wasn't just the police in Britain who were causing trouble: in Barcelona, during a demonstration sponsored by the Gay Liberation Front of Catalonia in June 1977, police fired rubber bullets into the crowd of 4,000 people.[9] A series of protests in Australia during June and July 1978 saw over 70 people arrested and over 1,000 people join a protest 'which organisers described as the biggest demonstration of its kind in Australia'.[10] A further 110 were arrested after a demonstration in Sydney in August, during Australia's Fourth National Homosexual Conference – several of those arrests coming after gay rights demonstrators clashed with anti-abortion supporters: 'we are not spouting pretty opinions,' one commentator wrote in the University of New South Wales' student periodical *Tharunka*. 'We are fighting for our right to exist. The arrests demonstrate that the "toleration" of dissent has ended, and we can expect to be blatantly jailed for our political activism.'[11] Australian rock singer

Carol Lloyd, formerly of rock band Railroad Gin and now recording with her own Carol Lloyd Band, was an out-and-proud lesbian whose career in music began with her band playing gay venues. She would spend the rest of her life fighting for respect and equality for LGBT people: 'We are the police that protect our kids and keep our streets safe. We are the doctors and health care workers that deliver our babies and keep us healthy. Blue collar, white collar, we are all the same and we all have love and we all deserve respect.'[12] Australia's original rock chick, with three Number One singles and two Number One albums to her credit, Carol passed away after a long battle with pulmonary fibrosis on 13 February 2017.

In New York, a violent attack by police on a black gay bar on West 43rd Street left 12 men hospitalised. 'About 10 cops came in, They had guns drawn and their clubs out. They told people to step away from the bar and they started throwing bar stools around,' one of the men in the bar told *Gay Community News*. 'They told everyone to stand facing the wall at the back of the bar and they just started beating people. They were shouting that two cops got jumped in Times Square and that we were to blame'.[13] A few months before the attack, the offices of Boston's *Gay Community News* had been destroyed in a suspected arson attack.

As if dealing with the police wasn't enough of a headache, in January 1978, 20 fascist thugs from the National Front 'went berserk' and smashed up the Royal Vauxhall Tavern, one of London's longest-established gay pubs – and one of the few still running today.[14] These attacks helped to politicise LGBT people: a group calling itself the Earl's Court Gay Alliance was set up to 'protect the local gay community'[15] and they would inspire LGBT people to become active and vocal members of the Anti-Nazi League, established by the Socialist Workers Party (SWP) in 1977 to oppose the rise of far-right groups in the United Kingdom.

Relations between Tom Robinson and Ray Davies quickly turned sour: Robinson was harangued by Davies on the Kinks' 1977 song 'Prince of the Punks' and Robinson took to the pages of the music press to castigate Davies. The two would make up, but not until long after a legal battle saw Robinson released from his contract and Davies no longer receiving publishing royalties from Robinson's compositions. 'Although we didn't end up having a terribly happy experience, if it hadn't been for Ray Davies taking us under his wing and giving us a chance to make a record – without his help and without his patronage – I definitely wouldn't have got in to the music industry,' Tom admits today:

> Even if it showed me things to avoid in the future, it still showed me what the terrain was like, so I do owe him a huge big debt of gratitude. Punk with its DIY ethic worked much better for musicians breaking through at that time. People like Elvis Costello, Ian Dury and the Blockheads, Graham Parker and the Rumour, Nick Lowe, lots of musicians of my generation took from the punk ethic the idea of taking charge of your career and how you were going to approach it, and punk rock came along at exactly the right time for us to be able to get away with calling the shots ourselves.

Leaving Café Society, and Ray Davies, behind him Robinson formed the Tom Robinson Band (TRB):

> I wasn't particularly keen for us to be identified as a 'gay' band because we weren't! I was the only one who was gay and we supported gay rights, all four of us, but we also supported racial equality and feminism. There were far bigger issues than just law reform for gay men at that time. It was all part of a bigger struggle: you either live in a fair and free society or you don't, so it was part of a political awakening that came through being gay and realising that you were seen as the scum of the earth by the authorities, and then sitting round with other people who had a common cause and who were also seen as the scum of the earth by the authorities. I formed TRB without any members: I went out and started performing as the Tom Robinson Band with musicians from other bands . . . and the eventual permanent members joined one by one. They were coming into a band that already existed and . . . it was part and parcel of the deal: if you want to be in my band you're going to be singing "Glad To Be Gay"!

Signing with EMI was a much happier experience for Tom than his earlier encounter with Konk: 'EMI gave us a big hand in how it was packaged, what the album sleeve looked like, which songs went on the record and all the rest of it. That was a very different experience from being complete beginners like when we were starting out with Café Society'.

Then, on 17 November 1978, Dan White murdered Harvey Milk.

Just seconds earlier White, a former member of the San Francisco Board of Supervisors, had used his police-issue revolver to kill Mayor George Moscone. Frustrated by Moscone's refusal to reappoint him to his seat on the Board (White had resigned on 10 November citing financial pressure), he took his gun into City Hall and, avoiding metal detectors by sneaking into the building through a first floor window, proceeded to hunt down Moscone and demand his reinstatement. During the ensuing heated argument, White pulled out his gun and shot Moscone several times. He then went to find Harvey Milk. Milk and White had clashed several times in the preceding 12 months, and Milk had lobbied against White's reappointment to the Board. Finding Milk near to White's old office, he ushered him inside, closed the door and opened fire.

Known as the 'Mayor of Castro Street', the popular and charismatic Milk had been the first openly gay person to be elected to public office in California. At the time of his election, it was estimated that as much as a sixth of San Francisco's 660,000 population was LGBT,[16] and the city's 130 recognised gay bars had a turnover of $14 million a year.[17] Milk, a vocal advocate for LGBT rights, had strong support within the city; it's no wonder then that Anita Bryant saw San Francisco as a modern-day Sodom and Gomorrah.[18]

The assassinations, the vigils held in Harvey Milk's honour, and White's subsequent trial all made headlines around the world. Milk had feared that his high profile would make him a target to assassins: a year earlier he had recorded a message for his supporters to be released after his death:

> I know that when a person is assassinated after they have achieved victory there are several tendencies, One is to go crazy in the streets, angry and frustrated, and the other is to have a big show and splash, a great service. Naturally I want neither. I cannot prevent anybody from getting angry, or mad or frustrated. I can only hope they'll turn that anger and frustration and madness into something positive, so that hundreds will

step forward, so that gay doctors come out, the gay lawyers, gay judges, gay bankers, gay architects. I hope that every professional gay would just say "enough", come forward and tell everybody, wear a sign, let the world know. Maybe that will help. These are my strong requests, knowing that it could happen, hoping it doesn't . . . and if it does I think I've already achieved something. I think it's been worth it.[19]

During the Pride march in London in 1980, a number of arrests were made, and ten men faced charges for varying misdemeanours including obstruction and minor assault. One man was charged with possessing an offensive weapon: a rusty prop meat cleaver that he wore as part of his headdress. But police oppression and attacks from right-wing hate groups were not the only issues facing the LGBT community. Britons were starting to become aware of a new disease that was decimating the LGBT community in the US and, on 4 July 1982 Terrence Higgins became one of the first people known to die of an AIDS-related illness in the UK. Very quickly, AIDS education became the number one priority within the international LGBT community. Governments, when they did respond to the growing epidemics, did so with scare tactics. The LGBT community, especially the younger members, needed someone (or something) more relatable.

When the London Gay and Lesbian Youth Video Project required some original music for an educational documentary they were working on, they pressed a young Scotsman by the name of Jimmy Somerville into service. The film, *Framed Youth*, went on to win the British Film Institute's Grierson Award for Best Documentary in 1983, and Jimmy and his friends Steve Bronski and Larry Steinbachek (who sadly passed away in December 2016), then all sharing a squat in the London borough of Brixton, went on to form electronic trio Bronski Beat. In the film Jimmy (credited as Jimi) tells his coming out story; his mother understood but he had not yet plucked up the courage to tell his father. It could almost be the plot of a song . . .

Somerville, Bronski and Steinbachek were openly gay and insistent that their music would reflect this. Signing a recording contract with PolyGram subsidiary London Records after only nine gigs, the band's debut single 'Smalltown Boy', the tale of a gay teenager leaving his family and fleeing his hometown for the big city, was a huge hit, peaking at Number Three in the UK Singles Chart, going to Number One in Italy, Belgium, and the Netherlands and making the US Top 50. Accompanied by a hard-hitting video, this was the first time that the reality of being a young gay man in Thatcher's Britain had been laid bare to the mainstream audience, an audience that would soon be asked to vote to re-elect a government with a strong anti-LGBT stance. 'I'm really aware of the impact that ['Smalltown Boy'] still has today on a younger generation and what it means to people and how it can tap into people. It's a very emotional and evocative plea, a cry from the heart. It's honest and raw and it still has the power to move people. That's special and I'm very proud to have been a part of Bronski Beat and to have created that.'[20] If anyone had any questions about the band's political leanings, then debut album *Age of Consent* made it pretty clear on which side of the fence they stood on: the record's inner sleeve (removed from the US release) featured a list of the different international ages of consent for gay sex. Two months after the album came out, Bronski Beat headlined *Pits and Perverts,* a fundraising gig held in support of striking miners, organised by Lesbians and Gays Support the Miners (and immortalised in the hit movie *Pride*). The following year, trade unions brought their banners to London's 1985 Pride march, and at the Labour Party Conference a motion to support equal rights for gay men and lesbians was only carried because of the votes cast by the National Union of Mineworkers and their allies.

On leaving Bronski Beat, Somerville formed the Communards with multi-instrumentalist Richard Coles, who Somerville had met when both were members of the London Gay and Lesbian Youth Video Project and who had appeared on a number of Bronski Beat recordings. Somerville, along with Tom Robinson, Billy Bragg and Paul Weller, helped form Red Wedge, a musical collective that supported the Labour Party and tried to encourage first-time voters to use the power of the ballot box to fight injustice: five years later, musicians in America would form the similarly left-leaning Rock the Vote. 'We supplied the camp element,' Somerville told *Q* magazine. 'We particularly wanted to do it in order to provide Red Wedge's gay visibility. Labour in those days still had a very cloth-cap

mentality and we wanted to help change that. We were very out and
proud then.' Mixing Somerville's love of disco with their political ideals,
'the Communards recorded just two albums, *The Communards* and *Red,*
and had several hit singles before splitting, and although nothing was
said at the time, Coles later revealed that he had caused the schism. Coles
had always struggled with his sexuality, attempting suicide in his teens,
and he did not take well to fame – indulging in all of the excesses that
come with stardom. In a moment of madness, he told Somerville that
he was HIV-positive; he wasn't, and to compound the deceit their close
friend, gay rights activist Mark Ashton (whose life is portrayed in the film
Pride) had recently died of the disease. The pair would not speak again
for years. Lost, Coles turned to religion, cleaned up his act and is now
an ordained minister in the Church of England, and a vocal advocate for
LGBT reform in the church. He is also married, to David Oldham, an
Anglican priest.[21] As well as enjoying a successful solo career, Somerville
has remained politically active, supporting equal rights, and is a fierce
critic of government plans to dismantle the welfare state.

HANDBAG

Publicity photo, c. 1975

CHAPTER 15

The Aggressive Style Punk Rock

'I'd always placed a premium on privacy. I didn't feel
comfortable identifying myself as a gay musician. I wanted
to be a musician and if I happened to be gay, that's great
too ... But Spin led with a saucy byline, something like "I'm
not a freak". I was like, "Oh, of everything I said, that's what
you're gonna put on the cover?" That's not me. I'm not a
freak. I'm a normal person'

Bob Mould[1]

Y ou can trace punk rock's roots back to the mid-1960s, to the proliferation of US garage bands which sprang up in the wake of the
Beatles, the Rolling Stones and the other British Invasion groups. Just as
the bands that inspired them had been encouraged to pick up a cheap
guitar by Elvis, Buddy and the 1950s skiffle boom, so the next generation
of nascent pop stars was spurred into action by the new sound emanating
from Liverpool and London.

Pop was old, boring and, above all, expensive. Young people who
wanted to make a noise could not afford the couture costumes, the
overblown banks of keyboards they saw Rick Wakeman and Keith
Emerson playing, and the ostentatious twin-necked electric guitars. No
one had the money: unemployment was at a post-war high thanks to the
economic recession of 1973–1975. They could not afford the gongs and
tubular bells favoured by Queen's drummer Roger Taylor, nor could they
buy (or did they want) the lights, smoke machines and other pyrotechnics

that most of the bands they saw on TV or in concert employed. Punk was back-to-basics music that anybody could get involved in, played on cheap, inherited or (very often) stolen equipment. Punk looked for inspiration to the raw energy of the New York Dolls, Iggy Pop and the Ramones. It was a reaction against commercialism, against singles charts filled with novelty records. Punk rejected fashion and conformity, although that, in itself, became a fashion statement of sorts. Objectified and vilified in the media, punk's halcyon days did not last long and the 'movement' (such as it was) quickly became commercialised, yet the reverberations are still being felt today.

'Seeing the Sex Pistols live was just a wake-up call,' says Tom Robinson. 'I didn't like it at the time; it was against everything that I believed about music, about how you had to be respectful to the audience and play in tune, sing in tune, and play your nice, melodic songs in time. But it was clear: it telegraphed a message that things were changing and it was time to wake up and smell the coffee.'

It seemed that wherever the Pistols played (when they were allowed to play, that is: many early shows were cancelled by local councils afraid of this new punk rock corrupting the local youth), they changed lives. Paul Rutherford explains:

We used to go to Eric's, to watch Liverpool bands like The Deaf School. Then the Sex Pistols played and we went to see that gig and that was just amazing. I went with Pete Burns, Lynne his wife, Jayne Casey, and it was from there that the punk thing really took off. I was asked if I could sing. Budgie happened to be the drummer in this group [the Spitfire Boys]; they just said "come along, have a sing song with us" and that was it. That was the lead-in for me. I was just a teenage kid, just 17. I didn't think I could be a musician until punk came along. The punk thing made it easy: it gave you the power to try these things you'd never tried before; to stand on a stage, to pick up an instrument or attempt to sing . . . you didn't have to be good. That was how you discovered that you had an innate sense for making music.'

Tom Robinson found that being gay wasn't an issue in the world of punk rock:

It was very gender-blurred and sexuality-blurred; everything was up for grabs ... After about 1979 punk rock became like a uniform, where you had to have a Mohican haircut, you had to have a leather jacket, you had to have bondage strides, chains and dog collars around your neck, but in 1976 when I saw the Sex Pistols a lot of the audience were wearing ordinary clothes. The people who were obviously 'punk' were making their own uniforms ... it was inventive: lots of ripped clothes, spattered with paint. It was much more DIY then, and along with the variety of clothes there was a variety of attitudes.

Handbag, described as 'Britain's first openly gay rock group,' began playing together during the glam rock boom, but found more acceptance as part of the capital's burgeoning punk scene. The trio built a steady following, playing a mix of punk gigs and Gay Lib benefits. 'Handbag came together with my coming out,' Paul Southwell, Handbag's bassist, singer and chief songwriter recalls:

I moved to London in 1971 when I was 20 and I came out. I joined the London gay scene and took to it like a duck to water! In 1971 the big thing was Gay Liberation, with Gay Lib dances, the Campaign for Homosexual Equality and that type of thing. We formed Handbag at about the same time. We didn't form Handbag as an out gay band, it's just that because we came out that was the tag we got. We didn't form Handbag to say anything politically or break any stereotypes down, it just so happened that it all came together. It just seemed logical; there was nobody else. We did lots of gigs. Denis Lemon and *Gay News* got behind us and we got some decent press. I don't know if it actually helped or hindered us in retrospect, but we did loads of gigs and then we got signed by Jet Records.

David Arden had discovered the trio – Southwell, Dave Jenkins and Alan Jordan – playing at London's Speakeasy and signed them to his father Don's company, home to the Electric Light Orchestra and Ozzy Osbourne (David's brother-in-law), in 1975. 'Everybody was trying to sign us,' says Paul, 'but we went with Don Arden, which was the worst thing we could have done. Even then he had a reputation for being a bastard! But they were offering nice things and we wanted to believe that they were nice people; we were a bit naïve really!' Their record label certainly wanted to make the most of the gay tag. 'Once upon a time you couldn't call a person black, but now they call themselves black people,' David Arden told *Beat Instrumental* magazine. 'Handbag are, well, queers! Queens! Call them homosexuals and they'd hit you with their handbags! Handbag are 100 percent gay. They are three "chaps" who look fabulous, whose music is outrageous . . . right out in the open. They slightly resemble Cockney Rebel and Roxy Music and they play all the right places, like the Gay Lib balls'.[2] While it's certainly true that both Roxy Music and Steve Harley's Cockney Rebel made the most of glam's camp aesthetic for their initial releases, by 1975 both bands had eschewed this for a more traditional rock look. Arden was looking backwards whilst everyone else was racing off in to the future. Southwell, thanks to his close association with the Gay Liberation Front, was becoming more and more political, and he wasn't afraid to speak his mind. Playing what Paul described as 'intelligent New Wave,' Handbag recorded an album for Jet, but the company dropped them and the record remains unreleased to this day.

'That was really disappointing,' Southwell notes:

> One minute you're being told that you're going to be launched and that you're going to be a star, and then suddenly it's "you've lost all your songs, we're not going to release you, goodbye!" We were back to square one. That put us back another two years, because to write an album, to actually get 10 or 15 songs together takes ages. It was incredibly disappointing. If Jet had gone with Handbag and put that album out there would have been so much publicity that even if it only sold 5,000 copies it still would have broken ground. Why go to all that trouble, spend all that money and then do nothing? I tried to find out why they wouldn't do it, but of course nobody would ever tell me. You would hear rumours, whispers, but I never found out why they wouldn't put it out.

Several venues refused to book the band because they were unashamedly gay. 'The initial idea was just to be outrageous,' says Southwell. 'We were kids; we were kind of punks if you will, and we just wanted to be a bit outrageous. We'd seen *The Rocky Horror Show* which had just opened in London, and thought, "oh, that's interesting," and we began to dress outrageously at gigs and of course that got us more attention and it also gained us some notoriety, which was a good thing and a bad thing because a lot of places wouldn't have us. A lot of venues didn't want to know'. Back in America another group, Mickey's 7, had also been inspired by *The Rocky Horror Show*, issuing *Rocket to Stardom* (which was marketed as 'the first gay sex rock LP') in 1975. The five members of the band were pictured on the cover flying through the air on a giant phallus. Mickey had his own fan club which promised, among other delights, 'intimate fotos and movies' for your bucks: the 7 in their name stood for seven inches . . .

Ronnie Scott's, a club better known for live jazz but which was looking to diversify, turned down a booking from Handbag because their manager, Jennifer Bell, was female. 'That's what it was like then. Eventually we did get a gig at Ronnie Scott's, so we did eventually break the doors down.' They played London's regular punk venues: the Roxy, Dingwalls, the Marquee and the Hope and Anchor, as well as hundreds of other paid gigs and just about every benefit they were asked to. Handbag entertained the inmates at HMP Wandsworth on two occasions; in 1975 they became the first out-gay band ever to perform in a British prison.

'I don't know if I ever really saw us as punk, but once the Sex Pistols had taken over the world if you weren't punk then you didn't get any work. So Handbag had to be punk, and that's when we started playing the Roxy and all the punk venues.'

Then, in 1978, an album appeared. 'That had nothing to do with me,' Southwell laughs. 'We'd signed to Jet, we'd done the album, we'd been released from the contract and lost everything, then about two years later we got another offer of a recording contract with a company called Circle International, which was owned by a guy called Reg McLean.' McLean also ran another label, Safari Records (a different company to the one that later signed Toyah and Wayne County and the Electric Chairs) and a publishing company, Voyage Songs. 'Reg said, "I've got a record label, would you like to do an album for me?" We didn't sign anything . . . and then suddenly this record came out in Italy! It should have been called *Handbag: Snatchin'*, but it came out as *Snatchin'* by

Handbag, they got it wrong . . . and they were the demos. They weren't supposed to be released . . . but anyway it came out and then, lo and behold, about a year later it was re-released under the title *The Aggressive Style Punk Rock* – punk had taken over the world, and the Italians must have thought, "this is a bit punky, we'll market this"! I would never have let that go out, with someone on the cover with a swastika on his face, but I had no control over it.'

Feeling that the band's name was holding them back, Handbag became Dino, Daz and the Machine, and continued to play the occasional benefit before splitting after five years at the coalface. 'We did about half a dozen gigs as Dino, Daz and the Machine,' Southwell explains, 'And then Dave and I did a handful of solo gigs at places like the Gay's the Word bookshop as a duo just to make some money . . . then it slowly faded out'. Southwell donated two Handbag songs to be used on the soundtrack for a movie, *David is Homosexual,* and he issued a self-financed solo EP, but with little promotion and even less availability (you could buy a copy from Gay's the Word or from Paul himself) it, too, went nowhere. 'By this time it was the early 1980s,' says Paul ruefully. 'I was coming up to 30 . . . Tom Robinson had had a hit, loads of my contemporaries were making money, and we weren't . . . so I decided to call it a day.' Southwell, now 65, now lives with his husband in Australia. Although officially retired, he still plays bass and sings with his current band, Timeslider. 'Looking back, I don't suppose that any of the gay songs would have been hits,' he says. 'However, we shall never know. I do think that Handbag did break down some barriers and I do think that we would have been remembered as the first gay rock band had they had the guts to launch us. But we shall never know. It might have just died a death like Jobriath. I think one of the problems was that because we were gay, gay people were coming to see us expecting us to play disco music. We didn't; we weren't really playing the right kind of music for a gay audience.'

Handbag may have been the only gay punk band in London at the time, but several other acts had LGBT members in their ranks, some out, some of them stubbornly closeted. Still gigging today, Chelsea were one of the many 'also-rans' of the British punk scene, never quite hitting the big time but building up a respectable following which has continued to support them for the last 40 years. Formed in August 1976 after former gay porn actor Gene October placed an advert in *Melody Maker*, they made their live debut two months later, supporting Throbbing Gristle (led by the genderfluid Genesis P-Orridge) under the name LSD. That incarnation didn't last out the year, but October's band mates went on to form Generation X, guitarist William Broad changing his name to Billy Idol in the process. Gene put together a new line-up, and convinced René Albert, the manager of Chaguaramas (better known as *shagger-amas*), a gay club in London's Covent Garden, to convert the venue into the capital's first live punk rock venue, The Roxy. Ironically, the headline band on the opening night was Generation X. The Roxy quickly became a favourite haunt of the city's punk and new wave musicians and fans. Chelsea made their recording debut in 1977, issuing two singles on the independent Step Forward label; their eponymous album followed in 1979. Kit Lambert, formerly co-manager of the Who, produced their third single, 'Urban Kids'. Henry Rollins, who cited October as an early influence, wrote about his less-than-friendly encounters with his idol in his 2004 book *Get In the Van*. Chelsea's line-up has changed constantly over the years, with October the band's only permanent member.

Paul Southwell and Handbag may have been denied the chance of fame, but Pete Shelley would become the face of LGBT punk as the country's first out-bisexual rock star. Shelley met Howard Devoto at Bolton Institute of Technology in autumn 1975 after Devoto advertised for like-minded musicians to join him in a new group which became the Buzzcocks (from the phrase 'it's the buzz, cock!') The band played their first gig in July 1976 at Manchester's Lesser Free Trade Hall; a few weeks before the pair had been the promoters of the Sex Pistols' epoch-defining but poorly attended gig at the same venue. Rather fittingly, this was the venue that had witnessed the newly electrified Bob Dylan being called 'Judas' by a disgruntled folk music fan. The Buzzcocks' debut release, the *Spiral Scratch* EP, was issued in early 1977, but singer Devoto left immediately afterwards, forming the band Magazine. Shelley stepped up as main vocalist and he and his cohorts signed to United Artists, issuing 'Orgasm Addict' as their debut major label release. Openly bisexual, (the single was reviewed in *Gay News* in November 1977, with the writer making reference to Shelley's sexuality), he saw punk as a leveller. 'It's a climate where people are accepting that everybody's different,' he told *Gay News*. 'Everyone wants to express themselves in that way that suits them best. And they are questioning things like the family and love.'[3]

The punk scene had rubbed along with London's LGBT crowd since its inception. SEX, the shop run by soon-to-be Sex Pistols' manager Malcolm McLaren (the group's name was dreamed up by McLaren to help promote the boutique), sold fetish and bondage wear to London's gay rubber and leather scene for years before it became the favoured hangout of Chrissie Hynde (who also worked the cash register), Adam Ant, Siouxsie Sioux and the rest. Before the Roxy there were no 'punk' clubs for the bands to play, but haunts such as the predominantly lesbian Louise's in Soho provided an early home for Siouxsie, the Sex Pistols and members of the Clash and the Slits. Boy George was a regular at Louise's, often joined by the openly bisexual Steve Strange; the pair – disaffected punks still in their teens who left the scene when they became sick of being gobbed on – would go on to reign supreme at the Blitz Club and introduce the world to the New Romantics. Strange (born Steven John Harrington on 28 May 1959 in Caerphilly, South Wales) began his performing career in the Malcolm McLaren-managed punk band the Moors Murderers, before forming Visage with members of the Rich Kids and Magazine. He and fellow Visage member Rusty Egan began organising 'Bowie nights' at Billy's, a subterranean nightclub in Soho, before moving to the Blitz in Covent Garden in 1979, where the soundtrack was a mix of glam rock, punk and electronica – and you were not coming in unless Steve liked the look of you. Many of the Blitz Kids formed their own bands, including Boy George, Steve Strange, Tony James (London SS, Chelsea, Generation X and Sigue Sigue Sputnik amongst others), Martin Degville (Sigue Sigue Sputnik), Jeremy Healy (Haysi Fantayzee) and all of the founding members of Spandau Ballet. Prior to scoring several chart hits with Visage, Strange and several other Blitz Kids (sadly not George) appeared in the iconic video for David Bowie's Number One hit 'Ashes to Ashes'.

London's gay and lesbian pub and club scene provided LGBT musicians with places to both perform and meet like-minded artists. The Coleherne, regular haunt of Tom Robinson and Paul Southwell, was also a favourite of Faebhean Kwest, guitarist with the London-based punk band Raped: 'I go to the Coleherne a lot but I'm bisexual and being bisexual means you have a 100 percent pick of people to take home,' he told *Gay News*.[4] Raped, who issued the EP *Pretty Paedophiles*, courted a gay image but despite songs detailing their experiences on the capital's gay scene, the group didn't go down well with LGBT audiences or with feminists, who objected to the name. In 1979 the band morphed into the more acceptable Cuddly Toys; their first single, 'Madman' was a cover of a song written by David Bowie and Marc Bolan shortly before Bolan's death in September 1977. Originating in Hull, and named after a William S. Burroughs novel, Dead Fingers Talk were led by a singer glorifying in the ridiculous name Bobo Phoenix, but born the slightly more prosaic Robert Eunson. Legend has it that the moniker was gifted to Rob by Genesis P-Orridge when they were both at Hull University. Dead Fingers Talk's regular live set featured the songs 'Nobody Loves You When You're Old And Gay', 'Can't Think Straight' and 'Harry', the tale of a particularly vicious attack on a gay man with a pair of garden shears which, guitarist Jeff Parsons explains, was 'like a piece of theatre. It was a comment on the anti-gay attitude which we didn't understand or agree with. Our way to tackle it was to satirise it. But a lot of people took it the wrong way. We had a good gay following who understood it but a lot of writers and audience thought we were advocating queer-bashing.'[5]

Raped and Dead Fingers Talk's sets were full of anger and violence, but Pete Shelley's songs were spiky, honest and usually sexually ambiguous; the band's biggest hit, 'Ever Fallen in Love (With Someone You Shouldn't've)', was purposefully, pointedly non-gender-specific (the earlier 'Love You More' was about a girl Shelley fell for who worked in Woolworth's). In February 1978, he announced that he was working on a gay opera which 'will last about 12 hours'[6] When the band split in 1981 after three Top 30 albums and 10 hit singles (they would reform in 1989), Shelley embarked on a solo career, issuing the completely unambiguous single 'Homosapien' which, of course, was banned by the BBC for containing an 'explicit reference to gay sex'.

Other punk bands were also exploring society's attitude towards LGBT people and sexuality in general: Elton Motello's 'Jet Boy Jet Girl', a song often confused with Plastic Bertrand's 'Ca Plane Pour Moi' (both songs use exactly the same backing track) is about the violent fantasies of a 15-year-old boy whose sexual relationship ('he gives me head') with an older man comes to an end when the older man rejects the teenager for a girl. 'Gay clubs were the one place, perhaps the only place, where we could go and meet,' says Shelley. 'It was very hard to go somewhere and not cause a fuss. But you could go in a gay club and no one would bat an eyelid about how you were dressed. They were used to the more flamboyant aspects of what punk was. And punk was more inclusive, there was room for girl bands that were actually saying something rather than standing there looking pretty.'

To label Jayne County an icon is to do her a massive disservice: she's been part of the fabric of LGBT life in the United States since the late 1960s, but it's for her outrageous stage antics and her punk anthem 'Fuck Off' that she will be forever venerated by punk fans. Born Wayne Rogers in a small rural community in Georgia with parents from a strict religious background, Wayne was in New York and took part in the Stonewall Riots. He shared a home with various members of Andy Warhol's Factory and appeared on stage in Warhol's *Pork*, played at legendary punk haunts CBGB's and Max's Kansas City and shared a management company, MainMan, with David Bowie. County later claimed that Bowie appropriated his image: 'MainMan gave me money so I could create ideas so Bowie could steal them, whitewash them, and use them for himself to create a fake version of what I was trying to create,' she told Gus Bernadicou of *Punk Globe* magazine in 2012. Shortly after issuing a 45 honouring Max's 40th anniversary (accompanied by his then-band the Backstreet Boys) and an appearance in court for attacking another singer with a microphone stand, County moved to London.

His third 45 release, 'Fuck Off', catapulted Wayne County to punk superstardom. Although issued on a tiny label with next to no distribution, County and his new band the Electric Chairs became stars of the British punk scene and 'must have played every fucking toilet in England'. County signed to Safari Records and 'Fuck Off' was reissued as part of the *Blatantly Offensive* EP in 1978. Cross-dressing on stage since the early 1970s, by 1980 Wayne had become Jayne full-time. Although Jayne has taken female hormones and had some minor plastic surgery,

Wayne County and the Electric Chairs Blatantly Offenzive EP, 1978

according to her 1996 autobiography *Man Enough To Be A Woman*, she has never had a total sex change: 'I'm used to my little friend by now, and quite honestly I'd rather save up the money for a facelift,' she says. County is the embodiment of the whole punk ethos and, as such, is the godmother of Queercore.

At the beginning of the 1980s, a similar scene emerged in America, where gay clubs that were struggling financially provided space for local punk bands. These bands fused punk and LGBT politics into a new musical movement. Queercore (also known as homocore) explores themes including prejudice, gender identity and the mainstream's disapproval of the LGBT community. It was in this environment that bands like the

Germs, the Dicks and Hüsker Dü, which included two gay men (Bob Mould and Grant Hart) in its three-man line-up, flourished. The Germs, led by the bisexual singer Darby Crash (born Jan Paul Beahm), had been banned from every club in Los Angeles because their shows would inevitably end in violence. Crash's sad, short life ended when he intentionally overdosed on heroin, aged just 22, a day before John Lennon was assassinated. The Germs were a huge influence on Nirvana, and Crash's bandmate Pat Smear would end up playing second guitar for Kurt Cobain's group as well as playing with Dave Grohl's post-Nirvana outfit Foo Fighters. 'Being gay wasn't shocking in the punk scene,' according to hit producer and Big Black frontman Steve Albini.[7]

This aggressive, primal music counters the out-and-out homophobia from such acts as the Meat Shits, whose leader Robert Deathrage freely admits that he wrote music to upset 'certain faggots in the music scene [who] succeeded in poisoning impressionable minds with their pro-gay/ anti-sexist propaganda'.[8] The Meat Shits demonstrated outright hostility and hatred towards the LGBT community; the message coming from The Angry Samoans was harder to decipher. Were they for real or was this all some pathetic joke from a couple of music critics old enough to know better? It's hard to take any band seriously when their set list includes songs such as 'They Saved Hitler's Cock' and 'My Old Man's A Fatso', but the lyrics are peppered with so many references to gays, faggots and queers that you have to wonder if they are trying to overcompensate. The original lyrics to their infamous 'Homo-Sexual' (from their 1982 album *Back From Samoa*) included the line 'Homosexual – I'm one too' (changed on the released version to 'Homosexual – we love you'). The lady doth protest too much, methinks, as Shakespeare might have put it, as The Angry Samoans' original lead guitarist Bonze Blayk (born Kevin Eric Saunders) underwent gender reassignment and is now living as a lesbian. She officially changed her name to Bonze Anne Rose Blayk in August 2011.

Queercore began with punk legends the Dicks – led by out-gay singer Gary Floyd. Formed in Austin, Texas in 1980 by Gary, Buxf Parrott, Pat Deason and Glen Taylor, the band's first single 'Dicks Hate The Police' was released that year and created quite a stir, not only for the sentiment but for the gigs the band played which would often see Floyd wearing make-up and looking not unlike Divine. Born in 1952 in Arkansas but raised in Palestine, Texas where his family moved when he was four years old, Floyd was drafted in 1972 but avoided being sent to Vietnam by registering as a conscientious objector. Instead he spent two years working as a janitor in a mental hospital and, after his 'discharge', he moved to Austin. Floyd caused quite a stir; he could often be seen around town, usually accompanied by his close friend Randy 'Biscuit' Turner (leader of Texas punk band Big Boys), looking like extras from a John Waters or Derek Jarman movie. 'Being queer has never been a big deal to me,' he said. 'If people don't like it, they can fuck off!'[9] Texas didn't know what to make of them, but Jello Biafra, leader of incendiary punk band the Dead Kennedys, was enthralled: Biafra told Raoul Hernandez of the Austin Chronicle that the first time he saw Floyd perform, he was amazed to discover 'a 300-pound communist drag queen who can sing like Janis Joplin'.[10] In the song 'Ode', from their 2004 album *Complete Discography*, the queercore band Limp Wrist paid homage to Randy Turner and Gary Floyd, along with many of the other pioneering gay punks in the hardcore scene who had paved the way.

In 1983, Floyd left Texas for San Francisco. Taking on new members Tim Carroll, Sebastian Fuchs, and Lynn Perko (formerly of all-women band The Wrecks), a second version of Dicks began to play together and record. Their album *Kill From The Heart* was released in 1983 on SST Records, followed by *These People* in 1985 on Biafra's Alternative Tentacles label. The group disbanded in 1986, and Floyd embarked on a new project with Dicks drummer Lynn Perko, the more blues-influenced Sister Double Happiness, who released several albums for SST and Sub Pop, before Floyd struck out on his own with a new group Black Kali Ma. In 2007, he formed the short-lived country band Gary Floyd and The Buddha Brothers, reflecting his new-found spirituality. He now records solo and occasionally plays with the original Dicks.

As had been the case with the British punk scene, queercore also offered space for all-woman and woman-led bands. Canadian group Lesbians on Ecstasy (who took their inspiration from the feminist music of the 1970s and mixed queercore with electronic music to create their own unique sound) and Washington's openly lesbian band Team Dresch, led by fanzine editor and DIY record label head Donna Dresch. San Francisco's outspoken lesbian collective Tribe 8 kept a tattered rainbow flag flying for early 1980s feminists, were signed by Biafra to Alternative Tentacles and joined the Women's Music circuit. Singer Lynn (sometimes Lynnee) Breedlove outraged some of the older members of the band's audience with her on-stage antics, frequently performing shirtless and wearing a strap-on dildo. Breedlove now tours the States solo, performing spoken word and stand-up comedy, and runs Homobiles, an LGBT non-profit ride sharing service in San Francisco. Queercore kept on through the 1990s, with Pansy Division (the four-piece formed in 1991, consisted entirely of out-gay musicians and toured regularly with punk/alt-rock band Green Day), Scott Free (who, over the years, has embraced punk, hip hop, dance and even musicals), Chris Cochrane's Suck Pretty and Extra Fancy taking the lead. Once again, Jello Biafra provided a home for Pansy Division, but in 1996 Extra Fancy became one of the few queer-core bands to ever sign to a major, when Atlantic picked up their album *Sinnerman*. The marriage would be short-lived: Atlantic dropped them just weeks after releasing the album, unable or unwilling (according to frontman Brian Grillo the company reneged on its 'commitment to breaking barriers')[11] to break the band into the big time. 'I cannot write songs pretending that I'm singing to a woman,' said Grillo, 'Because I like guys and I like having sex with guys'.[12]

Advertisement for Boy George's guest-starring turn
in the *A-Team* episode 'Cowboy George', 1986

CHAPTER 16

The 1980s: Small Town Boys

'We've never said anything about our sex lives to the
newspapers or to magazines, and we don't intend to'

Neil Tennant[1]

After getting sacked from his job looking after the cloakroom at
the Blitz Club, things were looking pretty dire for George Alan
O'Dowd. His band, In Praise of Lemmings, was going nowhere and
neither was he – until, that is, the former supermarket shelf-stacker
came to the attention of former Sex Pistols manager Malcolm McLaren.
McLaren was in the process of forming a new band, Bow Wow Wow,
which consisted mainly of an Adam-less Adam and the Ants. McLaren
had visualised a new pop character by the name of Lieutenant Lush being
part of that set up, and it was as Lush that George joined the former Ants
and their 14-year-old singer Annabella Lwin for a short while.

But George (born in London on 14 June 1961) was never cut out to
be someone's backing singer: from his earliest days, lip-synching along
to his mother's Shirley Bassey records, he knew that he was going to
be a star. Through friends he met first bassist Mikey Craig and then
drummer Jon Moss, and the idea of forming a band of his own started
to take shape. Moss had been in punk group London (managed by
Simon Napier-Bell) before becoming sticksman in the Damned for a
few months in late 1977 and early 1978, after original drummer Rat
Scabies walked out following sessions for their second album *Music
For Pleasure*. After the Damned he had briefly played in Adam and the

Ants – before they were poached by McLaren to become the backline of Bow Wow Wow.

Choosing the name Culture Club as it reflected the different ethnic backgrounds of the four members, although their first two 45s barely touched the UK singles chart the third, 'Do You Really Want to Hurt Me' went to Number One in most European territories and Number Two in the US, New Zealand and several others. The song's success was propelled by an appearance on *Top of the Pops* equally as incendiary as Bowie's infamous 'Starman' performance had been a decade earlier. Although the group's debut was as an eleventh-hour replacement for Shakin' Stevens, Culture Club would quickly achieve international superstar status, and Boy George himself would become a cultural icon. The band's *Top of the Pops* performance generated tabloid headlines that focused on George's androgynous look and his sexual ambiguity. No one then knew that George and Jon were involved in their own tempestuous relationship.

The timing was perfect. Not only was Britain ready for a new breed of pop star after the glamour-less punk and new wave years, but in America a new station, Music Television, or MTV, had recently started broadcasting and was desperate for film clips to fill its 24/7 music policy. British bands were old hands at making music videos; these short film clips had been a staple since the mid-1960s, and soon a second British Invasion took a grip, with Culture Club, Duran Duran, Adam Ant, Eurythmics, Ultravox and many more clogging up the US charts. Referred to as a 'gender-bender' in the press on both sides of the pond, George's refusal to discuss his sexuality made him seem more a delightful eccentric than a threat to the nation's youth. When he famously revealed that he would 'rather have a cup of tea than go to bed with someone,'[2] there was little reason to disbelieve him. Soon shops were filled with Boy George rag dolls, his face was on a thousand magazine covers and his records were hits everywhere. George's fame was at its zenith when, in February 1986, he appeared as a guest star on the hit US action-drama *The A-Team*. There was no stopping him. He was, as *Rolling Stone* put it, 'the harmless, lovable windup doll of pop, a cartoon-like fantasy figure who could sing like a white Smokey Robinson and trade glib one-liners with Joan Rivers and Johnny Carson. He was the pop star whom everyone from your grandmother to your little sister could like.'[3]

The 1980s were all about success and excess. Acquisition and avarice, it was all good and nowhere was the glamour and the greed celebrated more than on high-camp television blockbusters *Dallas*, *Dynasty* and *Falcon Crest*. But the early 1980s were also terrifying: gay men were dying from AIDS and no one outside of the LGBT community seemed to care. It wasn't until Hollywood A-lister Rock Hudson became ill that the rest of the world began to show an interest. By the start of 1985, more than 5,500 people had died from the disease in the US but the government had done nothing to try to tackle the crisis. When Hudson, in Paris seeking treatment, collapsed at the Ritz Hotel, his publicist turned to Rock's old friend Nancy Reagan, then America's First Lady, for help in getting the ailing star admitted to a military hospital. She refused. Her husband, whose economic policy had virtually crippled the country, put the blame squarely on sexual promiscuity, telling Philadelphia's College of Physicians that 'all the vaccines and medications in the world won't change one basic truth: that prevention is better than cure. Let's be honest with ourselves. AIDS information cannot be what some call "value neutral" After all, when it comes to preventing AIDS, don't medicine and morality teach the same lessons?'[4]

Hudson's predicament was compounded on 31 July, when *Channel 7 News* reporter Harold Greene suggested that it was 'possible that Rock Hudson transmitted AIDS to actress Linda Evans during love scenes' on *Dynasty*. The show's producer, Aaron Spelling, was incandescent. 'All that can be said about Rock Hudson has been said, yet they go on and on. We're just not going to become part of this witch-hunt. It's taken all this time for gays to come out of the closet. And now this is driving them back into the closet.'[5]

The ignorance was, perhaps, understandable – and Hudson's star status made him fair game for the media, yet his death in October that year shocked America and finally focused attention on HIV and AIDS. 'All at once the disease was linked with someone everybody knew and accepted as practically a member of the family,' *People* magazine wrote two months after his death:

Almost overnight, stimulated by massive media coverage, the US came to a consensus: AIDS was a grave danger to the national health, and something had to be done about it — fast. Since Hudson made his announcement, more than $1.8 million in private contributions (more than double the amount collected in 1984) has been raised to support AIDS research and to care for AIDS victims (5,523 reported in 1985 alone). A few days after Hudson died, at 59, on Oct. 2, 1985, Congress set aside $221 million to develop a cure for AIDS.[6]

Although the pop charts were reflecting a shift in attitude towards LGBT performers, the world of entertainment had not changed that much, and AIDS was now becoming an issue in the UK too. The government would finally take action in 1987 with its 'Don't Die of Ignorance' campaign, but as late as 1985 it was still acceptable for British comedians to demand that gay performers be 'banned from the entertainment business' and for AIDS to be the stick that the establishment beat us with. In an outspoken interview with the *Sunday People*, Bernard Manning described Rock Hudson as 'evil' for passing the disease on to 'his pansy partners like he was distributing death pills' and made disparaging comments about performers including John Inman, Larry Grayson, Leonard Sachs, Kenny Everett, Peter Wyngarde and Boy George.[7]

Not only was the HIV/AIDS propaganda being spread by the government incredibly homophobic, but in 1986, reacting to a *Daily Mail* story about the book *Jenny Lives With Eric And Martin*, available in a school library run by the Labour-controlled Inner London Education Authority, the powers that be claimed that 'there is no place in any school in any circumstances for teaching which advocates homosexual behaviour, which presents it as the "norm", or which encourages homosexual experimentation by pupils'.[8] During the 1987 election campaign, the Conservative Party distributed posters claiming that the Labour Party wanted similar books to be read in schools (according to Jill Knight of the Conservative pressure group The Monday Club) 'to little children as young as five and six,' which contained 'brightly coloured pictures' that 'showed all about homosexuality and how it was done,' and 'explicitly described homosexual intercourse and, indeed, glorified it, encouraging youngsters to

believe that it was better than any other sexual way of life'.[9] A year later
the government enacted Section 28 (also known as Clause 28), stating
that a local authority 'shall not intentionally promote homosexuality or
publish material with the intention of promoting homosexuality' nor
could it 'promote the teaching in any maintained school of the acceptability of homosexuality as a pretended family relationship'. The knives
were out.

The introduction of Section 28 galvanised the disparate gay rights
movement in the UK into action, with groups including Stonewall,
OutRage! and Schools Out (originally The Gay Teachers Association)
campaigning against the act, and pop stars recording songs in protest. Agitprop band Chumbawamba, keen supporters of LGBT rights,
released the single 'Smash Clause 28!', and Boy George's solo single 'No
Clause 28' was a damning indictment of the government's plans put to a
thumping dance beat. If anyone in Britain was still questioning George's
sexuality, they were in for a rather rude awakening. In June, at the behest
of Stonewall co-founder Ian McKellen, the Pet Shop Boys appeared at
the anti-Clause 28 benefit *Before The Act* at London's Piccadilly Theatre,
performing their recent Number One hit 'It's A Sin'.

Formed in London in 1981 by *Smash Hits* staff writer Neil Tennant
and Blackpool-born architecture student Chris Lowe, the pair had been
making music together for a couple of years before Tennant was sent
to New York to interview The Police: as luck would have it, he and
Sting had been to the same school. Neil took advantage of the situation, taking a demo tape the pair had worked up to Hi-NRG producer
Bobby Orlando (aka Bobby O), who had already achieved some success
producing Divine. Tennant was a huge fan: 'Meeting Bobby O was an
even bigger thrill than meeting Sting. I have admired his production
techniques with people like Divine as well as on his own records for a
long time.'[10]

Bobby O would produce their first single, a prototype of their giant hit
'West End Girls'. In all they would record 11 tracks with him – including
early versions of hits 'Opportunities (Let's Make Lots of Money)', 'Rent'
and 'It's a Sin'. Released by Epic in the UK, this early version of 'West
End Girls' failed to chart. The duo extracted themselves from their deal
with Bobby O (Bobby had apparently turned down working with Dead

or Alive in favour of the Pet Shop Boys)[11] and signed to Parlophone in Britain, formerly home to the Beatles and part of the giant EMI corporation. Their second single for the company, a re-recorded 'West End Girls', quickly shot to the top of the singles charts. Leaving Bobby O behind cost them $1 million,[12] but EMI had a monster hit-making machine on its hands.

Strange as it may seem now, in the 1980s the majority of Britain's (resolutely closeted) LGBT pop stars were unmoved, at least publicly, by the crisis in our hospitals, our schools and in our daily lives. At a time when people could still be sacked from their job for being gay or lesbian, and when pubs, clubs and other businesses could refuse to serve you simply for being gay, the community needed a figurehead, someone that could appeal to both the gay and straight communities – yet very few people wanted to stick their head above the parapet. Not Freddie Mercury, not Elton John and not George Michael. It was up to Tom Robinson, Jimmy Somerville, Boy George and the Pet Shop Boys to educate people. In America, the situation was worse, with a capella act the Flirtations, fronted by gay activist Michael Callen, one of the very few groups brave enough to put the fight against HIV and AIDS at the very heart of their set: the group also appeared in the film *Philadelphia*, performing an a cappella version of 'Mr. Sandman'.

When Elton and George Michael did decide to record together, the end product was the resolutely straight (and sexist) 'Wrap Her Up': neither of these two future gay icons was ready to risk harming their respective fan bases. Elton, who in 1984 married German recording engineer Renate Blauel, had 'come out' as bisexual to *Rolling Stone* in 1976, an act that was perceived to have damaged his career in the States, with letters calling John a pervert being sent to the magazine and many so-called fans refusing to buy his albums. It's no wonder that he felt he had to conform. Besides, he was also dealing with an onslaught of lies peddled by British tabloid *The Sun*, which splashed everything from a supposed predilection for rent boys to animal cruelty (in the September 1987 'story', 'The Mystery of Elton's Silent Dogs') across its front page: Elton sued, was offered £1 million in damages and roughly half as much again in costs by *The Sun* before the case (just one of a total of 17 lawsuits Elton filed against the paper around that time), got to court and received a full apology. Editor Kelvin Mackenzie and owner Rupert Murdoch lost not only a considerable amount of money and face: the paper also suffered a substantial slump in sales. The British public were becoming sick of the relentless bullying.

'Elton was out,' Tom Robinson, who worked with John on the albums *21 at 33* and *The Fox,* insists. 'He came out as bisexual and he subsequently fell in love with Renate and married her. That wasn't him going back in to the closet, he genuinely was sexually attracted to her.' Four years after marrying, the couple split and John came out as gay. 'I honestly didn't think it would hurt my career,' John revealed to *The Today Show* host Matt Lauer in 2012. 'It did a little bit. In America, people burned my records and radio stations didn't play me'. Yet after his marriage failed and *The Sun* coughed up it became increasingly obvious that the public were ready to accept him for what he was.

Bernard Manning and his outdated cohorts would have had a fit had they met Sleazy Christopherson and Neil Andrew Megson, aka Genesis P-Orridge, two men who made art from uncompromising sexual imagery and unsettling industrial sounds. The genderfluid Genesis (they prefer 'third gender') was once vilified by the British media as 'the most evil man in Britain' for their fixation with death cults, fascist iconography and occultism. The two (with Chris Carter and Cosey Fanni Tutti) would form Throbbing Gristle, invent industrial rock music and spawn first Psychic TV and then Coil, the first out-band to be based around a gay couple: Peter 'Sleazy' Christopherson and his boyfriend (and former member of Psychic TV) John Balance. Coil were at the forefront of British avant-garde music and were resolutely, unapologetically, in-your-face gay with a capital G. The front cover of the band's debut album featured a male backside framed by an upturned crucifix; they provided the soundtrack to two Derek Jarman films and contributed the music to the documentary *Gay Man's Guide to Safer Sex.* As well as working with P-Orridge in both Throbbing Gristle and Psychic TV, Christopherson was a designer and photographer, and one of the three partners of the album cover design group Hipgnosis, who produced iconic artwork for albums by Pink Floyd, Genesis, XTC and many others. For all of their chutzpah, Coil were only ever going to appeal to a fringe audience – unlike their sometime collaborator Marc Almond.

'Soft Cell came from punk,' says Almond (born Peter Mark Sinclair Almond in Southport on 7 July 1957: he changed his name to Marc in tribute to his idol Marc Bolan), 'Punk made me realise that I didn't need to be brilliant at playing instruments or making art – I could just create. It was about free expression.'[13] After meeting keyboard player David Ball whilst they were both studying at Leeds Polytechnic, he formed Soft Cell in 1977. A self-described 'garage band that used electronic instruments instead of guitars,' their initial, self-funded EP release *Mutant Moments* garnered interest from several record companies and the pair signed to Some Bizzare, the record label set up by Billy's DJ Stevo Pearce, issuing the single 'Memorabilia' and a track, 'The Girl with the Patent Leather Face' on the compilation *Some Bizzare Album*, which also featured future hit-makers Blancmange, The The and Depeche Mode – the group that would beget Erasure. 'Memorabilia' wasn't a hit, but their follow-up, 'Tainted Love' (originally recorded by Bolan's girlfriend Gloria Jones), proved to be a massive international success. 'Tainted Love' was the biggest-selling record of 1981 in the UK and was quickly followed by their debut album, *Non-Stop Erotic Cabaret*.

Almond has gone on record to say that, as Soft Cell were climbing the charts, he was being encouraged by his PR team to play the straight card: 'I was informed by my press department that they had come up with "girlfriends" for me,'[14] yet *Non-Stop Erotic Cabaret* was easily the most outlandish album to grace the British charts at that point. It's resolutely seedy and dark, and with its S&M overtones and colourful lyrics, the record is fiercely, defiantly queer. If Marc's TV debut, dressed from head to toe in black, festooned with bangles and wearing more eyeliner than any of the female artists on that week's episode of *Top of the Pops* hadn't been enough of a clue, then you'd have had to have been blind and deaf to ignore the gayness of *Non-Stop Erotic Cabaret*. Marc's look and obvious feyness were quickly lampooned (on hit British comedy series *Not the Nine O'Clock News* in 1982): taking the piss out of homos was still a-OK by the BBC.

Also signed to Some Bizzare, Coil covered 'Tainted Love' to raise funds for HIV/AIDS charity the Terrence Higgins Trust in 1985, issuing what would be the earliest fundraising record for AIDS awareness in the UK. Almond appeared in the video and would collaborate with Coil on their first two full-length albums, *Scatology* and *Horse Rotorvator*. Balance died on 13 November 2004, after he fell from a second-floor landing at the home he shared with Christopherson near Weston-Super-Mare. Christopherson relocated to Thailand, and died there in his sleep just over six years after his partner, on 24 November 2010.

Having already acted as the lynchpin to two major chart acts in the space of three years – Depeche Mode (who, like Coil and Soft Cell, had started their recording career at Some Bizzare) and Yazoo (with Alison Moyet), in 1983 keyboard player Vince Clarke was working on one-off collaborations with singers including former Undertone Feargal Sharkey and Paul Quinn. Andy Bell had long been a fan of Clarke's work, and answered an ad he placed in *Melody Maker* looking for new vocalists. 'We'd auditioned about 40 people and Andy was the 43rd,' Clarke told Paul Strange of *Melody Maker*. 'He was like a breath of fresh air'.[15] 'Electronic music just seemed to flow in my blood, especially *Dare* by The Human League,' Andy says. 'I had always loved "soft" punk, ska, electro and Motown ... the weirder the better sometimes: Nina Hagen, Lene Lovich, Siouxsie, X-ray Spex, Japan, Donna Summer and of course the Pretenders and Blondie – my favourite band.' Unlike Vince, Andy had no previous experience in the music industry, his singing experience having been limited to a church choir in his native Peterborough and fronting local band The Void before recording a one-off single ('Air of Mystery') with friend Pierre Cope as Dinger (the name taken from Andy's nick-name: "Dinger" Bell). 'It was pretty nerve-wracking, auditioning for Mr. Clarke but he was very much a hero of mine. I felt his music was so left field and unique, and I somehow felt that we belonged together. It took me quite a while to overcome being overly enamoured with him. I wasn't surprised I was chosen but I think I was a bit taken aback by how naïve I was to the whole business.'

His association with Clarke wasn't instantly successful: Erasure's first three singles all flopped in the UK, however their fourth – 'Sometimes' – peaked at Number Two in 1986 and began a string of major hits for the duo. It would take another couple of years before the band saw any kind of success in America, but they quickly became major stars in Europe and Asia. Bell was open about his sexuality from the off: 'There was no dif-ficult decision. I remember having "discussions" with my then-partner/

manager who thought it was a bad idea to come out! I was like "no way! It's important and I'm doing it anyway"!'

Dressed in feathers, plastered in glitter or wearing ABBA-esque pant-suits, Bell brought a camp sensibility to Erasure that was at odds with the more strait-laced Depeche Mode or Yazoo (who, renamed Yaz in the States, scored four Number Ones in the US dance charts) and, unlike those other acts the relationship has endured. Erasure have now been together for more than three decades, although Bell's brand of campery hasn't always been to everybody's taste: 'One gay San Francisco paper voted that I should go back in [the closet],' he once laughed.[16] Bell has continued to talk openly about being a gay performer, telling Billboard that 'my real obligation to the world is to show people that I am a happy person who happens to be gay. To me, it comes down to how you feel deep down inside. You can't change the world if you feel miserable and hate yourself.'[17] As he says today: 'You often felt there was a correlation between the media catching on that you were gay and radio airplay going down. Especially in the US. You knew about all the others who were getting away with it but hey, I'm glad I did it in an honest way. Our shows in North and South America were like Gay Pride parades!'

AIDS had decimated the disco scene, and the disease would have far-reaching effects on all forms of entertainment, with movie stars, painters, photographers, dancers and TV personalities felled by the scourge. Like Soft Cell, Department S had their roots in the punk scene and, like them, were also influenced by the emergent Blitz Kids. Lead singer Vaughn Toulouse (born Vaughn Cotillard in July 1959) was, like Marc Almond, also a huge Bolan fan: the band's early live set featured a cover of the T. Rex hit 'Solid Gold Easy Action'. Toulouse was openly gay and he named his band after the camp cult TV series of the late 1960s starring out-gay actor Peter Wyngarde. The group, which evolved from an earlier punk band Guns for Hire (who issued on 45 on Korova), released their first single, 'Is Vic There?' in December 1980, first on Demon and then – in March 1981 – via RCA. It became their biggest hit, reaching Number 22: the follow-up, 'Going Left Right', peaked at 55.

Department S called it quits in 1982. Toulouse went to work as a DJ under the name Main T and was signed to Paul Weller's Respond label, enjoying a minor hit with the Weller-composed 'Fickle Public Speaking'. Vaughn became part of Weller's extended Council Collective, writing sleeve notes for the Style Council (as The Cappuccino Kid) and appearing on their miners' benefit release 'Soul Deep'. Toulouse died in 1991 from complications of AIDS. AIDS proved to be no respecter of international borders, either. Federico Moura, leader of hit Argentinean pop band Virus, died from AIDS in 1988, just a year after he had come out. Brazilian songwriter Cazuza (Agenor de Miranda Araújo Neto), whose band Barão Vermelho (Red Baron) played the inaugural Rock In Rio festival in January 1985 with Queen, the B-52s and others, died on 7 July 1990. Cazuza, who was openly bisexual, gained a huge amount of media coverage as someone living with and fighting against AIDS, and his openness helped to change public perceptions and attitudes about HIV/AIDS prevention and treatment in South America.[18]

Klaus Nomi had drawn some attention already, performing as dancer and backing vocalist for Bowie's perverse appearance on the American late-night live television sketch show *Saturday Night Live* in December 1979. Bowie, naturally, got all of the press for the oddball performance that saw him perform 'TVC15' in a skirt and climaxed with a puppet Bowie whipping his puppet penis out. For one song, 'The Man Who Sold The World', Bowie wore an immobile costume inspired by Tristan Tzara's 1921 Dada play *The Gas Heart* – which would, in turn, inspire the costume worn on stage by his acolyte Nomi.

Or was Bowie the acolyte of this opera singer from outer space? Certainly it was Nomi that Bowie was keen to work with, spotting him and performance artist Joey Arias in New York's Mudd Club where, as Arias recalled, 'David exclaimed "Oh my God, Klaus! I just got back from Berlin and everyone is talking about you. We have to get together".'[19] Whichever way it worked, Nomi was so impressed with Bowie's Dada costume that he adapted it for the huge plastic tuxedo that he would wear on the cover of his first album, in videos and on stage.

Born in Bavaria in 1944 (as Klaus Sperber), Nomi gave his first performances in Berlin, singing operatic arias in the city's gay discos before moving to New York in 1972 and settling in the artistic, bohemian East Village. He acted, sang, appeared at the alternative cabaret New Wave

Vaudeville and earned money by working as a pastry chef at the World Trade Center. His startling, mime-like make-up and his unique sound brought together elements of pre-war Berlin cabaret, Bowie's showmanship and the world of opera. He was truly extraordinary; one reviewer claimed he sounded 'like Pinocchio on helium'. When he first sang opera at the New Wave Vaudeville, the audience did not believe that he was not miming to a recording. It is no surprise that Bowie loved him, nor that Morrissey would also fall under his spell. Klaus Nomi seemed to have come from another world. 'Some people think I'm not human,' he once revealed[20]. 'My mother visited me two years ago ... she was so shocked. I had black fingernails and black lipstick, and she said: "You look like the Devil – I can't believe it." I said "Mother, I AM the Devil!" That was enough for her.'

Signed to Bowie's record company, RCA, Nomi's eponymous debut album appeared in 1981 and included a mix of original songs, operatic arias and contrary covers of Chubby Checker hits; 'I always loved rock n' roll,' he told the *Soho Weekly News*. 'I bought an Elvis Presley EP, *King Creole*. I hid it in the basement, but my mother found it. She went to the record store where I bought it and exchanged it for Maria Callas'

Klaus Nomi in concert, 1981

operatic arias. Well I was very agreeable to that too. I like each as well as the other'. It was an intriguing mix, but something that was almost impossible to market successfully. A second album, *Simple Man*, was simply odd: the standout track (and lead single) was an insane elec-tropop version of 'Ding Dong The Witch Is Dead' from *The Wizard of Oz*. Nomi's musical career, which showed so much promise, was cut short when he was diagnosed with the still virtually unheard-of AIDS. Though his health was fading fast, his handlers kept him on the road, milking their cash cow even as his body failed him. He died in New York on 6 August 1983, at the age of 39, just three days after Jobriath had succumbed to the same disease; one of his last performances was as backing vocalist on his friend Man Parrish's 'Six Simple Synthesisers'. In 2007 the remnants of an opera that Klaus had worked on for a number of years appeared, reworked, as *Za Bakdaz*. Andrew Horn's excellent documentary film about the Klaus Nomi phenomenon, *The Nomi Song*, appeared in 2004.

Klaus Nomi had caused a small sensation when he appeared on the British TV show *The Old Grey Whistle Test* in 1982, but by that time audi-ences were becoming used to seeing the bizarre on their TV screens; Bowie's 'Ashes To Ashes' had introduced people to Steve Strange and the Blitz Kids, Soft Cell had already racked up a Number One single, and in Liverpool – undergoing a musical renaissance with New Wave acts Echo and the Bunnymen, the Teardrop Explodes and others – a new band with an very unusual name had recently formed. That band, which took its name from a headline about Frank Sinatra making movies, would cause shockwaves in the music industry that are still being felt today.

'Relax', by Frankie Goes to Hollywood, was the first single by a band with openly gay members to top the UK charts; Soft Cell's 'Tainted Love' had hit the Number One spot in 1981, but at the time of release singer Marc Almond had not come out (even though he would do so later). Both lead vocalist Holly Johnson and backing singer Paul Rutherford were out and proud, and the song's video – set at a Bacchanalian orgy inside a gay nightclub where the band were surrounded by S&M acts, water sports and cross-dressers – left little to the imagination. Shocking, offensive and gloriously hedonistic, 'Relax' was famously banned from the BBC by

Radio One DJ Mike Read, an act that propelled the single to the Number One spot where it stayed for five weeks. 'I don't regret what I did,' Read told *Jamming!* magazine in May 1984. 'From the outset, the band were very open about what they were about and the simulated sex scenes on their video made it clear that "Relax" was about gay sex'. 'It's only dirty if you have a dirty mind,' Johnson told Judy Cantor of the Associated Press. 'You really have to have a mind like a sewer'.[21]

During its run as the nation's biggest-selling song, the nation's broadcaster refused to play it: *Top of the Pops*, the most-watched music show of the day finally relented in time for their Christmas edition, but while 'Relax' was Number One it would not be shown. Within a few months 'Relax' had sold six million copies. The single would stay in the British charts for a year.

It was not the first song to be banned from the airwaves, nor would it be the last, but the ban helped Frankie become a massive, menacing, multi-platform phenomenon. In 1984, you couldn't move without bumping in to someone wearing a FGTH t-shirt (everything from the straightforward *Frankie Say Relax* to the incendiary *Frankie Say Arm the Unemployed*) or go to a club without hearing the latest remix of 'Relax', 'Two Tribes' or their cover of the Edwin Starr hit 'War'. The newspapers may have been shocked, but the kids dancing in the discos and queuing outside the doors of the record stores to buy their debut album *Welcome to the Pleasuredome* didn't care a jot about Holly's homosexuality. It was all about the music – and if that music happened to upset your parents, or a bore like Mike Read, then all the better. Johnson and Rutherford were part of a new generation of LGBT performers who were not going to apologise for being 'different'.

The first band since fellow Liverpudlians Gerry and the Pacemakers to score a Number One hit with each of their first three singles ('Relax' also stole the top spot from fellow Liverpudlian Paul McCartney), Frankie broke records and broke rules. 'The word "gay", at least in the record biz, is no longer pop poison. In fact gay has cachet – witness the success of the Smiths and Bronski Beat'.[22] Frankie were different: Johnson and Rutherford being so outrageously open about their sexuality should have limited their appeal, but it had entirely the opposite effect. Frankie Goes to Hollywood records were bought by New Wave fans, by indie kids, by rockers and by the people who bought dance records. The group appealed to both gay and straight audiences. They courted controversy in a way no act had done since the Sex Pistols eight years earlier. Breaking big in a vacuum caused by novelty acts like Black Lace and Renee & Renato (in exactly the same way that punk filled the void created by Brotherhood of Man and the Bay City Rollers), Frankie were all kinds of dangerous.

It may have appeared that Frankie were the post-punk Monkees, a group manufactured by studio wizard Trevor Horn and PR man Paul Morley, but Johnson and the rest of the band had been around for a number of years before hitting the big time: Johnson had been a member of Liverpool punk band Big In Japan and had issued a pair of solo 45s; Rutherford had been a member of local synth band Hambi and the Dance and, before that, the Spitfire Boys with future Banshees drummer Budgie. 'You don't start thinking you're going to be famous; it's just a bit of fun,' says Rutherford. 'It's not born out of a hunger to be famous, it's born out of a love of music – I don't think anyone imagined that they'd have a record deal when they were 17 – it was quite amazing. I was too young to sign the record deal, my mum and dad had to sign the contract!' The Spitfire Boys released one single, the Sex Pistols-inspired 'British Refugee'/'Mein Kampf' in 1977.

Frankie had been together for a few years and had already recorded a spot for Channel 4's hit pop show *The Tube* and two sessions for Radio One DJ John Peel before Horn and Morley (and their label, ZTT) signed them. 'Morley had his strategy all worked out,' Paul Rutherford confides. 'He wanted us to be like the Sex Pistols – all the outrage, controversy, but this time with all the sex.' Johnson and the others had been in a band called Sons of Egypt. When Rutherford returned from America, he sat in on their rehearsals and started to sing with them. 'I thought I'd see if I could help them get a gig, which I did. Hambi and the Dance had signed a really big deal with Virgin; they had a tour lined up around England and Europe, and it was like "do you fancy doing BVs [backing vocals] for us?" The punk thing had died a little bit really and it was something to do so I said "yeah"! So I went off on tour with them and that's how I got Frankie the support.'

*

1984 was a watershed year for LGBT acts in the UK. In the list of the 100 best-selling singles of the year, 'Relax' and 'Two Tribes' take first and second place respectively, and advance orders for Frankie's debut album *Welcome to the Pleasuredome,* topped 1.1 million.[23] The previous year had seen Culture Club top the list (with 'Karma Chameleon'), but the only other LGBT acts represented were Kajagoogoo (led by gay singer Limahl) with 'Too Shy', Marilyn ('Calling Your Name'), Wham! (although George Michael had yet to come out), Elton John and Tom Robinson. In the Top 100 for 1982, just three LGBT acts – Culture Club, Soft Cell and Wham! – made the cut, although at the time not one of them was out. Besides Frankie, 1984 saw both Wham! and George Michael as a solo act, Queen, Bronski Beat, Limahl (solo with 'Never Ending Story'), the Weather Girls, Hazel Dean, Elton John and Culture Club score huge hits, plus Evelyn Thomas chart with Ian Levine's gay disco anthem 'High Energy'. Unemployment was out of control, with more than three million on the dole and a quarter of under 25-year-olds unable to find work. Thatcher's Britain was failing the young. What they needed was escapism, and what they craved was glamour.

Suddenly, everyone was wearing make-up, and trying to work out who was who (or who was what) was becoming harder. The Cure's Robert Smith and Human League's Phil Oakey could be seen on Britain's TV screens in lipstick and lace; camp had gone mainstream, with Boy George and fellow Blitz Kid Marilyn appearing on the front cover of every magazine and on everything from Saturday morning kids' TV shows through to prime-time chat shows. Marilyn, born Peter Robinson in Kingston, Jamaica in 1962, was dubbed 'the unacceptable face of pop' by Britain's tabloids, viewed as the sexy counterpart to the cute and cuddly Boy George. The two had shared a squat together prior to George finding fame, but it had taken an appearance in the video for the Eurythmics' single 'Who's that Girl' for Marilyn to be discovered. His biggest hit, 'Calling Your Name', was written about his friend/nemesis. Soon others would try and jump on the gender bender bandwagon: singer Peter Helliwell, of the band Wide Boy Awake (who, naturally, featured ex-Ant Kevin Mooney in their line-up), reinvented himself as the androgynous Damian Grey. Damian may have felt that 'Boy George has as much sex appeal as a fish dinner,'[24] but any hope he had of being the Jobriath of the 1980s fell at the first hurdle.

In Frankie's wake, another Liverpudlian act, Dead or Alive, would reach Number One with 'You Spin Me Round (Like a Record)', bringing an infectious collision of Hi-NRG beats, Blitz Kids glamour and high camp to teatime TV. The British singles chart had never been so gay. Dead or Alive's singer was Paul Rutherford's friend Pete Burns, the former record shop assistant whose fierce look and uncompromising 'screw you' attitude had singled him out as one to watch long before he was seen performing 'You Spin Me Round' on *Top of the Pops*, as Boy George recalled: 'In the 70s I really wanted to go to Liverpool because I'd heard that this club, Eric's, was the place to be. He walked up to me and said: "you've copied my look"!' [25]

Paul Rutherford explains:

Me and Holly and Pete were just being who we were. You'd walk down the street in Liverpool dressed to the nines and didn't actually care about it. I'd been bullied at school so I'd got quite used to that – that stuff used to go way over my head ... we wanted to be noticed and we were going to be as outrageous as we wanted to be. It's a very defiant, Liverpool act. People used to come in to Probe [the record store where Pete Burns worked] to throw beer cans at us and call us queens and we'd fight back. We weren't scared; we were determined. I think that's why that whole thing happened in Liverpool, people became very defiant and it became this really great scene with people dressing up. The gay thing and the punk thing were always very close anyway, even in London with the Banshees hanging around the gay clubs. It was the gay clubs where you could find these people wearing make-up, just hanging out there.'

Originally formed in 1979 as Nightmares in Wax (their first single, 'Birth of a Nation' was issued in 1980), the band's debut album, *Sophisticated Boom Boom,* featured their first proper chart hit, a cover of the KC and the Sunshine Band disco floor-filler 'That's the Way (I Like it)', but it was 'You Spin Me Round' (included on their sophomore effort, *Youthquake*) that made him a star, spending almost a year in the charts. Ironically, when the band was signed to Epic, the company went into overdrive to market their bisexual frontman as the next Boy

George. 'Everywhere I went, people were asking me to sign autographs as George,' Burns admitted in his 2007 autobiography *Freak Unique*.[26] A media-manufactured feud followed, and 'gender bender' became part of the English language, but the hits soon dried up. Unperturbed, Burns and Dead or Alive concentrated their efforts on Japan, where the band enjoyed superstar status.

But for Pete Burns the price of fame was too great. Flamboyant and outrageous on stage, in private he found it hard coping with notoriety, and his obsession with his looks saw him spend any money he made on plastic surgery.

Burns died suddenly, of a massive heart attack caused by a pulmonary embolism, on 23 October 2016, sadly in the week that he was due to release a career-spanning 10-CD box set. His old adversary Boy George described him as 'one of our great true eccentrics'. Marc Almond added, 'we've had some mad times with Pete but he was a one-off creation, a fabulous, fantastic, brilliant creature and always sweet to me.' A few days after Burns' death, in a last act of largesse towards his old sparring partner, Boy George offered to cover the cost of the funeral.[27]

Despite what seemed to be blanket acceptance at home, when the time came for Frankie to try to crack the States, things changed, subtly perhaps, but perceptibly. The homosexuality of the two singers was toned down (something that pleased their three heterosexual bandmates), and because MTV refused to air the original video for 'Relax', an anodyne version was issued in its place. Despite choosing to make their live debut in the United States – before their biggest audience had a chance to see them in action – 'Relax' stalled at 67 on the Billboard charts. 'Two Tribes' fared little better, rising to 45 ('Relax' was repromoted in 1985 following the release of *Welcome to the Pleasuredome*, and this time hit the US Top 10). 'The gay thing was played down because of the boys in the band really, they weren't gay and being Liverpool lads they really didn't want that badge,' reveals Rutherford:

But we were so busy just doing it that we really didn't have time to take stock of what was really happening. We played up to it a hell of a lot! That was our nature; throw a few beers down our throats and we were off again. We were just a big bunch of Liverpool lads getting pissed and then the two gay ones would come along with their arses hanging out! It was fun, and it was funny but we soon got bored. It became as though we were being gay on demand. It's America, and you're not going to go on TV unless you play by the rules: we weren't very good at being told what to do, so we ignored all that ... we wouldn't make excuses: it wasn't us. That's what Frankie was really, an exercise in being really honest. That's why we split up in the end, because we were very honest with each other!'

'Rage Hard', the first single from their second album (*Liverpool*) peaked at Number Four in the UK in 1986, and the album itself reached Number Five. A worldwide tour was lined up to follow the release, but by April 1987 Frankie Goes to Hollywood had broken up – dates set for Australia had to be cancelled after the group split into two factions – Johnson versus the rest of the band. 'We had a very big career in a very short space of time,' Rutherford explains. 'We burnt ourselves out quite quickly. We fitted a lifetime in to those few years. It was exhausting but we didn't care, because it was also fun.' The same hypocrisy that had forced Rutherford and Johnson back into the closet saw MTV ban the video for Queen's single 'Body Language' because it showed Freddie Mercury in a women's sauna,[28] yet the broadcaster was happy to show all four members of the band in drag – and Mercury crowd surfing over a sea of nubile young men – when it programmed the film clip for 'I Want to Break Free' on heavy rotation.

The rise of two of the most influential American bands of the decade was aided by the massive amount of airtime afforded them by MTV. And like many others who came to fame in the decade, they would also have their lives forever changed by their run-ins with HIV and AIDS: one would lose a beloved founder member (and brother), the other would become one of the most outspoken acts of the century, with much of its political activity directed towards HIV and AIDS awareness and prevention. Both acts hailed not from New York or Los Angeles, but from Athens, Georgia: the B-52's and R.E.M. Both acts would produce some of the most defining music of the American indie/New Wave scene – and both featured

LGBT members. In the case of R.E.M. it was 'equal opportunity letch' Michael Stipe. Hailed as the politically aware voice of a generation, Stipe was the only queer member of the planet-straddling colossus; in the five-piece B-52s, singer and percussionist Cindy Wilson was the only straight member. Stipe came out, identifying himself as queer, at the height of his band's fame: when a gaunt-looking Stipe appeared at the Grammy Awards in 1992 wearing a baseball cap with the legend *White House Stop AIDS* emblazoned on it, rumours about his sexuality and health began to circulate. He really had little choice but to say something, but when he did, he did it on his own terms. He wrote in *The Guardian* shortly after the twentieth anniversary of the event:

> It was September 1994, and my band had released the two biggest records of our career. With *Out of Time* and *Automatic for the People*, we had sold more than 25 million records worldwide, and we were ramping up to tour for the first time in five years. I was more famous than I could have ever imagined. For the promotion of our next album, *Monster*, and its world tour, I decided to publicly announce my sexuality. I said simply that I had enjoyed sex with men and women my entire adult life. It was a simple fact, and I'm happy I announced it.[29]

Formed in 1976, with four of the band's founding members gay or lesbian, the B-52's odd mix of surf guitar licks and Yoko Ono-inspired vocals singled them out as at odds with the rest of the world even before the media started to pry into the various members' private lives: debut single 'Rock Lobster' sounded nothing less than otherworldly. Sadly, while recording the band's third studio album *Whammy!* guitarist Ricky Wilson discovered he had contracted AIDS. He died on 12 October 1985 at just 32 years old. The group had enormous success worldwide with hits including 'Love Shack' (the video for which featured an early cameo from RuPaul) and 'Roam'; singer Kate Pierson, who married her girlfriend Monica Coleman in 2015, added her distinctive vocals to fellow Athenians R.E.M.'s multi-platinum album *Out Of Time,* including on the worldwide hit 'Shiny Happy People'.

'These 20 years of publicly speaking my truth have made me a better and easier person to be around,' wrote Stipe. 'It helped develop the clarity of my voice and establish who I would be as an adult. I am proud to be who I am, and I am happy to have shared that with the world.' San Francisco-based Mark Eitzel, an occasional collaborator with R.E.M.'s guitarist Peter Buck, outed himself a decade before Stipe felt comfortable enough to do the same. 'I didn't get a good reaction,' the singer for the cult band American Music Club told Ben Walsh of *The Independent*. 'The record company wasn't happy and they wanted to put out that I was bi, not gay. It was the Eighties and a completely different world. In the rock 'n' roll world, even in San Francisco, it was not really acceptable to come out. Twenty years on, it's completely changed, thank goodness.'[30]

Mista Majah P, 2011

CHAPTER 17

Hope and Homophobia

'How people navigate life and communities is different from person to person and place to place. There's a still a lot of anti-gay sentiment, but despite the homophobia one is able to survive'

Dane Lewis, Executive Director of J-FLAG[1]

Inevitably there would be a backlash, and the 1990s saw a huge re-emergence of homophobia in many musical genres. Hip hop was rife with anti-gay imagery, used by everyone from Public Enemy, Eazy-E and Brand Nubian – who threatened to 'fuck up a faggot' on their 1993 hit 'Punks Jump Up to Get Beat Down' – through to acts we now associate with a more liberal attitude towards the LGBT community such as the Beastie Boys – ironic when founding member and original drummer Kate Schellenbach was an out lesbian who was in a relationship with The Breeders' Josephine Wiggs. Michael Franti's band the Disposable Heroes of Hiphoprisy were one of the few acts that fought back, releasing the track 'Language of Violence' on their sole album, *Hypocrisy Is The Greatest Luxury,* a tale of queer-bashing and the potential recriminations. Brand Nubian's Sadat X has since mellowed somewhat, saying, 'as you grow and see the world your views on life change. I say live and let live'.[2] Notorious for the homophobic, violent and misogynistic lyrics on many of his early recordings, Eminem was the *enfant terrible* of hip hop . . . until he performed a duet with Elton John at the 2001 Grammys: 'I love him,' Elton told *Rolling Stone* magazine in 2010. 'When David and I had our civil partnership, he sent us a present. In a case, on velvet cushions, were two diamond cock rings. So there's a homophobe for you.'

There have been a number of out-gay rap and hip hop acts, but very few of those have managed to cross over from their appreciative but small LGBT audience into the mainstream. Britain's QBoy began his career as part of gay hip hop trio Q-Form and released his debut solo EP, *Even the Women Like Him*, in 2004. In the summer of 2005 the producer, rapper and DJ organised PeaceOUT UK, Europe's first ever gay hip hop festival, and in 2011 he played a live set at the Glastonbury Festival. As of April 2017 he was DJing weekly at London's Heaven club, playing regular dates across Europe and promoting his current EP *Qing*. Nineteen-year-old out-gay rapper Karnage is quickly building a reputation on London's grime scene after issuing a brace of singles in 2016. In Oakland, award-winning California hip hop act Deep Dickollective (D/DC) were openly, unashamedly queer: 'we didn't want to be coy. We didn't want anyone to be able to get around queerness, to get around sexuality or race. We wanted that to be foreground, we didn't want them to make any mistake when they were listening to it,' co-founder Juba Kalamka told the press.[3] Kalamka was an early member of the influential 1990s crew Rainbow Flava, along with Minneapolis-based gay rapper Tori Fixx. The two men pioneered 'homo hop' or 'queer hip hop', terms coined by D/DC's Tim'm T. West.

Although the band folded in 2008 after issuing five albums, Kalamka is still active in the black and LGBT communities today. Juba's label, Sugartruck, also launched the career of San Francisco's trans rapper Katastrophe (Rocco Kayiatos), named Producer of the Year at the Outmusic Awards for his debut album *Let's Fuck, Then Talk About my Problems*. 'Poetry is about fallibility,' Katastrophe's label boss told the *San Francisco Chronicle*. 'He's got a little bit of both. He's got swagger, and he's got "I'm a sensitive guy" at the same time.'[4] Not everybody took homo hop seriously: in 2001, the US media started to sit up and take notice of a young rapper from Brooklyn called Caushun, who claimed to be 'a hairdresser for the stars by day' (influenced, perhaps, by Monti Rock) and 'one of the very few openly gay people' in the hip hop scene by night.[5] Unfortunately, despite some major magazine and television coverage, it was all a scam: Caushun's real name was Jason Herndon, and he had been hired by songwriter and producer Ivan Matias as a prank.

Gay rapper Joseph Thomas Lee, better known by his stage name Deadlee, scored two critically acclaimed albums, his 2002 debut *7 Deadlee Sins* and *Assault With a Deadlee Weapon* (2006) and was feted by the mainstream media in the States – including *Rolling Stone* magazine – for his sound, which blended hip hop with rock, and for his lyrics which tackled subjects such as race, class, sexuality and police brutality. In 2013, the year he changed his name to Joey LeMar (after he married his partner, the couple combined their surnames, Lee and Martinez), he told *429 Magazine*:

> Homo hop was just a catchy phrase to bring light to out LGBT rappers who are basically just doing hip hop as it was meant to be done. Hip hop was always about the struggle and the realities of life. The problem is it became mainstream and taken over by big corporate music companies who controlled the content. Sex of the hetero variety, violence, and money became the standard. Homo hop was one of those things we used to highlight homos who were being left out of hip-hop, but the name became a crutch. There is no real homo hop genre, it's just hip-hop. We were a very cohesive group all striving for the same thing. Like life, we all went in different directions but I think our impact was great. I get hit up weekly by new out rappers who thank me for opening doors. My producer at the time told me I was about 10 years ahead of everyone with my ideas and I see that now. We planted a seed and I see the fruits [of our labor].[6]

In January 2017, New York-based rapper ILoveMakonnen, whose debut single, the 2014 release 'Tuesday' was certified platinum and has been viewed on YouTube almost 140 million times, came out via Twitter, saying that 'I can't tell u about everybody else's closet, I can only tell u about mine, and it's time [to] come out'. 'The best decision I ever made in my life was coming out of the closet,' he says. 'I feel so much better and happier that I can truly just be me!'[7]

In New Orleans, a city that LGBT musicians had been calling home for decades Big Freedia has become known as the Queen of Bounce, a

local take on hip hop. Known as Freddie Ross but preferring the feminine pronoun for her stage persona, Big Freedia (pronounced Free-da)
has become an American sensation, performing bounce, known for its
'call-and-response' style and booty-shaking dance – a move that begat
the twerk. It's music to bounce to, based on repetitive sampled beats
(a favourite source is 'Drag Rap' by the Showboys which, sadly, has
nothing to do with *Showgirls* or with drag in the style of Gladys Bentley
or Julian Eltinge), and although Big Freedia may be the biggest star of
the scene, she began her career performing alongside Katey Red. Katey
is universally acknowledged as both the first out-trans rapper and as
the artist who gave birth to sissy bounce. Several musicians in New
Orleans, notably Katey and the lightning-speed rapper Sissy Nobby, use
the s-word defiantly; in much the same way as other people in the LGBT
community have reclaimed the word 'queer', New Orleans' sissy bounce
performers have taken the meaning of the word 'sissy' and turned it
on its head. Very few people would dare use the word in a derogatory
fashion in the presence of the fierce and intimidating Sissy Nobby or the
6' 2" Big Freedia.

Unfortunately, despite a clutch of visibly out artists and vocal support
for the LGBT community from some of the biggest players, the urban
music scene is still a no-go area for many LGBT musicians: in 2014 US
rapper T-Pain spoke out about homophobia in the industry, claiming that
certain rappers will not work with the R&B singer Frank Ocean – who
two years previously had admitted that he had fallen in love with another
man – because of his sexuality.[8]

A new breed of singers scorning 'batty boys' dominated reggae. The
Jamaican dancehall hit 'Boom Bye Bye' by ragga star Buju Banton incited
violence against gay men and rightly caused outrage, so much so that the
backlash almost destroyed his career: his shows were cancelled across
Europe and throughout America and he was dropped from the line-up
of Britain's multicultural WOMAD festival in 1992, due to be held in
Brighton, England's gay capital. In a very clear message from the organisers that homophobia would not be tolerated, his spot was filled by Boy
George.[9] A campaign, Stop Murder Music (the term 'murder music' had
been coined by British gay rights activist Peter Tatchell), was set up to

highlight artists that produce music that encourages violence against the LGBT community and to encourage people to boycott their records and concerts. In 2007, the organisers of London's Reggae in the Park concert were forced to cancel the event, which was to have featured Jamaican singers Sizzla Kalonji and Vybz Kartel, following intense lobbying by gay rights group OutRage! The Stop Murder Music campaign led to many singers signing the Reggae Compassionate Act (RCA), agreeing that 'there is no space in the music community for hatred and prejudice, including no place for racism, violence, sexism or homophobia'. Banton signed, then distanced himself from the RCA: the year that he signed the act (2007), his microphone was switched off as soon as he began 'Boom Bye Bye' at New York's CariFest reggae festival. In 2004, Banton had been charged, along with 11 other men, of breaking into a house in Kingston and attacking six men believed to be homosexual. One of the victims lost the use of an eye in the beating, but charges against the singer were dismissed in January 2006 because of a lack of evidence. Jamaica is still referred to as 'the most homophobic place on earth,' [10] where murder and mob violence is an almost everyday occurrence, and gay rights activists have been forced to flee their homes: lawyer Maurice Tomlinson received death threats after local newspaper the *Jamaica Observer* published an article about his wedding to his Canadian partner, and the couple were forced to relocate to Toronto.[11] Homeless LGBT people were, quite literally, living in the gutters: dozens of young LGBT people lived in a drainage gully in New Kingston after being driven from their homes for being gay. Local police repeatedly raided the site and eventually sealed off the gully, leaving the youths homeless again.[12] Yet despite all of this, in 2015 the country held its first Pride day; the following year events lasted for a whole week. As Dane Lewis, Executive Director of prominent human rights group J-FLAG (Jamaica Forum for Lesbians, All-Sexuals and Gays) says: 'We not hiding anymore, but we still have dancehall artists who feel as though they are required to have a least one song with homophobic lyrics in their repertoire. A lot of that is down to peer pressure: they feel that if they don't then their own sexuality will be in question.'

Very few Jamaican artists have dared to speak up on behalf of the LGBT community, as Dane Lewis explains. 'The only one who has been very public has been Tanya Stephens,' he says, talking about the singer who has urged her fellow artists to be more socially responsible. Tanya's 2010 song 'Still Alive' deals with discrimination against people with HIV, and it was used in a television campaign dealing with the issue. In 2011 Jamaican-born reggae singer Mista Majah P released *Tolerance,* an album that included songs supporting same-sex marriage and adoption rights for same-sex couples, as well as attacks on homophobic bullying. His most recent album, *Gays Belong in Heaven Too* challenges discrimination in the church, as well as including songs about LGBT rights in Uganda, Russia and Jamaica. The singer says:

> I wanted to challenge the homophobia of the churches, especially in Jamaica. The first thing most of them say is that to be gay is wrong because the Bible says so. Because people can use the Bible as an excuse to bash and hate on the LGBT community then these so-called Christian church goers take these words and infect the population with hate and homophobia, using God as a scapegoat and front man to get their message out there.'

The heterosexual singer has received death threats for his pro-gay stance:

> I was told I cannot come back to Jamaica because I am a traitor for speaking out about the treatment of gay people. The reaction from other reggae musicians is very hateful and discriminatory towards me and the LGBT community. They think I am a traitor because I want to change the culture of hatred toward gays. I have not gotten any support from any reggae artist: I was threatened by Sizzla's manager with a lawsuit for one of my videos ['What if Bounty Killer and Sizzla Are Gay?']. Bounty Killer and Sizzla are the two most homophobic reggae artist in Jamaica, that's why I leave my focus on them. I am trying to cut off the head of the snake, and I have got insults and death threats from these reggae artists, their management and fans.[13]

Mista Majah P, who now lives in San Francisco, says that his adopted home has helped change his attitude towards LGBT people in a very positive way. While living in Jamaica I used to see gays from afar with no interaction and only knew what I knew either from hateful reggae songs, homophobic pastors in the church or the general public who hated the very sight of anyone gay, who they would attack and spout hatred. Since living in the USA and the San Francisco area I have had the chance to walk, talk and interact with LGBT people, have gay friends, attend festivals and interview people from the LGBT community. I now know that what is sung about in reggae and talked about in Jamaica is totally bogus ... the gay community is very loyal and honest which makes me very proud to call a gay person my friend and glad that I am helping to kill that lie.

There *are* LGBT artists in Jamaica, but the local music industry has colluded to keep their stories out of the media. 'The music industry is so fickle; people are hesitant to speak out but we've heard comments from other artists,' Lewis reveals. 'They know who is gay in the industry and they have no issues working with them so it's a sort of unspoken tolerance that has been building up. The Stop Murder Music campaign has done a lot to help shift the landscape.' Life is still tough, but for LGBT people in the bigger towns and cities at least there is some kind of life. 'We have a very vibrant underground scene,' Lewis explains, 'people who know where the parties are – and we have proprietors who are willing to host us or rent us space. That's demonstrable of the shift that has taken place ... Social media has also provided an avenue for people to connect, and Pride is really important. Visibility is critical, especially in terms of encouraging other people to make personal connections.'

Anti-gay legislation in Russia – the Russian federal law 'for the Purpose of Protecting Children from Information Advocating for a Denial of Traditional Family Values' was signed into law by President Vladimir Putin on 30 June 2013 – has seen a vicious crackdown on LGBT rights and calls from religious leaders and community groups for Russian media and music fans to boycott Western artists such as Elton John. When gay artist Tom Neuwirth won the Eurovision Song Contest in 2014 as his alter ego Conchita Wurst, Russian politician Vladimir Zhirinovsky called his triumph 'the end of Europe,' adding that 'there is no limit to our outrage. There are no more men or women in Europe, just it.'[14] At a press conference, Conchita told reporters that the win 'was not just a victory for me but a victory for those people who believe in a future that can function without discrimination and is based on tolerance and respect.'

Conversely, many of Russia's best-known (and, thanks to state-sponsored television, most widely publicised) popsa acts – a kitsch, heavily synthesised, cartoon-like pop music – are either openly gay or adopt camp personas and are huge stars. Your average Popsa singer's antics seem entirely at odds with Russia's denial of basic LGBT rights. Popsa's biggest star, the former dancer and choreographer Boris Moiseyev, is a gay man who is reputed to be a close friend of Vladimir Putin.[15] He has angered gay rights activists in the country for speaking out against Pride events being held in Moscow, and both LGBT groups and religious organisations have picketed his shows. For a number of years, he claimed he was going to marry an American businesswoman and was a vocal opponent of same-sex marriage, specifically the wedding of Elton John and David Furnish, saying that 'this irritates people, and gays shouldn't irritate'.[16] The dichotomy of a gay singer protesting against gay rights is less surprising when you remember that this is the country where holding Pride events or even simply speaking out in defence of gay rights can land you in jail. Russia's biggest female rock star Zemfira is widely reputed to be a lesbian, and has been close to actress Renata Litvinova for a number of years, but given the country's stance on gay rights, it's unlikely that either woman will willingly open up about their relationship any time soon.

Russia is also the country that gave us t.a.T.u., the girl duo who shocked Middle America with a lesbian kiss. Although the two girls – Julia Volkova and Lena Katina – were shown kissing in the rain in school uniforms during the video for their international hit 'All the Things She Said', they have since claimed that neither woman is lesbian and in fact it was all for publicity. They are still the most successful Russian musical export of all time, with international sales in excess of 25 million and, until feminist trio Pussy Riot grabbed headlines after the women were jailed for daring to protest against Putin's links to the Russian Orthodox Church, were the country's best-known act internationally. The same year that t.a.T.u. hit the big time, the Russian techno duo Ruki Vverh!

(Руки Вверх!) released the song 'He Kisses You', a nice enough dance number about yearning after an old flame who has moved on. The song's video features footage of a man carefully applying make-up contrasting with film of another man and a blonde woman getting very friendly with each other. Two thirds of the way through the video, the young man removes the blonde woman's wig – revealing that she is, in fact, the man we saw applying make-up. In 2012, t.A.T.u.'s Julia Volkova teamed with singer Dima Bilan to provide Russia's Eurovision entry 'Back To Her Future'; Bilan had won the contest four years previously with the song 'Believe', having come second in 2006. Bilan has never opened up about his sexuality, but that hasn't stopped men claiming to be former lovers crawling out of the woodwork, or magazines and internet gossip sites speculating on his current partner. The same is true of Sergey Lazarev, who represented Russia at Eurovision in 2016: it's clear these men have to keep their private lives private if they are to continue to enjoy the level of celebrity that they do in Russia, yet both have spoken guardedly about their support for LGBT people and Lazarev has performed at Moscow's premier gay nightspot, BoyZ Club. The mainstream Russian media shies away from talk about the sex lives of celebrities; Bilan, Lazarev, Moiseyev and the 'king of Russian pop' Filipp Kirkorov are simply assumed to be metrosexual – or, like Liberace and Johnny Mathis, sexless. Kirkorov and Bilan have at least been among the few Russian celebrities to speak out against the country's ban on 'homosexual propaganda', despite being accused by Russian media of being 'prone to mannerisms and kitschy attire that have earned them accusations of being "closet gays".' [17]

'It's a very difficult life for homosexuals in Russia,' Pussy Riot's Ekaterina Samutsevich told *The Independent*. '[This law] will make life for non-traditional sexual orientation just simply hell and there will be no protection because at the moment the only protection is the law, and this law has very abstract provisions'. [18]

Hong Kong musical superstar Leslie Cheung committed suicide in 2003 by jumping from the twenty-forth floor of the Mandarin Oriental hotel in central Hong Kong. The multi-award-winning founding father of Cantopop (Cantonese pop music) came out as bisexual in 2001, although he had been in a relationship with another man, Tong Hok-Tak, for almost 20 years. At the time of his death he was being treated for depression.

Homosexual sex was banned in the People's Republic of China until 1997 and even then it still remained on the official list of mental illnesses until 2001. Today, the state controls the media and Internet access, conversion therapy is still used, same-sex marriage is outlawed and businesses are allowed to discriminate against LGBT people. 'Young people across China face homophobic harassment every day,' activist Xiaoyu Wang reveals. 'We're drugged and put in "conversion therapy". We're told that we're "sick" because of who we are and who we love.' Xiaoyu, a student at the Guangdong University of Foreign Studies, was horrified when police broke into her apartment after she and her girlfriend had posted pictures of the couple celebrating their engagement on social media.[19]

Unsurprisingly then, very few pop singers have dared to come out in China, although that is slowly starting to change. Anthony Wong (Wong Yiu-Ming) told the audience at his 2012 show at the Hong Kong Coliseum that 'People don't need to guess whether or not I'm a tongzhi [Chinese slang for homosexual] anymore. I'm saying I'm gay. I'm a homosexual. G-A-Y.'[20] Independent singer-songwriter Chet Lam has been open about his sexuality since he began his professional career in 2003, telling *The Advocate* that 'There is no Elton John in Hong Kong, only Chet Lam'. Cantopop singer Denise Ho publicly outed herself as lesbian at a Hong Kong Pride Parade in 2012. An outspoken civil rights campaigner, Ho has been viciously attacked by the Chinese state media, which has accused her of 'tarnishing China's image,' and branded her 'Hong Kong poison'.[21]

On 23 February, 2016 Ezekiel Mutua, of the Kenyan Film Classification Board, hosted a press conference from his Nairobi office to denounce the release, eight days previously, of a video by Kenyan rapper Art Attack. The subject of the Board's ire was a film produced by Art Attack to accompany his version of the song 'Same Love', based on the 2012 hit by US hip hop duo Macklemore and Ryan Lewis. In the video, bisexual singer Natalie Florence, professionally known as Noti Flow, is seen (briefly) kissing another woman. A male couple is pictured, partially clothed, laughing in bed. Noti is seen sitting on a park bench kissing another young woman and a young man (the gay gospel singer George Barasa, aka Joji Baro) is viewed walking through a forest. Images of Uganda's notorious *Red Pepper* news-paper, which regularly outs LGBT Africans on its front page, are shown,

Noti Flow (l) in a still from the 'Same Love' video

and the film ends with the suicide of a young gay man, unable to cope in a society that sees him as a criminal. It's hard-hitting stuff, but only a few people had seen Kenya's first ever gay-themed music video before Mutua alerted the press to its existence. Labelled 'the most unpopular person in Kenya' by *The Nairobi News*, at the press conference he stated that the 'culprits (will be) identified and arrested, and we are going to work with the police all the way ... to ensure that these things are stopped. We assure you that we will take action.' Mutua issued a 'cease and desist' letter to Google, demanding that the video be either removed from YouTube or blocked from being viewed in Kenya. Google refused and within days the video had been promoted around the world – thanks in part to the Kenyan Film Classification Board itself, which rather idiotically sent out a tweet with a link to it. Soon 'Same Love' had been viewed by more than a quarter of a million people.

Interviewed by the Nigerian podcast *NoStrings*, Art Attack revealed he:

felt the need to do a song about LGBT rights after some of my friends who are gays and lesbians started telling me about the bad things that were experiencing in Kenyan society. I live in Kenya, and I know how and what life is like for them, so I decided to record a song that will speak positively to the situation. We knew that this would not be appreciated by the larger Kenyan population who kick against homosexuality, but we needed to do what we have to do. It was such a huge risk; there has been a lot of controversy ... but we are only encouraging a positive message of love and respect, and discouraging violence against gay people. We are not telling people to be gay, but we are saying, "Let them be".'[22]

It was a brave move on the part of the avowedly straight rapper (Joji Baro had previously stated that all of the artists involved in making the video were LGBT, although most of the musicians did not want to be named for fear of reprisals), especially in a country where homosexual acts are punishable by up to 14 years in prison.

It was later reported, by US magazine *The Advocate* that some of the musicians involved in the song were 'living in fear', one of the actors in the video had gone in to hiding and others were facing arrest following the controversy stirred up by the song. In an email to the magazine, Art Attack revealed:

Dayon, who has been living in Kenya for the last five years, started receiving threats and hostility from his Kenyan neighbours after they saw the video and he had to flee to his mother country. As for the rest of us, a warrant of arrest has already been issued against us and we are living in fear. Our video has been banned and we have been alerted that we are to be arrested and charged anytime.[23]

'We hadn't seen a song that championed the rights of minority groups in Africa as this song has,' Art Attack told the BBC:

We did it with a purpose, and a reason and an intention, to stir up the debate. We knew this song would never get airplay on Kenyan radio or Kenyan television – it was made for YouTube and YouTube alone. We have some amazing, progressive, liberal Kenyans watching the video saying "this is amazing! This is beautiful and we support it totally".

I would say 60 percent are saying this is disgusting, this is abhorrent and we don't want this in Africa. We expected that.[24]

Noti Flow took to Facebook to express her outrage:

WTF??? The Kenyan Government has banned our song "Same Love", a collaborative effort between me and rapper Art Attack. The Government has also ordered the Kenyan Media NOT to distribute the song anywhere and asked Kenyans to avoid sharing or distributing the song on social media. Wow! What the hell? This is a simple song that celebrates same-sex rights and that acknowledges the rights of gays and lesbians. The Kenyan Government neglect Kenyan citizens on important issues like job opportunities but couldn't hesitate banning a simple song about people's sex orientations! Well, we will not be moved. We stand by our song and its message. Arrest us if you wish! We are unbowed.

Noti went on to star in Kenyan TV series *Nairobi Diaries*.

Other musicians took Art Attack's message to heart. In the months that followed, Nigerian singer-songwriter Chisom released the LGBT-themed song 'Why Love Is A Crime', which talks about the despair faced by many gay Africans, but homosexuality is still outlawed in 34 African countries, and in four – Mauritania, Sudan, Somalia and northern Nigeria – it is punishable by death.

Most Middle-Eastern countries still outlaw same-sex relationships, and the death sentence continues to be carried out in countries including Syria, Saudi Arabia, the United Arab Emirates, Iran, Libya and Yemen. Called 'the Arab world's most influential independent band' by the *Financial Times*[25] Mashrou' Leila is a Lebanese alternative rock band, formed in Beirut in 2008. They have released three albums and an EP to date, and each confronts taboo subjects including gay relationships and political corruption – an abrasive stance that saw the band briefly banned in Jordan. Their leader, Hamed Sinno, is an American-born but Beirut-raised Muslim who identifies as queer. In 2014, the band became the first Middle-Eastern act to be featured on the cover of *Rolling Stone* magazine.

With no management, no label and no financial backing, the band have organised their own tours (they've played widely in America and Europe as well as the Middle East) and have paid for promotional work and recording sessions via crowdfunding schemes. Only singing in Arabic, the band has become a voice for LGBT people in the Middle East. In June 2016, at a concert in Washington DC, just days after the horrific shooting at Orlando's Pulse nightclub that left 49 people dead and 53 injured, an angry Sinno told his audience: 'Suddenly, just because you're brown and queer you can't mourn and it's really not fucking fair. There are a bunch of us who are queer who feel assaulted by that attack who can't mourn because we're also from Muslim families and we exist. This is what it looks like to be called both a terrorist and a faggot.' The band followed this up with a performance of a song about an attack on a Beirut nightclub, Ghost.[26] On 3 July, he proudly carried a banner for Orlando at the head of the Toronto Pride march – Sinno's first ever Pride event.

In many ways, the Internet has made it easier for LGBT voices to be heard, especially in countries where war, violence and oppression are commonplace. In the twenty-first century you no longer need the might of a record company behind you to promote your work: with access to a decent Internet connection you can have your latest song or video online seconds after it has been completed. The same technology that is killing off the gay and lesbian bar scene in the developed world (who needs to go to a bar when you can meet your next boyfriend/girlfriend/casual shag via a free smartphone app?) is helping LGBT artists from some of the world's most oppressed regimes to find a worldwide audience. But even here in the west it's not always an easy ride. Singled out as 'one of Scotland's all-time great vocalists' (review in *The Scotsman*, 22 July, 2006), Sheena McDonald – known professionally as 'Horse' – scored eight British chart hits between 1989 and 1997. Touring with Tina Turner, and with her songs covered by artists including the out-gay singer Will Young, she married her partner in Lanark in January 2013, returning to the town she was born in but fled as a teenager after years of homophobic bullying. She told *The Daily Record*:

I had a terrible time growing up. People attacked and bullied me because I was gay in a small town I used to get chased by gangs. I had physical encounters. I was attacked by people with broken bottles but the verbal abuse was the worst. People would call me names and I was afraid when I was growing up. I didn't tell anyone at the time, not even my dad because I felt I was bringing shame on the family. It got so bad that one day I was walking and a police patrol car was sitting across the street. The policeman shouted, "There's that lezzie". I thought, "I'm in trouble now. If something happens, who is going to help me?" I left the town shortly after that.[27]

She has since become a vocal supporter of anti-bullying initiatives. 'One of my escape routes from bullying was being creative. The song-writing rescued me from very dark times. Children need to be taught that we are all different – either for wearing glasses, being a different colour or having red hair – and that we have to support each other.'

George Michael on stage during the Faith World Tour, 1988

CHAPTER 18

Scandal

'I give them plenty of things to gossip about. I like rumours circulating about me, but whether or not they're true – well, that's another matter'

Marc Almond[1]

Nothing sells newspapers like a good scandal, and whereas the public seemed not to care which side of the bed you slept on, British tabloids and US sleaze sheets were still obsessed with outing gay and lesbian performers. Reporters and the paparazzi would continue to sniff around Freddie Mercury, Elton John and the Georges like a pack of rabid dogs, camping out on the doorsteps of their London apartments and following their every move, desperate to catch the moment they fell – which, naturally, each one of them would do.

Besides the press, there was another, bigger, barrier to break. Acts relied on radio play for all-important exposure, and no US radio station – outside the college circuit, perhaps – was going to play your record if it were deemed to be too gay. It was a taboo that even openly gay performers were loath to smash. There would be no obviously gay-themed songs from John until he began working with singer and songwriter Tom Robinson, and even then he would struggle with directly referring to his sexuality in song, as Robinson reveals:

The only 'closety' thing Elton did, which he apologised to me for at the time, was when he sang the lyrics on "Never Gonna Fall In Love

Again". There was the line "I wish he wouldn't make me rabid/I wish he wouldn't turn me on" he just sort of squidged it so it sounded more like "I wish she wouldn't make me rabid". He was a bit shame faced about that but had the good grace to apologise and I didn't mind; I realised that his position in Middle America was such that he, *ahem*, didn't want to ram anything down anybody's throat! Fair play to him, when he made the video for "Elton's Song", which was about a school-boy crush at a public school, it had a younger boy being desperately in love with an older prefect, and it didn't pull any punches. I think the video itself got banned in America, but I don't think Elton was at all closeted'.

MTV may have been happy to give circumspect LGBT acts airtime, but in the early years it seemed that they would only do so if you were white, and the battle to win acceptance for black musicians would need to be fought first. During an interview, David Bowie asked presenter (or Video Jockey as they were styled) Mark Goodman outright about the station's policy towards minorities: 'I'm just floored by the fact that there are so few black artists featured. Why is that?' The VJ told him that the station was worried about reaction from 'some town in the Midwest who would be scared to death by Prince or a string of other black faces'.[2] It wasn't until Walter Yentikoff, then head of CBS, threatened to pull his entire roster from the station that they finally relented and programmed Michael Jackson's 'Billie Jean'.

In 1984, Boy George told *Rolling Stone* magazine that he was bisexual, that his last relationship was with a woman and that he was looking forward to becoming a parent one day. He may have been aping his hero's stance in the hope for acceptance, but it was still a brave move. His record company (Virgin in the UK, Epic in the US) wanted to keep milking their genderbending cash cow: they were not going to let him sabotage his career quite yet. However, after US televangelist Jerry Falwell took against him, accusing him of being a bad role model and stating that he would 'disappear as one more fad . . . like Tiny Tim and a host of other relics,' George – famous for his waspish tongue – struck back. 'This illusion that I am promoting homosexuality is obviously rub-bish,' he said. 'Sex is something that anybody will find out for themselves, and you cannot force somebody to be homosexual'.[3] 'Boy George is the Peter Pan of the androgynous set,' wrote *The Washington Post*'s Pamela Sommers. 'Outfitted in layers of baggy blouses and tunics, his long hair a mass of ribbons, shells and braids, his face made up geisha girl style, he's the innocent imp, the fey rag doll. Boy George does not threaten, does not challenge, does not – despite his unconventional get-up – exude any sort of sexual allure'.[4] It wouldn't take long for the wheels to come off the wagon.

By the middle of 1986, his life was in such a mess that *The Sun* claimed, 'Junkie George has Eight Weeks to Live'. The report, based on stories from his family and friends, claimed that he had developed a serious heroin habit. His publicist, Susan Blond, revealed that she knew the end was coming when trying to get him ready for a live TV show in New York: 'Because of the drugs he was taking the make-up wouldn't stick to his face ... the anxiety was just too much'.[5] In August 1986 Michael Rudetsky, a close friend, was found dead of a heroin overdose in George's home. The following December, he was arrested for possession.

With help, George cleaned up. The Pet Shop Boys returned him to the American charts in 1993 after a five-year gap with 'The Crying Game', his lush, synth-led re-reading of Dave Berry's 1964 hit, recorded for the movie of the same name, but then he discovered cocaine. In 2006 he was forced to spend five days' community service cleaning the streets of New York after another arrest for possession and for wasting police time by dishonestly reporting a burglary. In 2009, he was jailed for 15 months for falsely imprisoning a male escort in his Shoreditch flat; he served four months behind bars. The singer had denied the charge, claiming that the victim, 29-year-old Norwegian Audun Carlsen, had stolen photos from his laptop. George admitted handcuffing Carlsen to a wall in April 2007 but said he did so in order to trace the missing property. Carlsen later revealed that the pair had been snorting cocaine.[6]

Looking back, George feels that prison was 'a gift': 'I went into prison sober. I knew I had a lot of work to do. I've worked very hard at getting myself back in shape, getting my career back, getting my self-respect back. I knew it would take time, and it has. But I'm starting to feel the rewards of that work.'[7] The pop music chameleon used the experience to re-examine his life and in recent years has reinvented himself almost as many times as David Bowie, with a successful stage musical (*Taboo*), appearances on hit TV shows (*The Voice* and *The Celebrity Apprentice* among them), two volumes of autobiography, and a side career as a respected club DJ. Oh, and he also founded his own dance label, More Protein (with friend and former member of Haysi Fantayzee, Jeremy Healy), which has had hits with Jesus Loves You, E-Zee Possee, Eve Gallagher and George himself. 'My appetite for self-destruction and misery is greatly diminished,' he says. 'I'm not interested in being unhappy.'[8]

'My early influences were Charley Pride, Dolly Parton, Garth Brooks, Merle Haggard and all of the old country stuff that my mom and dad listened to,' country singer Drake Jensen admits:

> Then I was introduced to Culture Club: my mother played "Karma Chameleon" constantly and I often make the joke that she played it so much that she turned me gay! She played that song 150 times a day! She bought their *Colour By Numbers* album and played it so much. I identify a lot with Boy George. I would love to do something with him. That's my ultimate dream. I don't even care if it's music, I just want to go on a dinner date with him and talk about how much of a rebel we both were. He's taught me a lot: he literally fell flat on his face in front of the whole world and then came back with one of the best songs of his career. When I watched the video for "King of Everything" I was bawling and crying. I'd love to have a conversation with him, just to say: "thank you". I think that a lot of the fight that was in him, the things he suffered through ... I'm very much the same. He and I have a lot in common.'

In 2015, Boy George and Marilyn were reunited, with George producing his friend's comeback single 'Love or Money' the following year, Marilyn's first new recording in 30 years.

While George was dealing with his own demons, other LGBT acts were also struggling. Marc Almond, who by the mid-1980s had cast off any pretence at being straight or bisexual via recordings with Bronski Beat (on the hit single 'I Feel Love'/'Johnny Remember Me'), concerts in support of International AIDS Day and an appearance on the front cover of *Gay Times*, was almost killed in 1993. His penchant for the seedier side of life, which added such a beautiful sense of debauchery to his records, caught up with him when two of his 'acquaintances' tried to throw him from a sixth-floor window. The police arrived to find an injured Almond unconscious on the floor, but instead of pressing charges for attempted murder, he decided to check himself into rehab.[9] Like many of his fellow travellers, Almond has faced his own battles with drugs – he suffered from a 12-year long addiction to sleeping pills – and he admits to trying heroin, cocaine, crack, ecstasy and just about every other drug you can think of.[10] The clinic Almond chose to clean up in (the Promis Recovery Centre, near Canterbury) had previously treated Elton John and his former manager/boyfriend John Reid. Visage's Steve Strange spent many years battling heroin addiction, and in 1999 was arrested for shoplifting. It was only after details were dredged up by the newspapers that fans discovered Strange had suffered a breakdown two years earlier and had been 'prescribed a fierce cocktail of antidepressants and tranquillisers'.[11] He passed away from a heart attack on 12 February 2015, just two months after the release of the most recent Visage album, *Orchestral*.

When Frankie Goes to Hollywood imploded in 1987, Johnson and Rutherford both pursued solo careers, but a long-drawn-out court battle between the members of the band and ZTT put an end to their relationship. 'It became quite hard,' Rutherford admits:

> Holly wanted to be serious and he obviously had his eye on a solo career – he didn't want to share the stage with us any longer, and I understand that. It happened so fast and it was so big and every single day was a big day – helicopters here and there, private planes, bottles of champagne, tons of coke . . . it was pretty amazing but it wore our friendships out. The *Liverpool* album was done under absolute stress; maybe if we had more time it would have been better, we could have sold another million or whatever. It just wore out.

Paul's solo career never really stood a chance of taking off. 'It was an odd period for me because my partner had AIDS. I didn't have any fight left in me. Things were getting a bit difficult and I could see Island

Frankie Goes to Hollywood postcard, 1984

Records [who issued Paul's solo album *Oh World*] trying their best but I wasn't at *my* best really and I lost interest in my own career because I was too focused on him.' Holly Johnson helped break another taboo when, in 1993, he admitted that he was living with HIV. Luckily, medical treatment has come a long way since the early 1980s: Holly is still with us and still performing more than a quarter of a century after he first became aware that he was HIV-positive. In 2005, Erasure's Andy Bell told the press that he too was HIV-positive, having been diagnosed a decade earlier. 'Being HIV-positive does not mean that you have AIDS,' he wrote on Erasureinfo.com. 'My life expectancy should be the same as anyone else's, so there's no need to panic.'

Queen were no longer the draw they once were; by the end of 1983 it looked like it was all over for the former global superstars. After the success of 'Under Pressure', their massive hit duet with David Bowie, interest was waning. They still had a healthy fan base in Britain, South America, Australia and the East Asia, but with individual members releasing solo records, the band's attempt at a disco album (*Hot Space*) flopping and sales slipping in America the future wasn't looking too good. Tensions within the group – especially over Freddie Mercury's relationship with his personal manager Paul Prenter – were at an all-time high. Mercury was a man who clearly enjoyed all of the excess that fame afforded him, and a move to Munich for tax reasons allowed him to take advantage of the city's gay scene away from the prying eyes of the British media. However, his uninhibited behaviour was causing dissent in the ranks.

At a time when they should have been lying low and regrouping, the band walked into a PR disaster that came close to finishing them off. In October 1984, with a new album behind them (*The Works*: a Number Two hit in Britain but not even making the Top 20 in the US), Queen were castigated for playing a series of dates in Sun City, South Africa's notorious racially segregated resort, at the height of apartheid. Elton John, Rod Stewart, Cher and a number of other artists had already taken the money and played there, but Queen faced the world's opprobrium. The group received criticism in the music press for choosing money over morals, had to deal with the ignominy of a hefty fine from the Musicians' Union and were included on the United Nations' register of blacklisted artists.[12] Mercury followed this fiasco with his first solo offering. On *Mr Bad Guy*, the singer continued his flirtation with dance music: 'There Must be More to Life Than This' and 'Man Made Paradise' had originally been earmarked for *Hot Space*. Dressed in a sleeve that featured the singer in full clone mode, it sold reasonably well in the UK but bombed in America, only reaching Number 159 on the *Billboard* album charts. 'Queen might be in its twilight years,' wrote Robin Wells in his syndicated *World Of Music* column,[13] but within a month the global music event Live Aid (13 July 1985) would offer the group a platform to help them regain the position they had lost. They would remain global superstars until Freddie succumbed to AIDS on 24 November 1991; Mercury had tested HIV-positive in 1987 but had kept the diagnosis secret from all but his closest friends; however, his last years would be blighted by intrusion from the British media. Photographs of a gaunt and clearly ill Mercury were splashed across front pages, and reporters hung around his London home, desperate to catch him out. In his final statement, issued just the day before he died, he acknowledged the intrusion: 'Following the enormous conjecture in the press over the last two weeks, I wish to confirm that I have been tested HIV-positive and have AIDS. I felt it correct to keep this information private to date in order to protect the privacy of those around me. However, the time has now come for my friends and fans around the world to know the truth.' The press could not get enough: in the wake of Mercury's death, it was even suggested that Madonna, Elizabeth Taylor and Burt Reynolds had tested positive for HIV.[14]

In 1991, the duo of Elton and George re-formed, releasing a live version of John's 1974 hit 'Don't Let The Sun Go Down On Me', the proceeds of which were distributed among 10 different charities, including those raising funding for AIDS research. The following year both would take part in a concert to celebrate the life of Freddie Mercury; Elton went on to establish his own AIDS Foundation that, by 2012, had raised over $200 million to support HIV-related programmes in 55 countries. In 2005 Elton entered in to a civil partnership with David Furnish (his partner since 1993) that the couple upgraded to full marriage when the law changed in 2014. When they recorded the duet in 1991, George Michael had still to make his sexuality public; after he was arrested by an under-cover police officer for being 'engaged in a lewd act' in the rest room of a Beverly Hills park in 1998 he had little choice but to 'fess up.

Although Michael had spent his entire career fronting Wham! in the closet, his homosexuality was no secret to those who knew him – including the band's manager Simon Napier-Bell. 'He's incredibly sensible and incredibly stupid all wound up into one – as most artists are. He's the cleverest, smartest person . . .' Napier-Bell told writer Mark Ellen[15] before admitting:

He never meant to be in Wham! in the first place. Wham! was Andrew Ridgeley and never anything else. He wanted to create a group but he never saw himself in it – he was the Svengali and the songwriter, and Andrew and some other guy would be the band. So when he couldn't find the second person he thought, "I'll join the group and act the part for him", it was like a movie. Which is why he was right not to come out at the time, because he wasn't George – who was gay – but a copycat Andrew.

Wham! famously became the first Western group to play communist China, and Napier-Bell turned Ridgeley and Michael into worldwide stars, with sales in excess of 25 million in just four years. The duo split after a farewell performance in London's Wembley Stadium in front of 72,000 fans in June 1986 and Michael embarked on his phenomenally successful solo career – his first solo album, *Faith*, topped the UK, US, Spanish, Canadian and Netherlands charts – although he still did not come out until after his fateful encounter with that undercover officer.

Michael was, as Napier-Bell attested, a reluctant idol who did not deal well with fame and adulation – traits that Frank Sinatra found so abhorrent that he wrote to him in 1990, telling George to 'loosen up' and 'be grateful. You're top dog on the top rung of a tall ladder called stardom.'[16] In the early years, in an attempt to hide his sexuality, he manufactured a relationship with backing singer Pat Fernandez, a lie that was blown out of the water by the waspish tongue of his adversary Boy George. When Michael announced that splitting with Pat had 'broken his heart,' the Boy spat back 'Broke your heart did she? She lived with me for three years and all she managed to break was my Hoover!'[17] He would have been much happier simply making music. When he died, on Christmas Day 2016 at his country home in Goring-on-Thames, Oxfordshire, fans were shocked, but those who knew him better were less surprised. He had not been in good health: in 2011 he had nearly died from pneumonia, spending days in intensive care in a Viennese hospital and undergoing a life-saving tracheotomy. The condition damaged his lungs – and his ability to sing – irreparably. His friend and collaborator Sir Elton John took to Twitter to disclose that he was 'in deep shock. I have lost a beloved friend – the kindest, most generous soul and a brilliant artist.'[18]

The man who referred to himself as 'the singing Greek' was born Georgios Kyriacos Panayiotou to a Greek Cypriot restaurateur father and his English wife in 1963. With 11 Number One singles under his belt, and worldwide album sales in excess of 100 million, Michael was a genuine superstar. His reaction to being outed was pure genius: instead of hiding away at home waiting for the dust to settle he went on television to admit to his indiscretion, released a single ('Outside') with an accompanying video that made a joke of the whole affair and defiantly took a stand against the LAPD, who he – quite rightly – felt had entrapped him. He and long-time partner Kenny Goss had an open relationship, leaving George free to indulge, and although they split up in 2009 they remained close.

George Michael was a dichotomy: an intensely private man who craved sex in public places (he often found 'diversions' on notorious cruising ground Hampstead Heath). He was a man who shunned the spotlight but also one whose prodigious drug use saw him take unbelievably stupid risks (such as driving his car into the window of a photographer's shop) which would invariably end up on the front pages and which, on three occasions, saw him arrested: he would spend a month in prison in 2010 after he admitted crashing his Range Rover while under the influence of cannabis. One British tabloid had two paparazzi permanently stationed outside his London residence in case he screwed up again.[19]

Michael was, as Elton John pointed out, incredibly generous, donating large sums to charities, giving free concerts for NHS staff, playing benefits for striking miners (he was a strong supporter of LGBT and workers' rights) and, on several occasions, anonymously handing over cheques worth many thousands to people he encountered who needed help: the day after Michael died, TV presenter Richard Osman revealed that he once gave a couple who were trying to raise the money to pay for IVF treatment £15,000.[20] A former student nurse told reporters that he gave her a £5,000 tip when she was working as a waitress to help pay for her tuition.

Even though some of the biggest names in the industry were struggling with their own personal issues, their influence – good or bad – was paving the way for a new generation of musicians to be open about their sexuality. Patrick Fitzgerald, the leader of indie rock trio Kitchens of Distinction, was certainly taking note: 'It was a rubbish time to come out – the height of AIDS hysteria, and those folk who went on to more commercial success but kept their sexuality secret may have been more astute. I just never thought it was a problem. Don't care really, wouldn't have it any other way.'[21] After his band split, Fitzgerald, who went on to work as a GP before reforming KoD in 2013, recorded under the alias Fruit, issuing the single 'Queen of Old Compton Street' – 'a description of a modern London queen, which he himself is proud to be' (according to the press releases that accompanied the single) – in 1994. Chris Xefos, of US college radio favourites King Missile (and co-author of their sole hit 'Detachable Penis') felt the same: 'My biggest reason for being out is that I feel I function to my highest potential that way. People get wrapped up in trying to hide it; it's just easier to be out'.[22] Even Neil Tennant, who had resolutely refused to discuss his personal life in the media, came out in an interview with *Attitude* magazine:

When Bronski Beat came along, I was still assistant editor at *Smash Hits*. I loved those first few records. I loved the fact that they were gay, and that they were so out about it. It was the whole point of what they were doing. Jimmy Somerville was, in effect, a politician using the medium of pop music to put his message across. The Pet Shop Boys came along to make fabulous records, we didn't come along to be politicians, or to be positive role models. Having said all that, we have supported the fight for gay rights. I am gay, and I have written songs from that point of view.[23]

Questions about Suede's Brett Anderson, whose 'is he or isn't he' posturing echoed that of Freddie Mercury or any number of '70s camp pop icons, were finally answered in 2005 when he announced that he saw himself as 'a bisexual man who's never had a homosexual experience. I've never seen myself as overtly heterosexual, but then, I didn't see myself as gay. I sort of saw myself as some kind of sexual being that was floating somewhere.'[24] When guitarist Bernard Butler left Suede (known, for copyright reasons, as The London Suede in the US) he partnered up (musically speaking) with out-gay singer David McAlmont, scoring a hit with the Motown-inspired 'Yes' – a song Butler had originally offered to Morrissey. Similar questions have dogged Morrissey since he first became part of public consciousness, yet despite his appropriation of gay imagery and his veiled admission that he had, in fact, had a two-year affair with photographer Jake Walters,[25] he has denied being gay: 'Unfortunately, I am not homosexual. In technical fact I am humasexual. I am attracted to humans. But, of course . . . not many.'[26] He has, however, been a long-standing supporter of LGBT artists, and a number of LGBT musicians have gained useful exposure via a support slot at a Morrissey or Smiths concert, including David McAlmont (who supported him in London in 1995), Phranc and Melissa Ferrick.

The self-described 'all-American Jewish lesbian folksinger'[27] Phranc opened for the Pogues on tour in 1989 – but their audience did not always take to her, as her experience in Toronto proved: 'What's the way to deal with it when half the audience is screaming at me, calling me a faggot, dyke, queer, every name in the book?'[28] She had an easier time supporting Hüsker Dü and The Smiths (both in 1986), and she would later support Morrissey after he went solo. 'My sexuality is no big deal, but I do feel very strongly about it and I feel that there should be positive examples of us out there, gays and lesbians.' Growing up in Los Angeles, as Susan Gottleib, she came out when she was 17. 'I was singing in punk bands but I was pretty dissatisfied. With punk you can't understand the lyrics. I knew I had a lot to say that needed to be understood.'[29]

Melissa Ferrick began her career singing and playing in coffee houses in New York City but became famous overnight when, at the last minute, she replaced the opening act on Morrissey's 1991 tour. Signed to a long-term contract with Atlantic Records, Ferrick released her first album, *Massive Blur*, in 1993. However, like Ferron, Extra Fancy, Steven Grossman and any number of other LGBT artists had discovered before her, her relationship with the major label was destined to be difficult, and she was dropped like a stone when her first two albums did not sell enough copies for the conglomerate. Being sacked was 'difficult for me in all ways – physically, spiritually, emotionally,' she later revealed, and she started to drink heavily.[30] Sobering up she returned to music, signing with the indie label W.A.R. before, in 2000, founding her own label, Right On Records. In 1998 Ferrick joined Lilith Fair, the concert tour and travelling music festival started by Canadian singer-songwriter Sarah McLachlan and Vancouver-based independent record label Nettwerk. Hugely successful, Lilith Fair originally took place during the summers of 1997 to 1999 and, although it did not profess to have the same political or feminist stance of the Michigan Womyn's Music Festival, similarly consisted solely of female artists and woman-led bands. During its initial run, the festival raised $10 million for charity; however, an attempt to revive Lilith Fair in the summer of 2010 was less successful: ticket sales were poor and several dates had to be cancelled. McLachlan and her partners have now abandoned the concept.[31]

Major labels were still scared of the truth, especially in the US. Known for her confessional lyrics and raspy, smokey vocals, singer-songwriter, guitarist and activist Melissa Etheridge's eponymous debut album peaked at Number 22 on the *Billboard* chart, and its lead single, 'Bring Me Some Water', was Grammy-nominated. Born on 29 May 1961 in Kansas, when she signed to Island Records in 1986 she was warned by the label to keep her sexuality quiet.[32] Despite the demand, she came out as a lesbian in January 1993 at the Triangle Ball, an LGBT celebration of President Bill Clinton's first inauguration, telling the audience that her 'sister, k.d. lang has been such an inspiration,' and that she was 'very proud to have been a lesbian all my life,' a move which clearly influenced both the title and the material chosen for her next album. lang, who was also there to celebrate, told the audience that 'the best thing I ever did was to come out'.[33] Etheridge's 1993's *Yes I Am* and the accompanying Top 10 single 'I'm the Only One', catapulted her to stardom: the six-times platinum album would spend more than two and a half years in the US album chart. The next few years were busy for Etheridge – duetting with her idol Bruce Springsteen, co-parenting two children with then-partner Julie Cypher (in 2000 the couple revealed that David Crosby was the biological father of both of their kids) and recording successive hit albums. She and Cypher split, but soon after she met actress Tammy Lynn Michaels; the couple took part in a commitment ceremony in 2003, and three years later Michaels gave birth to twins. Despite being diagnosed with breast cancer in 2004 (she made a full recovery), Etheridge kept working, performing at the 2005 Grammy Awards (still bald from her chemo treatment), helping raise funds for victims of Hurricane Katrina and, in 2007, winning an Oscar for Best Original Song for 'I Need to Wake Up', from the Al Gore documentary on global warming *An Inconvenient Truth*. Etheridge and Michaels split in 2010. On 20 June 2016, Etheridge released 'Pulse', a song written in reaction to the mass shootings that took place at the LGBT nightclub in Orlando, Florida eight days earlier, which left 49 people dead and 53 others wounded. The Admiral Duncan, one of London's longest-established gay pubs, was the scene of a nail bomb explosion in April 1999 which killed three people and wounded around 70, but the Pulse attack was the deadliest incident of violence against LGBT people in US history. All money raised from the sale of 'Pulse' was donated to Equality Florida, the state's largest LGBT civil rights organisation.

Sia

Sam Smith

HiFi Sean

Beth Ditto

Conchita Wurst

Olly Alexander

Bright Light Bright Light

k anderson

CHAPTER 19

Out and Proud in the Twenty-First Century

'We all choose our roles, our situations; whether we choose to learn from them is the essential thing'

Boy George[1]

J ust as the old century was drawing to a close, a young Puerto Rican singer called Ricky Martin, who had originally found fame as a member of the massively successful Latino boy band Menudo, scored a massive hit with the song 'Livin' La Vida Loca'. The song was a huge international success; it took the Number One spot in the UK, US, Spain, Finland, New Zealand, Canada and Ireland, hit the Top 10 in ten more, and sold in excess of eight million copies worldwide. That phenomenal achievement helped to kick-start an explosion of interest in Latin pop, with Spanish-speaking artists including Enrique Iglesias and Shakira making a successful assault on the English-speaking market. With his first English-language hit, Ricky Martin was being hailed as the crossover kid, and – after a breakthrough performance at the 1999 Grammys – was catapulted into the limelight.

Sadly, this level of seemingly instant fame came with a catch, and certain sectors of the media immediately began to question his sexuality. The interest in Martin's love life was puerile and ugly, and smacked a little of racism: he's different; let's get him. Martin, they reasoned, *looked* gay; he had a large gay following (so does Kylie, and I cannot recall anyone trying to force *her* out of the closet) and he chose not to talk about his private life. *He must be gay!* True, his style owed a lot to the gay clubs of Puerto Rico and, following speculation from American tabloids, George Michael (of all people) and the academic and social critic Camille Paglia he was asked, in a December 2000 interview with *The Mirror*, to comment on the rumours. 'I don't think I should have to tell anyone if I am gay or not, or who I've slept with or not,' he answered, but the sniggering continued for almost a decade until, on 29 March 2010, Martin publicly acknowledged his homosexuality in a post on his official website.

He wrote, two years after becoming (via a surrogate) the father of twins:

> I am proud to say that I am a fortunate homosexual man. I am very blessed to be who I am. Many people told me: "Ricky it's not important", "it's not worth it", "all the years you've worked and everything you've built will collapse", "many people in the world are not ready to accept your truth, your reality, your nature". Because all this advice came from people who I love dearly, I decided to move on with my life not sharing with the world my entire truth. Allowing myself to be seduced by fear and insecurity became a self-fulfilling prophecy of sabotage. Today I take full responsibility for my decisions and my actions.[2]

Martin, whose career had hit a slump, was clearly re-invigorated by his admission: the two albums released after he came out sold better than his last 'straight' release (2005's *Life*), both receiving universally positive reviews and garnering several music industry awards.

Ricky had learned the hard way that they only way forward was to be honest with himself. 'There [were] many times when I went to bed hating myself – when I went to sleep at night, saying like, "You are not – you are not a good person",' he admitted:[3]

> I was very angry, very rebellious. I used to look at gay men and think, "I'm not like that, I don't want to be like that, that's not me". I was ashamed. When you're told you're wrong by everyone, from society,

from your faith – my self-esteem was crushed. I took my anger out on those around me. I look back now and realize I would bully people who I knew were gay. I had internalized homophobia. To realize that was confronting to me. I wanted to get away from that.[4]

As Martin discovered, life for LGBT people has changed dramatically over the 100 years since Tony Jackson wrote 'Pretty Baby'. In 2000, the age of consent in Britain was finally equalised, with sex between same-sex couples and between heterosexual couples legal from the age of 16: the homosexual age of consent had been set at 21 in 1967 but reduced to 18 in 1994. In September 2003, after three years of opposition from the House of Lords, Britain's Labour government wiped Section 28 from the statute books and, just two years later, the first civil partnerships took place in the country, with Sir Elton John (and his partner David Furnish) and Labi Siffre (and his partner Peter John Carver Lloyd) being some of the first LGBT musicians to take advantage of the change in both law and attitude. In March 2013, the law was updated once again and, for the first time, two people of the same sex could legally enter into a marriage together in Britain. Same-sex marriage is now available in more than 20 countries, with legal rights guaranteed to same-sex couples in at least as many more. However, many countries and territories still have laws which criminalise LGBT people and in 11 countries (along with Daesh or Islamic State) homosexuality is punishable by death.

This new sense of freedom and acceptance has seen a number of major stars feel safe enough to come out in recent years, including international hit-makers Sam Smith, Sia (who has collaborated with Zero 7, Christina Aguilera, Kylie Minogue, Beyoncé, David Guetta, Rihanna and Flo Rida among others), Adam Lambert (who, since 2011, has toured and recorded with Brian May and Roger Taylor of Queen), singer and plus-size clothing magnate Beth Ditto, who describes herself as a 'fat, feminist lesbian from Arkansas,'[5] and Olly Alexander, the lead singer of British band Years & Years who, at the time of writing, was working with the ubiquitous Pet Shop Boys. Lambert is one of the new breed of LGBT pop stars who, like Britain's Will Young, was discovered via a prime-time TV talent show. But both Lambert and Young are anomalies: most of the winners and also-rans who found a measure of instant celebrity on *American*

Idol, Britain's Got Talent and so on faded into obscurity just as quickly. It remains to be seen if out-gay performers Lucy Spraggan, Saara Aalto and the like can forge successful, long-lasting careers out of their moment on the spotlight.

We've also seen openly 'queer' performers such as Austria's Conchita Wurst and Israel's Dana International winning the Eurovision Song Contest. Perhaps more importantly, heterosexual actors, musicians and other artists who openly support LGBT rights have become more vocal and more militant: when Australian pop star Kylie Minogue and her English actor fiancé Joshua Sasse announced their engagement, they also made it clear that they would not marry until Australia legalised same-sex marriage. Kylie's huge LGBT fan base wholeheartedly approved.

In 2001, Sean Dickson, leader of Scottish indie rock band the Soup Dragons, decided to come out. Best known for their UK Top Five hit 'I'm Free' (a cover of the Rolling Stones' song), the group had disbanded a few years earlier and Sean, after forming the psychedelic pop band The High Fidelity, was fast becoming one of the UK's best-known DJs and producers. He was also married, and he and his wife were expecting a baby. 'It was a hellish decision,' he admits, 'to say those words and realise you were going to hurt those around you, especially those you love and care for very much. Maybe it was a bit selfish in retrospect, but I had to do what was right.'

With a friend, Dickson started a new club night in Glasgow, Record Players; one of the earliest acts to perform there was the Scissor Sisters. Then, through another friend, he met Mike. 'Falling in love is not a choice,' he says, 'But staying in love is. As I wrote in the song 'I Thank U' [released as a single by The High Fidelity in 2000], 'you left my right and you right my wrong'; that usually helps answer any questions for me when I have no answers for them.' In 2016, as HiFi Sean, he released a new album, *Ft.*, a celebration of dance music on which he collaborates with a number of iconic artists including Billie Ray Martin (of Electribe 101), Crystal Waters, Yoko Ono, Fred Schneider of the B-52s and David McAlmont. 'From a historical point of view, I think that being gay in dance music – like within disco for instance – was likely easier as it was way more hedonistic and flamboyant than the more macho Rock 'n' Roll stance in band culture,' he adds. 'The celebration of clubland has always, and will always, have to have a major payback to gay culture, as if it were not for those musical icons and revolutionaries back then who stood loud and proud where would we be today?'

In an interview with *Fader* magazine issued the same week as his debut album *In the Lonely Hour*, Sam Smith came out, hinting that repressing his sexuality had caused him to consider self harm.[6] The revelation did nothing to harm his meteoric ascendancy: in September 2015, Smith released 'Writing's on the Wall', the theme song to the twenty-forth James Bond film, *Spectre* and the first Bond theme to reach Number One in the UK. The song earned Smith an Academy Award for Best Original Song. As Sean Dickson says: 'Music and sexuality mean nothing to me as a package; I never cared or thought it made any difference. All I cared about was if the actual record, or song or artist et cetera, were any good. I still do to be honest. I don't think in musical genres and especially not in sexual genres.'

Dickson and Smith are not the only LGBT artists to have struggled with their sexuality. Once the leader of the critically acclaimed Czars, John Grant is one of biggest openly gay stars in the world today, with three hit solo albums, collaborations with Elton John and Sinead O'Connor and a slew of awards to his name. Heavily influenced by 'a lot of music that comes from the United Kingdom, especially during the late 70s and the 80s – things like Gary Numan, Blancmange, Visage, Depeche Mode, New Order, the Pet Shop Boys, XTC, the Psychedelic Furs – a lot of Trevor Horn-produced stuff,' he's also a huge fan of Boy George. But that fame has come with a price, not the least of which was, in 2012, discovering that he was HIV-positive. Add that to dealing with what he himself terms 'decades of brainwashing' from a traumatic childhood (his parents' religious beliefs lead to years of what he terms 'spiritual abuse'),[7] an anxiety disorder plus a self-destructive streak – with its roots in the homophobia and bullying he faced during his youth in Michigan – which saw Grant battle with drug and alcohol abuse, and it's a wonder he's producing music at all.

'When I was young, people were so disgusted by me,' he told NPR's Mark Daley. 'Before I even knew that I was gay everybody else had it figured out and, you know, they were letting you know.'[8] 'At home and at church I was told "you're going to spend an eternity being punished for this behaviour, which you have brought on yourself". If I had been able to express myself I would have found that there were some places and some people who would accept me, even back then and I find it sad that I was never able to access that, because for me it was just hostility wherever I went.' His third solo album, 2015's *Grey Tickles, Black Pressure*, features an eyeless Grant on the front cover; promotional shots included a blood spattered Grant wielding a croquet mallet. 'It's what I feel like doing every time someone calls me a faggot,' he admits.

Now living in Reykjavík, his lyrics can be as dark as an Icelandic winter ('grey tickles' is the Icelandic for 'mid-life crisis'; 'black pressure' comes from the Turkish for 'nightmare'), and he doesn't shy away from singing about his own sexual experiences, as he did with excruciating honesty on the song 'Jesus Hates Faggots' (from his debut solo album *Queen of Denmark*), which contains the lyrics 'I've felt uncomfortable since the day that I was born' and 'I can't believe that I've considered taking my own life'. With his background, it should not be surprising to find songs filled with hate and anger, but there is tenderness, too. 'Although my story is no more or less important than anyone else's, at least at this point I can admit to being a human who deserves to be happy no more or less than anyone else,' he says. 'If I had heard a song like "Snug Slacks" [from *Grey Tickles, Black Pressure*] when I was a gay teenager I think he could have saved me 10 or 15 years of heartache and pain,' Tom Robinson adds. 'It's great to hear somebody making music this unashamed and irresistible'.

Canadian musician Woodpigeon, aka Mark Andrew Hamilton, began playing music (on what his official biography claims was a stolen guitar) while living in Edinburgh in 2005, around the same time that he started to fully embrace his sexuality. 'The first time I ever felt like a complete person was when I moved to Scotland as a young adult,' he explains. 'There I got to live as an openly gay person. And I started to feel and understand why people feel so tied to where they live and why they go to such great lengths to defend pieces of land.'[9] Of shared Scots and Germanic descent – one set of grandparents fled Berlin after Hitler rose to power – Woodpigeon has been compared favourably to John Grant: the two men are friends, have toured together and share a confessional approach to lyric writing. 'I don't think that anyone who comes to see

Woodpigeon thinks that they are coming to a gay band – or a straight band for that matter – but I don't hide it and [being gay] is explicit in my lyrics,' he admits.[10]

John Grant was supported on his 2015 tour by Bright Light Bright Light, the stage name of New York-based Rod Thomas. Brought up in the valleys of South Wales, Rod learned how to play several instruments from an early age, and started busking in the London Underground after moving to the metropolis to study. With three successful albums behind him, plus plaudits from the Pet Shop Boys and Elton John, Bright Light Bright Light showcases Rod's love of pop, disco and electronica, yet he began his musical career a decade ago (under his own name) playing what he describes as 'organic, folk-y' music. Thomas is one of the most independent pop stars in the world, managing every part of his career himself, from booking his own gigs to running his own label, Self Raising Records, whose expanding roster includes Bridget Barkan, Beth Hirsch and Slow Knights, a musical collective put together by the Scissor Sisters' Del Marquis in which Thomas also features. He also publishes his own music, organises his own recording dates and is completely hands-on when it comes to the visual image Bright Light Bright Light presents to the public. 'A lot of the artists that influence me have really strong identities,'[11] he says. 'Lots of people who shape-shifted that were also very clearly identifiable like Kate Bush, Bjork, Elton John, Erasure, the Pet Shop Boys, David Bowie, people like that who worked in lots of different genres, and really showed that you could push boundaries and that you could try your hand at lots of different things but still remain quite clearly yourself. They were also people who let me dream and pushed my mind a little bit.' His influences, and his DIY ethic, are shared by Manchester-based composer/producer Ben McGarvey, who has released two albums and a trio of EPs under the name Minute Taker via his own Octagonal Records imprint. Nominated (in 2011) for *Mojo* magazine's New Voice Award, Ben creates his emotive and often dark songs using a mixture of acoustic and electronic instruments. Rod Thomas' style has changed quite dramatically over the years, and he has worked with Elton John, who became something of a mentor to the young Welshman, as well as John Grant, the Scissor Sisters and many other big names. 'It's not quite because of the community that we all met, but it does feel fucking brilliant to be accepted in to that world. There really is a danger; a lot of people still feel so completely isolated in their lives because of their sexuality, and it's not a given that the gay world is going to accept you: it can be really brutal. I feel really, really happy and really grateful to have found a place in the gay community where the music that I make is appreciated and I've got to meet some absolutely incredible people. That's the nicest thing about success.'

He's not one to rest on his laurels, though, and he understands that not everyone has been as lucky:

> There have been moments when I've been aware that being a gay man didn't make me desirable as a signing or as an option of an artist to push, but I've also not had any direct hurdles in my path really. I've been very lucky I think, especially in the decade in which I came to release my music, as things were a lot more liberal in general then. It wasn't as stigmatised and I also I wasn't trying to be Michael Bublé or Robbie Williams or someone. If I was going that route, or if I was an actor, then I would be much more hesitant to talk about my sexuality, because I know that that wider, mass-appeal audience does have an issue with how they treat out artists . . . I did find it harder when I was doing more organic, folk-labelled music because nobody in that world at that time was out, really. I felt like I didn't fit in to that world at all and I felt kind of at odds with myself and with that music scene in a way . . . everyone else was straight, other than Owen Pallett, who was a real anomaly in terms of how creative he was and how out and vocal he was. At the time I didn't feel like I had any gay contemporaries.

Born in Ontario, multi-instrumentalist and singer Pallett believes his work is implicitly influenced by his sexuality, saying, 'As far as whether the music I make is gay or queer, yeah, it comes from the fact that I'm gay, but that doesn't mean I'm making music about it.'[12]

It was when Thomas started to explore electronic and dance music that he suddenly found a world full of kindred spirits. Formed in 2001, the Scissor Sisters' eponymous debut was the UK's biggest-selling album of 2004 and spawned five hit singles. Named after a lesbian sex act (the original moniker was Dead Lesbian; they then became the Fibrillating

Scissor Sisters), original drummer Paddy Boom (born Patrick Seacor) was the only straight member of the five-piece, who fused glam rock, disco and electronica with 'a giddy swirl of '70s and '80s pop pastiches'[13] into a vibrant, dance-friendly pop sound that hit big with British audiences long before their home audience caught up. US sales of *Scissor Sisters* were not helped by retail giant Wal-Mart's refusal to stock it, claiming that it the album was 'a snarling, swaggering attack on conservatism'.[14] No matter; in other territories the Scissor Sisters could do no wrong, and soon the Sisters were writing hits for Kylie Minogue (the UK Number Two 'I Believe in You'), and collaborating with Elton John on their Number One single 'I Don't Feel Like Dancin''; the band's male vocalist Jake Shears (born Jason Sellards) and long-time Sisters collaborator John "JJ" Garden wrote the music for the stage adaptation of Armistead Maupin's *Tales of the City*. Many Scissor Sisters lyrics (usually written by Shears and Scott Hoffman, aka Babydaddy) deal with LGBT themes: 'Filthy/Gorgeous' is about transsexual prostitutes while 'Take Your Mama' deals with coming out to family members. The video for 'Filthy/Gorgeous', directed by John Cameron Mitchell, co-creator and director of the cult film *Hedwig and the Angry Inch*, aped Frankie Goes To Hollywood's 'Relax'. It was every inch as outlandish as the original, but 20 years on, videos set in sex dens were less shocking than they once had been.

As Rod Thomas and the Scissor Sisters have found, support from established names goes a long way towards encouraging acceptance: bisexual American singer Meshell Ndegeocello was one of the first acts signed to Madonna's Maverick label, and appeared on her mentor's *Bedtime Stories* album. Her song 'Leviticus Faggot' from the 1996 album *Peace Beyond Passion* tells the stories of people encountering extreme homophobia: 'I grew up in an environment where there was homophobia and it came out of a bunch of experiences all bundled up into one song, it just came from life. It's a story that a lot of people can tell.'[15] Meshell's 2012 album *Pour une Ame Souveraine (For a Sovereign Soul)* is a tribute to bisexual singer Nina Simone. That influence can go both ways; established artists looking for a career boost will often seek out the services of Linda Perry, one of the most in-demand writers and producers working in pop and rock today. The songwriter (now married to actress Sara Gilbert) first found fame when she fronted the band 4 Non Blondes ('What's Up' was a huge international success in 1993), but has become better known for writing and producing hits for a number of world-famous artists, including Miley Cyrus, Christina Aguilera, Gwen Stefani and Celine Dion, and for working with artists as diverse as Adam Lambert, Courtney Love, Robbie Williams and Adele.

Rufus Wainwright, the son of folk singers Kate McGarrigle and Loudon Wainwright III (and brother of singer Martha Wainwright), identified as gay while a teenager, coming out to his parents when he was 14:

> My mother wasn't happy when she found out. She'd found a maga-zine or something and so I told her. She basically told me, "Don't tell me something I don't want to hear." And I went, "Okay." And then I basically told her I was straight. She just wanted to live in denial for a while which I think a lot of parents want to do. I came out again much later, when I was 18. I made the announcement and then it was more accepted.[16]

He released his eponymous debut album in 1998 and since then has issued more than a dozen albums, written two operas and has taken part in the Cyndi Lauper-founded *True Colors* touring festival, which raised funds for LGBT campaign groups including the Human Rights Campaign, PFLAG and the Matthew Shepard Foundation. In the summer of 2001, Rufus was joined by the Pet Shop Boys, Soft Cell, the Magnetic Fields and others for *Wotaplava*, the world's first gay-themed touring music festival, with concerts in 18 North American cities. On 23 August 2012, he married his partner, German-born arts administrator Jörn Weisbrodt, in Montauk, New York.

Like Grant, Thomas and the Scissor Sisters, Wainwright is a keen collaborator, appearing as guest vocalist on the 2006 Pet Shop Boys album *Concrete* and on *I Am a Bird Now*, the 2005 Mercury prize-winning album by Antony and the Johnsons. Anohni was born (and given the name Antony Hegarty by his family) in 1971 in Chichester, West Sussex, England, although her family moved first to Amsterdam and then to New York before she was 10. A lonely, introverted child who 'saw my reflection in Boy George,' as a young teen she was 'listening to OMD, Kate Bush, Culture Club, Alison Moyet and especially Marc and the Mambas, which was this incredibly dark and emotional side project for Marc Almond. I was probably the only child in America who had those records, special ordering them at the age of 13.'[17] Like Meshell Ndegeocello, she was also heavily influenced by Nina Simone.

In 1990, while attending the Experimental Theatre Wing of New York University, Anohni co-founded the performance collective Blacklips, basing her gender-defying look on those teenage heroes: 'On the cover of "Torch" [the 1982 Soft Cell single] there is a picture of a transvestite without her wig, with her head shaved and smoking a cigarette. I modelled myself on that. It's what I looked like when I was 19 and playing at the Pyramid Club, shaved and smoking on a stool.'

Infamous for stalking the streets of New York with the words 'fuck off' written on her forehead, Lou Reed was an early fan: 'When I heard Antony, I knew that I was in the presence of an angel,' he said.[18] While singing in bars and touting tapes around record companies, Anohni formed a band, a loose collection of friends she christened Antony and the Johnsons. From the off, Antony and the Johnsons revelled in a queer aesthetic; Anohni lyrics were brutal, raw and defiantly sexual ('Cripple and the Starfish', from their debut album, describes an abusive gay relationship from the perspective of the abused partner) and Anohni distinctive voice and deft lyrics quickly became in demand among New York's elite, leading to her working with Reed, Yoko Ono, Rufus Wainwright and her idol, Boy George.

In 2015 Anohni, who had always been open about her transgender status and had bared her soul on such songs as 'For Today I Am A Boy' (from *I Am a Bird Now,* which opens with the couplet 'One day I'll grow up, I'll be a beautiful woman') revealed that she was now ready to live life as a woman, transitioning and releasing a new album, *Hopelessness.* In a radio interview with Radio One's Annie Mac, Anohni revealed that she had been using the name 'in my personal life for years now'. Anohni is the co-founder of the Future Feminist Foundation, a growing network of friends, thinkers and associates including Reed's widow Laurie Anderson.[19]

*

Record companies in Britain took note of the critical acclaim that the new wave of LGBT artists were having and went looking for similar artists. One of those approached was the London-based (Scots-born and Adelaide-raised) singer-songwriter k. anderson, who had been building a following for his folk-influenced, deeply personal songs. 'I've had a few interactions with the music industry over the years,'[20] he explains, 'and they are always interesting. In the wake of Rufus Wainwright's success I was seen by some as a British-lite version, and so had some sharks circling for a wee while. This was also around the time when self-releasing became a viable option for bands, and so I saw lots of acts record, release and promote their own releases. Being the control freak that I am this was super appealing to me, and I guess I romanticised how rewarding and easy it would be. The reality is much more tedious and involves far more hours of self-doubt and pity. But, somehow that feels about right.'

anderson self-released two EPs and a critically-lauded album, *The Overthinker*, although in recent years he has concentrated on getting his music out via download sites and by making award-winning videos for YouTube. It's hardly surprising that Tom Robinson would pick up on the buzz, featuring anderson's '14 Year-Old Me' and his most recent single 'Bitter Wind' on his BBC Radio 6 show. anderson's lyrics are equally as personal as those of Wainwright or Grant, and in a way echo the songs of Steven Grossman, although his own influences are more prosaic. 'Ani DiFranco, Lisa Loeb, Joni Mitchell . . . hell, there was a time when I was indiscriminately listening to music made by women wielding guitars,' he admits.

> The 1960s were a big influence on my music. Motown is the obvious starting place – my heart belongs to The Supremes – but also the Brill Building sound created by these young, naïve, brilliant musicians holed up in tiny offices in a random building on Broadway, NYC. Something about the romance of it all has always resonated with me. The thing about what I do, musically, is that it is so reliant on the lyrics being honest and about my own life and experiences, that it would just be jarring and strange if I watered it down and took out references to gender or, indeed, denied the fact that my sexuality is one of the

most important factors in helping to define my character; the way that I have had to navigate and negotiate the world around me due to the stigma and attitudes about homosexuality. It's never really been a question for me about whether or not to hide my sexuality in my songs and persona. Plus, it's just not really practical for me to pretend to be straight – it's stonkingly obvious when you meet me!'

The very fact that record companies would be looking for obviously LGBT artists to add to their roster is evidence that prejudice is – slowly – evaporating. Yet even in these enlightened days, some musical genres are still resistant to any performer being open and honest about their sexuality. When Trey Pearson of Christian rock band Everyday Sunday came out as gay in May 2016, he was immediately axed from appearing at Joshua Fest, a Christian music festival held annually in Northern California. Members of the production team threatened to walk out if Pearson performed at the three-day event. He did appear, as the surprise guest of fellow Christian rockers Five Iron Frenzy: the band had considered boycotting the festival to protest against Pearson's exclusion.[21] Luther Vandross was a giant of the recording industry, who sang backing vocals for David Bowie and co-wrote the song 'Fascination' which appeared on Bowie's 1975 album *Young Americans*. He also enjoyed fame as a solo star, selling in excess of 35 million records and was the recipient of eight Grammy Awards, including four for Best Male R&B Vocal Performance. Yet he died, in 2005 after a stroke, having never come out – seemingly worried about how the revelation would affect his career. 'Clearly, a lot of black gay performers feel they can't come out,' Michael Roberson, director of gay group People of Colour in Crisis, told *Pink News*. 'Yet it would be important, particularly to black gay young people, to see black gay role models'.[22]

Irish singer, songwriter and multi-instrumentalist Andrew Hozier-Byrne, who performs under the mononym Hozier, released his debut EP *Take Me to Church* in 2013; the video for the powerful title track (which also appeared on his first album, *Hozier*), features two men kissing passionately; the men are pursued by a mob who eventually track one of them down and beat him to a pulp. Conceived to raise awareness and offer support for gay marriage following the criminalisation of homosexuality in Russia, the track reached the Number Two spot in Britain and America and was nominated for a Grammy for Song of the Year. Hozier himself is straight, but the song made many in the media question his sexuality. 'I don't think it's the point,' he told the *Reuters* news agency. 'It doesn't come into it ... regardless of the sexual orientation behind a relationship, it is still a relationship and still love ... So people are free to make any assumption they want'.[23] Perhaps we're ready for a new, more accepting world where the male vocalists of a band like Australia's The Goon Sax can sing about wanting a boyfriend or imagining what it would be like to hold hands with the cute tall guy down the road without being automatically accused of being queer, or where artists like Britain's Rag 'n' Bone Man can openly support LGBT rights without having their own sexuality questioned. Not one interviewer has questioned The Goon Sax – Brisbane teenagers Riley Jones, Louis Forster and James Harrison who formed their band at high school in 2013 – about their sexuality. It's simply not relevant.

Or maybe it is. Sadly we still live in a world rampant with both overt and casual homophobia (Katy Perry may claim to support LGBT rights, but her first hit for Capitol was the distinctly homophobic 'UR So Gay'), a world lurching towards the Right politically with the LGBT community facing an erosion of our hard-won rights. That homophobia is still present in the mainstream media: when Boyzone singer Stephen Gately was discovered dead by his husband in their Spanish villa in October 2009, the accusations flew. In an article headlined 'Why There was Nothing "Natural" about Stephen Gately's Death,' *Daily Mail* columnist Jan Moir was the first to dance on his grave. It did not matter that Gately had died from a previously undetected heart condition and that the official post mortem attributed the singer's death to natural causes. 'Healthy and fit 33-year-old men do not just climb into their pyjamas and go to sleep on the sofa, never to wake up again. Whatever the cause of death is, it is not, by any yardstick, a natural one,' she continued. 'The circumstances surrounding his death are more than a little sleazy'. She continued to write that Gately's death 'strikes another blow to the happy-ever-after myth of civil partnerships' and that 'once again, under the carapace of glittering, hedonistic celebrity, the ooze of a very different and more dangerous lifestyle has seeped out for all to see'. The article provoked a massive outcry, not just from bereaved Boyzone fans and members of Stephen Gately's family, but from people worldwide outraged at Moir's shocking, ghoulish glee in the death of a young celebrity – and the obvious homophobia displayed in her column. The Irish edition of the newspaper refused to run the article. Moir's piece prompted a record 25,000 complaints to the press watchdog, and the online version of the article was quickly amended. Although she flatly refused to retract her words, Moir did apologise to his family for the timing of her article. Too late: the damage was already done.[24]

Social media has changed the landscape in more ways than one. Not only is it easier for an unsigned or independent act to find an audience for their music, but musicians are also able to interact with fans directly, bypassing onerous PR departments. Sometimes this can be a bad thing – after all, one of the functions of a decent PR department is to keep their charges out of trouble – but more often than not it allows artists the opportunity to be more human, and gives music consumers a level of access never before afforded them. Olly Alexander regularly uses his Instagram account to post pictures of himself with his partner Neil Amin-Smith, the violinist for electronic group Clean Bandit, and he's not alone. 'It's a bit of a double-edged sword,' says k. anderson:

> Yes, there are more and more independent LGBT artists breaking through, and that's largely because of the widespread use of the Internet and having infinite platforms to promote themselves on. But, and this is true of most currently successful musicians, the artistry is becoming less important than the image. There are a tonne of pretty young male singers who post endless pictures of themselves at the gym, and get a tonne of attention for it. But, when they then post their songs or videos they get a fraction of the attention. I'm not trying to say that there has ever been a point in time when the image hasn't been important, but there's something that's a bit relentless and vapid about the whole thing. No one is locked in a room writing songs for themselves anymore – instead they are almost tailoring their output to the audience they know intimately. Maybe that's a good thing, though?

While there's no denying that YouTube, Facebook, Soundcloud *et al.* are making it easier for LGBT artists to be heard, these platforms also allow people the opportunity to rediscover (or, more often than not, uncover for the very first time) music made 30, 40 even 50 years ago or more. Reissue programmes – like the one spearheaded by Chapter Music's Ben O'Connor and Guy Blackman – are, in Blackman's own words, 'providing neglected gay artists with long overdue validation and re-assessment, and filling a gaping hole in our historical awareness . . . when the *Strong Love* compilation came out in 2012 . . . we never imagined [it] would find a mainstream audience, but we wanted the songs to enter the digital world and have a permanent presence, so that anyone could come to them when they were ready.' Tracking down these artists and their recordings has had a profound influence on Guy's own work:

> I've had my own struggles and triumphs writing songs sensitively and honestly dealing with the experiences of being gay. I can trace a real change in my approach to songwriting back to the mid-2000s when we first started tracking down all these amazing 1970s and 1980s queer artists, and most of what we discovered came from JD Doyle's incredible Queer Music Heritage website. These musicians were brave enough to sing openly gay songs in different, more hostile times, and it gave me strength to try to do the same 30 years later. The reissues we've done are partly my way of saying thanks.

'This new interest blows me away,' adds John 'Smokey' Condon. 'I've done like 25 interviews, a photo shoot and now my music is going to be used in a film about Tom of Finland! All I wanted to do was sing, and sing songs about what I knew about, you know?'

In 2016, 35 years after *Finally* hit the streets, Blackberri is back, performing live, recording and starring in the short film *Eat the Rich.* 'I feel like I'm starting all over again,' he says. 'There's a whole group of young people who are discovering me and that's really kind of interesting. I've always had a young audience: when I used to travel across the country I would often meet some of those people, and now I'm meeting adults who say "I heard you when I was younger on the radio": I feel like I've raised about three or four generations of gay youth!' Chief among the songs being laid down for his new album is the track 'Your Boyfriend is My Girlfriend In Bed', a hysterically funny little song which has Blackberri has been including in his live set for a while now. It's easy to see how his use of humour and biting satire influenced LGBT artists Romanovsky and Phillips, the San Francisco-based act dubbed 'the gay Simon and Garfunkel'.

On 24 February 2017, Blackberri received a Lifetime Achievement Award for his work with the black LGBT community in the Bay area. The following day, Patrick Haggerty announced that he had recorded a new Lavender Country track, 'Red Dress', for the various artists' *Our First 100 Days* project, a benefit album for good causes under threat from the Trump administration. Other artists are also seeing the benefits of this renewed interest in our musical heritage. 'I'm absolutely gobsmacked,' admits Paul Southwell of Handbag. 'I thought it was dead and buried, I really did. I'm absolutely amazed that anybody is really interested.' 'It's wonderful, and I just knew we were right,' adds Paul Rutherford. 'I knew we were right to go through all of that angst. Frankie burnt twice as bright but lived half as long; it was like a big, mad firework and it couldn't have gone any further really.'

'I think it's fantastic that today's artists feel able to be open about their sexuality,' says Tom Robinson:

It's marvellous that people can just make music and it's kind of incidental what their sexuality is, certainly in the rarefied atmosphere of today's music industry on this side of the pond. Take Sam Smith: it's really good that he's done what he's done and has been as open as he has been and been as successful as he has been. It remains to be seen in post-Trump America whether a lot of those freedoms and tolerances do get whittled away. For myself, I'd like to live in a world where we don't have to have a label. Labels are all very well, but they help with the process of "othering" other people; it makes it "us and them", and we've suffered long enough from being a "them", with the other people excluding us because they put these labels on us. Be yourself, be proud of whoever you are and don't let anybody tell you how to live your life is the key advice to anybody, whether they're a musician or not.

Acknowledgements

A book like this could not have been written without the sterling work of countless other authors, whose books have been invaluable, occasionally frustrating but always inspiring. I hope I've covered all of them in the Bibliography; my profuse apologies to anyone I've missed. A personal note of thanks to John Aggy, Chris Albertson, Jonno Andrews, k. anderson, Andy Bell, Blackberri, Guy Blackman, John Condon, Ray Connolly, St. Sukie de la Croix, John Deane, Sean Dickson (HiFi Sean), Alix Dobkin, JD Doyle, Robbie Duke (Patrick Pink), Richard Evans, John Grant, Dean Griffith, Patrick Haggerty, Drake Jensen, James Lawler, Ian Leak, Dane Lewis, Mista Majah P, David Marshall, Michael Morin, Holly Near, Ben O'Connor, Andy Partridge, Phranc, Gemma Read and the team at the LSE for helping with access to the Hall-Carpenter Archive, Tom Robinson, Paul Rutherford, Paul Southwell, Rod Thomas, Mandy Weetch, Cris Williamson, Mitchell Winn, and the Women's Liberation Music Archive.

A big 'thank you' to the amazingly supportive teams at Duckworth in London and Overlook in New York, especially Gesche Ipsen, Peter Mayer, Matt Casbourne, Thogdin Ripley, Liz Dexter, Josh Bryson, David Marshall, Chelsea Cutchens and Shannon McCain. I am forever humbled and will always be grateful for your faith in me.

Finally, thank you, Niall, for your unending love and support. Now, where's that cup of tea you promised me?

Bibliography

Abbott, Lynn and Seroff, Doug – *Ragged but Right: Black Traveling Shows, Coon Songs, and the Dark Pathway to Blues and Jazz* (University Press of Mississippi, Jackson, MS, 2009)

Albertson, Chris – *Bessie: A Biography* (Barrie and Jenkins, London, 1972)

Aldrich, Robert and Wotherspoon, Garry (eds.) – *Who's Who in Contemporary Gay and Lesbian History* (Routledge, London, 2001)

Alpern, Tyler – *Bruz Fletcher: Camped, Tramped & A Riotous Vamp* (Tyler Alpern, 2010)

Amico, Stephen – *Roll Over, Tchaikovsky!: Russian Popular Music and Post-Soviet Homosexuality* (University of Illinois Press, Chicago, IL, 2014)

Armstrong, Louis – *Satchmo: My Life in New Orleans* (Prentice-Hall, Upper Saddle River, NJ, 1954)

Baim, Tracy (ed.) – *Out and Proud in Chicago* (Agate Surrey, Evanston, IL, 2008)

Baumgardner, Jennifer – *F'em!: Goo Goo, Gaga, and Some Thoughts on Balls* (Seal Press, Berkeley, CA, 2011)

Beatles, The – *The Beatles Anthology* (Cassell & Co, London, 2000)

Blesh, Rudy – *They All Played Ragtime* (Alfred A. Knopf, New York, 1950)

Brothers, Thomas – *Louis Armstrong's New Orleans* (W. W. Norton & Company, London, 2007)

Bullock, Darryl W. – *The World's Worst Records, Volume One* (Bristol Green Publishing, Bristol, 2013)

Burns, Pete – *Freak Unique: My Autobiography* (John Blake Publishing Ltd, London, 2007)

Cassidy, David – *Could It Be Forever?* (Headline, London, 2012)

Chauncey, George – *Gay New York: Gender, Urban Culture, and the Making of the Gay Male World, 1890-1940* (Basic Books, New York, 1995)

Clarke, Donald – *Billie Holiday: Wishing on the Moon,* (Da Capo Press, Cambridge, MA, 2000)

Cowton, Michael – *Pet Shop Boys: Introspective* (Sidgwick & Jackson, London, 1991)

Cullen, Frank – *Vaudeville Old and New: An Encyclopedia of Variety Performances in America* (Routledge, London, 2006)

De le Croix, St. Sukie – *Chicago Whispers* (University of Wisconsin Press, Madison, WI, 2012)

Dobkin, Alix – *My Red Blood: A Memoir of Growing Up Communist, Coming Onto the Greenwich Village Folk Scene, and Coming Out in the Feminist Movement* (Alyson Books, New York, 2009)

Dubowsky, Jack Curtis – *Intersecting Film, Music, and Queerness* (Palgrave Macmillan, Basingstoke, 2016)

Duchovnay, Gerald (ed.) – *Film Voices: Interviews from Post Script* (State University of New York Press, Albany, NY, 2004)

Earles, Andrew – *Hüsker Dü: The Story of the Noise-Pop Pioneers Who Launched Modern Rock* (Voyageur Press, London, 2010)

Faderman, Lillian and Timmons, Stuart – *Gay L.A.: A History of Sexual Outlaws, Power Politics, and Lipstick Lesbians* (Basic Books, New York, 2006)

Garber, Marjorie – *Bisexuality and the Eroticism of Everyday Life* (Routledge, London, 2000)

Goblinski, Gene (ed.) – *The 100 Most Influential Musicians of All Time* (Rosen Publishing Group, New York, 2009), p. 162

Hadleigh, Boze – *Hollywood Babble On: Stars Gossip about Other Stars* (Penguin Group (USA), London, 1995)

Hajdu, David – *Lush Life: A Biography of Billy Strayhorn* (Granta Books, London, 1997)

Hannaford, Alex – *Scissor Sisters* (Artnik, London, 2005)

Harbin, Billy J., Marra, Kim and Schanke, Robert A. (eds.) – *The Gay & Lesbian Theatrical Legacy* (University of Michigan Press, Ann Arbor, MI, 2005)

Haslam, Dave – *Life After Dark: A History of British Nightclubs & Music Venues* (Simon & Schuster, London, 2015)

Hasted, Nick – *You Really Got Me: The Story of The Kinks* (Omnibus Press, London, 2013)

Herzhaft, Gérard – *Encyclopedia of the Blues* (University of Arkansas Press, Fayetteville, AR, 1992)

Hobson, Vic – *Creating Jazz Counterpoint: New Orleans, Barbershop Harmony, and the Blues* (University Press of Mississippi, Jackson, MS, 2014)

Holmes, Thom – *Electronic and Experimental Music: Technology, Music, and Culture* (Routledge, New York, 2016)

Houlbrook, Matt – *Queer London: Perils and Pleasures in the Sexual Metropolis, 1918-1957* (University of Chicago Press, Chicago, IL, 2005)

Jones, Lesley-Ann – *Mercury: An Intimate Biography of Freddie Mercury* (Touchstone, New York, 2011)

Kirby, David – *Little Richard: The Birth of Rock 'n' Roll* (Continuum International Publishing, New York, 2009)

Kliment, Bud – *Billie Holiday, Singer* (Chelsea House, New York, 1990)

Levin, Floyd – *Classic Jazz: A Personal View of the Music and the Musicians* (University of California Press, Berkeley, CS, 2000)

Lieb, Sandra R. – *Mother of the Blues: A Study of Ma Rainey* (University of Massachusetts Press, Amherst, MA, 1981)

Lomax, Alan – *Mister Jelly Roll* (University of California Press, Berkeley, CA, 1950)

McAuliffe, Mary – *When Paris Sizzled: The 1920s Paris of Hemingway, Chanel, Cocteau, Cole Porter, Josephine Baker and their Friends* (Rowman and Littlefield, London, 2016)

McNeil, Legs and McCain, Gillian – *Please Kill Me: The Uncensored Oral History of Punk* (Grove Press, New York, 1996)

Marko, Paul – *The Roxy London WC2: A Punk History* (Punk 77 Books, London, 2007)

Marquis, Donald M. – *In Search of Buddy Bolden: First Man of Jazz* (Louisiana State University Press, Baton Rouge, LA, 1978)

Midlebrook, Diane W. – *Suits Me: the Double Life of Billy Tipton* (Peter Davidson, Boston, MA, 1998)

Miles, Barry – *London Calling: A Countercultural History of London since 1945* (Atlantic Books, London, 2010)

Miller, Neil – *Out Of the Past: Gay and Lesbian History from 1869 to the Present* (Alyson Books, New York, 2006)

Morris, Bonnie J. – *Eden Built by Eves: The Culture of Women's Music Festivals,* (Alyson Publications Inc., New York, 1999)

Morrissey – *Autobiography* (Penguin Books, London, 2013)

Myers, Paul – *It Ain't Easy: Long John Baldry and the Birth of the British Blues* (Greystone Books, Vancouver, 2007)

Norman, Philip – *John Lennon: The Life* (HarperCollins UK, London, 2009)

O'Brien, Lucy – *She Bop: The Definitive History of Women in Popular Music* (Jawbonew Press, London, 2012)

O'Meally, Robert – *Lady Day: The Many Faces Of Billie Holiday* (Arcade Publishing, New York, 1993)

Oliver, Paul, Russell Tony et al. – *Yonder Come the Blues* (Cambridge University Press, Cambridge, 2001)

Prono, Luca – *Encyclopedia of Gay and Lesbian Popular Culture* (Greenwood Press, Westport, CT, 2008)

Pryor, Richard and Gold, Todd – *Pryor Convictions And Other Life Sentences* (Pantheon Books, New York, 1995)

Repsch, John – *The Legendary Joe Meek: The Telstar Man* (Cherry Red Books, London, 2001)

Richards, Matt and Langthorne, Mark – *Somebody to Love: the Life, Death and Legacy of Freddie Mercury* (Blink Publishing, London, 2016)

Riva, Maria – *Marlene Dietrich* (Bloomsbury, London, 1992)

Rose, Al – *Storyville, New Orleans, Being an Authentic, Illustrated Account of the Notorious Red-light District* (University of Alabama Press, Tuscaloosa, AL, 1974)

Shapiro, Nat and Hentoff, Nat – *Hear Me Talkin' To Ya: The Story of Jazz As Told By the Men Who Made It* (Courier Corporation, North Chelmsford, MA, 1955)

Shapiro, Peter – *Turn the Beat Around: The Secret History of Disco* (Faber & Faber, London, 2005)

Sinfield, Alan – *Out on Stage: Lesbian and Gay Theatre in the Twentieth Century* (Yale University Press, New Haven, CT, 1999)

Slide, Anthony – *The Encyclopedia of Vaudeville* (Greenwood Press, Westport, CT, 1994)

Spoto, Donald – *Blue Angel: The Life of Marlene Dietrich* (G. K. Hall, Boston, MA, 1993)

Steele, Robert – *Careless Whispers: The Life & Career of George Michael* (Omnibus Press Limited, London, 2011)

Street, John – *Rebel Rock: The Politics of Popular Music* (Viking, New York, 1986)

Summers, Claude J. (ed.) – *The Queer Encyclopedia of Music, Dance and Musical Theatre* (Cleis Press, Jersey City, NJ, 2004)

Wald, Elijah – *Escaping The Delta: Robert Johnson and the Invention of the Blues* (HarperCollins, New York, 2004)

Wald, Gayle F. – *Shout Sister Shout! The Untold Story of Rock-n-Roll Trailblazer Sister Rosetta Tharpe* (Beacon Press, Boston, MA, 2007)

Watson, Steven – *The Harlem Renaissance* (Pantheon Books, New York, 1995)

White, Charles – *The Life And Times Of Little Richard: The Quasar of Rock* (Harmony Books, New York, 1984)

Whiteley, Sheila – *Women and Popular Music: Sexuality, Identity and Subjectivity* (Routledge, London, 2006)

Wieder, Judy (ed.) – *Celebrity: The Advocate Interviews* (Advocate Books, 2001)

Wilson, James F. – *Bulldaggers, Pansies, and Chocolate Babies: Performance, Race, and Sexuality In the Harlem Renaissance* (University of Michigan Press, Ann Arbor, MA, 2010)

Wintz, Cary D. and Finkelman, Paul (eds.) – *Encyclopedia of the Harlem Renaissance* (Routledge, London, 2004)

Wirth, Thomas H. (ed.) – *Gay Rebel of the Harlem Renaissance: Selections from the Work of Richard Bruce* (Duke University Press, Durham, NC, 2002)

Worden, Helen – *The Real New York* (Bobbs-Merrill Company, Indianapolis, IN, 1932)

Work, John Wesley – *American Negro Songs: 230 Folk Songs and Spirituals, Religious and Secular* (Crown Publishers, New York, 1940)

Image Credits

David Bowie on the cover of *Gay Times*, 1973. Photo from the LSE Library collection.

Freddie Mercury performing in New Haven, November 1977. Photo by Carl Lender/Creative Commons.

Fred Barnes in *The Black Sheep of the Family*. Author's own collection.

Camp Records order form, *c.* 1965. Author's own collection.

The Campaign for Homosexual Equality group march during London Pride, 1974. Photo from the LSE Library collection.

Press advert for *Lavender Country*. Author's own collection.

Drake Jensen, photo by Jonathan Edwards. © Corvidae Photos. Used by permission.

Early press photo of the classic Village People lineup, early 1978. Author's own collection.

Press advert for 'I Was Born This Way'. Author's own collection.

Poster advertising GLF fundraiser, December 1970. Photo from the LSE Library collection.

Press advert, 1978. Author's own collection.

Publicity photo, *c.* 1975. From the collection of Paul Southwell. Used by permission.

George Michael performing on stage during the Faith World Tour in 1988. Courtesy of Special Collections, University of Houston Libraries.

Marc Almond on the cover of *Gay Times*, June 1987. Author's own collection.

Klaus Nomi in concert, 1981. Author's own collection.

Boy George, Sydney, January 1, 2012. Photo by Eva Rinaldi/Creative Commons.

Frankie Goes to Hollywood postcard 1984. Author's own collection.

Rod Thomas, aka Bright Light Bright Light. Used by permission.

Mista Majah P, 2011. Copyright Mista Majah P. Used by permission.

HiFi Sean, photo by Paul Grace. Copyright Paul Grace. Used by permission.

k anderson. © k anderson. Used by permission.

Endnotes

Introduction

1 Author interview with Sean Dickson, February 2017
2 '"Eugene Onegin" is Final Novelty at the Metropolitan', *Musical America* Vol 31, Music Publications Limited, 1919
3 'Stock, Aitken, Waterman: the Biggest Hitmakers of the 80s', Mark Lindores, *Attitude*, 5 July 2015
4 'Judas Priest's Rob Halford: "I've Become the Stately Homo of Heavy Metal"', Alexis Petridis, *The Guardian*, 3 July 2014
5 'Tune In, Cheer Up, Rock Out', David Cavanagh, *Q*, October 1994

Chapter 1 – David Bowie Made Me Gay

1 'How I Came Out of the Closet and into the Streets', Kid Congo Powers, *Huffington Post*, 3 March 2014
2 'Holly Johnson Relaxed', Richard Smith, *Gay Times*, April 1994
3 Author Interview with Paul Rutherford, February 2017
4 Author Interview with Andy Partridge, February 2017
5 Author interview with Andy Bell, February 2017
6 'I Always Dreaded This Day; I Hoped he was Immortal', Boy George, *The Daily Mail*, 12 January 2016
7 'Marc Almond: "I've had the chance to be subversive in the mainstream"', Jude Rogers, *The Guardian*, 23 October 2016
8 Author interview with Tom Robinson, November 2016
9 'David Bowie: A Candid Conversation With the Actor, Rock Singer and Sexual Switch-hitter', *Playboy*, September 1976
10 'I Was the Filling in a "Cookie" with David Bowie and Mick Jagger', Marissa Charles, *The New York Post*, 17 January 2016
11 'David Bowie "Changed My Life Forever"', Marilyn Manson, rollingstone.com, 11 January 2016
12 Guillermo Del Toro quoted from Twitter, 11 January, 2016
13 *New Musical Express*, 12 March 1974
14 'Freddie Mercury: More than Flash', Bruce Britt, *Los Angeles Daily News*, 27 November 1991
15 *Somebody to Love: The Life, Death and Legacy of Freddie Mercury*, Matt Richards and Mark Langthorne (Blink Publishing, London, 2016)

16 *Mercury: An Intimate Biography of Freddie Mercury*, Lesley-Ann Jones (Touchstone, New York, 2011), p. 91

17 'Freddie's Song of Sadness', Annette Witheridge & Gerry Brown, *News of the World*, 24 November 1991

18 'Oh, You Pretty Thing', Michael Watts, *Melody Maker*, 22 January 1972

19 'Dusty Springfield', Ray Connolly, *Evening Standard*, September 1970

20 Author Interview with Ray Connolly, April 2017

21 'The Mad, Bad and Sad Life of Dusty Springfield', Roger Lewis, *The Spectator*, 2 August 2014

Chapter 2 – Pretty Baby

1   Interview with Johnny St. Cyr about Jelly Roll Morton, Tony Jackson, Morton's Compositions, and Arranging Old Tunes, Alan Lomax, 2 February 1949. *Association for Cultural Equity*, 2008

2   *Creating Jazz Counterpoint: New Orleans, Barbershop Harmony, and the Blues*, Vic Hobson (University Press of Mississippi, Jackson, MS, 2014)

3   *In Search of Buddy Bolden: First Man of Jazz*, Donald M. Marquis (Louisiana State University Press, Baton Rouge, LA 1978), p. 4

4   *They All Played Ragtime*, Rudy Blesh (Alfred A. Knopf, New York, 1950), p. 164

5   *Creating Jazz Counterpoint, New Orleans, Barbershop Harmony, and the Blues*, Vic Hobson

6   *Mr Jelly Roll*, Alan Lomax (University of California Press, Berkeley, CA, 1950), pp. 50-1

7   *Blacks in Blackface: A Sourcebook on Early Black Musical Shows*, Henry T. Sampson (Scarecrow Press, Inc., Lanham, MD, 2014), p. 67

8   'He Knew A Thousand Songs', Roy J. Carew, *Jazz Journal*, March 1952

9   *Storyville, New Orleans, Being an Authentic, Illustrated Account of the Notorious Red-light District*, Al Rose (University of Alabama Press, Tuscaloosa, AL, 1974), p. 110

10 *Louis Armstrong's New Orleans*, Thomas Brothers (W. W. Norton & Company, London, 2006), p. 66

11 *Hear Me Talkin' To Ya: The Story of Jazz As Told By the Men Who Made It*, Nat Shapiro and Nat Hentoff (Courier Corporation, North Chelmsford, MA, 1955), p55

12 *Mr Jelly Roll*, Lomax, p. 43

13 'He Knew A Thousand Songs', Roy J. Carew, *Jazz Journal*, March 1952

14 *Mr Jelly Roll*, Lomax, p. 45

15 Author interview with St. Sukie de la Croix, November 2016

16 'On and Off the Stroll', Columbus Bragg, *The Chicago Defender*, 17 October 1914

17 'On and Off the Stroll', Columbus Bragg, *The Chicago Defender*, 5 September 1914

18 *Hear Me Talkin' To Ya: The Story of Jazz As Told By the Men Who Made It*, Nat Shapiro and Nat Hentoff, Dover Publications, 1955, p88

19 *They All Played Ragtime*, Blesh, p. 162

20 *Satchmo: My Life in New Orleans*, Louis Armstrong (Prentice Hall Inc, New York, 1954,) pp. 96-7

21 'Jazz Artist Recalls Storyville Tunes', *Lodi News-Sentinel*, 15 August 1988

22 'Testimonial to Tony Jackson', *Billboard*, 5 March 1921

23 'Big Benefit', *The Chicago Defender*, 26 February 1921
24 *Film Voices: Interviews from Post Script*, Gerald Duchovnay (ed.), State University of New York Press, 2004, p234
25 *Mr Jelly Roll*, Lomax, p. 129

Chapter 3 - Bull Dyker Blues

1 '2011 Chicago G/L Hall of Fame to Induct 11 People', www.windycitymediagroup.com, 21 September 2011
2 *Mother of the Blues: A Study of Ma Rainey*, Sandra R. Lieb (University of Massachusetts Press, Amherst, MA, 1981), p. 18
3 Quoted in *The Collected Works of Langston Hughes: The Poems, 1921-1940*, (University of Missouri, Columbia, MO, 2001), p. 71
4 *Gay Rebel of the Harlem Renaissance: Selections from the Work of Richard Bruce Nugent*, ed. Thomas H. Wirth (Duke University Press, Durham, NC, 2002)
5 'Aeolian Company Announces First List of Race Records', *Talking Machine World*, 26 July 1932
6 'Hamilton Lodge Ball an Unusual Spectacle', *New York Age*, 6 March 1926
7 'Fag Balls Exposed', Buddy Browning, *Brevities*, 14 March 1932
8 *The Harlem Renaissance,* Steven Watson (Pantheon Books, New York, 1995)
9 'Children to Have Preference at Saturday Carnival Matinee', *Benton Harbor News Palladium*, 2 August 1929
10 *Ragged but Right: Black Traveling Shows, Coon Songs, and the Dark Pathway to Blues and Jazz*: Lynn Abbott and Doug Seroff (University Press of Mississippi, Jackson, MS, 2009), p. 261
11 *New York Age*, 16 November 1911
12 *New York Age*, 18 March 1909
13 *The 100 Most Influential Musicians of All Time*, Gene Goblinski (ed.), Rosen Publishing Group, New York, 2009, p. 162
14 *Yonder Come the Blues*, Paul Oliver, Tony Russell et al. (Cambridge University Press, Cambridge, 2001), p. 262
15 'Special Columbia Publicity', *Talking Machine World*, 15 October 1923
16 'Atlanta: Business Satisfactory Throughout Southern Territory', *Talking Machine World*, 15 July 1923
17 'Bessie Smith Scores Success', *Talking Machine World*, 15 August 1923
18 *Mother of the Blues: A Study of Ma Rainey*, Lieb
19 'Store Concert by Bessie Smith Helps Dealer Sales', *Talking Machine World*, 15 December 1925
20 *New York Recorder,* 11 December 1933
21 *Bessie*, Chris Albertson (Barrie & Jenkins Ltd, London, 1972), p. 117
22 *Bessie*, Albertson, p. 120
23 *Bulldaggers, Pansies, and Chocolate Babies: Performance, Race, and Sexuality In the Harlem Renaissance*, James F. Wilson (University of Michigan Press, 2010)
24 *Bessie*, Albertson, p. 32
25 'Reflections on the Origins of a Jazz Tune', *International Discophile*, Issue 1, Summer 1955, p176
26 'The Life And Death of Bessie Smith', Kay Mott, *The Philadelphia Enquirer*, 2 December 1961

27 'The Life And Death of Bessie Smith', Kay Mott, *The Philadelphia Enquirer*, 2 December 1961

28 *Chicago Defender*, 7 April 1934

29 'I Am a Woman Again', Bentley, Gladys: *Ebony Magazine*, August 1952

30 *Jet*, 28 January 1954

Chapter 4 – The Pansy Craze

1 *The Real New York*, Helen Worden (Bobbs-Merrill Company, Indianapolis, IN, 1932), p. 289

2 'Amuck on Bleecker St.', *The World (New York)*, 7 September 1890

3 'Brogan's Queer Bookkeeping', *The Press (New York)*, 8 September 1890

4 *New York Herald*, 5 January 1892

5 'Infamous Slide Closed By Herald', *New York Herald*, 8 January 1892

6 'Another Resort For Slide Patrons', *The New York Evening Telegram*, 11 March 1893

7 *Gay New York: Gender, Urban Culture, and the Making of the Gay Male World, 1890-1940*, George Chauncey (Basic Books, New York, 1995), pp. 219-20

8 'Ariston's Owner Bankrupt', *New York Sun*, 17 October 1903

9 'A Dressing Room Marvel', Ann Abblle Whitford, *Variety*, 4 December 1909

10 'Madame Critic', *The New York Dramatic Mirror*, 8 September 1915

11 'Old Impersonator, Julian Eltinge Dies', Martin Kane, *Madison Wisconsin State Journal*, 8 March 1941

12 'Julian Eltinge, Famed as Impersonator, Dies at 59', *Madison Capital Times*, 8 March 1941

13 'Old Impersonator, Julian Eltinge Dies', Martin Kane, *Madison Wisconsin State Journal*, 8 March 1941

14 'Love Calamities of the Cave Man Who is a Perfect Lady', *Syracuse Herald*, 18 December 1921

15 'New York Day By Day', O. O. McIntyre, 14 August 1923

16 'The Mirrors of Mayfair', *Broadway Brevities*, October 1923

17 *Rochester Times Union*, 17 December 1935

18 *The Stage*, 9 October 1920

19 *New York Morning Telegraph*, 25 May 1922

20 *Variety*, 27 May 1925

21 *The Encyclopedia of Vaudeville*, Anthony Slide (Greenwood Press, Westport, CT, 1994), p. 375

22 *Variety*, 12 April 1923

23 *The Sun, New York*, 29 January 1931

24 *The Encyclopedia of Vaudeville*, Slide, p. 375

25 'The Gay Boys Are So-o-o Pleased', *Syracuse Journal*, 4 April 1935

26 'All In A Day', Mark Hellinger, *The Syracuse Journal*, 14 August 1933

27 'Rival Gangs Shoot It Out in Broadway Resort', *Amsterdam Evening Recorder* New York, 24 January 1931

28 'All In A Day', Mark Hellinger, *The Syracuse Journal*, 14 August 1933

29 *Brooklyn Daily Eagle*, 10 May 1931

30 'On Broadway', Walter Winchell, *New York Daily Mirror*, 3 February 1931

31 'On Broadway', Walter Winchell, *New York Daily Mirror*, 26 February 1931

32 On Broadway', Walter Winchell, *New York Daily Mirror*, 27 July 1931

33 *Damon Runyon*, Jimmy Breslin, Random House Inc, 1992, p238

34 'New York Day By Day', O. O. McIntyre, *Canandaigua Daily Messenger*, 7 January 1932

35 'New York Day By Day', O. O. McIntyre, *El Paso Herald Post*, 17 December 1931

36 'Highlights of Broadway', Jack Lait, *Salt Lake Tribune*, 29 March 1931

37 'Days and Nights in Gotham', Gilbert Swan, *Charleston Daily Mail*, 17 March 1931

38 'About New York', Gilbert Swan, *Indiana Evening Gazette*, 24 November 1931

39 'Queers Seek Succor!', Stephen O'Toole, *Brevities*, 4 July 1932

40 'On Broadway', Walter Winchell, *New York Daily Mirror*, 17 August 1933

41 *The Day*, 10 November 1936

42 *Pittsburgh Press*, 9 November 1936

43 'Sylvester Russell's Review', *The Pittsburgh Courier*, 16 March 1929

44 'Sylvester Russell's Review', *The Pittsburgh Courier*, 19 March 1927

45 'Pansy Parlors – Rough Chicago Has Epidemic of Male Butterflies', *Variety*, 10 December 1930

46 'Seen and Heard at the Fair', *The Chicago Defender*, 10 June 1933

47 'Race Represented as World's Fair Opens in Blaze of Glory', Dewey R. Jones, *The Chicago Defender*, 3 June 1933

48 'Rival Gangs Stage War in Club Abbey', *Rome Daily Sentinel*, 24 January 1931

49 'Corona Detective Accused At Police Trial', *Daily Star*, Long Island, 14 February 1931

50 *Brooklyn Daily Eagle*, 31 March 1931

51 'In New York', Paul Harrison, *Hawk Eye Gazette*, 23 January 1935

52 *Rethinking the Gay and Lesbian Movement*, Marc Stein, Routledge, 2012

53 *Bruz Fletcher: Camped, Tramped & A Riotous Vamp*, Tyler Alpern, Tyler Alpern, 2010

54 *Chicago Whispers*, St. Sukie de la Croix (University of Wisconsin Press, 2012), p. 112

55 *The Sun (New York)*, 23 September 1936

56 Ibid.

57 'Bourbon Switches', *Long Island Star Journal*, 24 July 1956

58 'Voice of Broadway', Dorothy Kilgallen (syndicated column), 2 April 1955

59 *The Gay & Lesbian Theatrical Legacy*: Billy J. Harbin, Kim Marra, Robert A. Schanke (eds.), University of Michigan Press, 2005, p69

Chapter 5 – Europe Before the War

1 'What We Owe to Oscar Wilde', Hugh E. M. Stutfield, *Blackwood's Magazine*, June 1895

2 *Queer London: Perils and Pleasures in the Sexual Metropolis, 1918-1957*, Matt Houlbrook, University of Chicago Press, 2005, p245

3 'Prisoners Numbered at Old Bailey', *Lancashire Daily Post*, 20 February 1933

4 'Man's Weird Pose', *The Auckland Star*, 2 January 1932

5 *The Argus* (Melbourne), 9 October 1922

6 'Barnes' Engagement Broken', *New York Clipper*, 1 October 1919

7 'Frederick Jester Barnes (1885-1938)', Jason Tomes, *Oxford Dictionary of National Biography* (Oxford University Press, 2004)

8 *Hollywood Babble On: Stars Gossip about Other Stars*, Boze Hadleigh (Penguin
   Group (USA), London, 1995), p. 179
9 'Prison For Comedian', *The Daily Mail*, 12 November 1924
10 'Frederick Jester Barnes (1885-1938)', Jason Tomes, *Oxford Dictionary of National
   Biography*, Oxford University Press, 2004
11 'Fred Barnes' Appeal in London Traffic Court', *Variety*, 26 November 1924
12 'Yonkers Woman Wills British Actor $425,000', *Syracuse Journal*, 5 August 1927
13 'Obituary: Fred Barnes, Actor', *Daily Mercury*, 25 October 1938
14 'Too Daring Broadcast Turn Abandoned', *Saturday Journal* (Adelaide), 6 April
   1929
15 *On the Same Side: Homosexuals During the Second World War*, Stephen Bourne,
   BBC History Magazine, February 2012
16 'The Darling of Drury Lane', *The Independent*, 17 August 1999
17 'Pansies Blow U.S.!', Lepra Chaun, *Brevities*, 9 May 1932
18 *Bisexuality and the Eroticism of Everyday Life*, Marjorie Garber, Routledge, 2000,
   p122
19 'How an Up-To-Date Josephine Won Paris', Carl de Vidal Hunt, *Canton Daily
   News*, 16 January 1927
20 'Josephine Baker's Latest Exploit', *The American Weekly*, 12 October 1930
21 'Fags Ram Heinies!', Fred Schultz, *Brevities*, 19 September 1932
22 'The War, the World and the Cornish Land', *The Cornishman*, 15 October 1942
23 'Reichstag Fire Disclosure', *Western Daily Press*, 14 January 1946
24 *Marlene Dietrich*, Maria Riva (Bloomsbury, London, 1992), p. 52
25 *Blue Angel: The Life of Marlene Dietrich*, Donald Spoto (G.K. Hall, Boston, MA,
   1993), pp. 64-5
26 Quoted in *The Life And Times Of Little Richard: The Quasar of Rock*, Charles White
   (Harmony Books, New York, 1984)

Chapter 6 – Strange Fruit

1 'Lisa Ben: A Lesbian Pioneer', Kate Brandt, *Visibilities*, January 1990
2 Ibid.
3 *Billie Holiday, Singer*, Bud Kliment (Chelsea House, New York, 1990), p. 19
4 'A Southerner Looks at Prejudice', *Ebony*, January 1960
5 'Blues Singer Sentenced As Drug Addict', *Binghamton Press*, 28 May 1947
6 'A Southerner Looks at Prejudice', *Ebony*, January 1960
7 *New York Age*, 12 February 1949
8 'New York Is My Beat', Alan McMillan, *New York Age*, 24 October 1953
9 *Billie Holiday: Wishing on the Moon*, Donald Clarke, Da Capo Press, 2000, p398
10 *New York Sun*, 16 August 1944
11 'Mme. Knight Out', *Pittsburgh Courier*, 26 November 1949
12 *The Beatles Anthology*, The Beatles (Cassell & Co, London, 2000), p. 38
13 *Shout Sister Shout! The Untold Story of Rock-n-Roll Trailblazer Sister Rosetta Tharpe*,
   Gayle F. Wald (Beacon Press, Boston, MA, 2007)
14 'Liberace Says Story Hurt Career', *Buffalo Courier Express*, 10 June 1959
15 'I Am Not, Liberace Replies In Suit Against Cassandra', *Binghampton Press*, 8
   June 1959
16 Ibid.

17 'Any Chance of a Refund', *Daily Mirror*, 11 February 1987
18 'A More Reflective Leap On Elton John's "Diving Board"', npr.com, 23
    September 2013
19 'Peer is Cashiered on Grave Charges', *The Daily Mail*, 4 December 1947
20 'Lord Montagu on the Court Case Which Ended the Legal Persecution of
    Homosexuals', *Evening Standard*, 14 July, 2007
21 'Johnny Mathis: Realising I was a Drug Addict was so Traumatic', *Sunday
    Express*, 22 February 2014
22 'Happy Cry Baby', *The American Weekly*, 15 June 1952
23 *The Age* (Melbourne), 20 September 1954
24 *The Central Queensland Herald*, 17 March 1955
25 'Johnnie Ray Accused Of Morals Offense', *Philadelphia Enquirer*, 22 November 1959
26 *The Life And Times Of Little Richard*, pp. 40–1
27 *Little Richard: The Birth of Rock 'n' Roll*, David Kirby (Continuum International
    Publishing, New York, 2009), p. 176
28 'Little Richard Brings Flamboyance to Revivalism', *San Bernardino County Sun*, 1
    June 1980
29 *Lush Life*, David Hajdu (Granta Books, London, 1996), p. 79
30 Ibid., p. 65
31 *Pryor Convictions And Other Life Sentences*, Richard Pryor and Todd Gold
    (Pantheon Books, New York, 1995), pp. 100-2
32 'Nina Simone's Time Is Now, Again', Salamishah Tillet, *The New York Times*, 19
    June 2015
33 'In the Macho World of Jazz, Don't Ask, Don't Tell', Francis Davis, *The New York
    Times*, 1 September 2002
34 '"Dad" to Adopted Sons: Jazz Player Billy Tipton Kept Her Secret to the End',
    Los Angeles Times, 1 February 1989
35 Interview with Lesley Gore, Shauna Swartz, afterellen.com, 3 June 2005

Chapter 7 – Camp Records

1   Camp Records, 1964
2   From the original sleeve notes: *Sex Is My Business*, Fax Record Company,
    FAXLP-1007, 1960
3   From the original sleeve notes: *Nights Of Love In Lesbos*, Fax Record Company,
    FAX-LP 1009, 1962
4   *Out on Stage: Lesbian and Gay Theatre in the Twentieth Century*, Alan Sinfield (Yale
    University Press, New Haven, CT, 1999), p. 271
5   'New Talent Flood in UK', *Billboard*, 14 December 1974
6   www.queermusicheritage.com/mar2012a.html
7   'It's Show Time as the Australian Ballet Prepares to Stage Robert Helpmann's
    The Display', Valerie Lawson, *The Australian*, 18 August 2012
8   *The Canberra Times*, 30 September 1969
9   *The Canberra Times*, 4 February 1966
10 *The Canberra Times*, 29 September 1986
11 *The Canberra Times*, 30 September 1986
12 'Peter Allen on Broadway', William A. Raidy, *Syracuse Herald Journal*, 10 June
    1979

13   *Celebrity: The Advocate Interviews*, Judy Wieder (ed.) (Advocate Books, 2001), p. 85
14   Earl Wilson, *Long Beach Press Telegram*, 1 August 1974
15   *Who's Who in Contemporary Gay and Lesbian History*, Robert Aldrich and Garry Wotherspoon (eds.) (Routledge, London, 2001), p. 10
16   'Peter Allen on Broadway', William A. Raidy, *Syracuse Herald Journal*, 10 June 1979
17   'Thank You, Peter Allen, for Giving Australia the Permission to be Camp', Peter Taggart, *The Guardian*, 21 September 2015
18   *Billboard*, 14 October 1967
19   'I Bet Your Mama Was a Tent-Show Queen', Carl Wilson, *Hazlitt Magazine*, 22 April 2013

Chapter 8 – Do You Come Here Often?

1   *The John Lennon Encyclopedia*, Bill Harry (Virgin Books, 2000), p. 232
2   '100 Records That Set The World On Fire (While No One Was Listening)', *The Wire*, September 1998
3   'The Man Who Wrote "Telstar"', *Evening Standard*, 12 November 1963
4   'Joe Meek and Me', Jake Arnott, *Evening Standard*, 12 June 2009
5   'Joe Meek: Tragic Demise of a Gifted Musical Maverick', *The Daily Express*, 7 June 2009
6   Author interview with Robert Duke (a.k.a. Patrick Pink), June 2016
7   'Meek by Name, Wild by Nature', Jon Savage, *The Observer*, 12 November 2006
8   'The Tornados Part Two', www.robbhuxley.com
9   'The Tornados Part Three', www.robbhuxley.com
10   'Joe Meek: Tragic Demise of a Gifted Musical Maverick', *The Daily Express*, 7 June 2009
11   'The Tornados Part Two', www.robbhuxley.com
12   *John Lennon: The Life*, Philip Norman (HarperCollins UK, London, 2009)
13   *You Really Got Me: The Story of The Kinks*, Nick Hasted (Omnibus Press, London, 2013)
14   *It Ain't Easy: Long John Baldry and the Birth of the British Blues*, Paul Myers (Greystone Books, Vancouver, 2007), p. 134

Chapter 9 – Electronic Sounds

1   'Robert Moog, 71, Invented Music Synthesizer', Stephen Miller, *New York Sun*, 23 August 2005
2   *Electronic and Experimental Music: Technology, Music, and Culture*, Thom Holmes (Routledge, New York, 2016), p. 270
3   'Wendy Carlos Takes her Moog Music to East Side', Chris Morris, *Billboard*, 3 October 1998
4   Author interview with Rod Thomas, November 2016
5   'Walking With Elephants Star Says Gays are Another "Breed"', Tris Reid-Smith, *Gay Star News*, 4 June 2015
6   'Skin and Bone', *North Tonawanda Evening News (New York)*, 14 April 1979
7   *Intersecting Film, Music, and Queerness*, Jack Curtis Dubowsky (Palgrave Macmillan, 2016), p. 116

8 David Bowie, quoted in the *Sound + Vision* CD booklet, 1989
9 'People Talk', Kenneth R. Clark, *Jacksonville Courier*, 2 April 1979
10 *Rolling Stone*, 12 May 1979
11 'After a Sex Change and Several Eclipses, Wendy Carlos Treads a New Digital Moonscape', Susan Reed, *People*, 1 July 1985

Chapter 10 – After Stonewall

1 Quoted in 'What The A&R Men Want', *Beat Instrumental*, 1975
2 *Gay L.A.: A History of Sexual Outlaws, Power Politics, and Lipstick Lesbians*, Lillian Faderman and Stuart Timmons (Basic Books, New York, 2006), p. 1
3 'Homosexual Characters on Centre Stage', *The Canberra Times*, 28 August 1974
4 *The Advocate*, 12 September 1973
5 'Albums for Christmas', *Gay News*, December 1972
6 'Photographer for Roxy Music and Lou Reed Found Living in Semi-Obscurity in South Beach', Hans Morgenstern, *Miami New Times*, 11 April 2014
7 *Please Kill Me: The Uncensored Oral History of Punk*, Legs McNeil and Gillian McCain (Grove Press, New York, 1996), p. 4
8 'Lou Reed: A Deaf Mute in a Telephone Booth', Lester Bangs, *Let It Rock*, November 1973
9 'Lou Reed Backtracked from his Implied Bisexuality. But he Didn't Let me Down', Tom Robinson, *The Independent*, 28 October 2013
10 'A Family in Peril: Lou Reed's Sister Sets the Record Straight About his Childhood', Merrill Reed Weiner, *Cuepoint*, 13 April 2015
11 'Alice From Wonderland', Everett Henderson, *Gay: America's First Gay Weekly*, 11 May 1970
12 'Alice – A Fag?' *Spec*, August 1974
13 *Gay Times 31*, 6 September 1973
14 'Cassidy: Nothing to Hide', *Gay News 56*, 10 October 1974
15 'Could It Be Forever?' David Cassidy, *Headline* 2012
16 'Peter Straker, A Man Of Many Parts', *Gay News 13*, 1972
17 Advert, *Gay News 77*, August 1975
18 steveswindells.wordpress.com
19 'David Bowie: A Candid Conversation With the Actor, Rock Singer and Sexual Switch-hitter', *Playboy*, September 1976
20 'Elton's Frank Talk: the Lonely Love Life of a Superstar', Cliff Jahr, *Rolling Stone*, 7 October 1976
21 *Gay News 98*, 1 July 1976
22 'A Space-Age Minstrel', *Gay News*, January 1974
23 Sleeve notes to *Something In The Moonlight*, written by James Gavin, 2006
24 'Steve Grossman Sensitive, Attuned to Gay Experience', Mara Kelly and Suzanne Thompson, *The Mass Media*, 25 April 1974
25 'Gay Minstrel is Painfully Honest', *Berkeley Barb*, 23 May 1974
26 'Vibrations Reminisces Various Eras', *Sunday Herald Banner*, 2 July 1972
27 'By . . . Jack O'Brien', Jack O'Brien, *Schenectady Gazette*, 22 January 1974
28 *Billboard*, 13 October 1973
29 'Disc-cussion', *Sunday Gazette Mail*, Charleston, 28 April 1974
30 'Records', Adam Dawson, *Telegraph Herald*, 5 April 1974

31 'Got Tu Go Hustle', Steven Gaines, *New York Magazine*, 25 June 1979
32 '10 Singer-Songwriter Albums Rolling Stone Loved in the 1970s You've Never Heard', Gavin Edwards, *Rolling Stone*, 16 July 2015
33 'Grossman Offers Homosexual Songs', John Rockwell, *New York Times*, 7 May 1974
34 *Ann Arbor Sun*, 6 December 1974
35 'Tuning Up', *The Advocate*, 12 November 1981
36 'Jobriath: Oh! You Pretty Thing' Johann Hari *The Independent*, 12 April 2004
37 'Jobriath Revisited', Charles Herschberg, *Omega One*, 19 January 1979
38 'Jobriath: Oh! You Pretty Thing', Johann Hari *The Independent*, 12 April 2004
39 Author interview with Blackberri, November 2016
40 Jean-Jacques Rousseau, French philosopher, 1712-1778: 'When the people shall have nothing more to eat, they will eat the rich.'

Chapter 11 – Living With Lesbians

1   Author interview with Cris Williamson, December 2016
2   'The Bisexuals', Judy Klemesrud, *New York Magazine*, 1 April 1974
3   'Janis Ian Says Bill Cosby Spread Lesbian Rumors About Her as a Teen', Anna Silman, Salon.com, 29 July 2015
4   'Janis Ian and Patricia Snyder's Relationship Builds Upon Decades of Social Upheaval', Amy Sohn, *New York Times*, 10 September 2015
5   *Musica* No 2, May 1974
6   F 'em!: Goo Goo, Gaga, and Some Thoughts on Balls, Jennifer Baumgardner, Seal Press, 2011, p41
7   '20 Rock Albums Rolling Stone Loved in the 1970s That You Never Heard', Gavin Edwards, *Rolling Stone*, 11 June 2015
8   Author interview with Alix Dobkin, November 2016
9   'Obituary', *Bangor Daily News*, 30 August 2002
10 'Liberation Music, Angry and Proud, Enters Gay Life', Martin St. John, *The Advocate*, 11 April 1973
11 'Maxine Feldman: Folk Musician, Lesbian Activist', *Sing Out! The Folk Song Magazine*, 2008
12 'In Their Own Voices: Oral Histories of Festival Artists', Bonnie J. Morris, *Frontiers: A Journal of Women Studies*, Vol. 19, No. 2 (1998), pp. 53-71
13 *Vaudeville Old & New: An Encyclopedia of Variety Performers in America, Volume 1*, Frank Cullen (Routledge, London, 2007), p. 375
14 'Maxine Feldman: Folk Musician, Lesbian Activist', *Sing Out! The Folk Song Magazine*, 2008
15 'Stepney Sisters Turn on to Women's Rock', Marion Fudger, *Spare Rib*, May 1976
16 'Number One with a Star', Jean Williams, *Billboard*, 7 May 1977
17 *Closeup, Billboard*, 15 December 1979
18 *Gay Community News* (Boston), November 1980
19 Ibid.
20 Author interview with Holly Near, December 2016
21 *Gay Community News* (Boston), November 1980
22 'Canada's Ferron Wages a "Still Riot"', Roger Deitz, *Billboard*, 13 July 1996
23 Ibid.

24 Ibid.
25 'Out of the Cage: An Interview with Ferron', Douglas Heselgrave, *The Music Box*, December 2008
26 Ibid.
27 Ibid.
28 'Exclusive Interview with Ani DiFranco, the Ultimate Righteous Babe', Kathleen Bradbury, lavendermagazine.com, 20 September 2012

Chapter 12 – Lavender Country

1   Author interview with Patrick Haggerty, September 2016
2   chrissiedickinson.com/bio.html
3   'From Hank to HIV-Positive', Rheta Grimsley Johnson, *Kokomo Tribune*, 24 June 1994
4   'Doug Stevens Interview', stonewallsociety.com
5   Ibid.
6   'k.d. lang Recollection Review', Chris Roberts, bbc.co.uk, 2010
7   'Out and Riding High in Nashville', Jody Rosen, *The New York Times*, 24 May 2013
8   Ibid.
9   'Confessions of a Gay Christian Country Singer', Chely Wright, *Huffington Post*, 24 June, 2011
10 Ibid.
11 Author interview with Drake Jensen, September 2016
12 'Gay Ottawa Teen who Killed Himself was Bullied', *CBC News*, 18 October 2011

Chapter 13 – Can't Stop the Music

1   'The Full Monti Rock, and Then Some', Rick Lax, *Las Vegas Weekly*, 29 July 2010
2   'Village People', *Rolling Stone Magazine*, 19 April 1979
3   *Freddie Mercury: The Definitive Biography*, Lesley-Ann Jones, Hodder and Stoughton, 2011
4   'Elton and Rod Aren't Feuding', *Madison Wisconsin State Journal*, 10 December 1978
5   'Poor Image Upsets David Hodo', *Colorado Springs Gazette Telegraph*, 12 June 1979
6   'Wanted: Macho Men With Mustaches', Nicole Pasulka, *The Believer Magazine*, July/August 2013
7   'Movies', William E. Sarmento, *Lowell Sun*, 7 July 1980
8   'Tidbits', *Ironwood Daily Globe*, 17 February 1997
9   'Celebrity Spotlight', *Walla Walla Union Bulletin*, 17 July 2005
10 '1981: The Queer in Rock', Rob Schmieder, *Gay Community News (Boston)*, 23 January 1982
11 'The New Improved Sylvester', *Gay News*, 12 January 1978
12 Ibid.
13 'Disco Music Beats Live When Sylvester Performs', *Colorado Springs Gazette*, 15 May 1981
14 'Disco Singer Arrested', *Cumberland Sunday Times*, 16 March 1980

15 'Pipeline – National Pop Scene', Becky Lynn, *Monahans News*, 1 May 1980
16 'Forum Entertainment', *Billboard*, 24 March 1979
17 'The New Improved Sylvester', *Gay News*, 12 January 1978
18 'Divine in Conversation With Paul Tams', *Men In Town*, November/December 1987
19 Author interview with John Condon, November 2016
20 Author interview with Guy Blackman, February 2017
21 Author interview with Paul Southwell, November 2016
22 'More Than A Miracle', *Gay News 92*, 8 April 1976
23 'Hollywood', *The Advocate*, 4 June 1975
24 *Gay News 74*, July 1975
25 'Disco Action', Tom Moulton, *Billboard*, 22 February 1975
26 'Happy and Carefree This Way', *Gay News 74*, July 1975
27 'Come Back to The Disco, Jimmy Somerville', Gregg Shapiro, chicago.gopride.com, February 2015
28 'Drag and Glitter-Rock Star Hibiscus Dies', *Gay Community News, New York*, 22 May 1982
29 'Boy's 1969 Death Suggests AIDS Invaded US Several Times', Gina Kolata, *New York Times*, 28 October 1987
30 *New York Times*, 11 May 1982
31 'Gay Community Frowns on Disco Diva Donna Summer', *Jet*, 18 September 1989

Chapter 14 – The 1970s: Political and Pink

1   Twitter, 13 May 2011
2   *Homosexuality and Citizenship in Florida*, the Florida Legislative Investigation Committee, January 1964, p. 7
3   'Gay Community Disputes Singer's Alleged Claims', *Lethbridge Herald*, 3 March 1977
4   'Homosexual Rights March', *The Canberra Times*, 28 June 1977
5   *Rebel Rock: The Politics of Popular Music*, John Street (Viking, New York, 1986), p. 75
6   *London Calling: A Countercultural History of London since 1945* (Barry Miles, Atlantic Books, London, 2010), p. 408
7   'Coleherne Gays "Near Riot"', *Gay News*, 17 June 1976
8   'Police Swoop on Nightspots', *Gay News*, July 1975
9   'Homosexual Rights March', *The Canberra Times*, 28 June 1977
10 'Homosexual March', *The Canberra Times*, 16 July 1978
11 'Mass Arrests at Gay March', *Tharunka*, 4 September 1978
12 'Queensland Shows its True Colours', David Alexander, *Star Observer Magazine*, November 2014
13 'Cops Stage Violent Attack on New York Bar', *Gay Community News*, 16 October 1982
14 'Gang Of 20 Attacks Gay Pub', *Gay News 136*, 9 February 1978
15 'Coleherne Gays "Near Riot"', *Gay News 97*, 17 June 1976
16 'White's Memory of Shootings "Hazy"', *Casa Grande Dispatch*, 1 December 1978

17 '"Conscience of Gay Movement" Wants Movement Shifted to Courts', *South Mississippi Sun*, 3 December 1976
18 'San Francisco Gay Community Gains Clout', *Las Cruces Sun News*, 5 December 1977
19 'Milk Had Recorded Message', *Colorado Springs Gazette Telegraph*, 28 November 1978
20 'Red Wedge', Johnny Black, *Q*, March 1996
21 *Richard Coles: My Journey from Pop Star to Celibate Vicar*, Patrick Strudwick, *The Independent*, 13 October 2014

Chapter 15 – The Aggressive Style Punk Rock

1 Interview, *Uncut*, May 2014, quoted in 'Bob Mould's Fears Over 'Coming Out'', *Daily Express*, 28 April 2014
2 'What The A&R Men Want', *Beat Instrumental*, February 1975
3 'Punk: Wot's In It For Us?' Keith Howes and Alan Wall, *Gay News* 136, 9 February 1978
4 Ibid.
5 'Dead Fingers Talk History', Jeff Parsons, www.punk77.co.uk, December 2005
6 'Punk: Wot's In It For Us'? Keith Howes and Alan Wall, *Gay News* 136, 9 February 1978
7 *Hüsker Dü: The Story of the Noise-Pop Pioneers Who Launched Modern Rock*, Andrew Earles (Voyageur Press, London, 2010), p. 105
8 'Interview by Dale Roy with Robert Deathrage of the Meatshits 2001', www.canadianassault.com
9 'A Growing Number of Pop Musicians are Being Open About Being Gay', Jim Farber, *New York Daily News*, 3 October 1991
10 'Gary Floyd: Once a Dick, Always a Dick', Raoul Hernandez, *The Austin Chronicle*, 12 May 2000
11 'Atlantic Dumping', *The Advocate*, 17 September 1996
12 Interview, *Genre Magazine*, September 1995

Chapter 16 – The 1980s: Small Town Boys

1 'Seize the Opportunity', *NME*, December 1986, pp. 20-7
2 *Woman*, 8 October 1983
3 'Boy George's Nightmare', Michael Goldberg, *Rolling Stone*, 28 August1986
4 'Reagan Says Aids Solution Rests With Morals', George E. Curry, *The Chicago Tribune*, 2 April 1987
5 'Rock Hudson: Victim Of TV Malpractice', Howard Rosenberg, *Los Angeles Times*, 2 August 1958
6 'Rock Hudson', *People*, 23 December 1985
7 'If You've Got It, Don't Flaunt It', Jeremy Jehu, *The Stage*, 5 December 1985
8 *Department of Education and Science circular* DES206/86, 6 August 1986
9 *Hansard*, 6 December 1999
10 *Pet Shop Boys: Introspective*, Michael Cowton (Sidgwick & Jackson, London, 1991), p. 26
11 Ibid., p. 35

12 Ibid., p. 41

13 'Marc Almond: "I've had the Chance to be Subversive in the Mainstream"', Jude Rogers, *The Observer*, 23 October 2016

14 *Somebody to Love*, Richards and Langthorne

15 Paul Strange, *Melody Maker*, 26 October 1985

16 'Erasure Singer Honest About HIV', Jim Farber, *New York Daily News*, 14 April 2005

17 'Andy Bell in the Public Eye', Larry Flick, *Billboard*, 25 June 1944

18 *Who's Who in Contemporary Gay and Lesbian History*, Aldrich and Wotherspoon (eds.), pp. 78-9

19 'Joey Arias talking to Kim Hastreiter', *Paper*, 11 January 2016

20 Interview, Maureen McLaughlin and John Beal, *Soho Weekly News*, 1979

21 'Frankie's Johnson say Have Fun! That's It, Really', Judy Cantor, *The Daily Herald*, 8 July 1985

22 'Say It Again, Frankie', Joe Brown, *Washington Post*, 4 November 1984

23 'Prince, Frankie Go to Town', Nelson George, *Billboard*, 10 November 1984

24 'Uncomfortable Compromise for Newest Gender Bender', Jeremy Jehu, *The Stage*, 31 May 1984

25 'It Was a Lovely Feeling Dying', Josie Griffiths, *The Sun*, 8 November 2016

26 *Freak Unique: My Autobiography*, Pete Burns, (John Blake Publishing Ltd, London, 2007)

27 'Boy George to Cover Funeral Expenses for Pete Burns' Family', Meka Beresford, *Pink News*, 30 October 2016

28 'Have You Heard?', *Lowell Sun*, 21 October 1982

29 'Queerness is a State of Mind Brought About by Understanding', Michael Stipe, *The Guardian*, 26 October 2014

30 'American Music Club's Mark Eitzel Strikes a Hopeful Tone', Ben Walsh, *the Independent*, 8 February 2013

Chapter 17– Hope and Homophobia

1   Author interview with Dane Lewis, January 2017

2   Annotation from Sadat X on the lyrics to 'Punks Jump Up to Get Beat Down' at genius.com

3   'Deep Dickollective – Oakland Gay Hip-hoppers', Lisa Hix, *San Francisco Chronicle*, 22 June 2006

4   'Heavy Handed but Tender-hearted, Transgender Hip-hopper Katastrophe is a Rebel With a Cause', Rona Marech, *San Francisco Chronicle*, 25 February 2005

5   'Words of Caushun: The Gay Rapper Goes On the Record', Will Doig, *Metro Weekly*, 22 May 2002

6   'Interview: Deadlee on the Struggle Against Discrimination in Hip Hop', fourtwonine.com, 12 April 2013

7   Twitter (@iLoveMakonnen), 20 January 2017

8   'T-Pain: Rappers Will Not Work With Frank Ocean Because He is Gay', *The Guardian*, 11 February 2014

9   'WOMAD Drops "Anti-Gay" Ragga Star', Brian Attwood, *The Stage*, 19 November 1992

10 'The Most Homophobic Place on Earth?', Tim Padgett, *Time*, 12 April 2006

11 'This Man Is Challenging Jamaica's Ban On Homosexuality', J. Lester Feder, Buzzfeed.com, 8 December 2015

12 '12 Grim Lands, Seven Bright Spots in LGBTI Preview of 2015', Colin Stewart, 76crimes.com, 12 January 2015

13 Author interview with Mista Majah P, February 2017

14 'Conchita Wurst's Eurovision Win Slammed by Russia', *Daily Mirror,* 11 May 2014

15 'Gay Russian Attacks Activists for Pushing Homosexual Acceptance', *Pink News,* 3 June 2008

16 *Roll Over, Tchaikovsky!: Russian Popular Music and Post-Soviet Homosexuality,* Stephen Amico (University of Illinois Press, Chicago, IL, 2014), p. 74

17 'Russian Pop Stars Chime in on "Sodomite Propaganda"', www.sputniknews. com, 20 December 2012

18 'Winter Olympics 2014: Pussy Riot Join Campaign for Sochi Boycott', Robin Scott-Elliot, *The Independent,* 17 October 2013

19 'Gay and "Sick" in China', allout.org, 19 December 2016

20 'Pop Star's Stadium-Style Coming Out', *Wall Street Journal (China),* 25 April 2012

21 'Denise Ho: the Cantopop Queen on a Crusade Against China's Communist Party', Tom Phillips, *The Guardian,* 19 September 2016

22 'Let Homosexuals Be! – Art Attack', nostringsng.com, 7 March 2016

23 'Kenyan Creators of Banned "Same Love" Remix Are "Living in Fear"', Elizabeth Daley, *The Advocate,* 24 February 2016

24 'How Kenya's "Gay Love" Video Ban Backfired', www.bbc.co.uk/news/blogs, 11 March 2016

25 'Hamed Sinno, Frontman of the Arab World's Hottest Indie Band', Harriet Fitch Little, *Financial Times,* 7 October 2016

26 'Mashrou Leila's Hamed Sinno Speaks out on Being Muslim', cnn.com, 15 June 2016

27 'Music Star Horse McDonald Returns to Home Town that Shunned her for Being Gay to Wed Love of Life', John Dingwall, *The Daily Record,* 8 January 2013

Chapter 18 – Scandal

1 Interview, *The Tube,* January 1984

2 David Bowie interviewed by Mark Goodman, MTV 1983

3 'Boy George, Jackson Bad Examples?', *Twin Falls Times-News,* 9 July 1984

4 'Gender-bending: The Road to "Everyperson"', Pamela Sommers, *Washington Post,* 15 March 1984

5 'At Peace With Himself', Gary Graff, *Syracuse Post Standard,* 8 April 1993

6 'Boy George Ruined my Life and Never Said Sorry', Ben Griffiths and Tom Worden, *The Sun,* 3 January 2016

7 'Boy George Describes Prison Sentence "a Gift"', Julia Hunt, *The Mirror,* 14 April 2016

8 Ibid.

9 'Lights, Cameras, Addiction: Rehab has Become the Latest Trapping of Fame', *Daily Record,* 7 June 2000

10 'Marc Almond: From Bedsit to Plague Pit', Mark Fisher, *The Guardian,* 18 July 2011

11 'Strange but True', Simon Hattenstone, *The Guardian*, 18 May 2000

12 'Queen Give Sun City Pledge But Offer No Apologies', *The Stage*, 19 June 1986

13 'World Of Music', Robin Wells, *Chicago Heights Star*, 16 June 1985

14 'Outing by Disease', Deborah Hastings and John Horn, *New Philadelphia Times Reporter*, 8 December 1991

15 'Simon Napier-Bell Tells Mark Ellen About Six Decades of Excess', *The Times*, 9 August 2014

16 'Read the Advice Frank Sinatra Had for George Michael in 1990', Patrick Shanley, *The Hollywood Reporter*, 26 December 2016

17 *Careless Whispers: The Life & Career of George Michael*, Robert Steele (Omnibus Press Limited, London, 2011)

18 Elton John, Twitter, December 26, 2016

19 'George Michael: "I'm Surprised I've Survived my Own Dysfunction"', Simon Hattenstone, *The Guardian*, 5 December 2009

20 Richard Osman, Twitter, December 26, 2016

21 'Interview: Kitchens Of Distinction', Brett Spaceman and Jon Leonard, *[sic] Magazine*, 24 January 2009

22 'A Growing Number of Pop Musicians are Being Open About Being Gay', Jim Farber, *New York Daily News*, 3 October 1991

23 'Neil Tennant: I Wouldn't Normally do this Kind of Thing', Paul Burston, *Attitude*, August 1994

24 'Anderson: I'm Bisexual', *Contact Music*, 3 June 2005

25 *Autobiography*, Morrissey (Penguin Books, London, 2013)

26 'Morrissey: "Unfortunately, I am Not Homosexual – I am Attracted to Humans"', Aaron Day, *Pink News*, 20 October 2013

27 'Lesbian Singer Phranc Draws Diverse Audience', Peter B. King, *Winnipeg Free Press*, 29 November 1989

28 Ibid.

29 'People', *Winnipeg Free Press*, 20 June 1991

30 'Interview with Melissa Ferrick', Matthew S. Robinson, *MusicDish.com*, 15 March 2001

31 'With Sales Lagging, Lilith Fair Faces Question Of Relevance', Laura Pellegrinelli, www.npr.org, 19 July 2010

32 *She Bop: The Definitive History of Women in Pop, Rock and Soul*, Lucy O'Brien (Penguin Books Ltd, London, 1995), p. 213

33 *Women and Popular Music: Sexuality, Identity and Subjectivity*, Sheila Whiteley, (Routledge, London, 2006), p. 166

Chapter 19 – Out and Proud in the Twenty-First Century

1 Interview, *Syracuse Post Standard*, 8 April 1993

2 Originally posted at rickymartinmusic.com/news, 29 March 2010. No longer on website, but referenced at bbc.co.uk, http://ew.com/article/2010/03/29/ricky-martin-gay and others

3 'Ricky Martin On Revealing He's Gay & His Family's Reaction', www.accesshollywood.com, 3 November 2010

4 'Ricky Martin: I Used to Have Internalised Homophobia', Jenni McKnight, Metro.co.uk, 27 August 2013

5   'The Insiders Guide to Beth Ditto', www.cnn.com, 24 November 2006

6   'Sam Smith Opens Up About Life and Love', Jessica Robertson, *The Fader*, 28
     May 2014

7   John Grant interviewed by Ian Leak, March 2016

8   'For John Grant, There's Power In The Personal', Mark Daley, www.npr.org, 2
     January 2017

9   'Woodpigeon's Die Stadt Muzikanten is Rich and Cinematic', Lara Purvis,
     www.dailyxtra.com, 27 January 2010

10 'Pages from Mark Hamilton's Songbook', Kevin Allen, www.dailyxtra.com, 2
     March 2008

11 Author interview with Rod Thomas, December 2016

12 'Final Fantasy', Sarah Liss, *Now*, 23 June 2005

13 'Scissor Sisters: On the Cutting Edge', Richard Harrington, *The Washington Post*,
     7 January 2005

14 *Scissor Sisters*, Alex Hannaford (Artnik, London, 2005), p. 112

15 'Remembering Nina Simone with Meshell Ndegeocello', www.outinperth.com,
     12 November 2012

16 'The Wainwright Stuff', Randy Shulman, *Metro Weekly*, 10 March 1999

17 'The Boy who Would be George', Tim Geary, *The Telegraph*, 16 March 2005

18 'The Trials of St Antony', Barbara Ellen, *The Guardian*, 3 July 2011

19 'Antony Hegarty: It Takes Nerve to Get Through your Sense of Shame on
     Stage', Fiona Sturges, *The Independent*, 14 July 2012

20 Author interview with k anderson, October 2016

21 'Gay Christian Rocker Trey Pearson on Being Ousted From Festival Bill', Chris
     Willman, *Billboard*, 12 September 2016

22 'Friends Claim Luther Vandross was Gay', pinknews.co.uk, 3 October 2006

23 'Irish Rocker Hozier Says Sexual Orientation "Not the Point"', Edward Baran,
     Reuters, 2 February 2015

24 'Why There Was Nothing "Natural" About Stephen Gately's Death', Jan Moir,
     The Daily Mail, 16 October 2009

Index